Notice So soon
as the Pub. House
debt is paid
I request the C.S.
Board Directors
to start a daily
newspaper called
Christian Science
Monitor This
must be done
without fail
M B G Eddy

Received by messenger
July 28, 1908
William B Johnson

First note sent by Mrs. Eddy ordering establishment of the *Monitor,* July 28, 1908. Mr. Johnson was a member of The Christian Science Board of Directors and Clerk of The Mother Church.

Commitment to Freedom

THE STORY OF

The Christian Science Monitor

BY

ERWIN D. CANHAM

Illustrated with Photographs

1958

HOUGHTON MIFFLIN COMPANY BOSTON

The Riverside Press Cambridge

LIBRARY OF CONGRESS CATALOG CARD NUMBER: 58–9055

FIRST PRINTING

The Riverside Press

CAMBRIDGE · MASSACHUSETTS

PRINTED IN THE U.S.A.

Dedication

To my mother, whose understanding and love of Christian Science set the path of my life, and to my wife, who has made its traversing so happy.

Discourse was deemed man's noblest attribute,
And written words the glory of his hand;
Then followed Printing with enlarged command
For thought — dominion vast and absolute
For spreading truth, and making love expand.

Wordsworth

Acknowledgments

WITHOUT THE unfailing support of The Christian Science Board of Directors, The Trustees under the Will of Mary Baker Eddy, the Board of Trustees and Manager of The Christian Science Publishing Society, this book would not have been possible. The Directors have permitted access to and quotation from materials in the Archives of The Mother Church. The Trustees under the Will have permitted quotation from Mrs. Eddy's writings. The Trustees of the Publishing Society have permitted quotation from the minutes and correspondence of their Board, from the columns of *The Christian Science Monitor,* the *Christian Science Sentinel,* and *The Christian Science Journal.* The Manager has handled the business details and facilitated the writing and production of the book with endless patience and good judgment.

In the gathering of material, many, indeed, have been of invaluable assistance. Paul S. Deland has collected historical data actively for over a decade and assembled it with the aid of Miss Sadie L. Porter. Both were tireless in the checking of details. The *Monitor* history file they produced and managed remains as a source of original materials. Miss Miriam E. Loveland, Custodian of the Archives of The Mother Church, and her assistant, Mrs. Susan T. Jackson, were patiently painstaking in verifying important facts. The library staff of *The Christian Science Monitor,* led by Chester W. Sanger, helped continuously in finding and checking data. The Longyear Foundation kindly permitted quotation from the autobiography of Alexander Dodds, which is in their library in Brookline, Massachusetts. The Library of Congress permitted examination of the papers of Frederick Dixon, in their Manuscripts Division, and publication of the photograph of Mr. Dixon. Many details concerning Mr. Dixon were made available through the persistent interest of Alexander Primrose of Chipping Campden, England.

I am grateful for the use and quotation of the personal memoirs of many *Monitor* workers: Walter W. Cunningham, Ernest R. Sherburne, Winthrop P. Tryon, Amos Weston, Oscar L. Stevens, Forrest Price, Miss Emily Henderson, Mrs. David P. Wyman, Miss Mabel E. Burnside, Mrs. Jean Edgar Taylor, Miss Irene Armstrong, Volney D. Hurd.

Herbert T. Stanger, H. Phelps Gates, and M. Alvah Blanchard gave me indispensable help in the analysis of their respective departments of the *Monitor.* Franklin Smith assisted with personnel records and Mrs. Dorothy E. Webster with facts and figures. Several chapters of a once projected book by Robert W. Desmond were usefully interesting. Gordon N. Converse and Burt B. Mader gave fruitfully of their high artistic and technical talents in preparing the illustrations.

Mrs. Willis J. Abbot has been unstintingly helpful with material concerning her distinguished husband. Mr. and Mrs. Luther P. Cudworth, Mrs. Clifford P. Smith, Mr. and Mrs. Bliss Knapp, Mrs. William P. McKenzie, and Mrs. William R. Rathvon contributed significant and interesting recollections.

In the arduous typing and editing of the manuscript, Miss Mary Lou Gloor and Miss Elizabeth Howe were as efficient as they were tireless.

E.D.C.

Contents

Illustrations

Introduction

THIS DOES NOT PRETEND to be a neutral history of *The Christian Science Monitor.*

How could it be? The author has been on the *Monitor*'s staff since he was a cub reporter in 1925. He has been aided by others who have worked for the paper uninterruptedly from the beginning. We believe deeply in the paper's ideals.

And so, in this account, we try to tell something of what lies behind the paper. It is an inside story. If this leads us here and there into small religious dissertations, we hope our purpose will be understood by those who are not Christian Scientists. To tell about *The Christian Science Monitor* without some references to Christian Science would be incomplete and misleading. Readers surely want to know why the paper thinks and acts as it does.

The primary purpose is to tell the facts about a newspaper which is to professionals a kind of daily astonishment. In telling them, there has been another difficulty: to avoid institutionalism and false pride. We have to remind ourselves that the *Monitor* is good enough to tell its own story. We know, too, that the *Monitor* has a long way to go to be worthy of its ideals and objectives. Everything it does, or has ever done, can be done better. The second half century is full of opportunity and need for doing a better job.

Now, at the outset, let us define terms.

What is *The Christian Science Monitor* anyway? What is it trying to do? How is it guided and controlled? How does it relate to other newspapers and to public affairs of its time?

The *Monitor* is one of very few daily newspapers in the world owned by a church. It is published by The Christian Science Publishing Society, which was established on January 25, 1898. The Publishing Society is one of the activities of the Christian Science Church, officially known as The First Church of Christ, Scientist, in Boston, Massachusetts.

Christian Science is a religious system which affirms spiritual healing as an essential part of its teaching and practice. It finds an abundant authority in the Bible and urges its daily study. The religion was discovered and the church established by Mary Baker Eddy after a long search for health and a deeper understanding of Christianity. She received a sudden influx of inspiration in 1866 and a striking healing resulted when she turned to the New Testament in an hour of great need.

Following this experience, Mrs. Eddy devoted several years to intensive study of the Bible to seek out the laws underlying the healing practice of Christ Jesus. She embodied the results of her prayerful study in a book which she published, with no little difficulty, in 1875 and first entitled *Science and Health.* In a discussion of the newspaper which Mrs. Eddy later established, it is not irrelevant to mention the absolutely central role that the printed word played in her religious work.

As the textbook of Christian Science, and definitively entitled *Science and Health with Key to the Scriptures,* this book has had a most remarkable history. It has gone through hundreds of editions with sales running into many millions. It is used every day by Christian Scientists in their thoughtful and studious application of their religion.

William Dana Orcutt, who was not a Christian Scientist but helped print Mrs. Eddy's book as an official of the University Press and the Plimpton Press, wrote in *Mary Baker Eddy and Her Books* that "with the exception of the Holy Bible, the Christian Science textbook . . . holds every printing and publishing record." Be this as it may, the book was and is the very center of Mrs. Eddy's teachings and of the Christian Science religion. The printed word thus has an ineffable meaning for all Christian Scientists. Publication, both of this textbook, of other volumes, and of periodicals, was a vital and dynamic part of Mrs. Eddy's presentation of her religious discoveries.

In 1879 a small group under Mrs. Eddy's leadership voted to organize a church "designed to commemorate the word and works of our Master, which should reinstate primitive Christianity and its lost element of healing." * In 1892 this church took its present form. It has more than 3200 branches in 48 countries.

Christian Scientists have a deep consciousness of the spiritual nature of man. Their teaching derives from the first chapter of Genesis: that God made all and made it "very good," that He created man in His image and likeness; and that, as Jesus declared, God is Spirit. The Christian Scientist thus regards the spiritual or true man as being as incapable of evil as his Maker. Sick, sinning, mortal man is seen as a merely material misconception of the true man. This false conception, the Christian Scientist believes, can be corrected by an increasing understanding of man's spiritual selfhood. Healing and regeneration result.

Such an approach explains the attitude of confidence in good which underlies the entire experience of the *Monitor.* The newspaper, like the individual Christian Scientist, does not ignore or dismiss the assertions of evil which confront human experience. It has to deal with them. But it does not believe these evils are the truth about man, and it seeks to replace

* Mary Baker Eddy, *Manual* (Boston, 1895), p. 17.

and correct them with more upright and noble concepts and deeds.

Hence the *Monitor* has always been profoundly dedicated to a crusading, reformative approach to human affairs. But it is an affirmative reformation, rather than an alarmist attitude. It springs from the profound purpose of the *Monitor* to contribute to the regeneration of all mankind.

The Christian Science Church does not publish a newspaper for the purpose of maintaining contact with its members, or for stimulating them to deeper religious zeal or greater church activities. The paper is not published to advertise Christian Science. It is published as a public service, in the words of Mrs. Eddy in its first editorial "to injure no man, but to bless all mankind." This public service does in fact serve to promote and extend the religion of Christian Science, which is the basic obligation of The Christian Science Publishing Society, set forth in its Deed of Trust.

The *Monitor* is a "religious newspaper" in the sense that its fundamental obligation is to a religious purpose, its net revenues are turned over to The Christian Science Board of Directors, and many of its decisions and actions are motivated by profoundly religious criteria. By law and public authority, under the federal postal regulations and taxation rules of city, state, and federal governments it is defined as a religious newspaper.

In a broad, nontechnical and nonlegal sense, the *Monitor* is not a religious newspaper. Down through the years, from the very outset, the *Monitor* was designed to be a "real newspaper," as its first editor, Archibald McLellan, defined it before it was ever issued.

The *Monitor*'s special method, in its task of serving mankind, is to give proper emphasis to significant news. It does not leave out news just because it is unpleasant, nor seek to throw a rosy glow over a world that is often far from rosy. To describe the *Monitor* as a "clean" newspaper is correct but incomplete. It also strives to expose whatever needs to be uncovered in order to be removed or remedied. It seeks to put the news in a sound perspective, giving greatest emphasis to what is important and reducing the merely sensational to its place in an accurate system of values. It seeks also to amuse and entertain, but in wholesome and socially desirable terms.

In short, the *Monitor's* contents must measure up to a system of value judgments which would be agreed upon by thoughtful and intelligent readers as accurate and adequate. Behind these judgments is the paper's purpose to help in uplifting human thinking. It seeks to do this formidably serious task in as bright and readable a manner as possible. It knows that nothing anybody prints is of any value until it is read. It is easy to get into human minds with sensation, with passion, with conflict. But such a penetration is rarely useful, often harmful. To interest human minds with information which is really important to people and their lives is, paradoxically, a much more difficult task. But it is an infinitely rewarding one.

The *Monitor* seeks to perform its public service in the local area where it is published, in the nation, and in the world. Though critics have sometimes defined the *Monitor* as "not a Boston newspaper," it has almost always had a local edition, having been committed to do so by a careful statement printed in the *Christian Science Sentinel,* the church weekly, before the paper first appeared. Its local news in its earliest issues and for many years — including the present — has been diligent. Its local reporting staff is expert. Its specialists — as at the Boston City Hall or Massachusetts State House — have often won praise. Thus it strives to serve and inform the community in which it is published.

But the *Monitor* circulates throughout the American continent and in 120 lands overseas. It has a large readership in the various parts of the United States, notably on the Pacific Coast and in the Middle West. It has always been aware of the problems of the nation as a whole and of its regions, and has maintained news bureaus, staff and special correspondents, throughout the country from its earliest days. Its coverage of such matters as farm problems, water usage in the scarcity areas, power development, conservation, justice to Indians, and regional political problems, has always been intent and well informed. Year in and year out, it devotes more space to coverage of events throughout the United States generally than does any other daily newspaper. A former Presidential nominee from the Middle West once told this writer that he had been an intent reader of the *Monitor*'s domestic dispatches long before he became aware of its foreign service.

The *Monitor*'s constant interest in world affairs has long been regarded as its chief distinction. From its first issue, it received analytical dispatches covering the chief problem areas of the world. At the same time it recorded progressive human achievement. As the years went by, its staff came to be more and more carefully trained in the affairs of significant areas of the world. Nowadays it maintains a sizable group of staff correspondents in news bureaus throughout the world. It has a very much larger corps of special correspondents who are not full-time members of its staff. It has also a number of area specialists who write background interpretive articles concerning parts of the world where censorship or other restrictions impair direct coverage.

From 1910 the *Monitor* published an "international edition," which circulated generally and put the emphasis on world news. Since 1917 all its editions have borne the subtitle on page one, "An International Daily Newspaper." This expression does not imply a commitment to supranationalism or a world state. The *Monitor*'s internationalism is strictly of the sort expressed by Mrs. Eddy in her phrase "to bless all mankind," in its first editorial. It is dedicated to the enlightenment of all whom it can reach. Its audience is global. It gives relative news emphasis to matters of greatest real importance to the largest groups of its readers. It carries at least as much and perhaps more significant American news to readers overseas, and overseas news to Americans, than any other publication.

The basic over-all authority for *The Christian Science Monitor,* as for the other Christian Science publications, and for other activities of the Christian Science movement, is vested by the Church Manual in The Christian Science Board of Directors. This is a group of five full-time members. They are not the kind of Board of Directors which meets once a month or once a year and ratifies or revises the work of a group of company officials. They keep in close touch with all important branches of the church work.

This is especially true of the *Monitor.* It was inevitably the case in the *Monitor*'s earliest years, when Mr. McLellan was also a member of the Board of Directors. But such overlapping in office has not existed since his time. Nowadays, and for many years, the chief executive of the *Monitor*'s news and editorial department has a weekly appointment with the Board of Directors, at which time he informs them of all important current activity and receives their instructions.

The Board is responsible for basic *Monitor* policies. It decides what line the paper is to take on various issues. Its interest in maintaining the quality of the *Monitor* is deep and constant. It frequently extends to matters of detail which are, in fact, the essence of an effective newspaper.

The Board of Trustees of The Christian Science Publishing Society is responsible for the business operations of the *Monitor,* as for the other publications. They are a three-member Board, also meeting several days a week in official session, keeping in close touch with and reaching decisions on the various business operations of the Publishing Society. In the years 1919–22 a severe legal battle, essentially between the two Boards, for control of the publications took place and will be summarized in Chapter 16. The issue was settled for all time by the Supreme Judicial Court of Massachusetts, which found that basic authority was vested in the Board of Directors, where Mrs. Eddy had placed it in the Church Manual.

When a vacancy arises in the Board of Directors, a successor is at once elected by the remaining four members of the Board. The members of the Board of Trustees also elect their members when vacancies arise, but the Board of Directors has authority to declare vacancies in the Board of Trustees.

The editor of the *Monitor,* the managing editor of the *Monitor,* the manager of the Publishing Society, and the editor and associate editors of the *Journal, Sentinel* and *Herald* are appointed by the Board of Directors, as stipulated by the Church Manual. Hence the editors of the *Journal* and *Sentinel,* as well as the manager, have regular meetings with the

Directors and fulfill their basic responsibilities to the Board.

The manager, while an appointee of the Directors, is also a full-time executive officer to the Board of Trustees, and carries out their decisions regarding the business operations of the Publishing Society. He sits with the Board during its regular official sessions.

The editor of the *Monitor* is responsible to the Board of Trustees through the manager for the business operations of the editorial department — such as salaries, hiring and promotion of personnel, and expenditures. He has regular meetings with the Trustees and more frequent meetings with the manager. If by any chance the editor's news and editorial responsibilities to the Directors should seem to come into conflict with his business responsibility to the Trustees, he is given a right of direct appeal to the Directors. The manager has the same right.

All this means two important things: first, that there is no question where ultimate authority rests over the policy and operation of *The Christian Science Monitor;* and second, that the two boards, the manager, the editor, and other officials, constitute a collective kind of leadership which is as rich in experience as it is in safeguards. The warm mutual confidence which has always prevailed, except during the litigation period, has greatly furthered the effective operation of the newspaper. This co-operation works in large part because of the common spiritual dedication underlying the newspaper and earnestly shared by its staff.

From 1927 to 1939 the *Monitor* editorial department was administered by the Monitor Editorial Board. This body, of from three to five members, bore the same organic relationship to the Directors and the Trustees as does an individual editor. However, the manager of the Publishing Society and one member of the Board of Trustees were members of the Editorial Board. This arrangement brought both the manager and a trustee deep into the operations of the editorial department, a position which might not have worked at all well if there had not been abundant good will and mutual confidence on the part of all involved, and if the ultimate authority of the Board of Directors had not been always operative. For a brief period, from 1939 to 1947, there was a Monitor Editorial Council, including as its members all three Trustees, the manager, and five members of the *Monitor* editorial department. The Editorial Council was a strictly advisory and consultative body, with no executive or administrative role.

The *Monitor* has no partisan political commitment or affiliation. It is linked to no vested interest except the one frankly expressed in its name. It has been economically self-supporting for the major part of its existence, deriving its revenues from subscriptions and advertising. This has given it a position of exceptional independence.

The normal framework of business administration has prevailed: a manager, an advertising manager, circulation manager, production manager, and various other technical department heads. On the business side, the *Monitor* has had many unique problems to solve: distribution of over 90 per cent of its circulation to points remote from its place of publication; selling of advertising to advertisers in all parts of the world and solicitation on a broad rather than a local basis; production of many different editions daily with heavy changes between the editions; maintenance of a plant which is efficient and functional on the one hand and a showplace for a steady stream of visitors on the other; support of an editorial operation, including maintenance of bureaus and correspondents at remote points, which is expensive but does not derive revenue from syndication of material to other newspapers. All these and many other technical problems have been solved.

It is difficult to say with positive assurance just what effect the *Monitor* has had on other newspapers and on the public affairs of its time. These are things that cannot readily be proved. But there are strong indications that the *Monitor*'s steady insistence on significant, constructive, responsible news and interpretation has had a real influence on the maturing of newspapers in the United States and elsewhere in the world.

Certainly the irresponsible yellow journalism which existed when the *Monitor* was established — and was one of Mrs. Eddy's prime motivations in founding the paper — has been greatly modified. The sensational journalism of today, though plenty of it exists, bears not much resemblance to the sensational journalism of 1908 and through the 1920's.

In its early years, the *Monitor* preached the doctrine of "clean journalism" almost as much as it practiced it. Part of its articulate missionary work was to sell itself to an increasing readership. Part of it was to remind other newspapers of their duties, by word as well as by deed. As time went on, the word became less necessary than the deed. The *Monitor*'s position became better known, its editors and staff members took a more and more active role in newspaper organizations dedicated to the betterment of newspapers.

One of the *Monitor*'s editors was instrumental in the foundation of the American Society of Newspaper Editors and another has served as the Society's president. Another *Monitor* editor — the chief editorial writer — was a founding father and later chairman of the National Conference of Editorial Writers. Others have presided over Sigma Delta Chi, the journalistic fraternity, the Overseas Writers, the Women's Press Club of Washington, and various other organizations. Several *Monitor* staff members have been Nieman Fellows at Harvard University. Others are active in the affairs of the American Press Institute, the International Federation of Newspaper Editors, of which one has been vice-president, the International Press Institute, and the Pulitzer Prize Awards Committee. These are but a few of the contexts in which the *Monitor*'s contribution to better journalism is practiced.

The paper has been awarded the N. W. Ayer cup for typographical excellence. On many occasions it has been among the top three or four newspapers in the running for this coveted recognition. One of its correspondents has received the Pulitzer Prize. It has received the Maria Moors Cabot award for its Latin American coverage, and been recognized with many other professional distinctions. Several of its staff members have been decorated by various governments for the paper's contribution to better understanding.

Doubtless the most effective and important influence of the paper on journalism is its daily impact in newspaper offices throughout the nation and the world. The *Monitor* may well be the most widely quoted newspaper in the world, taking everything together. It would seem to be read by more newspapermen than any other. Its voice of moderation, judgment, and responsibility speaks in the editorial sanctums of over 4500 other editors daily. It would be presumptuous to claim too much for this influence; it is difficult to judge. But its role is certainly important, disinterested, informative, helpful.

All these qualities, and many others, are needed more than ever in the mid-century world. The complications that face humankind are vast and puzzling. Information and interpretation, today more than ever, are required if the world's people are to avoid the greatest of disasters. More accurate and honest statement of the problems facing the planet's peoples is the essential preliminary to an awakening of mankind from its materialism and selfishness.

Information is the key to understanding. It must be genuine information, alert to long-range relationships and inner values, as well as pitfalls. The local newspaper performs its useful role in telling people of the needs and events of their neighborhood. This is important too. And it is legitimate for people to be amused. The entertainment factor in newspapers need not be degrading, any more than it is in all human life, if it is kept within balance. But in addition to these functions, the newspaper has the imperious responsibility of telling people what is happening in the world and what it means, helping them to transcend mere human judgments. Without information, people cannot rise to the grave decisions they face in this crisis-laden period, nor take them with sufficient wisdom.

Human civilization, everyone agrees, is at a crossroads. Always, we seem to stand at a crossroads of some sort. It is a hackneyed phrase. But today the crisis is more critical than it has ever been in human history. For civilization faces the issue of survival. Nothing less. Extinction of the human race has become a technological possibility. Damage to the human race of appalling magnitude is more than a possibility. It is a present threat.

In deciding rightly at this crossroads, mankind needs honest and accurate information, responsible, and spiritually enlightened. And everyone needs to be reminded of the basic truths which run through the religious teachings of mankind: the doctrine of the infinite significance of God's individual man, the universal brotherhood of men, and the applied lesson of the Golden Rule as it is taught in many faiths. *The Christian Science Monitor* aims never to make religion obtrusive, but it does not hesitate to point out that a better awareness of spiritual values and duties is the essential preliminary to action for the salvation of society. To emphasize such facts is to get at the real meaning of events. It is journalism of the highest order.

Half a century ago a lone woman, in her eighty-eighth year, foresaw the service a newspaper could perform in these terms of high idealism. Her vision created *The Christian Science Monitor*. Her instructions brought it into being. The church she established furnishes the framework in which it is published. In all the history of journalism, surely there is no more extraordinary and unexpected phenomenon.

✧

PART ONE

THE MONITOR IS FOUNDED

1883–1908

✧

1

A World of Change

THE YEAR was 1908.

The ferment of a new century — and of new forces and ideas — stirred the world.

In the United States, a Presidential election was taking place. Theodore Roosevelt was bringing his only elective Presidential term to a tumultuous conclusion. William Howard Taft, his personally designated successor, was soon to win a substantial victory over William Jennings Bryan, the perennial Democratic nominee. But more important than the election was the surge of conflict over political, economic, and social reform. Tides of human liberation had begun to flow. They would not soon recede, though they were sometimes dammed.

The need and danger of the opening century, the challenge to citizens and their press were starkly headed "Insufficient Freedom" in a statement Mary Baker Eddy, Founder of *The*

Christian Science Monitor, gave to the New York *World* in December, 1900. These two words remained a key and a challenge at mid-century. Freedom is the *Monitor*'s commitment.

In Europe as 1908 unfolded, the mellow Edwardian succession to the Victorian age was swiftly and steadily stiffening into the imperial rivalries which led to the First World War. Already Germany under Emperor William II had challenged Britain's naval power. The Balkans were in recurrent crisis. Revolution and reform were running a race in tsarist Russia. The Ottoman Empire, which had maintained a kind of stability in the ancient area where three continents come together, was tottering toward collapse.

In Asia, Japan had just shown how well it was learning to organize military power by defeating Russia. It had entered into an alliance with Great Britain which alarmed many Americans. The venerable Manchu Empire in China was well along the road to revolution. In the Philippines, Uncle Sam, reluctant imperialist, was getting at the job of training and organizing an Asian people for independence. Mr. Taft, as a matter of fact, not long before had come back from Manila where with great dedication and good cheer he had admirably begun the benevolent education of the Filipinos. Elsewhere in Asia — in Kipling's imperial India, in the tidy Dutch East Indies, in teeming, vivid French Indo-China — the seeds of nationalism were in the soil but few foresaw their early flowering.

Yet it was in every respect a world on the edge of profound change. Permeating all the factors of ferment was the total difference made by man's new relationship with nature. For half a century or more, men had been breaking material barriers. They thought they had come a great distance, and in relative terms they had. Power resources were being developed which would help to lift the great burden of toil that had always hung heavy on the back of mankind. Steam and electricity were multiplying many fold the work capacity of the world. The newly available forces were shrinking the world. Steamboat and railroad, telegraph and cable, motorcar and airplane had appeared one after another, each drawing men closer together, multiplying their problems and their potential achievements.

Men's ideas had also begun to change. The smugness of the nineteenth century was giving place to the challenge and questioning of the twentieth century. Except in the fields of political and economic reform, the meaning of these changes was little manifest. It remained an age of optimism and confidence. Few, indeed, realized how deeply the unfolding century would require pathfinders and guides in a period of confusion and complexity.

Newspapers were none too well equipped to rise to the responsibilities that soon would be recognizably theirs. The growth of mass circulations, especially in the United States and Britain, had led to a period of mass sensationalism, and sensationalism had built up more circulation. William Randolph Hearst and Joseph Pulitzer were still fighting the titanic jaundiced battle which had risen to crescendo during the Spanish-American War. Lord Northcliffe and his emulators in Britain were minting the new literacy into the very profitable coin of popular, if yellow, journalism. Among the more serious and responsible newspapers of the world *The Times* of London had just barely emerged from the very real hazard of bankruptcy and collapse. The *New York Times* was steadily growing in capacity and service, though it was not the institution it has since become. In Paris, Berlin, Rome, Tokyo, Chicago, and elsewhere great organs were in transition, most of them the voices of political parties. Many of them were to disappear before many more decades had gone by. But the dominant elements in most newspapers were violence and scandal.

Despite the ferment and the hopes not many foresaw the period of growth and of change, of danger and of opportunity, into which the world was about to plunge. In the United States, nothing seemed more remote than the possibility of participation in two great world wars, with ever-increasing involvement in the affairs of nations. And, while many men of vision saw something of the meaning of technological change, none of them could possibly anticipate all that the impact of the motor age and atomic fission would mean. Anybody in 1908 who could have forecast the size of the American (or the world) population in 1958, or its electrical power output, or any other of its material indices, would simply have been put down as mad. Scarcely anyone looked out at the stars and foresaw the prospect of space travel.

The half century that loomed ahead in 1908 had vast need of honest, alert, and dedicated newspaper voices with substantial and continuing influence on their contemporaries. It needed voices that would not be choked or shrill with the tawdry excitement of sensationalism. It needed a newspaper setting an example to others of a sense of historical perspective, with ability to escape from the present, willingness to look beyond today's banner headlines to yesterday's or tomorrow's significance.

Very few could have imagined that such a newspaper voice would come through the agency of a church, as a result of the vision of a woman who had been living and working for almost twenty years withdrawn from the world, who had just gone through severe legal battles, and who faced urgent church needs which might be expected to demand every bit of her time and energies.

The simple fact that Mary Baker Eddy envisioned the role and serviceability — the spiritual mission — of a daily newspaper among the various activities of a busy and engrossing church movement is the first and perhaps the most remarkable of the many extraordinary facts about *The Christian Science Monitor*. That she saw it not as a merely religious daily, not as an extension in daily terms of the kind of journalism she had practiced on a bi-monthly, monthly, and weekly scale since 1883 and 1898, but as a regular daily newspaper of general interest, is additionally remarkable. That such a publication could also serve as a spiritual beacon light without losing its regular role as a newspaper is vital.

Moreover, that such a paper could be organized from scratch in little more than one hundred days, that it could turn out at once to be an excellent product, that it could survive not only the expected rigors of newspaper publishing but the especially severe trial of a long legal battle over its control, were further proofs that this was no ordinary journalistic enterprise. Finally, that at the end of its first half century the newspaper should be stronger than it has ever been, economically self-sufficient, possessed of prestige and respect commensurate with its opportunity and capacity to be of service, dedicated more deeply than ever to the task of leavening human thinking, rounds out a pattern without parallel.

2

Mrs. Eddy Prepares

On Sunday afternoon, January 26, 1908, Mary Baker Eddy moved from Concord, New Hampshire, where she had lived since 1889, to her new home in Chestnut Hill, Massachusetts, a suburb of Boston. The precise reasons for her move were not immediately apparent to the officers of her church. She had just gone through a bitter legal struggle, the "Next Friends" suit, in which a newspaper-promoted effort to seize control of her properties and undermine her church had failed. The routine of her life in Concord had been well established and fruitful, and designedly secluded. Why she should wish to undertake the major inconvenience of a move she did not explain.

As the late spring and early summer of 1908 progressed, a few of those closest to Mrs. Eddy in her household at Chestnut Hill, and the members of The Christian Science Board of Directors, may well have realized that something startling was under way. The project, a most carefully guarded secret, was nothing less than the establishment of a daily newspaper.

Just when Mrs. Eddy first conceived the role of a daily newspaper is not entirely clear from the existing evidence. Already, in 1883, only a scant eight years after she had put the final touches to the first edition of *Science and Health with Key to the Scriptures,* she had established her first periodical, *The Christian Science Journal,* originally a bimonthly.

In the first issue of the *Journal,* in words carefully revised for re-publication in 1896, she wrote: "At this date, 1883, a newspaper edited and published by the Christian Scientists has become a necessity." * Later in the same article, she said: "Looking over the newspapers of the day, one naturally reflects that it is dangerous to live, so loaded with disease seems the very air. These descriptions carry fears to many minds, to be depicted in some future time upon the body. A periodical of our own will counteract to some extent this public nuisance; for through our paper, at the price at which we shall issue it, we shall be able to reach many homes with healing, purifying thought." †

Many have felt that when Mrs. Eddy said that "a newspaper edited and published by the Christian Scientists has become a necessity," she was referring to the daily newspaper which she established a quarter of a century later. The word "newspaper" was introduced, perhaps significantly, only in the 1896 revision. In 1883 she used the word "organ," writing: "An organ from the Christian Scientists has become a necessity."

Certain it is that in 1883 she already saw the need of improving modern journalism, although she placed the emphasis not so much on general news as on disease-laden propaganda. But it required a quarter of a century for the ideal she envisioned in 1883 to unfold in practical experience.

From the context, it is evident that the "newspaper" or "organ" which had become "a necessity" in 1883 was *The Christian Science Journal.* In the very following sentence, describing the task of the proposed publication, Mrs. Eddy

* *Miscellaneous Writings* (Boston, 1896), p. 4, line 12; hereafter cited as 4:12.
† *Miscellaneous Writings,* 7:17–24.

wrote: "Many questions important to be disposed of come to the College [Massachusetts Metaphysical College, where Mrs. Eddy taught her students at this period] and to the practising students, yet but little time has been devoted to their answer. Further enlightenment is necessary for the age, and a periodical devoted to this work seems alone adequate to meet the requirement." Such a periodical, devoted to denominational questions which came to Mrs. Eddy and the practicing students, was precisely what Mrs. Eddy then established in *The Christian Science Journal.* It differed almost totally in function from the kind of general newspaper she set up twenty-five years later.

Yet the ideal and objective of a newspaper were clearly in Mrs. Eddy's thinking, even in 1883. From the outset of her publishing activity she saw the need of conveying information of public and world affairs to her students. The *Journal* in 1883 and soon after, contained a number of items of general interest, rather than simply of religious significance, and it carried some secular advertising. When, in 1898, Mrs. Eddy established the *Christian Science Sentinel,* which at first was called *The Christian Science Weekly,* it also included a generous quota of general news. In the first issue, which came during the Spanish-American War, there were 26 items. No less than 19 of them dealt with problems concerning the war. Three out of 14 columns of reading matter in the periodical were devoted to news.

It was evident from the way in which Mrs. Eddy included general news in otherwise strictly religious periodicals that she felt a real need for bringing significant news material to the attention of Christian Scientists. She herself was remarkably well informed. In 1907, the famous lecturer and journalist William E. Curtis called upon her in Concord for an interview. The visit is described by Michael Meehan, himself not a Christian Scientist, who was editor of the Concord, New Hampshire, *Patriot* at the time. Mr. Meehan wrote that Mr. Curtis "made a statement about affairs in China, touching which Mrs. Eddy asked for more detailed and definite information, and quite unconsciously, seemingly, she took the topic entirely out of his grasp, and for more than an hour, dwelt on the details of the Chinese situation, with such a wonderful insight and with such intimate knowledge of its social, political and economic conditions, as to quite confound the man . . .

"As we drove from Pleasant View, Mr. Curtis marveled how a woman who so completely excluded the world could possibly know so much about the world's affairs, and particularly how she could have acquired such accurate and comprehensive acquaintance with the history and national habits of the Chinese, a people so little known, and with the court customs and unpublished intrigues of its rulers." *

Mrs. Eddy's various comments on public affairs were always timely, and perceptive. In early 1908, an impelling issue of the outgoing Roosevelt Administration was the question of naval armament. President Roosevelt had advocated more vigilant preparedness. It was the time of the "big stick." In the April 11, 1908, issue of the *Christian Science Sentinel,* Mrs. Eddy had witten: "For many years I have prayed daily that there be no more war, no more barbarous slaughtering of our fellow-beings; prayed that all the peoples on earth and the islands of the sea have one God, one Mind; love God supremely, and love their neighbor as themselves.

"National disagreements can be, and should be, arbitrated wisely, fairly; and fully settled.

"It is unquestionable, however, that at this hour the armament of navies is necessary, for the purpose of preventing war and preserving peace among nations."

Three days later, on April 14, 1908, President Roosevelt sent a message to Congress advocating increased armament, saying, "If we desire to secure peace, one of the most powerful instruments of our rising prosperity, it must be known that we are at all times ready for war."

There are many instances recorded by members of her household of the close attention Mrs. Eddy paid the flowing panorama of current history. She was greatly interested in the evidences of man's mastery of his material environment. She

* Lyman Powell, *Mary Baker Eddy: A Life Size Portrait* (New York, 1930), p. 205.

followed the technological wonders of the day, and was keenly interested in the conquest of the air.

When the English aviator Claude Grahame-White made the first flight over Boston in 1910 in his Bleriot monoplane, Mrs. Eddy eagerly followed the event. She had a number of the members of her household go to the beach at Squantum, near Boston, where the flight took place, in order to report to her in detail just what occurred. She asked one of her secretaries to arrange, if possible, for a flight over her house at Chestnut Hill, so that she might see the plane in motion. Mr. Grahame-White felt the overland flight to Chestnut Hill was too far for him to attempt. He preferred flying over the ocean, although on the day in question he covered 35 miles.

Mrs. Eddy subscribed to and read many current magazines. She also annotated them and often called interesting passages to the attention of members of her household. The files of these magazines are an indication of her interest in current events. One of the most carefully marked of the magazines is the *Literary Digest*. For example, Mrs. Eddy read and annotated an issue describing President Theodore Roosevelt's State of the Union Message to Congress in 1905. She underlined a passage observing (on December 16) that "there is more need to get rid of the causes of war than of the implements of war."

Mrs. Eddy also underlined a passage reading: "As for the Monroe Doctrine, 'we have adapted our application of it to meet the growing and changing needs of the hemisphere' but it will not be used 'as an excuse for aggrandizement' or 'a cloak for territorial aggression.' " Such a reference by President Roosevelt was certainly necessary after he had intervened in Panama two years before to make possible the foundation of the republic and the cession of the Panama Canal Zone.

Other noteworthy markings by Mrs. Eddy in this Presidential message concerned Theodore Roosevelt's proposal to regulate corporations dealing in interstate business. She drew attention to these words: "As the case now stands, they [corporations dealing in interstate business] 'occupy the position of subjects without a sovereign,' because 'State control is not broad enough and the laws passed by Congress are inadequate.' " The problem, the President says, is with the national laws in that they are "negative and prohibitive," and are enforceable, if at all, only by "incessant appeal to the courts."

These passages shed a good deal of light on Mrs. Eddy's analysis of the problems of the twentieth century, headed "Insufficient Freedom" and quoted on page 88. The concept of the need for more freedom, spiritual and material, for the individual and for private enterpise, which she emphasized in several of her public statements — and which has been a constant objective of the *Monitor* — is the "commitment to freedom" which gives the title to this volume. The theme is emphasized in another underlined passage, this time in the *Literary Digest* on September 27, 1902. Under the title "Dictation by Labor-Unions" occur these marked words: "No industry has a right to more than that amount of the worker's energy which can normally be replaced by the food and rest allowed to him. Workers worn out at an early age by too great exertion must be maintained in some way by society; either their friends or relatives subsidize them, or they become chargeable to some public or private charity." These words, anachronistic as they sound at mid-century, are nevertheless a recognition of the need for proper hours, compensation, or some form of social safeguard.

Enough has been quoted to show the scope and intentness of Mrs. Eddy's interest in public affairs, but it is a mere scraping of the surface. The collection of her magazines, not to mention the wide range of her public writings, amply documents her concern with the flow of the news and of the meaning of events — political, economic, cultural.

In still another important respect Mrs. Eddy's interest in newspapers had been developing for years. She herself and the religion she founded had received a very mixed reception from the press. Some newspapers were objective and honest in their coverage of the new religion and its Founder. But others had been consistently hostile and vindictive, sneering with malice or ill-timed jests. The early years of this century were at the height of the "muckraking" period in American journalism. Much of the investigation which newspapers and magazines performed during these years was salutary and constructive. Many vicious social abuses were exposed, and their removal was advanced by crusading journalism. But the behavior toward Mrs. Eddy of two of the leading "muckrakers" shows how sensationalism can cause grave abuses.

In 1906 the New York *World* and *McClure's Magazine* sent representatives to Concord with the apparently intent purpose of deriding and destroying Mrs. Eddy and Christian Science. The most fantastically distorted and fabricated charges were published. Their refutation was constantly at hand in Concord. Honest reporting could not have avoided it. Two leading Concord newspapermen, Michael Meehan and George H. Moses of the Concord *Evening Monitor,* later an eminent United States Senator, both reported abundant facts which refuted the claims made by the *World* and *McClure's.* Boston and New York dailies and national press services sent reporters to Concord, they interviewed Mrs. Eddy, and their reports were unmistakable denials of the slanders coming from the two determined muckrakers. Among the most detailed and persuasive of these refutations was an interview Mrs. Eddy granted to Arthur Brisbane, the famous Hearst editor, who had also been an old Pulitzer star.

Describing Mrs. Eddy's thinking as being "perfectly clear" and her answers as "instantaneous," Mr. Brisbane gave a vivid picture of her graciousness, clarity, and spiritual strength. There were plenty of other witnesses. Nevertheless, the New York *World* went so far out of any normal journalistic role as to promote in 1907 a suit designed to wrest from Mrs. Eddy and her trusted officials all control of her church and its activities. The suit, which ended triumphantly to Mrs. Eddy's advantage, may well have convinced her that the time was at hand when the Christian Scientists should set the newspaper world a better example. Instead of criticizing the newspaper press, or even replying with justified fervor to the attacks upon her, Mrs. Eddy may indeed have decided that the best contribution she could make would be that of a more ennobling newspaper. But the newspaper she established was not for the purpose of counterattacking her enemies. She realized that the best possible course in the face of vindictive and malicious journalism was honest and constructive journalism. She knew, too, that such an organ would do the most good for her church.

The motivation of the New York *World* in promoting the Next Friends suit against Mrs. Eddy is obscure, and whether Joseph Pulitzer himself had authorized the action is dubious. Neither Christian Science nor Mrs. Eddy is mentioned in his biography, *Joseph Pulitzer, His Life and Letters,* by Don C. Seitz, long an executive of the *World.*

Mr. Pulitzer's other newspaper, the St. Louis *Post-Dispatch,* is today often coupled with *The Christian Science Monitor* in references to the United States' most distinguished and independent newspapers. Joseph Pulitzer, Jr., who was greatly responsible as publisher for the growth and eminent service of the *Post-Dispatch,* was for many years a careful reader and outspoken admirer of the *Monitor.* Whenever a *Monitor* representative would meet him at newspaper conventions, or on visits in St. Louis, he regularly indicated a large and informed interest in the *Monitor.* His newspaper has for many years paid the *Monitor* the compliment of reprinting many of its special articles and editorials, with credit, and has even sought the right to purchase some of them for joint publication. Since the *Monitor* does not syndicate its copy to other publications, such a plan was not feasible. But it is pleasant to record that the antipathy of 1907 turned ultimately into respect. The *Monitor,* conversely, has had the privilege of reprinting many editorials from the *Post-Dispatch.*

Mrs. Eddy had taken several steps prior to 1908 which might have been interpreted as foreshadowing an important new publishing enterprise. As early as 1902, only four years after the weekly *Sentinel* had been established, she summoned Archibald McLellan of Chicago to Boston to become editor of the *Journal* and the *Sentinel.* In a letter discussing her decision, she wrote: "Until I start a widespread press, we should have in Boston a born editor." *

* Clifford P. Smith, *Historical Sketches* (Boston, 1941), p. 131.

The exact significance of this striking observation is not clear. It was in a letter addressed to Mr. and Mrs. Edward A. Kimball, two of her most trusted students. In the letter, Mrs. Eddy requested Mr. and Mrs. Kimball to remain at hand in Boston while she carried out the task of training a new editor. She describes vividly in the letter the difficulty and time involved in developing a person for this responsible post. The remark shows, at least, that Mrs. Eddy was thinking in broad and sweeping terms of new publishing plans. "A widespread press" could scarcely be a more expansive phrase whether it referred specifically to a daily newspaper or to some other project.

There had been a flurry in 1898 concerning a daily newspaper. In that year, Mrs. Eddy had sent a letter to Judge Septimus J. Hanna, then editor of *The Christian Science Journal* and *Sentinel,* specifically disapproving a proposal that a group of Christian Scientists buy control of an important Boston newspaper. The purpose of owning such a newspaper, in the recollection of one member of Mrs. Eddy's household, would have been to some degree what the *Monitor* became: to give an accurate and impartial version of world affairs. The plan went so far as to be presented to Mrs. Eddy. Her disapproval indicated at least that she did not consider the time ripe in 1898 for Christian Scientists to own or control a Boston newspaper. This project was very different from that of a newspaper published by The Christian Science Publishing Society. It more nearly resembles the proposal described in the following chapter, which was made to Mrs. Eddy by John L. Wright in March, 1908. Then, too, the idea of a paper simply owned by Christian Scientists, as contrasted with a paper published as an integral part of the Christian Science movement, was rejected.

Already, in 1898, Mrs. Eddy had executed a Deed of Trust which vested ownership of the building and real estate occupied by The Christian Science Publishing Society in the Board of Trustees. She gave to them all the publications of the movement, reserving an option which she never exercised to withdraw the copyright of *The Christian Science Journal* in her own name. She provided that all the moneys and assets of the publications were to be held in trust by this Board of three Trustees, whose duty was to be the management of the business affairs of the Publishing Society, with all profits turned over to The Mother Church at specific intervals. In short, Mrs. Eddy made ready the legal instrument and the practical arrangements under which a major publishing enterprise could be carried out.

In 1907, while she was still at Concord, she authorized issuance of an appeal for contributions with which to build a new Publishing House at what is now 107 Falmouth Street. Although the structure begun in 1907 was not big enough for the task of printing and publishing a newspaper, it was an important start in that direction. Again it was part, conscious or unconscious, of careful preparation for a great undertaking.

3

The Instructions Are Given

ON MARCH 12, 1908, by a remarkable coincidence which may have had something to do with bringing her long maturing plans to a head, Mrs. Eddy received the following letter from John L. Wright, a Boston newspaperman who was a Christian Scientist. Mr. Wright wrote:

> During the last two years I have felt a growing desire to have a part in establishing a Scientific daily newspaper. It seems to me that such newspapers are greatly needed, that Boston is the natural place for the first one, and that perhaps the time for it has come. I am not thinking of a daily official Christian Science paper, or one containing in its title the word Christian Science, but of a general newspaper owned by Christian Scientists and conducted by experienced newspapermen who are Christian Scientists; so presenting news more as Christian Scientists would like it presented than any newspaper now presents it. I have heard a number of Scientists express a desire for, or the expectation of such a paper as perhaps

the next thing to result from the Christian Science movement.

I desire of course to be divinely led in whatever I may undertake in the matter. I do not want to do anything that you would not wish done. Hence, I am taking the liberty to write to you so that if you see any reason why such a project should not be entered upon in the near future you can readily prevent it, at least as far as I am concerned.

The disappearance so largely of the more stable, sane, patriotic newspaper, the usurpation of the newspaper field in great centres by commercial and political monopolists, and the commercialization of newspapers — their management mainly for dividends, with almost everything subordinated and many things eliminated to that end, constitute, I believe, a great misfortune to the country. All Scientists, I am sure, have wearied of seeing the pictures and glaring and detailed descriptions of crime, death and other depressing representations that daily confront one at first glance at almost any newspaper. Such occurrences of course are regarded as "important" in the offices of the large newspapers because accounts of them prominently displayed swell circulation. On the other hand, news of the constructive, helpful, encouraging, uplifting activities of life is sacrificed, often being minimized if not thrown away.

I think many would like to read a paper that takes less notice of crime, etc., and gives attention especially to the positive side of life, to the activities that work for the good of man and to the things really worth knowing. I do not think such a paper would have the largest circulation by any means, at present, but it seems to me the time has come when it could gain a very considerable circulation. I believe there is need of daily newspapers that will place principle before dividends, and that will be fair, frank and honest with the people on all subjects and under whatever pressure; that will not compromise with evil. It seems to me that a newspaper should be active in the interests of civic righteousness. . . .

Hoping I am not presuming too much in sending you so long a letter, and that I shall be notified soon if you disapprove of my suggestion, I am with profound gratitude,

JOHN L. WRIGHT

On this letter, in Mrs. Eddy's handwriting, is the following note:

Beloved Student:

I have had this newspaper scheme in my thought for quite a while and herein send my name for our daily newspaper

The Christian Science Monitor.

This title only classifies the paper and it should have departments for what else is requisite.

This note, undated but evidently written not long after March 12, 1908, represents as far as we know the first coupling of the words *The Christian Science Monitor,* and the first explicit declaration by Mrs. Eddy that she had in mind the establishment of a *daily* newspaper. It is the first documentary reference to *The Christian Science Monitor,* and there is no record of any earlier verbal reference.

At the least, Mr. Wright's letter evoked Mrs. Eddy's specific naming of *The Christian Science Monitor* and impelled her to state her long held plan for the establishment of a daily newspaper. Hence it is of very considerable importance in the history of the newspaper. However, it clearly did not give Mrs. Eddy the idea of a daily newspaper. That had been in her thinking, as she said, for years. A similar proposal to Mr. Wright's had been considered and rejected in 1898.

But the practical and cogent way in which Mr. Wright argued his thesis may well have interested Mrs. Eddy. In some respects, his proposal differed from the kind of newspaper she had in mind, and which was established a few months later. His suggestion was for what would ultimately be a chain or group of newspapers, and he was proposing "the first one." Mrs. Eddy had no such idea. She saw the importance of a single newspaper, of universal application and interest. She knew the disadvantages of "minds many" and of decentralized or conflicting control. Mr. Wright disavowed "a daily official Christian Science paper, or one containing in its title the words Christian Science." Mrs. Eddy's concept, as she affirmed in her penciled note, was definitely for a newspaper with the words "Christian Science" in the title, and her organ was to be official in the important sense that it was to be owned by the

Church. Her concept of its mission was more profound. She had no thought of selling shares to private persons, as Mr. Wright proposed.

But elsewhere in his letter, Mr. Wright struck responsive chords, which were prophetic of the nature and commitment of the newspaper that shortly came into being. He was one of the group of newspapermen engaged later in 1908 to prepare the paper, and he remained on its staff until 1922. He was at first city editor, and later an editorial writer. There is no record that Mrs. Eddy's reply to Mr. Wright's letter was ever sent. Nor is there any hint that he ever did anything further about his plan. Perhaps word was discreetly conveyed to him to await developments.

The project did not slip from Mrs. Eddy's thinking. Just a few weeks afterward, on May 3, she drafted a letter addressed to Archibald McLellan, who was editor of *The Christian Science Journal* and *Sentinel* as well as a Director of The Mother Church, and to Allison V. Stewart, also a Director of The Mother Church, and Publishers' Agent in charge of publication of Mrs. Eddy's writings. In this draft letter, which was never sent, she wrote: "The time has come when we must have a daily paper entitled Christian Science Monitor. Allow no hesitation or delay on this movement. I will loan you all the money I can raise to help do it. When I proposed having the weekly Sentinel students held back at first; they may hold back this time but I in the name of God direct you to do this. Answer me immediately."

The fact that Mrs. Eddy drafted this letter, following her notation on the Wright letter in March, must have been a plain indication to her secretaries and perhaps to a few other members of her household that she intended to publish a newspaper. That so sensational a bit of news did not penetrate beyond the household, though it would have been exceedingly meaningful to the Trustees of The Christian Science Publishing Society and many others at the church headquarters, is a tribute to the discretion of her staff.

The reason why Mrs. Eddy did not send the May 3 letter

becomes apparent in the next letter she wrote on the subject, dated July 3. In this message, written in her handwriting, addressed to Mr. Stewart and also not sent, she said:

> I am impressed to write what must not be named before the debt of our Publishing House is paid — and it is this.
>
> We should have a daily newspaper it is very important to our cause and the bulk of this cause demands it.
>
> I hereby state that so soon as said debt is paid I will head a subscription list for this purpose with $100 subscribed and I ask that you entitle this newspaper The Christian Science Monitor. Please keep silent on this matter till our Church debts are paid. I want to name it to you and hear from you on this subject.

Not until July 28, in a letter received at the offices of The Christian Science Board of Directors, did an actual instruction go forth. This letter, again in Mrs. Eddy's handwriting said:

> *Notice.* So soon as the Pub. House debt is paid I request The C. S. Board of Directors to start a daily newspaper called *Christian Science Monitor.* This must be *done* without fail.

Here was a clear and ringing order. But the Directors, while not shirking their own responsibilities in the matter, felt that the Board of Trustees of The Christian Science Publishing Society were the proper authorities to undertake the publishing job. They were also — one of them has averred — deeply impressed by the magnitude of the task. They sought to gain time to consider it carefully. So the Directors communicated with Mrs. Eddy at Chestnut Hill through her secretary, Adam H. Dickey. They suggested that the orders for founding a newspaper should go from Mrs. Eddy to the Board of Trustees, and they asked for further clarification of the scope of the project.

While this was being done, Mrs. Eddy again communicated to the Directors, through a typewritten note to Mr. McLellan, who as editor of the periodicals she no doubt considered the official most directly concerned with the *Monitor* project. To him, on August 3, she wrote: "Have on the cover of the

Christian Science Monitor, 'First the blade, then the ear, after that the full corn in the ear,' and have that illustrated with a pretty design."

This quotation, from Mark 4:28, was indeed placed at the top of the *Monitor's* editorial page, which then as now, was the back page of the entire publication. But the American Standard Version was used on recommendation of the Board of Trustees to Mrs. Eddy, so as to avoid ambiguity over the word "corn," in this form: "First the blade, then the ear, then the full grain in the ear." And the "pretty design," used then as now, consists of a sheaf of five ears of grain.

Mrs. Eddy's condition "as soon as the Publishing House debt is paid" had now been met. Ground had been broken for erection of the Christian Science Publishing House in the autumn of 1907 and the work had been rapidly carried through during the first months of Mrs. Eddy's residence in Chestnut Hill. A handsome and conservative three-storied structure of Bedford stone had gone up at the corner of St. Paul and Falmouth Streets. It is just across St. Paul Street from The Mother Church Extension and it faces the Church Park. The building, which extends from Falmouth Street through to Norway Street, is in fact in three sections. It is now used for the administrative offices of the church. The first section, extending about a third of the way down the block, was the segment which had to be completed before Mrs. Eddy was ready to launch the *Monitor* project. The Publishing Society moved into these new quarters in August, 1908. Thus the way was clear for Mrs. Eddy to write the Board of Trustees and start the newspaper definitely on its way.

Here is the historic letter which officially launched *The Christian Science Monitor:*

Christian Science Board of Trustees,

Boston, Mass.

Beloved Students:

It is my request that you start a daily newspaper at once, and call it the Christian Science Monitor. Let there be no delay. The Cause demands that it be issued now.

You may consult with the Board of Directors, I have notified them of my intention.

MARY B. G. EDDY

These terse and unequivocal instructions seem to have come to the Trustees as a bolt from the blue. Although the Directors had known of Mrs. Eddy's intentions for at least twelve days — and perhaps longer, since three draft letters from Mrs. Eddy predated that time — and some members of her household must have known of her project for a daily newspaper since March, the secret had been extremely well kept.

Perhaps the best proof concerns William P. McKenzie, then a member of the Board of Trustees, a Christian Science lecturer, and subsequently a member of The Christian Science Board of Directors. His wife, Mrs. Daisette D. S. McKenzie, writes:

In the summer of 1908, Mr. McKenzie and I accepted the invitation of Mr. and Mrs. Albert Metcalf to occupy their summer farm in Dublin, N.H., for a vacation. We had been only five days on the farm when Mr. McKenzie received a telegram from Boston to take the first train back, as business of great importance had arisen. In order to get the very first train, Mr. McKenzie rose at four o'clock in the morning and walked three miles, on the possibility of flagging a train which would get him into Boston when the office opened. He was successful in stopping the train and found on his arrival that our Leader had sent word of the immediate starting of a daily newspaper. I believe that she indicated that it must be done within three months. Their faith in God and in the inspiration and guidance of our beloved Leader sustained the Trustees in this seemingly enormous task before them.*

The picture of Mr. McKenzie hiking cross-country in the dawn to be at his post in Boston is very evocative to all who knew him. He was a very gentle person, a poet, a brother of Dr. R. Tait McKenzie, the sculptor, and his love and dedication for Christian Science knew no bounds. He would never have gone away on vacation if he had had the slightest

* From a letter written by Mrs. McKenzie to Paul S. Deland, then managing editor, *The Christian Science Monitor,* December 29, 1948.

advance notice that the newspaper project was under way.

Another personal episode raises an intimate picture. It happened that on Monday, August 10, the day the Trustees received their startling note from Mrs. Eddy, they were to dine, together with their wives, at the home of one of their number. Their dinner-table conversation, says the wife of one of the Trustees, was unusually constricted. Only the ladies, it seemed, had anything to talk about. And as soon as dinner was over, the men retired to their host's study, firmly closing the door behind them. They wished, of course, to talk over their *Monitor* project, but they were unable to disclose its nature to their good wives. And so the ladies spent the evening wondering, audibly and silently, what in the world could have happened!

The meeting which Mr. McKenzie reached after his early morning hike was held at 10:30 A.M. on August 10. The Trustees were all present. As well as Mr. McKenzie, they were Judge Clifford P. Smith and Thomas W. Hatten. Archibald McLellan was present from the Board of Directors to deliver the letter from Mrs. Eddy. The Trustees' minutes record that they "immediately commenced making plans for the new daily and arranged a consultation with the Directors concerning it for tomorrow morning."

The two Boards met, as specified, on August 11. Their minutes state: "It was agreed between the two boards that the Directors are charged with the duty of providing the building or place for the publication of the Monitor and that the Trustees are charged with the duty of organizing and starting the new paper subject to such special authority in regard thereto as is vested in the Directors by the Church By-Laws or in Mr. McLellan by our Leader."

A brief word is desirable about the men who made up The Christian Science Board of Directors and the Board of Trustees of The Christian Science Publishing Society, to whom Mrs. Eddy sent her momentous message. What sort of people were they who had to carry out the challenging mandate?

The Directors were five: Ira O. Knapp, William B. Johnson, Allison V. Stewart, Stephen A. Chase, and, as previously mentioned, Archibald McLellan. The Trustees were three: Messrs. McKenzie, Smith, and Hatten. These were strong and seasoned men. Many of them had been staunchly helpful to Mrs. Eddy in the difficult periods through which her young church had passed.

Mr. Knapp was a New Hampshire patriarch, a man of striking appearance with a long white beard who became interested in Christian Science along with his wife Flavia Stickney Knapp in 1884. In 1889 Mrs. Eddy made him the recipient of a trust deed for the land on which the Original Mother Church was to stand. From September 1, 1892, he was a member of the church's Board of Directors, and a much trusted member of the official family.

Mr. Johnson had also been closely relied upon by Mrs. Eddy since the late 1880's. He had served for three years in the 1st Massachusetts Regiment during the Civil War. After holding other posts in Mrs. Eddy's very new church organization, he became its Clerk in 1889, and still held that position in 1908.

Mr. Stewart, also a long trusted supporter of Mrs. Eddy, had in December, 1907, been appointed publisher of her books and a Director of the Church in January, 1908. Since September, 1906, he had been a Trustee of the Publishing Society, relinquishing that post when he became a Director.

Mr. Chase was a businessman from Fall River, Massachusetts. In 1884 he became interested in Christian Science, was named to the Board of Directors by Mrs. Eddy in 1892 and at the same time was appointed treasurer of the building fund for the erection of the Original Mother Church building. Later he was elected Treasurer of The Mother Church and still held that position in 1908. Mr. McLellan is described in Chapter 8.

Of the Trustees, Mr. McKenzie and Judge Smith continued to play large roles in the affairs of the Church until the 1940's. Mr. McKenzie was of Canadian birth. His interest in Christian Science began in the 1890's, and his earnest zeal and dedicated poetic spirit came to the attention of Mrs. Eddy. He was appointed to The Christian Science Board of Lectureship in 1898, and to the Board of Trustees in the same year. In 1932 he became a Director. Judge Smith, who had served on the bench while a young man in Iowa, also served Christian Science in responsible posts for many years, thirty-seven of them in Boston. At the time of the *Monitor's* founding he was also First Reader of The Mother Church. Later he became Manager of Committees on Publication, and still later was in charge of the Bureau of History and Records. Mr. Hatten had come to Boston in 1892. He was appointed to the Board of Trustees in 1898, where he remained until 1917. For a short period of 1901–2 he had been a member of Mrs. Eddy's household.

From these brief summaries, it will be seen that those called upon by Mrs. Eddy to take over-all responsibility for the new undertaking were seasoned, substantial, and practical men. In terms of judgment and knowledge of business and professional affairs, they constituted impressive boards. But above all they had a deep sense of religious zeal which enabled them to tackle and solve the unprecedented problem that was placed in their hands in August, 1908.

4

◊◊◊◊◊◊◊◊◊◊◊◊◊◊◊◊◊◊◊◊◊

The Work Begins

THUS IT CAME ABOUT that a board of three Trustees, none of whom had had professional publishing experience before he entered upon his duties in The Christian Science Publishing Society, an editor who had not been a professional writer or journalist, and a Board of Directors who were similarly inexperienced in the techniques of a publishing enterprise found themselves suddenly faced with the considerable task of setting up a daily newspaper. And they were told "let there be no delay"!

There was none. Within little more than a hundred days, spurred by their Leader's ringing mandate and inspired by the feats of organization and construction which had recently been performed in erecting the Original Mother Church and its Extension, and which they had found to be habitual and normal in Christian Science, these men carried out what in 1958 would be considered a total impossibility in the time utilized.

They started from scratch. The job was gigantic. They had to secure professional assistance and make a plan. It would be necessary to demolish a block of three-story brick apartment buildings which stood on the spot where the Publishing House had to be extended. Tenants of these dwellings, many of them away on summer holiday, must be interviewed and cared for. The Publishing House enlargement must be designed and erected. Machinery also must be designed, ordered, constructed, and set up. A skillful professional staff must be recruited and organized. News services must be acquired, at home and abroad. Above all, the policies and methods of operation of a completely new and very challenging venture must be worked out. A unique task of newspaper pioneering must be thought through from the very ground up.

Instantly, on August 11, the Trustees responded to Mrs. Eddy that they were able and ready to begin the task. They wrote:

> Your letter of August 8th was delivered to us yesterday. The announcement contained in your letter is good news. We are confident that this move is timely; that the Monitor will be a mighty instrument for the promotion of Christian Science; and that it will be a success from a business standpoint. We rejoice to have this additional opportunity of assisting you in your plans for the welfare of humanity.
>
> As soon as we received your letter we immediately began the work of starting the new Daily and we shall proceed with it without delay. To-day we consulted with the Board of Directors. Tomorrow and next day we will confer with two practical newspaper men from Pittsburgh and Chicago whom Mr. McLellan has called here as advisers.

From this letter it is apparent that Mr. McLellan, who as the designated editor of the *Monitor* and a member of The Christian Science Board of Directors, had known of Mrs. Eddy's plans at least since July 28, must have been doing some exploring of available newspapermen who were Christian Scientists. These investigations had been carried out through the Christian Science Committee on Publication.

The Committee is a noteworthy institution. Starting from a single Committee in Boston, the operation has grown so that wherever in the world there is a Christian Science organization there is also a Committee on Publication. Each "Committee," customarily a single individual, and typically a person of substantial experience in business or public affairs, is charged with the task of giving out correct information about Christian Science and rectifying misstatements and misunderstandings which may be made by others concerning Christian Science.

The Committees also function in relation to legislative or other governmental bodies to make sure that the basic religious rights of Christian Scientists are maintained. The Committees are available, as in the instance of Mr. McLellan's search for experienced newspaper men, to provide information and do contact work which may be required for the Mother Church. For over half a century, the committee system has worked admirably in protecting the public position of Christian Science and conducting necessary business in a simple, practical manner.

So it was in 1908 that Mr. McLellan turned to the Committee on Publication, and through it made contact overnight with two experienced journalists.

For the Board of Trustees' first consultation, they summoned to Boston Alexander Dodds of the Pittsburgh *Post* and *Sun,* and John J. Flinn, of the Chicago *Inter-Ocean.* The three trustees, Mr. McLellan, who had been designated by Mrs. Eddy to be editor of the *Monitor,* and the two newspapermen dug deep into their practical problems. They met on the morning of August 13 and composed a letter to Mrs. Eddy outlining their task.

This letter is an amazing document. It outlines in rather detailed terms just what had to be done and how the Trustees and editors proposed to do it. It represented the lapse of only three days, culminating in a few hours' talk with working newspaper men, brought into the project then for the first time. To experienced newspapermen, the letter may well seem a striking feat of practical, if general, analysis. It is doubtful if a project for the establishment of a metropolitan daily newspaper was ever composed more quickly, or set forth in simpler terms. Here is what they said:

This is Thursday, and since receiving your message on Monday we have been continually at work finding out what must be arranged in order to publish a daily paper. As it is a very large enterprise, careful consideration has been necessary, and we have had to gain advice from men in that work.

To begin with, the machinery required is complicated, and two presses will be required to print a daily eight-page paper. For the Boston Herald six are used. Each press will cost $25,000, and must be set on a solid foundation, which in this neighborhood will require piling. For all the plant required for stereotyping $10,000 would be involved. Ten linotype machines would be necessary, twenty-three being used in the Boston Herald office, and the cost of each machine is $3,300. It takes several weeks for orders to be filled.

This mechanical department will, with some additions, involve the expenditure of over $105,000. This whole sum need not be paid at once. The machinery is valuable, and it is customary for publishers to pay a certain sum down, and settle the balance by installments.

We have counselled with newspapermen as to the number of men needed. Mr. John J. Flinn tells us that the Chicago Inter-Ocean has over 300 persons employed. We have gone over, item by item, our smaller needs with Mr. Alexander Dodds of the Pittsburgh Post and Sun, who is a managing Editor, and it seems as if at the beginning our paper could be handled by 90 to 100 employes. At the rates we would have to pay, the rates prevailing in newspaper offices, the payroll would be at least $400 a day, for six days a week, or $125,000 a year.

We have not figured on a Sunday edition. We are agreed to recommend an afternoon paper. This will avoid the necessity of having the editors work nights and Sundays, as every morning paper has to be prepared during the day and night previous to its issue. The price per year is proposed at $3.50, as in the West prices range from three to four dollars a year for dailies, and we should expect wide circulation on this continent.

New quarters will be required for the daily paper, since practically the whole of the new building is required for our present work. The Directors have consulted the architect and expect that a suitable building could be ready, with night and day work on the contract, in 90 days.

Mr. Dodds, who has had experience in starting and managing newspaper plants, has said that builders of printing presses will expect at least 90 days to fill orders, and by conference with an agent we find this is the case here in Boston.

You may be disappointed to know that preparation for this magnificent enterprise will require time. The good men who will be needed are already in demand in their present places, and before leaving must make such arrangements as will be just and kind to their present employers. Expensive and complicated machinery must be carefully built, tested, and transported. But Christian Science work has always been wrought better than the ordinary expectation.

Summing up the expenses, apart from the building, we find that for the printing plant an investment of over $105,000 will be necessary, and for the payroll, for one year $125,000. The expense for paper for the editions as printed is usually paid by the money received for subscriptions. The revenue of a paper is from its advertising. This might possibly within the first year meet the expense of the payroll. As circulation increases higher prices can be charged for advertising, and in time a profit will appear.

The revenue from the Publishing Society paid to the Church has been about $90,000 a year. If we were to expend as much as that in one year on this enterprise we would have nothing for the Mother Church which now depends somewhat upon this revenue. We have no larger fund to draw upon if we are to keep the business in the proper state of solvency. Nevertheless we know the newspaper can be financed, since you see it to be the right time for the enterprise.

Thus the Trustees gave Mrs. Eddy a candid report on the scope of her undertaking. In view of her engagingly modest offer — in her unsent note of July 3 — to subscribe $100 toward the project, it may be assumed that the magnitude of the task surprised and impressed her. Such was the case. In a letter on the following day, August 14, from her secretary, Adam H. Dickey, there were these comments:

Your letter of the 13th instant addressed to Mrs. Eddy comprising the report of your plans for starting a Christian Science daily paper is at hand. After reading this report our Leader expressed surprise at the amount of capital that would be required. Her original thought on the subject was, that you should proceed to get out a small paper of about eight pages and with a circulation of about fifty or sixty thousand copies, at a much less outlay than the amount stated in your letter. Her intention was not to branch out at once into metropolitan greatness, but rather to begin in a comparatively small way and grow into bigger things with the progress of time. However she does not wish to hamper your movements by placing restrictions on the amount you shall spend, but wishes you to go ahead with wisdom and economy as your guide.

Our Leader hopes you will not find it necessary to consult with her with regard to details, but proceed with the work in your own way doing the best you can.

Here was a frank and generous mandate.

The adventures of the next one hundred days were spectacular. Until October 17 they had to be carried out in secrecy, for only then was it officially announced that the Christian Scientists were to publish a daily newspaper. Money, however, was needed at once. Christian Scientists throughout the world had just finished paying for what they thought was a new and complete Publishing House. As recently as October 12, 1907, the *Christian Science Sentinel* had announced that the Publishing Society was to have a new home, and issued a call for funds. In August, 1908, the building had just been completed and paid for! And here in the *Sentinel* of September 19, 1908, was this startling and cryptic announcement:

"The Christian Science Board of Directors respectfully announces to the Field that it has become necessary to enlarge the new publishing house in order to accommodate the presses and other machinery required for the printing of the Christian Science publications. Contributions from those who wish to assist in the erection of this addition to the publishing house will be thankfully received by Mr. Chase, Treasurer."

Even this kind of appeal brought a warm response, and the specific announcement of the *Monitor,* which came soon after, stirred the field deeply. By May 15, 1909, they had completed the subscription of the building fund.

No sooner had the Trustees received Mrs. Eddy's go-ahead signal on August 14, than they began the most definite and sweeping of commitments, while the Directors proceeded to carry out their part in clearing the land and erecting the extension of the Publishing House. As early as August 19, the Trustees signed a contract with the Goss Printing Press Company for two presses and a stereotyping plant to be delivered and erected within 60 days. The price for the presses was $40,000, with 5 per cent cash discount, a 20 per cent saving over the price of $25,000 apiece quoted in the letter to Mrs. Eddy. The Directors were notified that the building and foundation must be ready for the presses not later than October 10. To move tenants, demolish brick buildings, set new foundations — on piles — and be ready to install elaborate equipment within two months is a very considerable mechanical achievement. It was done, and the presses were in place on their foundations, shrouded in tarpaulin, before the rest of the building had been completed around them.

Types and typesetting machines were investigated, and Mrs. Eddy herself — despite her injunction about not being consulted on details — took pleasure in selecting a body type which was attractive and suitable. It was a lightface 8-point roman letter. She also approved the headline type and corrected the form in which the paper's title was to appear. A year's supply of newsprint was ordered. The numberless details needful for the organization of a serious newspaper were all under way.

One of the most striking achievements was the preparation of a sample copy of an eight-page newspaper as early as September 15. Thus, within a month of the signal to proceed, and two months before the first official *Monitor* appeared, these dauntless pioneers were able to put into shape a perfectly respectable newspaper prototype. Later, beginning on November 19, they produced three days' trial-run newspapers.

The sample newspaper of September 15 reveals that in the few short weeks that a very small staff had been at work — by that time it included few beyond Archibald McLellan, Alexander Dodds, and John J. Flinn — a great deal of practical thinking had been going on. Many attributes of the *Monitor* which are among its strongest elements a half century later were conceived during these first few weeks.

For instance, it had been decided to carry the editorial page as the back cover. This distinctive and emphatic placement has helped to give *Monitor* editorials a special force. The paper, which for many years has been habitually printed in two sections, continues to make vigorous use not only of the back page of the entire paper, but of the back cover of the first section and the front cover of the second section.

This sample edition of September 15 also included, in the position just preceding the editorial page, "The Home Forum." This unique newspaper feature, still a vital element in the *Monitor,* bears the same title to this day. It seeks still to serve high cultural interests.

Page one in the sample edition reveals a news judgment which is as typical of the *Monitor* today as it was half a century ago. The front-page photograph is a view of the Wright airplane during Army tests at Fort Myer. Then as now, the *Monitor* had an intense interest in men's mastery of material limitations. The reader may well find on the *Monitor*'s front page today a photograph of some important advancement in natural science or technology, more likely than not in aviation. It may be assumed that Mrs. Eddy was attracted by the photograph of the Wright plane, in view of her special interest in aviation.

This sample newspaper, the first *Christian Science Monitor* ever produced, was printed at the Heinzman Press, a commercial printing establishment in Boston. Printed, that is, except for the title. To preserve secrecy, the words "The Christian Science Monitor" were left blank at the printer's. On September 15, Ernest C. Sherburne, a young man then employed since 1898 as a printer in the Christian Science Publishing House, was kept after work by Mr. McKenzie and asked if he could keep a secret. Upon being reassured, he was shown the sample issue, complete except for its title, and asked to set up and print the name "The Christian Science Monitor" across the top of the first page of the dummy.

Thus apprised of the exciting new adventure, Mr. Sherburne asked to be transferred to the new paper's staff as a reporter. This was done, and until 1946 Mr. Sherburne remained a highly useful member of the editorial staff. In early years, he took many photographs. The article and pictures on page one of the first *Monitor* issued to the public describing the lock and dam by which the Charles River Basin was created, are his. Later he was appointed dramatic editor, and did the paper's principal theatrical reviewing for over two decades.

While the building was being erected and after the presses and other basic equipment had been ordered, the task of recruiting a staff went forward. This was done in two ways. Through the Committee(s) on Publication and various personal contacts, able men throughout the nation — and in some cases overseas — were being sought.

On October 17, in the issue of the *Christian Science Sentinel* which made the first public announcement of the new newspaper, there was published a request to Christian Scientists who were in the newspaper business to send in their names and addresses and professional experience. Both methods were effective.

The private canvass had turned up by October 16 a group of major news and business executives. In a letter of that date, the Trustees notified Mrs. Eddy of their progress. They had engaged Thomas C. Winans of Pittsburgh as advertising and circulation manager. Somewhat hopefully, as it turned out, they wrote that "his large business capacity enables him to take charge of both the Advertising and Circulation Departments, which usually have separate Managers." This dual job did not turn out to be feasible, and in April, 1909, Mr. Winans became advertising manager alone while Samuel H. McCutcheon was appointed circulation manager.

As to the rest of the executive organization, Mr. McLellan functioned as editor of the *Monitor,* as he did for the other Christian Science publications, and David B. Ogden, manager of The Christian Science Publishing Society, served as manager of the *Monitor.* These appointments were verified by Mrs. Eddy.

The Trustees proceeded, in their letter of October 16, 1908, to give Mrs. Eddy the further personnel appointments they had made. The managing editor was to be Mr. Dodds, whose role was already a central one in all the planning and arranging. The chief editorial writer was to be John J. Flinn, who had also been one of the two key men called in to give the initial advice. The city editor was to be John L. Wright of the Boston *Globe,* the eager young man who had written Mrs. Eddy on March 12, and who had called forth her first identification of *The Christian Science Monitor.* The news editor was to be Oscar Stevens, from the Boston *Transcript.* Mr. Stevens was soon made assistant managing editor, and his place as news editor taken by John Phillips, of the Chicago *Examiner.* As financial editor and political writer (so they said in the letter, though the political writer part was never carried out) the Trustees had engaged Forrest Price, from the Pittsburgh *Chronicle-Telegraph.* As foreman of the composing room, they had selected Amos Weston, from the Boston *Herald.*

The Trustees further told Mrs. Eddy that they had made arrangements for special weekly articles from Frederick Dixon of London (of whom more will be heard later), William D. McCrackan in Switzerland, Edward C. Butler of Mexico City, Charles H. Gibbs of Sydney, Australia, and Albert Cope Stone of Melbourne, Australia. Regular or occasional letters were also being commissioned from the Philippines, Panama, Mexico, Alaska, England, Germany, France, and South Africa. This kind of planning shows that from the outset, the Trustees, manager, editor, and managing editor were envisioning a newspaper of the very broadest scope.

To the group specified in this letter, the Trustees speedily added a number of others. Among them were Paul S. Deland, the only member of the original staff who was still on the staff in 1958; George M. R. Holmes, sports editor, who filled that post monumentally until 1940; Winthrop Pitt Tryon, music critic, who though retired still writes regularly for the paper; and James L. Bruce, Lawrence Brainerd, T. Harold Rhodes, and Ernest C. Sherburne, as reporters; Leon V. Stone, who retired only in 1958, was hired as the first copy boy.

The total roster of the *Monitor's* very first payroll is not available, but a few weeks later, on February 24, 1909, it included 99 persons divided as follows: Advertising, 9; Circulation, 5; Mailing, 5; Editorial, 9 (which must have included features); News, 24; Composing, 31; Press and Stereotype, 16. This, newspapermen will agree, is a modest but a respectable staff. Few publications can have assumed a task as ambitious as the *Monitor's* with a more moderate roster.

The request for names and addresses of Christian Scientists who were connected with the newspaper business, published on October 17 in the *Sentinel,* produced so great a response that in the very next issue, on October 24, the Trustees withdrew the notice, saying: "It was not known that so large a number of Scientists were now engaged in newspaper work, and so many applications have been received that the invitation to apply is now discontinued." As a matter of fact, about 1000 responses were received from editors, writers, reporters, skilled printers, stereotypers, pressmen, etc.

Meantime, also in the October 17 *Sentinel,* was the historic first announcement of the *Monitor.* In a signed editorial, Mr. McLellan described the proposed newspaper in terms which indicate that a great deal of clarifying thought and discussion had gone on. Already a most crucial corner had been turned. This was the decision to make the *Monitor* a "regular" newspaper, not merely a church organ.

It would have been very natural to make the *Monitor* a daily version of the *Sentinel* and *Journal,* especially in view of its spiritual mission. It would have been easy and obvious to publish the sort of newspaper other churches have published and still publish: denominational, parochial, diocesan, or otherwise church-oriented. The great innovation, the crucial difference vitalizing *The Christian Science Monitor* was that it was a regular newspaper, performing its spiritual mission all the more effectively for that very reason. This fact Mr. McLellan made clear in his initial editorial. He had to drive it home in a second editorial on November 14.

On October 17 Mr. McLellan defined the nature of the forthcoming newspaper in these terms:

> It is their intention [the Trustees of The Christian Science Publishing Society] to publish a strictly up-to-date newspaper, in which all the news of the day that should be printed will find a place, and whose service will not be restricted to any one locality or section, but will cover the daily activities of the entire world . . .
>
> All over the land there has been and is a call from the fathers and mothers . . . who are asking for a paper that will supply vital current news, the things we want to know and ought to know about our fellow-men, but which are submerged in the daily tidal wave of crime and disaster which the ordinary newspaper would have us believe sweeps over the world. There is a field, and a wide one, for a clean newspaper, and it is this field which the Monitor is entering.
>
> It will be the mission of the Monitor to publish the real news of the world in a clean, wholesome manner, devoid of the sensational methods employed by so many newspapers. There will be no exploitation or illustration of vice and crime, but the aim of the editors will be to issue a paper which will be welcomed in every home where purity and refinement are cherished ideals. It is intended that the Monitor shall contain, in addition to the usual news features of the best city papers, such special departments as will make it a home paper of the highest grade, — one which will appeal to good men and women everywhere who are interested in the betterment of all human conditions and the moral and spiritual advancement of the race. From the "news" standpoint the Monitor will be of far wider scope than a merely local daily would cover, and will be read with interest from Maine to California and from Canada to Mexico. Even our friends across the sea will find the Monitor interesting from this standpoint.
>
> While all Christian Scientists are requested to subscribe for the Monitor, for we believe it is only by their support that the success of an absolutely clean and unsensational newspaper can be assured, it is not believed that they alone are interested in a paper of this character. Indeed, it is hoped and believed that all others who have seen the need of a reform in journalism will find in the Monitor

the ideal newspaper for which they have longed, and that they too will support it on its merits.

A month later, further emphasizing these points, Mr. McLellan wrote:

. . . judging from the personnel of the staff and the quality of the news service which they [the Trustees] have been able to secure, they believe they are justified in saying that the Monitor will be even better than was promised.

To those who have inquired whether the Monitor is to be a real newspaper, we say Yes. To those who have asked whether it will be "simply a Boston newspaper," we say No, except that a special New England edition, which will give the current local news of that section, is to be issued each day.

From these affirmations, it will be seen that Mr. McLellan and his associates had a very clear idea of what they were about. Starting only with Mrs. Eddy's instructions to publish a daily newspaper, they had thought through what kind of paper it was to be and was not to be. The ideals and purposes they set forth in these prepublication statements are precisely the ideals and purposes that have prevailed in the half century since. The sense of mission is there. This clarity of function is manifestly one of the *Monitor*'s greatest assets. The paper knows where it is trying to go: it always has known. The *Monitor*'s goal is not an easy one, and it is not one which is popular in mass circulation terms. It calls for the best in the reader, as well as in the newspaper. But this clear definition of purpose, matched by a reasonable and steadily enlarging capacity to carry it out, has helped the *Monitor* down the years.

5

◇◇◇◇◇◇◇◇◇◇◇◇◇◇◇◇◇◇◇

Obstacles to Surmount

If by October 17, those responsible for the tremendous new adventure of preparing a daily newspaper knew what kind of a paper must be produced, that did not mean there were no obstacles yet to be overcome. The basic job was challenging enough. But there were unexpected hurdles. For example, the composing room equipment, type, cabinets, makeup tables, and so on, had been ordered from the American Type Founders Company in Jersey City. The shipment was put on a Boston-bound boat. That night the vessel collided with another in Long Island Sound and the shipment went to the bottom.

Amos Weston, first foreman of the composing room, writes: "We Monitor workers saw the story of the collision in the morning papers, knew that our composing room equipment had been on that boat, and we immediately communicated with the type company. The company was very alert, and knowing well what delay would mean in issuing a new paper, in an incredibly short time, had a duplicate order on the way to Boston. With some lively activity on our part, we soon made up lost time and the first edition came out as scheduled."

Another unexpected difficulty arose concerning the telegraphic wire and stock ticker service and financial news bulletins. All arrangements had been made for this indispensable facility. But at the last moment Forrest Price, the experienced Pittsburgh newspaper man who had been appointed financial editor, was informed by the superintendent of the Western Union Telegraph Company in Boston that wire service could not be provided in time. He said that the telegraph wires in Boston extended uptown only as far as Mechanics Building, a full block and a half short of the Publishing House. A city ordinance required that the wires should be run underground. There was no time to dig a conduit and place the wires in it before the paper was to make its appearance on November 25.

That news [wrote Mr. Price in his reminiscences] was staggering. We simply had to have the wire service. The Monitor could not come out without it. A meeting was hastily called at which were present Messrs. McLellan and Dodds and the Trustees. I laid before them what looked to me a very serious situation. But apparently none of them was as perturbed about it as I was.

Mr. McLellan at once got in touch with the New York Committee on Publication whom he informed of our dire predicament. The New York committeeman laid the matter before Col. Robert Clowry, then president of the Western Union Telegraph Company. It happened that Col. Clowry was somewhat interested in Christian Science. A short, sharp investigation convinced him that it would be a good thing both for the cause of Christian Science and the Western Union Company if we were to be given wire service as and when desired.

The very next day following, the Boston superintendent of the Western Union Company called upon me, and asked me in detail just what we wanted. I informed him that we must have the wire service ready by Thanksgiving Day. He said that Col. Clowry told him to give us everything "within reason" that we desired. He added that it might require some special arrangements on our part with the city of Boston to have the telegraph wires temporarily run overhead from the Mechanics Building to the Monitor office, but he was sure everything would work out satisfactorily to all concerned.

The wires and stock tickers were installed on time, and the first edition of the Monitor looked very much like a real newspaper.

This incident, like the others that marked the *Monitor's* prepublication problems, illustrates very well a Christian Scientist's approach to such matters. The explanation goes deep. His religious convictions persuade a Christian Scientist of the allness and goodness of God. What may appear to others to be mere optimism, sometimes blind if not fatuous, is in fact a profound confidence that the laws of the universe — which he knows are God's laws — are consistent and beneficent. He feels a deep sense of harmony with the truths of being. He has an indomitable expectancy of good. It may seem unreasonable ("unto the Greeks foolishness," as St. Paul said, I Cor. 1:23) but to him the power of God's good is ever present and ever potent.

Such confidence, far more profound than a mere surface cheerfulness, gives the Christian Scientist an added capacity based upon his harmonious adjustment with his environment, for he feels constantly that he lives and moves and has his being in God. Faced with a problem, he focuses at once on the means and nature of a solution, being perfectly confident that a solution can be demonstrated (as he puts it) because in God's spiritual universe such maladjustments cannot and do not happen. He strives to demonstrate here and now an understanding and application of this divine and infinite harmony.

But at the same time, the Christian Scientist does not ignore what he calls the "human footsteps." Indeed, these practical measures are to him the application of divine truth in human affairs. So, as in the case of the telegraph wires, the Christian Scientists had long since set up a system — the Committees on Publication — by means of which they could make speedy and effective contact with the person capable of taking authoritative action. Their prayer, their "knowing the truth," again to use a Christian Science phrase, did not consist in sitting down, closing their eyes, and imploring God to make the telegraph wires sprout from Mechanics Building to the Publishing

House. Their prayer consisted of knowing where and how to turn, so that a human problem could be solved in practical terms.

The person who is not a Christian Scientist may well ask how such procedure differs from what anybody of common sense and experience would do. The Scientist's answer lies in the "expectancy of good," in the deep sense of oneness with God's universal law, in the calm and confidence with which one can proceed to get a job done. If a non-Christian Scientist thinks this doesn't work, he should try it.

And so, one by one, the obstacles were removed. With the official announcement of the forthcoming paper, many who had already been engaged for the staff were relieved: now they could tell their wives. Nobody was more gratified at this opportunity than the editor himself, Mr. McLellan. His wife had read an item in a Chicago newspaper which reported that John J. Flinn had resigned his position on the Chicago *Inter-Ocean* to become editor of the Christian Science publications in Boston. When Mrs. McLellan saw this, she wondered what was to become of her husband, who was already the editor!

Forrest Price also welcomed the end of the secrecy. Mr. Dodds, who knew Mr. Price as a Pittsburgh newspaper colleague, offered him the job of financial editor of a new newspaper that was soon to make its appearance in a distant city. He assured Mr. Price that it was to be a high-class publication "with ample financial backing and conducted by men of unimpeachable integrity." Both men were Christian Scientists. Mr. Price writes, "He and I had previously discussed such a journalistic enterprise without either of us knowing at the time what was in store for us." This wistful remark, coupled with the letter John Wright had written Mrs. Eddy, indicates how the idea of a Christian Science newspaper and the ideals and purposes involved had been stirring in the consciousness of Christian Scientists who were newspapermen. It reveals why so many of them were so eager and responsive when the *Sentinel* announced that jobs were available.

At any rate, Mr. Price accepted the job Mr. Dodds offered him, although on the condition that the city of publication was not New York. He arrived in Boston in October, about a month before the publication deadline. And he remained as financial editor until his retirement in 1936. His previous career, in Pittsburgh, had been largely in political reporting. Many were the colorful tales he recalled of Boss Quay, William McKinley, William Howard Taft, and William Jennings Bryan. He made the transition from political writer to financial editor — in which he had some previous experience — with great expertness and helped make and keep the *Monitor* authoritative and useful in the financial field.

Why did Mrs. Eddy give her officials the challenging deadline, under which "let there be no delay" was translated into "the day before Thanksgiving," and why was there so much secrecy, up to October 17? Again the reasons are to be found in Christian Science itself. Mrs. Eddy felt, taught, and put into practice the importance of maturing right ideas in quiet, protected from the harsh and divergent pulls of variant human viewpoints. Earnestly, prayerfully, quietly she sought answers in the sanctuary of her own communion with God. Only when she had received her answer was she ready to expose the infant idea to the turbulence of many human minds, and then only when the idea was ready to be put into practice as swiftly as possible without further pulling and hauling.

In the words of Mr. McKenzie, "Mrs. Eddy instructed her workers that a needful work should be established, if not completed, before there was talking about it." * As a matter of fact, Mr. McKenzie confides that Mrs. Eddy "expected the newspaper to make its appearance immediately, and it had to be explained how the printing office and presses must be constructed first, and how much machinery must be assembled, and how many men recruited. She agreed to the delay, but urged that the publication begin its work 'as soon as possible.' "

Although the men and women around Mrs. Eddy — her church and Publishing Society officials, her household — were consecrated and courageous, they were not free from human fears and uncertainties. Some of them, at least, had very grave

* From his article in the Progress Issue of *The Christian Science Monitor,* November 20, 1933.

doubts about the wisdom of establishing a newspaper. Well they might have, for an ordinary newspaper is a risky undertaking at best, and a newspaper owned and published by a church is as problematical as it is unique.

In the years before and since Mrs. Eddy's bold decision, church newspapers have been established many times. Those concentrating on church news are generally able to fulfill their special purposes well enough. But the church-supported newspapers dealing in general news and seeking a nondenominational readership are few indeed.

One or two only come to mind, and then with basic differences from the *Monitor*. The Church of Jesus Christ of Latter-Day Saints owns an excellent daily newspaper in Salt Lake City, the *Deseret News*. The *Osservatore Romano,* published at the Vatican, performs an important service as an official voice. There are newspapers supported by religious political parties, as in France, West Germany, the Netherlands, and Italy. But these are politically rather than church operated.

It is understandable that some of those around Mrs. Eddy, despite their confidence in her, were hesitant about the *Monitor* project. Indeed, Adam H. Dickey, who was Mrs. Eddy's secretary when the *Monitor* was established and was the person to whom she said, "Mr. Dickey, take your pencil . . ." and dictated the initial order, has testified that the Directors themselves at first had doubts about starting the project. When the Directors, upon receiving Mrs. Eddy's first instructions on July 28, waited and suggested that she should send the letter to the Trustees instead, they were in Mr. Dickey's words "sparring for wind." It did not take them long to see that Mrs. Eddy had been carefully maturing her plan, that she had taken the problem to God, and had received her answer. So whatever doubts there may have been at the very beginning, on the part of a few, were soon replaced by buoyant confidence. The atmosphere, for instance, as expressed by Mr. McLellan in his *Sentinel* editorials, was confident and keen.

On one subject, however, Mr. McLellan, Mr. Dodds, and some of those in Mrs. Eddy's household were most eager to get her to change her plans. They wished to have the words

"Christian Science" deleted from the paper's title. It was their opinion that the words would be a severe handicap upon sales to the general public. Various arguments why the words "Christian Science" should be deleted were advanced. There were repeated attempts to persuade Mrs. Eddy to alter the name.

The episode is graphically described by Irving C. Tomlinson in his book *Twelve Years with Mary Baker Eddy*. Mr. Tomlinson, who served during that period in Mrs. Eddy's home, wrote: "I remember so well that thrilling occasion when Mrs. Eddy took her stand for the naming of The Christian Science Monitor. Some Christian Scientists were shaking their heads dubiously over the situation, the editors, members of the technical force, some of the members of Mrs. Eddy's household, and others. It was secretly whispered about that greater success would attend the newspaper if the words 'Christian Science' were omitted from the name." And so, records Mr. Tomlinson, an interview was obtained with Mrs. Eddy. Mr. McLellan endeavored to win her to this view. But to no avail. "The members of the household were on tiptoes, waiting outside the door of Mrs. Eddy's room, while the final decision was being made. The conference was brief. A moment or so, and the editor emerged. Said he, 'Mrs. Eddy is firm and her answer is "God gave me this name and it remains." ' "

The reasons lying behind this decision are clarified further in an address given on December 22, 1926, by Mr. Flinn. He said:

> Mrs. Eddy had stood out with the assurance and positiveness of conviction so characteristic of her decisions throughout her whole career, for a title which would leave no doubt regarding the exact identity of the newspaper which she was engaged in founding. Many arguments had been advanced, all of them well-meant, some of them quite forceful, others extremely plausible, from a material point of view, in support of the contention that the term "Christian Science" should not appear in the title. How much or how little attention Mrs. Eddy paid to these arguments, or whether she paid attention to them at all, I do not know. I do know, however, that she was not influenced in the slightest degree by the plea that the

omission of the term "Christian Science" in the caption of the newspaper would assure it easier access to the homes of non-Scientists. It was reported and widely believed at the time that she had replied to one person offering the suggestion that the title which she had decided to give the newspaper would be certain to arouse antagonism, in words substantially these: "Well, if antagonism is to be aroused for this reason, let it come and be disposed of now; then we shall not have to meet it hereafter."

Mr. Flinn continues:

The all-important fact remains that she was understood to be immovable in the position that to evade or to attempt to evade the issue would not only be unwise but unscientific; that here as at all times, and in every particular, the Truth must be expressed and adhered to. The impression that we all received of Mrs. Eddy's attitude toward the name of the newspaper was: That since the Monitor was to represent Christian Science in journalism, the only thing, because the right thing to do, was to stamp it at once with its proper designation.

From this time on, all discussion upon the name ceased. It was remarkable how completely the thoughts of all were changed by Mrs. Eddy's positive position into a better understanding of one of the fundamentals of our faith, that there should never be evasion of any obligation involving the assertion of the Truth.

Mr. Flinn's declaration that "all discussion upon the name ceased" applies to talk within the ranks of Christian Scientists, and especially among these connected with the *Monitor*. It does not apply to friends and well-wishers who do not appreciate the fundamentals of the question. Thus, down through the years, a good many people have urged *The Christian Science Monitor* to change its name, and have promised it would achieve vast circulation gains thereby.

One of these was J. Ramsay MacDonald, onetime British Prime Minister and leader of the Labor Party. Speaking one day to Willis J. Abbot, editor and contributing editor of the *Monitor* from 1922 to 1934, Mr. MacDonald said: "Your paper is a wonderful one. It seems so honest, so fair, so tolerant. Its attitude of internationalism makes it fairly unique. But, my dear Mr. Abbot, don't you think you and your associates could extend its circulation into quarters now closed to it, and thereby exercise a much wider influence, if you would take those provocative and limiting words 'Christian Science' out of its title?"

Mr. Abbot replied: "Yes, Mr. MacDonald, there is much in what you suggest. But to reach into those closed sections of society one would have to sacrifice much of the affection and love of the members of our church who are supporting the Monitor loyally and are proud to see it carrying the banner of Christian Science bravely before all the world. But your question suggests one to me. Could you not gain a hearing in quarters now closed to you, and thereby exert a wider influence for good, if you take that limiting and provocative word 'labor' out of the title of your political party?"

Mr. MacDonald found it a very apt retort. But, as Mr. Abbot continued to point out * it was more of a retort than an answer. The answer can be given on many levels. On the level of merest practicality, it is surely much better for any product to identify itself clearly. Suppose the newspaper were named "The Monitor." Would it advance its interests for people to go around saying and sometimes whispering: "You know that paper 'The Monitor'? It's really owned by the Christian Scientists!"

On a deeper level there is the commitment to truth, candor, honesty, pointed out by Mr. Flinn. And, from still another point of view there is the distinctiveness, the curiosity, the uniqueness all evoked by the full title. The title is surely a great and tangible asset because of this very distinctiveness.

Conversely, there is the service that has been rendered to Christian Science by the newspaper that bears its name. In the most legitimate of senses, the newspaper is a public relations organ for the religion, and so should be identified. It has carried the name into far corners of the earth.

Any oddity that ever adhered to the title has long since worn off. Day in and day out, the *Monitor* is quoted in newspapers and parliaments the world around. Every available statistical

* Willis J. Abbot, *Watching the World Go By* (Boston, 1933), p. 324.

evidence indicates that it is quoted at least as frequently as any other daily newspaper. Some papers, having great regional prestige, will be quoted in their particular region more often than the *Monitor*. But putting the whole world together, including small and large newspapers and other media of information and opinion, it seems probable that the name *The Christian Science Monitor* is regularly carried into as many human minds as that of any other newspaper. And done so without self-consciousness or handicap.

In respect to the paper's name, as in other crucial matters that arose in the crowded one hundred days, Mrs. Eddy's decisions with their farseeing purposes cleared the air for all time. One by one the obstacles were surmounted.

6

The Trial Run

By two weeks before the first publication date, the basic staff had been assembled. They had begun learning their jobs. Here was the crux of the matter. Newspapermen who had been trained in far different schools had to master a completely new form of journalism. There were no precedents, no established standards, no rules. Everything was pioneering.

What actually happened was that about a dozen staff members sat around a large library table, with Mr. Dodds presiding. He outlined the aims and ideals which the staff was to turn into operative journalism. Mr. McLellan gave the group the benefit of his many contacts with Mrs. Eddy concerning her expectations and convictions for the paper. Mr. Dodds told them they were to turn traditional newspaper practice upside down. That is to say, instead of emphasizing sensation, passion, conflict, and disorder they were to record the important and constructive developments in the news, whether local, national, or worldwide.

"This seemed like quite an undertaking," says Paul S. Deland, who was a member of the group, "but it wasn't long before we found that we were not turning things upside down. We were turning things right side up. It was the other newspapers that were upside down."

"We were instructed," Mr. Deland has written, "to devote our efforts to making as interesting as possible all events of intrinsic merit and permanent value. This was a relief and satisfaction to a newspaper man who had previously been required to glorify out of all proportion the transient and inconsequential happenings that, as has been aptly said, were to be 'ashes' the next day . . . Each story was discussed, and while the general form was that of the regular newspaper, what a difference in the substance and treatment!"

The *Monitor* did not seek to withhold tragic or distasteful news from its readers. It did not suppress news of crime or disaster. It placed such news in perspective, recording such events modestly but factually, without giving them sensational display, and reserving its bigger headlines and larger space for events or situations of long-range importance to humanity. In terms of a sober chronicle of what happened, the *Monitor* files stand up as a useful guide to its times.

To recognize and decide how to handle such news required a good deal of retraining of the eager and possibly overawed staff. Despite Mrs. Eddy's injunction not to come running to her for detailed instructions, the *Monitor* officials went to her, and always found a keenly interested response.

The precision and vigor of her views are well illustrated by the following message sent through Mr. Dickey on November 24:

Dear Mr. McLellan:

I have submitted to Mrs. Eddy the sample copies of "The Christian Science Monitor" which you and Mr. Dodds left with me last evening.

Our Leader prefers the heavy style of type shown in the title of the paper which I enclose herewith, but insists that the article 'The' properly belongs in the title and wishes it placed there. This will necessitate making another design that can be as easily read as the one enclosed.

The placing of the motto beneath the title on the editorial page is satisfactory to Mrs. Eddy, and in other respects she is well pleased with the appearance of the newspaper.

Mrs. Eddy directed that a religious article should always appear on "The Home Forum." The first one, in the issue of November 25, was signed. It would appear to be through Mrs. Eddy's direct instruction that the signatures were left off soon thereafter. The fact of but a single daily religious article, and the fact of its anonymity, are two significant points.

Mrs. Eddy did not believe that the *Monitor* should be just a denominational organ, speaking only to Christian Scientists or to prospective converts. The *Monitor* must be a "real" newspaper. But it could and should carry a regular daily article of explicitly applied Christian Science thinking. It should not be devoid of a spiritual message. The *Monitor* itself as a total entity exemplifies the civic attitude and purpose of Christian Science itself.

Finally the "trial run" newspapers were produced in mid-November and submitted to Mrs. Eddy. They were not without the usual difficulties. One such slip is reported by Forrest Price, who writes: "When Mr. Dodds took a dummy sheet of the new paper out to Chestnut Hill to show Mrs. Eddy before the first issue came out, he returned with a very red face. The motto at the top of the editorial page (which, it will be recalled, Mrs. Eddy had specifically ordered in one of her earliest instructions) read: 'First the blade, then the ear, then the full grain in the YEAR.' He had not noticed the serious typographical error before handing the paper dummy to Mrs. Eddy for her inspection. He let us know all about it when he got back to the office, and in no uncertain terms."

Finally the great day of November 25 came. The weather was murky, and ships had been held in the stream unable to dock in New York and Boston harbors. "At nine o'clock on the date of the Monitor's first issue," Mr. Tomlinson wrote in his diary, "all the workers were called by Mrs. Eddy to her study. Present — Frye, Sargent, Miss Alice Peck, Adam Dickey, Mr. Rathvon and I.C.T. The morning dark and foggy. Mrs. Eddy asked if it were a dark morning. 'Yes,' replied one, 'a heavy fog makes it darker than usual.' Mr. Frye said that according to sense it was dark. Mrs. Eddy replied: "Yes, but only according to sense. We know the reverse of error is true. This, in Truth, is the lightest day of all days. This is the day when our daily paper goes forth to lighten mankind . . . !' "

Mrs. Daisette D. S. McKenzie, whose husband was then a Trustee, describes Mrs. Eddy's joy at receiving the first copy: "She had been informed that the paper was to arrive, and when the messengers entered her office, she came forward with both hands extended and received the paper and clasped it to her heart. They reported that the scene was most moving. Her great hope which she had cherished so long had at last found expression."

Mr. Tomlinson records further that he saw Mrs. Eddy in her study perusing with deepest interest the first copy of the paper. And so it went, for the remaining years until Mrs. Eddy passed on in 1910. The first sheet off the press was sent to Mrs. Eddy each day, the religious article and each editorial rubber-stamped with the name of the writer so that she might know who wrote each important article that went into the *Monitor*. "Mrs. Eddy read discriminatingly, critically, and appreciatively each article," wrote Mr. Tomlinson, "and if there were any comments, they were sent to the editor."

In addition, proof sheets of the religious articles were sent to her in advance for correction, and for some time she frequently made changes in them. But this guidance was designedly kept to a minimum. The goals and purposes of Christian Science journalism had been set: it was up to the staff to learn how to fulfill them.

These purposes were given their most eloquent and everlasting definition in the editorial which Mrs. Eddy wrote for the *Monitor*'s first issue. In the dummy issues which were prepared — the sample copy of September 15, and the trial copies just before November 25 — there was no provision for an editorial by Mrs. Eddy.

The leading editorial in the final trial copies was entitled "A Word of Appreciation." It appeared as the second editorial in the actual issue. It was a tribute to Mrs. Eddy for her leadership in establishing Christian Science journalism down the years from the *Journal* to the *Sentinel* to the *Monitor.* This editorial, suitable though it was, did not have the ring and lift which a personal word from Mrs. Eddy would have.

She herself foresaw the need and opportunity, and met them. In a handwritten letter to Mr. McLellan, dated November 11, 1908, she said: "Please have my article last sent to you appear in the first issue of the Christian Science Monitor." Thus it came about that the *Monitor* had the privilege of a leading editorial by its Founder, an editorial which defined its purpose and mandate in simple, eloquent, authoritative terms. This is indicative of the way in which Mrs. Eddy thought and acted, independently and unexpectedly, throughout the whole experience of founding the *Monitor.* The signed editorial made all the difference in the world.

It uses as its peg a letter written to Mrs. Eddy on November 2 by Frank Bell, managing editor of the Harrisburg *Telegraph.* Mr. Bell, too, typified the Christian Scientists throughout the newspaper world who were tremendously moved by Mrs. Eddy's project. Mr. Bell later became a Christian Science teacher and lecturer, well known throughout the world. Among his students in Christian Science was one of the *Monitor*'s great friends and contributors, the late Marquess of Lothian, British Ambassador to the United States. Mr. Bell had written:

Dear Leader — As a newspaper man I thank you for The Christian Science Monitor in prospect, and I feel sure that such will be the sentiment of hundreds of newspaper workers all over the land when The Monitor in fact shall have demonstrated the feasibility of clean journalism.

A definition of "monitor" is "One who advises," and I foresee that when this Christian Science Monitor shall have proved that there is such a thing as newspaper success along non-sensational lines, there will follow a widespread readjustment of news policies, for which I am sure none will be more truly thankful than an army of honest, conscientious toilers in the ranks of newspaperdom.

Gratefully yours,

FRANK BELL
Managing Editor, Harrisburg Telegraph

And so, using this heartfelt voice of gratitude as a starting point, Mrs. Eddy wrote the most important and definitive editorial *The Christian Science Monitor* has ever published:

SOMETHING IN A NAME

The gentleman, Mr. Frank Bell, has caught my thunder; therefore he will not object to the lightning which accompanies it.

I have given the name to all the Christian Science periodicals. The first was The Christian Science Journal, designed to put on record the divine Science of Truth; the second I entitled Sentinel, intended to hold guard over Truth, Life and Love; the third, Der Herold der Christian Science, to proclaim the universal activity and availability of Truth; the next I named Monitor, to spread undivided the Science that operates unspent. The object of the Monitor is to injure no man, but to bless all mankind.

Here are the words of which *The Christian Science Monitor* has sought ever since to be worthy: ". . . to spread undivided the Science that operates unspent. The object of the Monitor is to injure no man, but to bless all mankind."

". . . to spread undivided the Science that operates unspent." In these words Mrs. Eddy affirms the inexhaustible abundance of divine wisdom, the "Science" which is the truth of God and man, and which liberates and uplifts all human experience. The *Monitor*'s job is to spread this wisdom, knowing that the supply will never run out. And to spread it "undivided"—without compromise or dilution. It is a commitment to the leavening of all human thinking.

". . . to injure no man, but to bless all mankind." Here is the essence of the *Monitor,* in a brief phrase. It is the paper's mandate. It is an expression of unswerving idealism. Yet it is not to be interpreted in mawkish fashion. "To injure no man" has not inhibited the paper from uncovering evil in whatever guise, for it is clear that such exposure can be impersonal and constructive. The objective of such journalism is to bless all involved, by helping them into their true manhood through regeneration. It is a mandate which is not easy to fulfill, but it keeps the *Monitor's* flag nailed high on the masthead.

7

The First Issues

WHAT SORT of newspaper did they produce and issue on November 25? They had been enjoined modesty, learning to walk before flying. The advance expectation had been a simple 8-page paper. But so many advertisements came in, through the vigorous efforts of the advertising department and the loyal activities of Christian Scientists, that it had to be enlarged to 12 pages. There were, as a matter of fact, 19 columns of advertising, out of 84 columns in the paper. There were only 7 columns to the page, compared to 8 since 1924. Each page was about half an inch wider than it is today, and each column of reading matter included about 868 words, plus headlines.

A 12-page paper including 19 columns of advertising and 65 columns of editorial material was a quite respectable publication. The total editorial material — some 56,420 words plus headlines and pictures — was undoubtedly as much or more than many newspapers of the day were presenting to their readers. When one considers that it was all informative material, and did not include comic strips or other space-consuming "entertainment" matter such as has now grown to large proportions in many papers, the total represents a very good start.

In its content, the paper showed weak and strong elements. Obviously the staff, despite their vast and evangelical enthusiasm, had still a great deal to learn. They had had only a few days of practice. They had a clear goal. But the ways to approach it all had to be worked out, explored, charted.

In view of the uncertainties it is amazing that the staff produced a paper of such relative professional competence. It is an interesting newspaper. Read with the hindsight of fifty years, it includes many remarkably prophetic passages. Some of its articles were right on the news beam. Others were naïve, although in their guilelessness there is some genuine reader-interest. A later newspaper wit described the *Monitor* as one day "leading the paper with the story of a rock garden in Seattle." There were touches of such innocence in the first issue.

A story in column six of page one of the national edition recounted the efforts of the Odd Fellows and the Knights of Pythias in Lexington, Kentucky, in developing homes for the care of widows and orphans, and it referred to a successful Christian Science lecture in that city. Such references to special Christian Science activities soon vanished from the paper. It was re-emphasized that the *Monitor* must not become a "house organ" for the Christian Science church.

There were also extensive differences between the front-page content of the national edition and the local edition. It is surprising that the staff should have worked out such differences on the first, difficult publication day. Evidently they were determined to show at once how good a job they could do, applying the plans of varying coverage between New England and the nation which they had worked out.

The items about Lexington might have justified a place somewhere inside the paper, though they were not developed sufficiently to bring out real meaning. Publishing them on page one was part of the process of learning to walk. And it may be observed that the dividing line between constructive, "clean" news that is important and such news, when it is commonplace or even a trifle inane, is not always a self-evident and easy line to draw. You have to learn, and the *Monitor* staff were taking their first tentative steps.

Nevertheless, their first front page contains a number of items of first-class significance and long-range perception. The lead story in column one was of the tariff revision battle then opening in the House Ways and Means Committee — one of the great domestic political struggles of the first decade of this century in American history. It was one of the major cleavages later leading the Taft Administration away from the Theodore Roosevelt position. No story was more important in the period. This particular dispatch is of a running phase of the struggle.

Leading the paper in column seven is a dispatch on the American armaments budget. Again this is a story of looming importance in 1908, unconsciously prophetic of the dire issues of 1958. "Arms Budget Asks Millions for Defense," ran the headline. The story revealed that it was fifty million dollars that was being asked. Even then a good part of it was for "rivers and harbors." What any reader of 1908 would have said to a $41,000,000,000 peacetime defense budget is too appalling to contemplate. And yet, there in 1908, the Arms Budget story was leading the paper.

The front-page photo display and accompanying story was of the progress of the Charles River Dam, which created the Charles River Basin in Boston, contributed vastly to the beauty of the city, helped provide an ultimate home for so portentous an institution as the Massachusetts Institute of Technology, and gave the setting for "Research Row," or the "Billion-Dollar Mile" — facing the Basin — along which some of the world's greatest natural scientists work in the interest of applied research on industrial problems and opportunities. Nowhere has more work been done to alter the relationship between men and nature than by the research completed and the men trained here on the banks of the Charles. Nothing of this awesome development, of course, could possibly have been in the thinking of the *Monitor*'s editors when they gave top pictorial prominence to the Charles River Dam. Yet it is interesting that they hit such a bull's-eye.

It was in this fabulous complex of technical research that M.I.T.'s Radiation Laboratory set up the first radar antenna and screen in the United States and developed, following British pioneering, the great military and peacetime tool of radar. The late President Karl T. Compton, of M.I.T., told me once that he happened to be in Washington when the Radiation Laboratory completed the task of setting up the first radar antenna — a single antenna — and got their first "blip" on the radar scope. The first object that came into view was the pineapple which adorns the dome of The Mother Church, adjacent to the Christian Science Publishing House. The staff was eager to tell Dr. Compton the good news, but they could not break security. So they concocted one of those famous cryptic telegrams, like that sent from Chicago to President Conant of Harvard University about Dr. Enrico Fermi's first successful atomic pile. The M.I.T. workers sent Dr. Compton this message: "Saw Mary Baker Eddy with one eye." Thus they conveyed to the M.I.T. president the significant fact that with a single antenna the radar experimenters had seen the dome of The Mother Church.

Elsewhere on page one of the first edition was a story which in the light of subsequent developments takes on enhanced meaning. It describes the attention being given to increased yields of corn. It drives home to readers the fact that far greater quantities of corn can be produced on a given area than had ever been supposed before, and that the quality and uniformity of the corn can be enhanced by simple seed-selection methods. In view of the revolutionary changes which increased farm productivity has brought about in the United States, this story is notably and not unwittingly prophetic.

The most important overseas story on the *Monitor*'s first front page is typical of the paper's interests down through the years. It is the start of a series discussing the Balkan crisis. The article, viewed in historical retrospect, is very good. It diagnoses events in the Balkan peninsula as part of the economic duel taking place between England and Germany. It traces the rise of Germany's challenge, capped with the proposed Berlin-to-Baghdad railway. It speaks, again with foresight, of the growth of Balkan nationalism, and of religious rather than dynastic divisions.

Throughout even this first edition runs a thread of vital contact and interest in the great issues of the day, issues which were far more than transitory and have remained of important concern throughout the ensuing half century. One of these is conservation of natural resources, which under Theodore Roosevelt had become a burning problem, getting still hotter in the Taft Administration. Another is the development of the Pure Food and Drugs Act, and truth in advertising, both covered in a page-one story recording statements by Dr. Harvey W. Wiley, the great leader in one of the century's most important cleanups.

From these few samples it will be seen that despite inexperience, despite a kind of innocence, the *Monitor*'s fundamental commitment to the illumination and solution of the deepest human problems led it at once into areas which — fifty years later — stand out with abiding significance and value. Some of these issues excited people at the time. Others did not. But in retrospect they are meaningful; this word best describes the *Monitor*'s addition to journalism. It is more accurately descriptive than "clean" or "constructive."

At the same time, the *Monitor* tried to keep a light touch. It embellished the bottom of page one with the story of a thirty-pound lobster brought in to T Wharf that day. And on "The Home Forum," along with more elevating cultural material and the religious article, it ran jokes. And such jokes!

"Oh, sir, please, I have swallowed a pin," exclaimed a servant maid running into her employer's study. "Never mind, Mary, never mind," said her employer soothingly, "here's another."

[Or this:]

"Most people," said the thoughtful thinker, "take life seriously."

"Well," replied the light thinker, "there is no reason why they should not. It is a serious thing to take life."

There was a little item that must have been of surpassing interest to ladies, with their long and noble tresses. It recorded the invention of an electric hair dryer. And so it went.

The editorials took all the back page, not just two columns, as became the practice in 1934. They were set in three columns. A full page of editorials was quite a diet, stretching to some 5000 words a day. The first editorial page included not only Mrs. Eddy's editorial and the tribute to her, "A Word of Appreciation," which took the entire first column between them, but a semireligious editorial on "The Importance of the Unimportant." The inclusion of this editorial, with its specific references to Christian Science, reveals again the pioneering stage of the paper. For several months, somewhat similar editorials were published. Such treatment would have been suitable in a strictly denominational medium. It was out of keeping with the *Monitor's* pledge to be a "real newspaper," though published by a church and serving the interests of the church by serving the public interest. And so, after April 23, 1909, the religious references ceased as abruptly as if someone had turned a switch. The last overtly religious editorial, published on that date, was called "Nothing Is Really Lost."

This elimination of frequent conscious religious terminology is not mentioned in the available documents, except that Amos Weston, the first foreman of the composing room — who was much more than a technician, being a perceptive and dedicated *Monitor* worker — writes: "The editorial zeal to present Christian Science to Monitor readers was evidently curbed. I never heard an order being given on that subject. It seemed to have been Mrs. Eddy's method to give to Mr. McLellan and Mr. Dodds, who principally contacted her on Monitor policies, her general ideas on a subject and leave it to them to work out the details."

In any event, the frequent references on the editorial page or in the news columns went out of the paper after April 23, 1909, and stayed out. At this time, Mrs. Eddy herself was carefully watching the paper, especially its editorial page. The drastic change was made at least with her knowledge and tacit approval. It represented a decisive confirming of the fact that the *Monitor* was to be a regular paper, was not to slip over into the doctrinal and house-organ category. At all times, the *Moni-*

tor was dedicated to show in action the inner importance of the truths by which it lived.

The exceptions to the rule against denominationalism should be explained to avoid any misunderstanding. As stated, the *Monitor* every day runs a religious article on its "Home Forum." This piece of religious writing clearly signals its nature. It is, as a matter of fact, of considerable interest to non-Christian Scientist readers, and not without influence.

One incident affecting the religious article on "The Home Forum" is recalled with particular pleasure. The editor of a small city newspaper told me once that every Saturday he publishes a religious editorial, regularly contributed by individual clergymen in the community. Whenever one of them fell behind his deadline, and did not get his copy to the editor on time, the editor would clip a religious article from the *Monitor*'s "Home Forum" and run it instead. "They'd meet their deadlines fine for a few weeks after that," my editor friend remarked with some satisfaction. "But you always get more than your share!"

The *Monitor* has always published Christian Science news of outstanding importance. It has done this at somewhat greater length than would other newspapers in the community, but the difference is only one of degree. Thus, at the time of the Annual Meeting of The Mother Church, the *Monitor* prints several columns of reports and summaries of the meeting. Other newspapers print briefer accounts, unless some exceptionally important news is announced. The *Monitor* prints the texts of Christian Science lectures delivered in The Mother Church or in downtown Boston seven times a year. Some other newspapers also print full texts of Christian Science lectures, and before there were the pressures of the present time for newspaper space a substantial number of papers would run these texts. Nowadays only a few papers can find space for the texts, though many papers print briefer accounts of the lectures. And finally, once in a great while, the *Monitor* is used to give brief official announcements to Christian Scientists when time is important. But these items are never obtrusive.

Thus it is that the *Monitor* seeks to avoid a denominational cast over its journalistic service. This corner was turned in part in the great decision announced in the *Sentinel* before the *Monitor* ever appeared: that it would be a "real newspaper." The issue was confirmed when, under Mrs. Eddy's intent observation, the denominational cast was removed from editorials.

This does not mean that an occasional reference to the teachings of Christian Science applied to some public issue is out of place. From time to time, but with careful discrimination, when the special viewpoint of Christian Science seems to add an indispensable element of insight, clarity, and healing, the *Monitor* will admit such an observation. Christian Science thinking does indeed underlie all the conclusions presented in *The Christian Science Monitor.* There is no intention to conceal or camouflage how important Christian Science is to the ideas and services of the *Monitor.* It is fundamental. The fact was affirmed when Mrs. Eddy insisted that the words remain in the paper's title. But it is equally true and important that the paper seeks to present its ideas honestly and objectively to a nondenominational audience. Quite frequently, even today, The Christian Science Board of Directors have to stand firm against natural and eager requests of Christian Science churches and other groups related to Christian Science to have special attention in the *Monitor.* The working rule is: "Only if the material would be newsworthy to other newspapers," and not always then.

8

◇◇◇◇◇◇◇◇◇◇◇◇◇◇◇◇◇◇◇◇

The "Colonel" and His Staff

GREAT WAS THE EXCITEMENT, great the relief and gratitude, when the pioneer staff finally produced the first copy of *The Christian Science Monitor* and launched it upon the world.

Two pleasant incidents embellished the first few days. First, Mrs. Eddy sent the staff of the composing room a letter of congratulation for the great work they had accomplished, and accompanied it with a bunch of pansies. The pansies were evidently divided among the staff, and one of them still had his pansy, carefully tucked away in a little box, as the half-century anniversary approached.

Second, during the first week, the staff was very pleased to be given full pay for Thanksgiving Day, on November 26, when no paper was published. In those days it was not customary to pay for holidays. The workers, who had come from various newspapers and printing establishments where very different working conditions then prevailed, were appreciative. Morale got off to an excellent start. The composing room staff sent this message to the Trustees: "We, the undersigned, members of The Monitor Composing Room, feeling the kindly spirit that prompted your generous gift to us of the holiday just passed, desire to express our appreciation and heartily thank you for the same."

The International Typographical Union's wage scale was always paid in the *Monitor* composing room with additional bonuses for extra production. There has customarily been a chairman, chosen by and from the members of the force, who collects union dues and presides at monthly "chapel" meetings. (The chapel, for the benefit of those not familiar with typographical union terminology, is the branch union organization in a given shop.)

During the construction period, prior to the first issue, there was one threat of a strike, but it was avoided. The nature of the dispute seems not to have been recorded. Down through the years, labor relations have been extremely good. There has never been an actual strike or walkout or suspension of work. The paper has never missed a day's publication. Of not many other major daily newspapers can this be said. In 1957 when all other Boston newspapers were forced to suspend publication for three difficult and costly weeks, the *Monitor* did not miss an edition. The situation which led to the Boston newspaper strike had been foreseen and wise steps taken to prevent it from reaching the *Monitor*. The mechanical force has by no means been made up entirely of Christian Scientists. Throughout the mechanical departments, unionization has been the usual practice. The Publishing Society has sought at all times to compensate its workers at least as well as they would be paid if they worked in any other Boston establishment where more rigorous collective-bargaining relations prevail.

But in addition, down through the years, the Publishing Society has not only provided more agreeable, well-lit, well-ventilated, and convenient surroundings in which to work, but it has constantly maintained a wholesome and congenial atmosphere, and the Trustees have provided many fringe benefits long before such things were demanded by unions.

The working atmosphere, particularly in the editorial department, is the subject of regular chaffing by professional newspaper visitors. It has even been falsely reported that men in the *Monitor* editorial department always wear their coats at work! This doesn't happen to be so, especially in summer. But it is true that the news room is not littered (the waste baskets are ample and well used) and so the place is tidy. The floor is swept, and regularly washed. The desks are kept picked up. If men sometimes take off their coats, it is also true that they always take off their hats. They don't smoke. And they don't yell and run around a great deal, although much work has to be done on rapid and recurrent deadlines. There aren't any spittoons.

All this, it must be admitted, does make a difference from some old-school newspaper offices. Yet, except for the no-smoking rule, it isn't very different from practices in other large and well-conducted newspapers today. The rule against smoking should be explained. Christian Scientists do not smoke, nor do they drink alcoholic stimulants. These concepts are part of their religious conviction — which is to maintain man's freedom from enslavement to any false appetite. Addiction, especially to habits which also become social evils, is contrary to the basic teachings of Christian Science. The point is twofold. Christian Scientists do not take or believe in stimulants anyway, and they strive to be free from slavery to any form of false habit or addiction. In cases where the addiction demonstrably and gravely impairs the ability to think in an upright and responsible manner, or produces tragedy and needless expense for individuals and families, these arguments are reinforced.

The custom of not smoking in the office has had a great many repercussions down through the years. The staff has always welcomed the rule, including those members who were not themselves Christian Scientists, since it meant that a much more tidy, clean, less distracting, and breathable atmosphere could be maintained. But visitors have more than once had their problems. The most memorable was the visit of the late General (then Colonel) Evans Carlson, fresh from the Far East, before the days of Carlson's Raiders during the dismal early stages of the Second World War. General Carlson was calling on Charles E. Gratke, then foreign editor, and casually remarked: "I suppose it's all right to smoke here." "Oh, quite all right," replied Mr. Gratke with a whimsy typical of his sharp wit. "Of course, nobody ever has." Neither did General Carlson.

I'm not sure the Gratke technique would have done for everybody. Once when Erika Mann, daughter of Thomas Mann, was chatting with me she fumbled in her bag for a cigarette and I asked her not to smoke. To embellish the situation, I told her the Carlson-Gratke story. She replied: "It's a good thing you didn't tell me that before you asked me not to smoke. I should certainly have tried to be the first one."

On another occasion, an old newspaper friend came to see me on business one forenoon, visibly and embarrassingly suffering from a hangover. With his hands shaking, he fished for his package of cigarettes. I told him not to smoke. Years later I learned, with much happiness, that the incident gave him just the moral courage to stop smoking altogether, and to stop drinking as well. A fine career was saved.

There is no denying that the atmosphere in editorial, business, and mechanical departments of the Christian Science Publishing House is unusual. Music played its part in the very early days, although there has never been "Muzak" or such audible tranquilizers laid on. But in the early days, there came a time when the composing room force wanted to enrich their day musically. Frank Doyle, a worker who possessed a good deal of musical talent — being a teacher of singing among other things — persuaded the whole force to chip in and buy an Edison phonograph for use at lunch time.

In those days everyone brought a lunch, so excellent concert music was added to the minor sounds of rustling sandwich paper and munching of food. "It was a good thing," commented Wendell W. Wyman, an original employee who was for many years foreman of the composing room, "to have something to distract us and cool us off."

The situation, in a fast-moving newspaper day, is not always so mellow. Old-timers in the composing room remember with transfixed horror the occasion in the original Publishing House when the sports page was wheeled into an elevator to make its normal descent to the stereotyping room in the basement three floors below. But the elevator wasn't there, only the shaft, and the sports page made a tragic descent. It took a long time to put it back together again.

Another incident reaffirms the fact that our decorum is not always staid. Bertram B. Johansson, now Latin American editor, and recent holder of a Reid Fellowship in India, came from Iowa. His first job on the *Monitor,* during the Second World War, was as a city reporter. One day he was sent to Deer Island, in Boston Harbor, where the city maintains a pig farm.

The political appointee who nursed the swine was totally at a loss when our photographer asked him to call the pigs, who were wandering all over the island, so that a good lively action photograph could be taken. The pig-herder hadn't the slightest idea how you call a pig. But Mr. Johansson, coming from Iowa, had. Clearing his throat and loosening his belt, cupping his hands to his lips, he let go with a good Middle Western "Sow-e-e-e-e." The Boston pigs came running from all over the island and nearly bowled over the attendant.

The photographer told the editor with great pride of the reporter's prowess. So, next morning, when the newsroom was a hive of activity, the editor stepped to Mr. Johansson's desk and asked him to stand up quietly and give everybody the benefit of his hog-call. He did, and the Linotype operators from the composing room down the corridor came running in, thinking the war was over.

The atmosphere, then and now, is an important part of the picture. It is really possible to get a lot more work done when the place is clean, the air is good, and the talk is not loose and loud. It is and always has been a thoroughly professional shop, even when it doesn't look like it. There is also an external factor which keeps the staff on its best behavior. The whole Publishing House is constantly being inspected by guided tours of visitors. Sometimes the guides, in an excess of zeal, have delighted the staff. The corridor to the present newsroom is lined by the small private offices of editorial writers. Once a guide, taking a party down this corridor, was heard to say: "We mustn't talk along here. The editorial writers are thinking!"

Another guide, a dear old gentleman who had taken parties around for many decades and whose monologue had become rather formalized, used to say as he brought his flock into the newsroom, "An edition has just gone to press, and the workers are relaxing at their desks." Since this was rarely true, the workers could only assume the guide felt the atmosphere of tranquillity required an explanation. It really wasn't that tranquil.

Miss Emily Henderson, a candid little lady who first came to work at the Publishing House in 1906 and still visits us from time to time, writes in her reminiscences:

> Amusing things would come up in the work in the early days, from correspondence. One laugh went around about someone who wanted to come and sit on the cellar stairs and "breathe the holy atmosphere." It seems as if about everyone who comes to the Publishing House to work expects to find that the Kingdom has actually arrived, that the wonderful calm was continuous without a break. I remember how I was disillusioned regarding this, when I saw the order clerk running frantically along Huntington Avenue for fear the rain would spoil her new summer hat. Quite human-like, to be sure. After a few of these observations, one gains understanding and more charity and goes on from there. But I will say that for the most part human nature is pretty much under control at the Christian Science Publishing Society.

Beneath such false concepts of the arrival of the Kingdom of Heaven on earth, there lay a genuine sense of spiritual dedication which contributed vastly to the success of the enterprise, from start to finish. Without this spiritual dedication, it is certain the undertaking would have failed. It was an implicit and essential part of the whole. Something of its meaning, in daily operational terms, is indicated in a letter from Mrs. David P. Wyman.

As F. Gertrude Waterman, she was one of the original Linotype operators, and Mr. Wyman, who became her husband five years later, was also an original composing room worker. Her letter makes two points which reveal some of the inner values. She writes: "My husband, known by his fellow workers as 'Pete,' was employed at the Boston Herald and was perfectly satisfied with his position at the time, but on being asked if he would like to come to work on The Christian Science Monitor, felt it a duty and a privilege to accept. So he was employed two weeks before the paper started. While he was willing to come on a much smaller salary than that to which he was accustomed, it was not long before the amount was raised spontaneously by the Trustees, and was much more than he had received previously."

Mrs. Wyman herself had had some little trouble with the union, which she had been accused of joining in order to get a job, and so she was delighted when Mr. Dodds and Mr. Weston accepted her as a Linotype operator. She writes: "The day I was to interview Mr. Dodds and Mr. Weston was the day my father was to be buried. Mr. Dodds wrote me a very beautiful letter and quoted from Mrs. Eddy's Miscellany, page 296, line 13 to end of article. It meant so much to me at that time that a very busy man as he was, should stop long enough to do it. I have always been grateful."

The quotation referred to the recent passing of Joseph Armstrong, publisher of Mrs. Eddy's books. She wrote in part: "Evil has no power to harm, to hinder, or to destroy the real spiritual man. He is wiser to-day, healthier and happier, than yesterday . . ." That Mr. Dodds, in the extraordinary rush of the last two weeks of preparation for the new paper, should have written to console a young girl in her bereavement, like the action of the Trustees in spontaneously increasing her future husband's salary, tells a great deal about the basic relationships which, along with many other similar elements, made the survival of *The Christian Science Monitor* possible.

What sort of men were they who were leading this bold and chancy enterprise? The key man, of course, was Mr. McLellan. Scarcely second in importance was Mr. Dodds. These two quite clearly carried through the initial planning, setting the

Mary Baker Eddy as she began Christian Science journalism in 1883.

Mary Baker Eddy at Concord, New Hampshire, not long before she established the *Monitor.*

4

Hoping I am not presuming too much in sending you so long a letter, and that I shall be notified soon if you disapprove of my suggestion, I am with profound gratitude,

Your would-be faithful follower,

John L. Wright

First Reader, First Church of Christ, Scientist, Chelsea, Mass.

Beloved Student

I have had this newspaper scheme in my thought for quite a while and herein send my name for our daily newspaper The Christian Science Monitor. This title only classifies the Paper and it should have departments for what else is requisite

Mrs. Eddy first names *The Christian Science Monitor* in a letter, apparently not sent, about March 12, 1908. Mr. Wright was a Boston newspaperman.

Box G. Brookline, Mass.

August third, 1908.

Mr. Archibald McLellan,

Boston, Mass.

Beloved Student:-

Have on the cover of the Christian Science Monitor, "first the blade, then the ear, after that the full corn in the ear". and have that illustrated with a pretty design.

Lovingly yours,

Mary B. G. Eddy

Second note sent by Mrs. Eddy, establishing motto and "pretty design." From the samples submitted the design on right was chosen.

Box G. Brookline, Mass.

August 8,1908.

Christian Science Board of Trustees,

Boston, Mass.

Beloved Students:-

It is my request that you start a daily newspaper at once, and call it the Christian Science Monitor. Let there be no delay. The Cause demands that it be issued now.

You may consult with the Board of Directors, I have notified them of my intention.

Lovingly yours

Mary Baker Eddy

Mrs. Eddy's letter which started official work.

First paper printed: experimental

A DAILY PAPER FOR THE HOME

THE CHRISTIAN SCIENCE MONITOR

ALL THE NEWS WORTH READING

"First the blade, then the ear; after that the full ~~corn~~ grain in the ear."

Volume 1, Number 1 — BOSTON, MASS., TUESDAY, SEPTEMBER 15, 1908. — Price Two Cents the Copy

Modern Glasgow Is Very Stately but Gloomy City

Solid of Structure, Somber and Plain Like the Sterling Inhabitants of the Bonny Land of the Scots.

IS GREAT WORKSHOP

Wonderful Industry and Activity Noted on Every Side in City that is a Great Workshop.

Orville Wright Is Making Records With Aeroplane

Circles Parade Grounds at Fort Myer Forty-eight Times and Remains in Air Almost an Hour.

IN PERFECT CONTROL

He Surpasses With Ease the Half Hour Flight Made by Aviator Delagrange in France.

VIEWS OF THE WRIGHT AEROPLANE DURING ARMY TESTS AT FORT MYER

New Hampshire Politics Mixed Result in Doubt

Supporters of Quinby and Pillsbury Claim Their Candidate Has Republican Nomination for Governor.

ELLIS A CANDIDATE

Few Delegates are Pledged and it is Claimed Ellis Will Draw His Support from the Unpledged Members.

Submarine Fleet May be Sent to Pacific Ocean

Project now on Foot at Washington to Tow the Little Fighters on a Long Voyage.

WILL UNDERGO TEST

Going South This Winter, and They May Make Their Start for the Far East From Cuba.

Chinese Annoy the Australians

Government Forbids Manufacture, Use, or Possession of Opium—Many Chinamen ...

Forests Ablaze in Minnesota

Aid Sent to Those Left Homeless by the Fires at Grand Marais. Towns Surrounded by Flames.

Church Will Aid Gov. Hanley

Indiana's Executive Appeals to the Methodist Conference in his Fight. Urges ...

Warfare Play on New Basis

Col. Maus Wants to Use Balloons, Wireless Telegraph and Automobiles in California Maneuvers.

Test Ride Over Officers Are Fit

U. S. Treaties are Adopted.

Capitalists Will Buy Cave of Winds

Masons to Have Bay State Home

Grand Lodge Appoints Committee to Secure Options on Suitable Sites for the Structure.

Harriman Plans Free School

Railroad Man Said to Have Consulted Experts Regarding Practical Institution for Worthy Young Men Needing Help.

Will Direct Torpedo Fleet.

REAR ADMIRAL BROWNSON, NEW CHIEF OF THE BUREAU OF NAVIGATION.

Rich Woman Weds Farm Hand

Unemployed Parade.

Women Rescued by Two Sailors

Up Twenty-three Hours.

Centennial of a Sunday School

German Spy Makes Confession

Sample copy produced only thirty-five days after instructions were received. Handwritten correction by Mrs. Eddy and notation by Calvin Frye.

Right Must Triumph Because It is Part of the Divine Plan

—A DAILY THOUGHT FOR EACH OF US.

EDITORIAL

Boston, Mass., Tuesday, September 15, 1908.

Presidential Veto Power

Now that billion-dollar congresses have become usual there is greater need than ever for an amendment to the national constitution which will enable the President to veto any particular item of an appropriation bill. Such an amendment if submitted to popular vote would carry almost unanimously. There is little or nothing that could be said against it; nothing perhaps except that if this proposed amendment were to be submitted other proposals to amend the constitution might insist upon being submitted at the same time.

The framers of our national constitution intended to confer the veto power as an executive check upon all legislative acts. If they had foreseen the extent to which congressmen and even senators would work to promote the supposed interests of their own constituents rather than the interests of the nation or the welfare of humanity and the manner in which items are added to appropriation bills solely to obtain the support of senators and congressmen who demand certain expenditures for the benefit of their own localities, the framers of the constitution would doubtless have conferred the power to veto particular items of an appropriation bill without vetoing the whole measure. The principal measure may be wise and just. It may be a measure of immediate importance. It may be encumbered nevertheless with "riders" with which selfishness has saddled the bill by taking advantage of public necessity. In this situation, with the constitution in its present form, the President must needs veto the whole measure or approve it with whatever waste or extravagance it may contain.

The people have accepted a larger army and navy, more territory to be governed, and a wider scope of government as sufficient reasons for larger appropriations; but they have not ceased to demand wisdom and economy on the part of the government; and every check on waste or extravagance should be provided which experience or changed conditions show to be useful or necessary.

THE VOTERS MUST DECIDE

Mr. Bryan's familiarity with the Scriptures is well established. His search of the Good Book for political wisdom or admonition never fails. Monday, at Chicago, he chose for the text of his political preachment Solomon's warning: "As a man thinketh in his heart, so is he." The pertinency of the text to the present campaign is readily apparent. The issue is of men, rather than of platform promises. The voters will decide between Mr. Taft and Mr. Bryan as President for the next four years. In the comparison of deeds, Mr. Bryan is admittedly at disadvantage with his opponent. Mr. Taft has seen much of public life and has been in intimate touch with great questions of national policy. He has thus proved his fitness for the office. Mr. Bryan has had less opportunity for performance, his official career having been confined to two terms in Congress. Mr. Bryan now appeals from the judgment of parties and of platforms to the judgment of men, and seeks to take the standard of the wise man for the comparative measurement.

Legal Training in the United States

The recent action of the Association of American Law Schools in adopting resolutions limiting its membership to schools granting diplomas only on the completion of a three years' course of study is interesting from many points of view. The motive underlying it seems to have been misinterpreted by a contemporary, which regards it as principally directed against schools that allow credit for ill-defined apprentice service in a lawyer's office. Doubtless this consideration was not without influence, but there are schools in which a two years' course of study is sufficient for a diploma, but under exceptional conditions. Such schools are as much affected as those which designedly make graduation easy to attract students. The eminently respectable law school of Boston University, it will be remembered, at once withdrew from the Association on the adoption of the resolution and was followed by the New York University Law School. Each has a two years' course, but in the former, at least, only college graduates are elegible to it, and the required standing is ten per cent. above that of students in the three years' course, an arrangement very different from one productive of pettifoggers.

From another point of view, that of educational progress, the decision of the Association is significant of the trend of the times towards the substitution of the collective system of instruction for what remains of the old individualistic method. Everywhere now the leading professors have their schools, and it is as seldom one comes upon a lawyer in the prime of life who is a graduate of an office, as upon a clergyman whose preparation for taking orders has been in the study of a theologian. Time was when in both theology and law studies leading to the pulpit and the bar were carried on under the tuition of individuals. There were great preachers and great lawyers who illustrated this era, which, if not altogether past, is rapidly passing away.

In the application of the school to the study of law the United States has dragged far behind the nations of Continental Europe. The universities of Bologna and Paris had great law schools even in the Middle Ages, with courses on general principles assimilating those of today. We were influenced by the British traditions, for neither Oxford nor Cambridge has what may be called law schools in the modern acceptance of the term. On the other hand, the sparsely settled condition of our country, the absence of great cities, the crudeness of our social system, the newness of everything combined to prevent the evolution of schools of lawyers for lawyers similar to the Inns of Court. Our great lawyers, men of the stamp of Webster and Marshall, acquired their law at the bench, so to speak, and from such instruction as they could receive or obtain in offices.

"THE LAST ENEMY."

BEN HAWORTH-BOOTH.

My barque is hastening onward to a bourne
  Of summer seas; and soon the boatswain may
  Pipe me the signal at the close of day
Or 'neath the opening eyelids of the morn.

The storm upon my window wakens me;
  Upon the clamorous night my spirit peers,
  Where leafless boughs and lonely glimmering meres
Reach forward to the fog-enfolded sea.

On such a night as this 'tis hard to tell
  Thine heart that on the darkness and the deep
  One Hand alone doth guide and guard and keep,
'Tis hard, but it is true—and all is well.

On such a night I used to deem, of yore,
  'Twere fearful to depart, to wander forth
  Upon the howling tempest of the north,
Over the frozen fields and shuddering shore;

To pass away upon the wild night air—
  A formless fear, a sightless, senseless thing!
  'Twas terrible! but now the morn doth bring
A wisdom far more wise, a faith more fair.

We are the sons of Life—not sons of death—
  And in His great design all, all is well;
  Can mourning mummeries or the funeral bell
Prove that we perish with the passing breath?

There dies indeed the noisome taint of earth
  That Truth has not destroyed—but naught beside—
  The sin, the selfishness, the pain, the pride;
But life lives on, and faith attains new birth.

Webster was one of these clerk-students in the office of Christopher Gore, then famous among the advocates of his time, and much sought as an instructor of legally minded youth, who had to pay handsome premiums for the privilege of receiving his instruction. Our first law schools were simply expansions of this system, an eminent jurist gathering about him classes, and by his ability developing the gathering into an institution. The most famous of all these private schools was that founded by Tapping Reeve, at Litchfield, Conn., shortly after the Revolution, which had an existence of half a century.

It had many imitators but few equals. All these private schools were supplanted by those of the universities, and these in turn seem to be entering upon an era of increased requirements for admission and graduation. This tendency is in part stimulated by the practice of nearly half the States of the Union which has substituted for the old free and easy method of admission to practice examination by expert boards. The result has been that admittance to the bar has become practically equivalent to demonstrating the possession of the degree of bachelor of law. In Massachusetts graduation from a reputable law school is not legally a prerequisite condition for admission to the bar, but the nature of the examination is such that the possession of a diploma is practically requisite to passing. All who have it do not pass, but almost all who pass have it. Despite the increasing rigor of the test there is no diminution of the number of lawyers. The profession is congested in every large city, and the only room is at the top, whither Websters and Marshalls climb. The Websters are rather men who make schools of law than men made by law schools, but who shall not say that the great Daniel would not have appreciated facilities similar to those of the present.

Dr. Grenfell and His "Miracle"

Mr. Grenfell, whose heroic Christianity among the Labrador fishermen has won him world-wide celebrity, wrote recently to his friend, Mr. W. R. Moody, informing that gentleman that he had been saved from death by a "miracle." This led to enquiries by the curious, and Dr. Grenfell has written another letter explaining what he meant. He was out on the ice when an off-shore wind broke up the field, leaving him solitary and alone on a comparatively small cake which the wind was carrying rapidly out to sea. "I could expect," he says, "short of a miracle, nothing but death out there. Somehow one scarcely felt justified in praying for a miracle, but we have learned down here to pray for things we want, and anyhow, just at that moment the miracle occurred. The wind fell off suddenly." Even "stranger" than the experience of Dr. Grenfell is pronounced to be by the religious press, is the comment of the *Interior* upon it. "This," says that journal, with all gravity and in all seriousness, "is the nearest and plainest demonstration of the imminent presence of a personal God who is 'keeping watch above his own,' and after a man has had one such experience in life he is beguiled no longer with pantheistic notions of a 'great impersonal force' within that is deaf to prayer and empty of will." This is certainly dim enough to suit the most densely orthodox, but it would be comparatively illuminating were it not that the *Interior* had already attributed the escape of Dr. Grenfell to a mere accidental change in the direction of the wind.

Premier Stolypin's apologies for his government's efforts to suppress the Tolstoi birthday festivities are late, but hindsight is better than total and persistent blindness.

And speaking of the successful opening of the public school season, New York's turnout of 640,000 pupils and 17,000 teachers seems to be entitled to the numerical prize, anyway.

Forestry as Insurance Against Fires

The forest fires which swept over the Mesaba range in Minnesota, destroying one town and causing a loss of over $5,000,000 worth of property were fed largely by the tangle of deadwood and brush which had accumulated in years of forest neglect. The intensity of the average forest fire is due to similar conditions. Improved forestry prevents such tinder heaps. It costs money for labor to clear the woods of brush and to remove fallen trees and deadwood, but such work does something more than save all the living powers of the soil for the growing trees. It prevents the accumulation of fuel with which to feed sweeping flames. Is it not worth while? But a diminutive percentage of the loss in British Columbia and in Minnesota, to say nothing of smaller fires in other parts of the country, would have been required to apply to these tracts the principles of practical forest preservation. The value of forestry as an insurance against fire loss is capable of mathematical demonstration.

Honest Construction Must Prevail

Some recent conflagrations, notably one in Boston involving a loss of $1,500,000, has set insurance men and economists to discussing again the tremendous, unnecessary, and shameful destruction of property by fire in this country annually. A list of conflagrations throughout the world since 1835, from which all fires in which the estimated loss was less than $10,000,000 have been eliminated, exhibits the following appalling comparison between the United States and other countries.

1835—December 16, New York	17,000,000	1877—June 4, St. John, N. B.	15,000,000
1842—May 4, Hamburg	35,000,000	1882—December 11, Kingston, Jamaica	10,000,000
1848—August 16, Constantinople	15,000,000	1892—July 8, St. John's, Newfoundland	20,000,000
1851—May 4, St. Louis	15,000,000	1896—October 5, Guayaquil, Ecuador	22,000,000
1861—December 12, Charleston, S. C.	10,000,000	1900—April 27, Ottawa, Hull, Ontario	10,000,000
1866—July 4, Portland, Me.	10,000,000	1901—May 3, Jacksonville, Fla.	10,000,000
1870—June 5, Constantinople	25,000,000	1904—February 7, Baltimore	50,000,000
1871—October 8, Chicago	165,000,000	1904—April 19, Toronto, Can.	12,000,000
1872—November 9, Boston	70,000,000	1906—April 18, San Francisco	350,000,000
1876—September 3, St. Hyacinthe, Canada	15,000,000		

Fire insurance statistics show that within the last five years the loss of property in the United States from fires alone reaches a total of $1,257,716,855, an average of $251,000,000 a year. A saving of even 50 per cent. of this amount annually would construct for us a great canal system, build, equip and maintain colleges, museums and libraries, and provide recreation parks in the tenement districts of our great cities. The most lamentable feature of the matter is that in ninety-nine per cent. of the cases these fires are preventable. As in another well-known field of human endeavor, effort is mainly directed toward the cure rather than toward the removing of the cause of the disease. We spend millions annually in fire extinguishing apparatus and in the maintainance of fire-extinguishing departments, but we pay little or no attention to the matter of preventing the erection of buildings of inflammable material or to the removal of structures whose character menaces the better class of buildings in their vicinity. Dishonest construction, faulty workmanship, carelessness in electric wiring, ignorance of the causes of spontaneous combustion, and criminal negligence on the part of those entrusted with the care of buildings, account for a majority of the fires.

When men are moved by something higher than selfishness, when they are guided in their dealings with each other and in their conduct toward the community by nobler impulses than those which move them now—when men will do unto others as they would be done by—fire-traps which imperil life and property will no longer be erected, nor will workmen consent to have part or parcel in the frauds which are too often practiced by architects and contractors upon those who are seeking and willing to pay for good construction. A widespread sense of the demands of common honesty will do more toward reducing the losses by fire in the United States than costly fire-extinguishing apparatus and laws against incendiarism and arson.

With the view of making it clear that Marshfield, Mass., is not the only place in the world where fame at times cuts no sort of figure, an anecdote growing out of the recent celebration of the Linnean Society in England is told. In the parish of Down, so the story runs, Mr. Darwin was much beloved. He was rather a puzzle, however, to the villagers. One of his friends once asked the gardener how Mr. Darwin was. "Oh," he said, "my poor master has been very badly. I often wish he had something to do. I have seen him stand doing nothing before a flower for ten minutes at a time. If he only had some regular work I believe he would be much better." The Marshfield story, however, is of a little different order. A stranger went to Marshfield for the express purpose of paying his respects to Daniel Webster during that great statesman's lifetime. Accosting a resident, he enquired the way to Senator Webster's home, but was informed that no such person lived in the town. On being assured that he certainly did, the resident replied that it was impossible, as he himself had lived in the place for thirty years, and had never heard the name before.

A Western exchange relates how one day recently in a department store a woman had much difficulty in controlling her young son, who it was plain entertained little respect for his maternal guardian. One could not but ask why. A little observation revealed the reason. Within two or three minutes that woman had told her child at least three falsehoods. She said a policeman was coming for him, that the elevator man would get him, and that she had candy for him—all of which the boy plainly disbelieved. It ought to be said that there are probably other mothers very like this one in other parts of the country, and that, like this one, they are all probably wondering why their children are not obedient and respectful.

Modern newspapers have their mission hand in hand with the other great reform movements of the nation. Too much care cannot be exercised as to the reading matter presented.

President Roosevelt's advice to the returned Olympian athletes to now lay heroism aside and go to work, might be pondered upon profitably by many.

Editorial page of sample copy.

Mrs. Eddy on daily ride from Chestnut Hill, in 1909. Coachman is Frank E. Bowman; to the right, Calvin A. Frye, Mrs. Eddy's long-standing, faithful secretary.

Work swiftly progresses — piles driven, steel riveted, two months after orders were received.

THE CHRISTIAN SCIENCE MONITOR

STOCK EDITION. BOSTON, MASS., WEDNESDAY, NOVEMBER 25, 1908.—VOL. I., NO. 1. PRICE TWO CENTS.

CARNEGIE DOES NOT WANT TO BE TARIFF WITNESS

Steel Magnate Says He Has Served His Time in Matters and Views Are Well Known.

71 YEARS OLD TODAY

Chairman Payne of Ways and Means Committee Makes Public Correspondence With Multi-Millionaire.

CONSTRUCTION WORK RAPIDLY PROGRESSES ON GREAT DAM ACROSS THE CHARLES RIVER BASIN

Lock and Sluices Completed and Machinery Installed in New Lock-House on Boston Side of Stream.

LOCK IN OPERATION

LOCKS AND SLUICES IN CHARLES RIVER DAM.

ASK INJUNCTION AGAINST CHELSEA SHOE WORKERS

Walton V. Logan Alleges Union Men Interfered With Employes at Factory After Strike Was Declared.

NAMES EIGHT MEN

UNVEIL STATUE OF GEN. SHERIDAN AT WASHINGTON

Salute of 17 Guns Fired in Honor of Civil War Hero When Son Pulls Aside Covering of Memorial.

NOTED MEN PRESENT

SHIP RELIEF IS SAFE AT LUZON

CALL TROOPS TO QUELL STUDENTS

THANKSGIVING SERVICE.

CITY WINS $5000 IN LAND CASE

Judgment Is Entered in Case of Property Purchased From Cemetery Trustee and Superintendent.

BOSTON LIBRARY IS GIVEN A RARE BOOK COLLECTION

Mrs. Louise Chandler Moulton and Philip Bourke Marston Volumes Include Many Autograph Copies.

FIREMAN SAVES ENTIRE FAMILY

Brave Rescuer Swung From Roof 70 Feet Above Sidewalk in New York to Aid Seven Persons.

SAVES CHILDREN AND WIFE AT FIRE

NIGHT SCHOOLS FOR DES MOINES

Success of Plan Last Year Causes Educational Board to Resume Sessions This Season.

GOV. GUILD MAKES GOETTING ADVISER

EXPERT REVIEWS CONDITIONS IN THE DISTURBED BALKAN COUNTRIES

Interesting Phase of Economic Duel Between England and Germany Discussed.

LANDMARK HISTORY

Installment Stories of Situation in Near-Far East Presented for Readers of The Christian Science Monitor.

SARDINIA BEACHED BECAUSE OF FIRE

Liner Burned Just Outside Malta While on Her Way From Liverpool—Many Lives Lost.

NO DEMOCRACY, ZUEBLIN SAYS

Second Lecture in Course on "The American Municipality" Deals With the Training of the Citizen.

Largest Lock Gates in America.

Two Centrifugal Pumps.

BROCKTON CHURCH DEDICATION NEAR

SPEAKER'S CLUB FOR HARVARD MEN

NEW FACTORY SOON TO START

THANKSGIVING DAY FORECAST

37,000 TURKEYS FOR HOME MARKET

CONTINUED ON PAGE TWO.

First edition, front page.

THE CHRISTIAN SCIENCE MONITOR

"First the blade, then the ear, then the full grain in the ear."

EDITORIAL

Boston, Mass., Wednesday, November 25, 1908.

Something In a Name

By Mary Baker G. Eddy

The gentleman, Mr. Frank Bell, has caught my thunder; therefore he will not object to the lightning which accompanies it.

I have given the name to all the Christian Science periodicals. The first was THE CHRISTIAN SCIENCE JOURNAL, designed to put on record the divine Science of Truth; the second I entitled SENTINEL, intended to hold guard over Truth, Life and Love; the third, DER HEROLD DER CHRISTIAN SCIENCE, to proclaim the universal activity and availability of Truth; the next I named MONITOR, to spread undivided the Science that operates unspent. The object of THE MONITOR is to injure no man, but to bless all mankind.

HARRISBURG, PA., Nov. 2, 1908.

Rev. Mary Baker G. Eddy, Brookline, Mass.

Dear Leader—As a newspaper man I thank you for THE CHRISTIAN SCIENCE MONITOR in prospect, and I feel sure that such will be the sentiment of hundreds of newspaper workers all over the land when THE MONITOR in fact shall have demonstrated the feasibility of clean journalism.

A definition of "monitor" is, "One who advises," and I foresee that when this CHRISTIAN SCIENCE MONITOR shall have proved that there is such a thing as newspaper success along non-sensational lines, there will follow a widespread readjustment of news policies, for which I am sure none will be more truly thankful than an army of honest, conscientious toilers in the ranks of newspaperdom.

Gratefully yours, FRANK BELL,
Managing Editor Harrisburg Telegraph.

A Word of Appreciation

It is fitting that the editorial columns of the first issue of THE CHRISTIAN SCIENCE MONITOR should carry a tribute to the Rev. Mary Baker G. Eddy, discoverer and pioneer of Christian Science.

Brought into being with her approval, THE MONITOR plainly shows that, after nearly 43 years of consistent pioneering and untiring leadership, Mrs. Eddy is still foremost in progress.

Her pioneer work in the re-establishment of spiritual healing as taught and proved by Christ Jesus is revolutionizing human thought as regards disease and sin.

Her pioneer work in the rehabilitation of primitive Christianity is bearing fruit in a worldwide religious reform, demanding that those who declare the Christ as their Saviour shall give evidence of their faith by their works.

As the discoverer and founder of Christian Science, Mrs. Eddy started in 1883 a monthly publication called "The Christian Science Journal," the first periodical to circulate a current literature that healed. Mrs. Eddy's ideal, even then, was a "newspaper edited and published by Christian Scientists." (Miscellaneous Writings, page 4.)

Recognizing that her message was inherently cosmopolitan—to all mankind and to all peoples—she established in 1903 "Der Herold der Christian Science," a monthly magazine in the German language.

When the weekly paper, the "Christian Science Sentinel," was published in 1898, she was again a pioneer, advancing a step nearer her purpose to have a newspaper which purpose today, after 25 years of patient preparation, finds fuller expression in THE CHRISTIAN SCIENCE MONITOR.

Christian Scientists are not unduly enthusiastic nor apart from fact when they claim that Mrs. Eddy's life is proof both of her inspired mission and her personal integrity.

She is marvelous because of her spiritual scientific understanding of God, her consecration to Principle, and her patience in demonstration. It is just as characteristic of her to wait 25 years for "a newspaper edited and published by Christian Scientists," as it is for her to have such a newspaper at the end of 25 years.

She is profound because she is simple—direct in logic, sturdy in argument, steadfast in conviction, impersonal in the great religious activities which have made her the world's benefactor.

Looking without prejudice upon Mrs. Eddy's achievements—a reformed medical system, a healing literature, a spiritualized philosophy, a scientific Christianity, the signs everywhere of man thinking, Mind dominate and matter dethroned—witnessing, too, the insistent retirement from public notice of the human personality that has done these things, it is inconceivable that Mrs. Eddy *could* be actuated by anything less than a deep conviction of Truth and a sincere desire to help humanity.

Eminent as a woman, eminent as a religious reformer, Mrs. Eddy is uniquely eminent as an author. Pioneer there as elsewhere, she is the originator of a noble literature, the aim of which is to elevate the human consciousness to an understanding of the allness of good and the nothingness of evil.

As the student of the art of sculpture must gain dominion over the clay before he can set forth his ideals in a manner acceptable to the connoisseur, so Mrs. Eddy has been obliged to struggle long with words and phrases of original material meaning before she could express her spiritual concepts in a way which the literary critic would pronounce workmanlike.

Her first purpose was not to write prettily but to get her message to the public. Much of her recent labor has been to improve the literary setting of this message. To-day her great work, "Science and Health with Key to the Scriptures," is a study in appropriate literary expression. It marks Mrs. Eddy not only an original thinker in the domain of metaphysics but a stylist of marked and notable characteristics.

Christian Science, as taught by Mrs. Eddy, is before the world to be judged by what it does. All may not be willing to strive for the ideal of perfection which she places as the goal of human endeavor; but we are convinced that no one, who perceives ever so slightly what Mrs. Eddy means by Christian Science, will quarrel with her or with her teachings.

It seems to be in the regular order of things that if Mr. Whitelaw Reid is desirous of returning to America, and Mr. George von L. Meyer is desirous of going to the Court of St. James, such an arrangement may be brought about as will enable Mr. Reid to step from the British ambassadorship into the cabinet, probably as secretary of state.

The Importance of the Unimportant

What a man is doing may not indicate what he would like to do, therefore by his vocation you may not always judge the man. He may be working under discipline, guided by the direction of wiser minds, controlled by the demands of an organization. Ruskin suggested that a man's tastes would reveal what he was. Get acquainted with a man's unfulfilled desires and you may know what he is becoming. If it is the unspoken prayer in the heart that decides the tendency of the life, then it is important for a man's welfare that he alertly guard "the imagination of the heart." The dreamy current of unguided thought which wanders in the mind of an idle man is usually supposed to be of no importance. The passing from mind to mind of suggestions unmoral, or frankly immoral, is considered uninfluential pastime. The perusal of writings where the transient flashing of wit is supposed to compensate for the salacious inferences is defended. But as well say that the *ignis fatuus* that glimmers over the marsh compensates for its malarial breath. In whatever way they find entrance to a man's mind it is true that "evil communications corrupt good manners." Furthermore it is manners that express the man.

The explanation of the success which follows effort in Christian Science is often sought. Critics say that will-power, personal magnetism, concentration of mental energies, strength of determination, account for results; but they are all wrong. Interesting demonstrations are made by children, for themselves and others. In the child is not found controlling personal magnetism, but rather simplicity and limpid purity of thought. And it is not the humanly measured strength of thought in the Christian Scientist, but the purity and rightness of his thought which accounts for his success. By right-thinking a man is brought into affiliation with the active good controlling the universe. The pure in heart not only shall see, but do see God.

Under the discipline of Christian Science teaching men awake to see the importance of what they had considered unimportant. They had lazily accepted the verdict of critics against other men, they had entertained causeless prejudices, they had fed little fires of resentment within and hated honest men without cause, and felt that they were doing no wrong since all this was concealed in the realm of thought. Also they had been open to the influence of the panic fear of others, hospitable to the expressed anxiety and prophecy of evil in current talk, and wholly unaware of the influence on their lives of such mental conditions. When the light of truth comes there is a complete reforming of the habits, tastes and desires. Ideal conditions are not reached at once, and no one should unkindly judge the Christian Scientist who is in process. All that makes for righteousness, mercy, and good will he considers important. You must judge him by his aims—by his prayers, if you will.

One Thousand Miles Nearer To Central America

The idea of constructing a ship canal across the Florida peninsula is far from being a new one, although it has been revived and brought into prominence lately by a discussion in a convention of the Gulf Coast Inland Waterways Association held at Columbus, Ga. It is as old, almost, as the idea of a canal across the isthmus of Panama.

It has long been felt by those who have been enthusiastic in their advocacy and support of the Panama canal project that if this great waterway is to be as valuable as it ought to be to our Eastern seaports it can only be made so by the construction of the Florida canal. The latter would place the commerce of the Atlantic states 1,000 miles closer to the republics of Central America than it is now, and reduce to an equal degree the distance between the Atlantic seaports and the Pacific, on the completion of the Panama canal.

Very little cutting, comparatively, would have to be done in order to make a waterway across the Florida peninsula above the Everglades. It would be necessary in the first place to make a connection between the Atlantic and Lake Okeechobee at a point, perhaps, just north of Fort Worth, and, in the second place, a connection between Lake Okeechobee and the Caloosahatchie river.

The $50,000,000 which it is estimated the canal would cost would be expended mainly in deepening the present watercourses and in dredging. The gulf terminus of the canal would in all probability be at Fort Myers, or, more properly, Punta Rassa. The carrying out of this project would be a boon to the export trade of the country.

England's Fear of an Invasion Unwarranted

At a time when the people of Germany are almost a unit in condemning the attitude of their Emperor toward their neighbors, and particularly toward England, it is regrettable that Lord Roberts should, by his declarations in the House of Lords, fan the dying embers of international bitterness into new life.

In telling the peers what the Kaiser might do, in the matter of invading England, he leaves the unhappy impression on the British mind that this is the thing which the former will do at the earliest opportunity, unless certain precautions are taken to prevent him from doing it. He fails to take cognizance of the fact that the Kaiser has quite recently been shorn of much of his personal power, and that even though he might now have the disposition to make war upon England he lacks the ability to do so.

The German people are desirous of living in peace with their neighbors. They have seldom gone to war unless under the very greatest provocation. They have much in common with the English people, with whom they are on the friendliest terms. Aside from all other considerations, it would not be to their interest, and they know it, to engage in a strife which might result in sweeping their great and growing commerce from the seas.

It is high time that the war lords in England were being silenced also. The English and the German peoples are perfectly content to live in peace, if only the professional fighters of both countries will permit them to do so.

There does not appear to be any reason why the New England states should not get together for mutual and general advancement. They are already bound together sentimentally; they might just as well be bound together practically. And there need be no sectionalism in the alliance.

Did Bret Harte Know the California of '49?

It has been charged of late that Kipling in the earliest and the best, because the most natural, of his writings—in the sketches that gave us at once most pleasure and most instruction—did not paint the true India. It has been charged of late that Lafcadio Hearn, in those pictures of the Orient that have charmed two hemispheres, did not paint the real Japan. And now comes Professor Josiah Royce of Harvard with the startling declaration that Bret Harte, whom thinking Americans are more and more disposed to regard as the most distinctively and originally native of all our writers, did not paint the real California of the '49 period. Says the professor:

> As a Californian I can say that not one childhood memory of mine suggests any social incident or situation that in the faintest degree gives meaning or confirmation to Bret Harte's stories. But it is also true that Bret Harte never saw the mines in '49 and '50, and that years later he collected the chance material of his stories from hearsay. It is also true that the social order which he depicts is an order that never was on land or sea, and that his tales are based upon a deliberately false romantic method.

Unfortunately for Professor Royce all the evidence is against him. It is true that Bret Harte was not in California in 1849 or 1850, but he was in California in 1856 when the civilization introduced by the "Argonauts" was beginning to make itself felt, and all through the period of which '49 and '50 were simply the beginning. Those who worked with pick and shovel in those days, in the gulches and canyons of the Sierra Nevada have since testified to the marvelous accuracy of Bret Harte's descriptions and portraitures. Some who were adventurers, gamblers and saloonkeepers in the gold fields during the '50s have borne like testimony in later years. The files of newspapers of the period testify to the fidelity of Bret Harte's art to truth. The civilization which the Forty-Niners brought to California was only an exaggerated form of the civilization in the river towns of Illinois and Missouri—the states which did more than any others to people California at that day—for years before and after the outbreak of the California gold fever, and Mark Twain, John Hay and scores of other observers and writers have testified to this.

The best testimony of all, however, is that conditions, situations and episodes, like unto those painted by Bret Harte, modified only by the changes that have affected every quarter of the country and every class of people in the country, have since existed and developed in other mining camps from Virginia City to Leadville, from Butte to Cripple Creek.

The fact that Professor Royce's childhood memory does not suggest any of the incidents or the situations observed, pictured and immortalized by Bret Harte, should have no weight even with Professor Royce himself. No doubt many thousands of things have occurred round about him even in his manhood hours of which he has taken no note. As a learned professor he ought to know, and in all probability does know, that it does not follow from the fact that we fail to see things or to be impressed by them that these things have no existence, and are not visible to others.

When the People Hoard Their Dollars

One of the many peculiar phases of the recent financial and commercial depression was what might be called the rejection by the people of the subsidiary coin.

That is to say, when the money panic came the average person held on as long as possible to his whole dollars, whether paper or silver. As a consequence the demand for halves, quarters, dimes and nickels fell off amazingly.

When the depression began there was about $3,000,000 of subsidiary coin in the United States treasury, but during the next seven months this amount was increased to $24,500,000, or at the rate of over $3,000,000 per month. However, notwithstanding the presidential campaign and the doleful predictions made by partisans on every side as to what would happen unless their particular candidates were elected, the demand for "small change" began to make itself felt once more in Washington, and since then fully $10,000,000 of the amount accumulated has found its way back into its legitimate channels, a fact that indicates the return of public confidence.

The people are once more "breaking" their dollars. They are beginning, in other words, to see that there was no cause for the "panic"—no cause for the "depression"—no reality to their fear beyond that which they themselves gave to it. Nothing has changed but the human sense of things. Belief brought on the panic. Understanding is destroying its effects.

New England Conference Unique and Important

The conference of governors and governors-elect of the New England states, which has just closed in this city, was in many respects one of the most unique and important gatherings held in the country during recent years. There have been state conferences in the past, it is true, but their purpose has been sectional in a political sense, or, in an economic sense, antagonistic to other divisions of the Union. Disagreeable memories are associated with most of them, painful memories with some of them.

In the present instance, however, the object has been purely to conserve and promote the interests of one section without infringing in the least upon the interests of other sections. Indeed, the purpose was broad and patriotic, in that the conference was not striving to do for New England anything that it would not be glad to have the rest of the country take a hand in.

Many facts were brought out which are of vital importance to New England and its people. But this was by no means all. The discussions which took place in the conference contain food for national reflection, and the gathering may be pronounced one of national importance in so far as it will assist in concentrating the thought of the country upon the paramount question of conserving and developing our natural resources.

We have it from one who must be classed as a student of eminent scientists, if not an eminent scientist himself, and who has written to a New York contemporary on the subject, that geology, anthropology, and prehistoric archeology all go to prove that there is a maximum and a minimum period for the existence of man upon the earth, viz.—from 20,000 to 100,000 years. There is here, it may be noticed by the careful reader, a margin of 80,000 years, which is a very liberal one indeed, considering that the sciences which get the credit for fixing the maximum and minimum periods of man's existence are popularly reputed to be exact.

First edition, editorial page with Mrs. Eddy's editorial.

Archibald McLellan, first Editor and Mother Church Director.

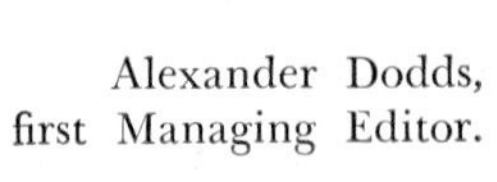

Alexander Dodds, first Managing Editor.

Frederick Dixon, Editor 1914–22.

Willis J. Abbot, Editor 1922–27, Contributing Editor 1927–34.

Roland R. Harrison, Executive Editor 1924–29, Manager 1929–39, Administrative Editor 1939–41.

Editorial Council, 1945. Left to right: Frank L. Perrin, Contributing Editor; Charles E. Gratke, Foreign Editor; Paul S. Deland, American News Editor; Erwin D. Canham, Managing Editor; Donovan M. Richardson, Chief Editorial Writer.

paper on paths which it has followed ever since. The depth and scope of their perception of what the paper should be, and how it could carry these plans into practice, were altogether remarkable. A good many others on the original staff were professional journalists of a high order of competence. The group as a whole deserves immense credit for their pioneering work. While the leadership was manifestly strong, the teamwork and integration were important. Then, as now, the achievement of the paper is very greatly due to strength in depth throughout the staff. Nor should the constant role of the Board of Trustees and manager be underestimated. It was altogether a team success.

Archibald McLellan was a native of New Brunswick of Scotch parentage. In early life he moved with his parents to Boston, and received his education in the Boston public schools. He worked in business for some years, and then took up the study of law, graduating from the Kent Law School in Chicago.

Thereafter, Mr. McLellan was associated with the R. G. Dun Mercantile Agency, later known as Dun and Bradstreet, for nearly twenty years, living for most of that period in Chicago. "A lawyer by profession and awake to everything which appeals to reason," writes Michael Meehan, the Concord journalist who knew the early Christian Science officials, "he was early attracted to the Christian Science movement, and soon became an ardent adherent of the teachings of Mrs. Eddy." He took a prominent part in the development of Christian Science in Chicago.

In 1902, with Mrs. Eddy's emphatic statement that she needed a "born editor" in Boston until she was ready for a "widespread press," Mr. McLellan was called to Boston to assume the editorship of all the Christian Science publications. At that time he gave up his other professional and business connections. In addition to his position as editor of the periodicals, he became a member of The Christian Science Board of Directors, and in 1907 was selected by Mrs. Eddy as one of the three trustees to take charge of and manage her financial affairs.

Mr. McLellan was a man of substance, of long business experience, thoroughly capable of carrying a heavy load of responsibility. That he also became a skilled writer is readily evidenced in the many signed editorials he wrote in the *Journal* and *Sentinel* from 1902 to 1917. Just how many editorials he wrote for the *Monitor* does not appear from the records. It is to be inferred that he wrote on important occasions, but not as many as if he were simply a writing newspaper editor.

Mr. McLellan was a thoughtful Christian Scientist, with a large grasp of Mrs. Eddy's purposes in founding the *Monitor*. It would not have done to place the control of the infant newspaper in the hands of merely a competent newspaperman. At the outset, when so many precedents had to be created and so much new ground plowed, newspaper talent had to be infused with spiritual insight. This will be always true, of course, but it was particularly important in 1908 that the first editor should have been a responsible church official as well as an experienced man of affairs. There could hardly have been a happier choice than Mr. McLellan.

His writing and speeches show the depth and quality of the man. Mr. McLellan's practical vision of the *Monitor*'s role, as well as a report on its progress are set forth in a speech he made before a large and enthusiastic crowd in Chicago on October 28, 1910.

"Briefly told," said Mr. McLellan, "we are trying to publish . . . all the news it is worth while reading,—such a paper as right minded men and women have long demanded, but which it has heretofore been thought could not be successfully maintained."

"All the news it is worth while reading"—there was a slogan to compare with "All the news that's fit to print" and other famous newspaper tags. Defining the function further, Mr. McLellan said it was "a paper which goes into the highways and byways of humanity and by its very character proclaims the potency of good to meet the seeming aggression of evil with a tangible proof of supremacy."

"At the end of five months," disclosed Mr. McLellan, "it had been demonstrated that the Monitor could be expected to pay its own way and to have something left over to provide for future needs and growth." Then he gave a pledge which has remained policy ever since: "The Monitor is not published with the intent to earn dividends for stockholders, for there are no stockholders and dividends are not needed or expected. The readers of the Monitor are its only beneficiaries. It has been, and is (and has always remained), the policy of its publishers to expend on the Monitor every dollar of its income, and this policy will be continued indefinitely."

The three important elements in newspaper success, pointed out by Mr. McLellan, are policy, readers, and advertising. The *Monitor* had a basic policy: "to injure no man, but to bless all mankind." It was steadily building up its readership. And its advertising was coming in very satisfactory volume. Indeed, the *Monitor*'s advertising standards required rejection of much advertising which was not straightforward or reliable. Said he: "During its first year, the advertising declined by the Monitor equalled in volume and monetary value that which was accepted as up to its standard."

Already, in two years, the worldwide distribution of the *Monitor* was phenomenal. Its Thanksgiving issue in 1910 carried seven tons of newsprint to London. Shipments went to Australia, China, Japan, Egypt, South Africa, and of course all of Western Europe. With the aid of gift funds the *Monitor* in its earliest year was available in every leading American consulate throughout the world, in foreign steamship booking offices, in public libraries, and many other public places. Its international reputation was speedily built up by actual distribution of the paper to the ends of the earth, and actual, first-hand familiarity with it by perceptive and discriminating readers everywhere.

Thus, as Mr. McLellan pointed out, the paper had standards and ideals, it was doing an acceptable job at carrying them out, and it had developed remarkable techniques for calling itself to the attention of the public it was committed to serve.

Mr. McLellan was a genial and robust man, with more than a touch of the William Howard Taft about him. His broad mustache lifted in a pleasant curve, his brow was open, his color bright, his eyes even and steady. He was a man of authority and confidence. His contribution to the *Monitor* was certainly very great, for he gave it strength and stability within the Christian Science movement, while its staff learned their technical and professional lessons. His judgment in recruiting and supporting the newsmen who joined the original staff was eminently sound.

In the fall of 1912, Mr. McLellan was one of a party of Eastern newspapermen to tour Glacier National Park. On the trip, according to others who took part, he was virtually the commandant, winning the sobriquet of "Colonel" by sheer force of bearing, following the trail and sitting his horse with all the enthusiasm of his Scots Covenanter forefather. From the pen of one of his companions on the trip, Frederick G. Birchall, who later served as managing editor of the *New York Times,* came this tribute:

> Once in a while in this life it is one's privilege to meet a Christian gentleman. "Colonel" McLellan was all that through and through. During the short month in which we were traveling companions I conceived the warmest regard and the highest personal respect for him. Our views upon some few things were as wide apart as the poles, but that did not at all affect the personal regard I felt for him.

Mr. Birchall, who was one of the ablest of newspapermen and not a person to overstate his convictions, tells of an afternoon near the end of the trip when to him everything and everybody seemed "out of joint." At last he thought of the "Colonel," and after a while found him alone on the observation platform, quietly reading.

"Instinctively as I stepped out," said Mr. Birchall, "I felt as if I were intruding on holy ground; but he looked up at me with his ever ready smile, slipped his little book into his coat pocket, and was at once at my disposal for a friendly chat. I realized then that of us all he alone had a place of refuge from all discomforts, even 'the secret place of the most High,' and inwardly rebuking myself for my unwarranted intrusion on his meditations, I soon excused myself and withdrew. Never shall

I forget his influence, for as no other man I have ever met he lived what he professed."

Those closely associated with him say that Mr. McLellan was a very hard-working man, rarely retiring before the small hours of the morning, dedicated profoundly to his responsibilities. He is described as a somewhat shy person, despite his abundant business experience. In his eyes was a friendly smile, sometimes wistfully appealing for informal and personal contact through the barrier of his dignity. He was a person quite ready and prepared to take responsibility. Thus it was that his role in guiding the young newspaper was singularly appropriate and successful.

Second only to Mr. McLellan in the pioneering work on the *Monitor* staff, of course, was Alexander Dodds. The men were nearly twenty years apart in age. Mr. Dodds was a vigorous and enterprising young man, heavy-set, high-spirited, thirty-four years old when he came to Boston. He was bluff and hearty, not above a practical joke, steeped in newspaper life, and yet conscientious and dedicated to his religion. He was a yachtsman, and a fire "buff." He had a fire-alarm signal in the newsroom, and insisted to the staff that a constructive angle could be found in every fire!

Mr. Dodds was of Scots-English extraction. He was born on Easter Sunday, 1874, in Allegheny, Pennsylvania. His family had at one time been comfortably wealthy, but the money had been lost in his father's generation. He had only one year in high school. He wanted to be a physician, but lacking resources to get education in the formal way he had gone to work in a drugstore. A year or two behind the prescription counter soon disillusioned him with what he described as "the under side of a physician's life," the dominance of people by drugs and stimulants, and — having met and admired newspapermen — he got a job as a reporter on the Pittsburgh *Times*.

Finding the work congenial, again in his own words (as recorded in his "Autobiography" which is in the collection of the Longyear Foundation, Brookline, Massachusetts), Mr. Dodds "decided to fit myself for newspaper management." Thus he left the *Times* and took a job in the mechanical department of the Pittsburgh *Press*. Over a period of nine years he worked his way through all the departments of the *Press* — mechanical, art, editorial — ending as assistant to the publisher. In the latter role, he was left in full charge of the *Press* when the publisher went off to the Spanish-American War. He was then twenty-four.

The Pittsburgh *Press* was then, Mr. Dodds wrote, "young and raw" and devoted entirely to the cause of union labor. It had been established only in 1884, as the *Evening Penny Press*, and was not purchased by the Scripps-Howard chain until 1923. So in 1898 Mr. Dodds transferred to an older and more dignified paper, the Pittsburgh *Dispatch*, and became its night managing editor, the youngest man to hold such a position in Pittsburgh, he proudly records.

Soon thereafter, Mr. Dodds's health broke down, he was hospitalized and doomed to death. But he did not die, and not being able to return to the *Dispatch*, he bought a half-interest in the Sharon, Pennsylvania, *Daily Telegraph*.

There, one day, a lady entered seeking to persuade the editor to give more favorable news treatment to Christian Science. Knowing nothing of Mr. Dodds's ill health, she asked him to read Mrs. Eddy's *Science and Health with Key to the Scriptures*, just to inform himself about the new religion. Mr. Dodds began to read out of curiosity, and continued to read even though he often found himself quarreling with what he read.

Before long, his friends began to comment on his astonishingly restored state of health. He found himself totally healed of valvular heart disease, chronic gastritis, and other illnesses. He also lost his addiction to social drinking, then decidedly a newspaper occupational hazard. All this happened, Mr. Dodds wrote, before he really began to understand much of what he read in *Science and Health*. It was two years, he explained, before the light of understanding penetrated his consciousness. By that time he had been able to give up eyeglasses, use of drugs, and smoking. He had returned to Pittsburgh, had become night editor of the *Gazette*, and was sent for a period to

New York as its correspondent. He went back to Pittsburgh in 1904 and became managing editor of the *Gazette-Times,* and later of the Pittsburgh *Sun* and *Times.*

In 1906, Mr. Dodds visited Boston to attend the dedication of The Mother Church Extension, the great new edifice of which Christian Scientists were so proud. There he met and was able to be of service to Alfred Farlow, the Committee on Publication, and he was casually introduced to Archibald McLellan. These contacts paved the way for the telegram which went to Mr. Dodds on August 10, 1908, saying: "If you can do so please come to Boston soon as possible at my expense to consult on matter of importance." The telegram was from Mr. McLellan and it began the professional association of the two men in the exciting experience of founding the *Monitor.*

Mr. Dodds's early newspaper training admirably fitted him for the job of setting up a newspaper. That he had decided while in his teens to fit himself for newspaper management, and that he had worked for nine years in the various departments of a struggling newspaper, could hardly have been more pertinent. His youthful vigor and drive, his exuberance, his wealth of practical experience in a rough-and-tumble newspaper town, combined with his deep religious idealism, gave him real insight into what was wrong and might be made right in American newspapering.

Immediately, Mr. Dodds was given wide authority, the Trustees formally voting him complete charge of the *Monitor.* All employees were subordinate to him with the sole exception of Mr. McLellan. He had a hand in the employment of mechanical as well as editorial personnel. Evidence of his professional skill runs through all the early arrangements and is plainly apparent in the resultant newspaper. His capacities of leadership manifested themselves at once in the planning stages and in the methods of staff training that were adopted.

In such telltale respects as make-up, headline writing, and copyreading the *Monitor* was from the outset thoroughly expert. It was "modern" in the 1908 version, and although it was produced on afternoon deadlines, which sometimes requires more hasty results than those of morning papers, it was made up with meticulous care. Astonishingly few typographical errors and failures in printing appear.

Many technical details reveal skilled and imaginative thinking. Page two, which in those days was often reserved by other papers for the bits and pieces of "jumps" from page one, was in the *Monitor* a page of major overseas articles. Photographs were used on most news pages and all feature pages, although it was some years before they attained the technical excellence in photoengraving and printing which has gained the *Monitor* a high reputation. The *Monitor,* like numerous other newspapers, sent its pictures to be photoengraved at a commercial shop. Its pictures in 1908 were quite as good as its contemporaries'. Indeed, its venerable and dignified neighbor, the Boston *Transcript,* did not begin to print photographs at all until after the 1908 period. Perhaps the *Monitor*'s example helped.

The *Monitor* began in 1908 and maintained for several years one unexpected policy: it put its sports page in its second-best news position, page three. For what might seem to be a sober-sided newspaper, deeply interested in world news and affairs of state and consequence, to feature sports news on page three reveals some careful reasoning. It tells a good deal of Mr. Dodds, and something of Mrs. Eddy.

Mr. Dodds realized that the *Monitor* needed to achieve reader-interest. It eschewed the sensationalism of current yellow journalism. It would not play up scandal and the merely bizarre. Where better to look for decent, wholesome human interest than in the field of sports? Furthermore, Mrs. Eddy had always been interested in and had praised deeds of physical heroism and unusual skill. She felt they showed mastery over the human body and material limitations. She wrote: "The feats of the gymnast prove that latent mental fears are subdued by him . . . Had Blondin believed it impossible to walk the rope over Niagara's abyss of waters, he could never have done it. His belief that he could do it gave his thought-forces, called muscles, their flexibility and power . . . His fear must have disappeared before his power of putting resolve into action could appear." * Within a year the *Monitor*'s sports page was voted "the best in New England" by the students of a New England university.†

In the combination of Messrs. McLellan and Dodds, the *Monitor* had an ideal partnership for its founding period. The dedicated, perceptive, supporting religious official and experienced businessman as editor, and the ingenious, dynamic practical newspaperman as managing editor were made to order. The results show it. And the results also indicate the quality that ran down through the staff.

In addition, the Board of Directors as a whole, the Board of Trustees, and the manager of the Publishing Society all played their vital roles. The Directors, with one of their own number as editor, took a deep and constant interest in the well-being of the new venture. The Trustees, who had worked so manfully in the crucial hundred days during which was carried out the vast enterprise of building the Publishing House extension and setting up the paper's complete organization, were continuously helping the growth and stability of the paper. The manager, charged with responsibility of ensuring the financial and business aspects of the undertaking, set it upon an orderly and progressive path.

Mr. Dodds soon found he needed a first-rate assistant. For this job he chose the fifth man hired for the editorial staff, Oscar Stevens of the Boston *Transcript*. Mr. Stevens was first news editor, and his job was to select and drill the reportorial and feature staff. But soon he was named assistant managing editor, and John Phillips of the Chicago *Examiner* was made news editor. Mr. Stevens played an important and useful role on the staff for the next fourteen years. He passed on in early 1958. Few, indeed, of the entire 1908 roster are still here in 1958. One alone, Paul S. Deland, remains actively on the staff. Mr. Deland has had an altogether remarkable part in the *Monitor*'s history. Starting as copy editor, he was city editor for a long period of time, financial editor briefly, American

* *Science and Health with Key to the Scriptures,* p. 199, lines 19–31; hereafter 199:19–31.

† *New England Magazine,* September, 1909.

news editor for a very extended and fruitful period, managing editor, and associate editor.

Doubtless the second most important full-time member of the 1908 staff was the man in charge of the editorial page, John J. Flinn. He was perhaps as seasoned as any member of the staff, having worked on the Chicago *Inter-Ocean* for many years. That eminent newspaper, which was swallowed up by consolidations in 1914, had been owned by a liberal Republican leader in Chicago, Herman H. Kohlsaat. It was the first American newspaper to use color printing on rotary presses. It was for long years a force in mid-continent journalism.

Mr. Flinn's job of running a full-sized editorial page in the *Monitor* was a challenging one. The consistent vigor of the page, the moderate but unquenchable liberalism and humanitarianism which it manifested, showed both balance and brightness.

In short, the 1908 staff was surprisingly talented and its work was unusually free from the experimental slips, the false starts, that might have been expected. The files of the newspaper they produced speak for themselves.

9

The Commitment to Freedom

How WAS the fledgling newspaper received?

"It will be a wonder," said the *New York Times,* speaking of Mrs. Eddy's paper, "if she makes it pay."

"Good luck to the coming Christian Science newspaper," wrote the Boston *Herald* hospitably. "Starting a daily paper is an enterprise that usually tests the courage and resources of the bravest and most resourceful souls. The graveyards are full of their remains."

Mr. McLellan replied, in the columns of the *Sentinel,* that the progress of the Christian Science movement had been marked from the beginning by a series of steps such as "usually test the courage and resources of the bravest and most resourceful souls," and added that under Mrs. Eddy's example and leadership "these steps have been taken successfully."

The newspaper world was distinctly interested. One of

James Gordon Bennett Junior's young men wrote a supercilious little piece about the *Monitor* and it was carried on the New York *Herald*'s front page next morning. Even this critic admitted, however, that the paper was "modern in typographical make-up," that "its plentiful advertising does not blacken the page," and that it was not sensational. Indeed, he remarked: "Readers afflicted with heart trouble may open up the newspaper with absolute safety." No Christian Scientist would contradict him.

Few newspaper contemporaries would have said the venture could possibly succeed. Many of them sent it their best wishes: indeed, an extraordinarily large number paid generous tribute to the *Monitor*'s aspirations. It has been that way ever since. The typical attitude of other newspapers has been one of friendly support and interest. Rarely, indeed, has any hostility or prejudice been displayed.

The *Monitor* manifestly appeals to the genuine idealism which inspires many newspapermen. More than a few of them understand and agree with its deepest purposes. They would like to follow its example more closely, but the commercial imperatives under which they work are held to debar them. Nevertheless, a great number of them have followed its example in one respect or another, and still a greater number quote from it frequently. Already in 1908 and 1909, this good will and emulation were expressed in many quarters. It was seen that the *Monitor* was not so odd as might have been expected, and its journalistic practices, while unusual, were carried out with professional flair.

An examination of the *Monitor*'s files is extraordinarily interesting largely by reason of its particular differences from other newspapers. Most of the ephemera being absent, the scandal and speculation and gore, what you have left has a very high percentage of historically informative material.

The *Monitor*'s task for the pioneering staff was at once more difficult and easier than on another paper. It was more difficult because new newspaper standards had to be devised: at least standards differing from the typical American newspaper.

Yet it was not so different in approach from serious European newspapers like *The Times* of London, *Le Temps,* and the great German, Italian, Russian, Dutch, Scandinavian, and other journals as they existed half a century ago. But the task was easier because the staff did not have to dissipate its energies in stealing photographs of a suicide victim or chasing ambulances.

People have forgotten how bad many newspapers were in 1908. Some readers today are very critical of newspapers, and with some reason. The more "monopolistic" newspapers have become, the more critical are their readers, because newspapers now are produced for a mass audience. A half century ago, the six or eight newspapers that typically existed in a medium-sized city catered to consistent groups in the citizenry. Each one's prejudices and distortions suited its particular readers. Today the community-wide mass-audience newspaper must serve such diverse groups that it is bound to seem not quite satisfactory to many of them. That is the main reason there is so much criticism of newspapers these days.

In fact, newspapers have on the whole steadily improved during the past five decades. The *Monitor* is not nearly so much of a contrast as it was in 1908. No American newspaper today does what a great many yellow journals did in 1908.

Here is Will Irwin's description of "the climax of the yellow craze, an episode in social history which we may yet come to regard with as much amazement . . . as the Mississippi bubble. Now did the World and Journal go insane with violent scareheads, worded to get the last drop of sensation from the 'story' and throw it to the fore; now did they make fact out of hint, history out of rumor; now did they create, for their believing readers, a picture of a world all flash and sensation; now did they change their bill day by day like a vaudeville house, striving always for some new and startling method of attracting a crowd . . . At its best the form stretched truth to the bursting point; for it consisted in warping facts to suit a distorted, melodramatic point of view. From this to outright falsehood was but a step, taken without perception by men no longer capable of seeing the truth. The fact became but a peg whereon to hang the lie." *

This was the kind of journalism at whose hands Mrs. Eddy had suffered, and toward which she sought to hold up a standard of responsibility and integrity. Reading the files of the yellow press of 1908 is today an exercise in the incredible and the loathsome. Reading the files of the *Monitor,* or of any responsible paper, is to walk down the corridors of history, with vision blurred only with contemporaneity. And what interesting things there are to see!

The *Monitor* came on the scene at an extraordinary vital and important moment in national and world history. Its columns reflected at once the challenge and vigor of the times. Politically, economically, technologically, socially the period was one of challenge and interest. A better time could not have been chosen for a newspaper with a mission. Already as 1908 turned into 1909 the lines of challenge were visible.

There was, first of all, the question of President-elect Taft and his Administration. Would he, as promised, carry on the reforms of the Theodore Roosevelt Administration? Specifically, would the Republican Party in Congress be able to revise downward the mountainous tariff barriers erected in 1897 under the name of Senator Nelson Dingley of Maine? At once Congress became the scene of conflict between the regular Republicans led by multimillionaire Senator Nelson Aldrich of Rhode Island and the more liberal Republicans and insurgents who had followed Theodore Roosevelt.

The *Monitor* made no secret of its convictions. They were not partisan, but they were perfectly definite. The paper evaluated the outgoing Roosevelt Administration and found much it could approve.

But it was not prepared to approve the short-cuts of legality which Theodore Roosevelt had found suitable. It said editorially: "Mr. Roosevelt is one of the ablest men who have ever held the presidency, and despite the fact that his critics allege he has taken some liberties with the fundamental law, he leaves

* From Edwin H. Ford and Edwin Emery, eds., *Highlights in the History of the American Press* (Minneapolis, 1954), p. 278.

the White House with all believing in his honesty and his good intentions for the welfare of the nation."

In a highly interpretive article from Washington, the paper concluded:

> Until Roosevelt came the public had grown cynical. A public man who was really to be trusted and who took the public into his confidence and was taken into the confidence of the public — this was something history had not given since Lincoln. It was something the people had almost despaired of ever seeing. The tribe of politicians had come to be a synonym for the self-seeking, the tricky, the double dealing and the untrustworthy. Roosevelt came before the public and gradually won their confidence. That confidence never has been impaired, and the result is that he goes out of office today after all the bitter attacks upon him and after one of the most disastrous business panics the country has suffered from — two causes sufficient in themselves to destroy any ordinary politician — as one of the best-loved Presidents the country has ever known.

Despite this the *Monitor,* reflecting much national opinion, turned to the Taft Administration with relief. As this same dispatch says, "Taft's way of doing things will be more conducive to the recovery of business. Of course, Taft will do the same things Roosevelt did but he will do them in a different way." That was a pretty general view in March, 1909.

Incoming President Taft was warmly hailed. His experience as jurist, as Governor-General of the Philippines, as Secretary of War, all seemed likely to lead to a very successful term of office. The *Monitor* felt the Republican Party was committed to revise the tariff downward. It was very disappointed when the Payne-Aldrich bill emerged as at best an equivocal revision. Yet it insisted on the importance of a Tariff Commission, as a means of handling tariffs by a better method than the traditional log-rolling in Congress. The *Monitor*'s objection to a high tariff was that it would send costs of living, already very lofty in comparison to wages and salaries, still higher. Its attitude in 1908–9 was very similar to its attitude toward the Smoot-Hawley Tariff Act in 1930. And when, three years later, the Reciprocal Trade Agreements Act came along, the *Monitor* was heartily in favor of tariff-making under terms set up by Congress but administered by the Executive Branch of the government. So, in 1958, the *Monitor* continues to support tariff adjustment in a manner as free as possible from the pulling and hauling of special interests lobbying in Congress, and based as completely as can be on the genuine national interest.

The attitude of the paper toward international trade has been consistent from start to finish. It is a genuinely liberal attitude. It does not ignore the need for special safeguards from time to time to protect some domestic industry, such as a newly established and important industry in 1908 or an industry like watch-making in 1958, which may require maintenance in the interest of national defense. But the paper has everlastingly emphasized the need for a healthy flow of foreign trade, imports as well as exports, if the prosperity and peace of nations are to be achieved.

The economic liberalism which the *Monitor* has always expressed stems no doubt in part from the common sense and intelligence which its complete independence from political or industrial or financial commitment made possible. It was beholden or linked to no political party, was under the wing of no financial or industrial combination. It was utterly independent of any vested interest except the one proclaimed in its title.

And the "vested interest" of Christian Science itself gave the *Monitor* a position of liberalism, in the genuine and original sense of the word, from *liber* — free, not servile or mean, not narrow or contracted. By the same token, it was truly conservative — "preserving, safe." Translated into terms of the political and economic controversies of the half century, the *Monitor* was inevitably on the side of more freedom.

This position had been affirmed by Mrs. Eddy when, in December, 1900, she responded to a question from the New York *World*. Under the heading INSUFFICIENT FREEDOM, Mrs. Eddy wrote, "To my sense, the most imminent dangers confronting the coming century are: the robbing of people of life and liberty under the warrant of the Scriptures; the claims of politics and of human power, industrial slavery, and insufficient freedom of honest competition; and ritual, creed, and trusts in place of the Golden Rule, 'Whatsoever ye would that men should do to you, do ye even so to them.' " *

In her Communion Address on June 4, 1899, Mrs. Eddy had said: "I reluctantly foresee great danger threatening our nation, — imperialism, monopoly, and a lax system of religion." † This message was delivered at the height of the controversy over American expansion in the Caribbean and the Philippines, and at a time when Germany, France, Britain and other nations were scrambling to seize and dominate such parts of the world as had not already been partitioned among the empires. It is very clear, therefore, that the application of Mrs. Eddy's teaching to the current and impending controversies of the twentieth century gave her newspaper a definite line to follow. "Insufficient Freedom" was a magnificent mandate, a challenge to all that was wrong in the social and political order. And it was made explicit: "industrial slavery" . . . "insufficient freedom of honest competition" . . . "trusts." It is no wonder that the editors of the newborn paper had no difficulty in taking clear positions in behalf of wise, careful, genuine reform which contributed to more freedom for the individual.

In other contexts, during the same period, Mrs. Eddy made her political independence positive. In November, 1908, responding to a query from the Boston *Post,* she said: "I am asked, 'What are your politics?' I have none, in reality, other than to help support a righteous government; to love God supremely, and my neighbor as myself." ††

To have no politics did not mean that Mrs. Eddy refrained from taking a position on political problems and issues. It is the same with the *Monitor.* The paper is not politically partisan, but it takes a position on all important political issues.

Mrs. Eddy often expressed her abhorrence for war, but also

* Mary Baker Eddy, *The First Church of Christ, Scientist, and Miscellany* (Boston, 1913), 266:1; hereafter cited as *Miscellany.*

† *Miscellany,* 129:3.

‡ *Miscellany,* 276:23.

accepted the necessity of national armament. She was asked in 1898 by the Boston *Herald*: "Should difficulties between the United States and Spain be settled peacefully by statesmanship and diplomacy, in a way honorable and satisfactory to both nations?" She replied, "I will say I can see no other way of settling difficulties between individuals and nations than by means of their wholesome tribunals, equitable laws, and sound, well-kept treaties." The careful qualifying words are important: "wholesome . . . equitable . . . sound, well-kept." She added: "But if our nation's rights or honor were seized, every citizen would be a soldier and woman would be armed with power girt for the hour. To coincide with God's government is the proper incentive to the action of all nations. If His purpose for peace is to be subserved by the battle's plan or by the intervention of the United States, so that the Cubans may learn to make war no more, this means and end will be accomplished."

A little later, during the Russo-Japanese War, she requested the members of her church to pray for an amicable settlement "that God bless that great nation and those islands of the sea with peace and prosperity." When, two months later, peace between Russia and Japan was announced, Mrs. Eddy was requested to comment by the Boston *Globe,* especially on President Roosevelt's role. She said:

War will end when nations are ripe for progress. The treaty of Portsmouth is not an executive power, although its purpose is good will towards men. The government of a nation is its peace maker or breaker. I believe strictly in the Monroe doctrine, in our Constitution, and in the laws of God. While I admire the faith and friendship of our chief executive in and for all nations, my hope must still rest in God, and the Scriptural injunction, — "Look unto me, and be ye saved, all the ends of the earth." The Douma recently adopted in Russia is no uncertain ray of dawn. Through the wholesome chastisements of Love, nations are helped onward towards justice, righteousness, and peace, which are the landmarks of prosperity. In order to apprehend more, we must practise what we already know of the Golden Rule, which is to all mankind a light emitting light.

This is not the place for an exegesis on these various interesting declarations and many others. They tell much of Mrs. Eddy's concept of the severe problems she foresaw coming in the twentieth century, and of her approach toward their settlement. Such ideas would naturally be of decisive effect in guiding the newspaper she established and which is published by the church she founded. They are the foundation of policy. And the policies specifically worked out during the two years when Mrs. Eddy was carefully examining the editorial page have been especially helpful in determining policy down through the years.

The *Monitor* therefore took its stand on the side of those who exposed and denounced evils, who demanded that the social order should be improved, but always within the framework of the Constitution, and above all reflecting the Golden Rule. This kind of liberal humanitarianism constitutes a charter which stands up very well down through the years, and remains profoundly conservative.

So it is in examining *Monitor* positions in 1908 and the years immediately thereafter that we find the paper comes much closer to the verdict of history than do many of its contemporaries. While it was generous and kind to President Roosevelt as he left office, it did not join his friends who began almost at once to attack the Taft Administration and to prepare for TR's return to office. It could see at the time the value of such constructive legislation as the Mann-Elkins Act of 1910, which brought the railroads under tighter governmental rein, the extension of Interstate Commerce Commission authority, the great development of Civil Service reform, the Postal Savings Bank Act, the establishment of parcel post, and finally the federal income tax. These are hailed by historians today. During the mid-century years there has been a re-evaluation of the Taft and Theodore Roosevelt Administrations by professional historians, considerably to the advantage of Taft.

The paper did not see just the sunny side. Faithful to Mrs. Eddy's injunction against "industrial slavery, and insufficient freedom of honest competition," the *Monitor* of April 6, 1909, tartly stated: "The Standard Oil Company is almost universally regarded as a combination of industrial bandits exercising a many-sided and far-reaching capacity for industrial and political harm." The paper's Washington correspondent described its chairman, John D. Archbold, on the witness stand, as writhing and twisting "on the inquisitorial spit wielded generally over the toasting fire of interrogations by Prosecutor Frank B. Kellogg."

The *Monitor*'s humanitarianism in 1908–9 took on more than once some of the touches of more conventionally crusading journalism. With slashing irony its New York correspondent described Miss Marjorie Gould's debut on January 7, 1909. He told of "5000 orchids," while as many destitute men and women huddled in breadlines, at warehouses, and in car barns, in the bitter cold. The paper did not hesitate to treat social problems with outspoken vigor. It was hitting out at the excesses and abuses of "industrial slavery," while supporting the free competitive system which — under the stimulus of constructive reform — could rectify them.

The *Monitor* was immediately interested in the two challenges to peace in the world of 1908. One arose from friction between the United States and Japan. The Flowery Kingdom, emerging as a great power in the years following its defeat of Russia, had ambitions conflicting with the United States's new position in the Eastern Pacific. Large numbers of Japanese laborers, their wives, and their numerous children, had been pouring into the broad and sunny valleys of California. The people of the Golden State, fearful of a second wave of oriental immigration, began in 1906 to pass restrictive and punitive legislation.

Theodore Roosevelt persuaded the Californians to repeal the most extreme restrictions. He negotiated the "Gentleman's Agreement" with Japan by which the flow of coolie labor was curbed. But in 1908–9 fears of Japan's intentions were rife, and the yellow press was shouting of the "yellow peril."

The *Monitor,* which had a good many readers in California, constantly urged them to remain calm in the face of Japanese immigration. On February 1, 1909, it had a strong dispatch from California denying Japan's capacity to fight a major naval war for fifteen years. On February 2 it emphasized in a lead editorial the Japanese foreign minister's commitment to peace. Thus, while detecting and describing Japan's aspirations for power and influence, the *Monitor* set these in a framework of realism. It strove constantly to counterbalance and correct the irresponsible warmongers in the United States. It decried on innumerable occasions, the mesmeric reiteration of the "inevitability" of war.

As to the Balkans, the *Monitor* was most expertly informed. While clearly aware of the dynastic, nationalistic, economic, and clerical rivalries of Eastern Europe, the *Monitor* nevertheless supported to the bitter end all efforts to adjust them peacefully. Like reasonable men of good will, the *Monitor* could see various adjustments which would have avoided war, and pointed them out. It never glossed over the war crises of 1909 or 1911. When fighting finally broke out between Bulgaria and Turkey in 1913, it gave full and expert coverage. The *Monitor,* needless to say, never glorified war or advocated it as an instrument of national policy, but it did not cry "peace, peace," when there was none. It committed itself soberly to analysis of the problem of war.

If the *Monitor* gave careful attention to the obvious news — war and politics — it was singularly attentive to the less manifest trends which often turn out to be of deep and lasting significance. Its first issues pay frequent attention to the problem of hard-surfaced roads. The portentous meaning of rapid popular transportation was scarcely evident in 1908, but the *Monitor* missed no opportunity to tell of the incipient good-roads movement. Every week, from the earliest issues and for a long period, it carried to New England readers weekly maps showing interesting automobile tours.

Part of the interest in automotive transportation stemmed from Mrs. Eddy herself. Though she preferred a fine pair of horses and handsome carriage for her daily drives, she was clearly aware of what the automobile could mean to the future. In one of the few pieces of documentary instructions which she sent to the Publishing House after the *Monitor* was established, she admonished the editors not to play up stories of automobile accidents. She said there were several reasons for this, among them the undesirability of making enemies of those who were developing the automobile business.

It was apparent that constant emphasis on automobile accidents might have engendered fear of the automobile and inhibited its progress. Fear publicity is rarely ever effective as a deterrent. The *Monitor* has always had its doubts concerning the many crusades, including those dealing with disease, which heavily utilize the element of fear. And so, already in 1909, Mrs. Eddy in midwinter — when there was not much motoring anyway — put her staff on the right track. She did not forbid them to print stories about automobile accidents. She knew there might be times when such incidents should be reported, as part of an accurate and preventive newspaper function. She simply urged them not to overdo it.

Although Mrs. Eddy did not wish to make enemies unnecessarily, she was never afraid of standing up and talking to evil whenever it was right and necessary to do so. She permitted the *Monitor* to speak out frankly on a wide range of social evils. She did not say: "Do not speak severely of Miss Marjorie Gould's debut; it might make an enemy of Mr. Jay Gould." She never exercised the slightest restraining hand on the *Monitor* when it did unpleasant things that had to be done for the sake of wiping out "industrial slavery" or any of the other social evils she had identified. She was simply against irritations that served no public purpose, or that would hamper the newspaper's deeper duties.

A little later in 1909, Mrs. Eddy intervened to prevent other needless pinpricks. On April 5, 1909, she wrote again to Mr. McLellan to warn against "the harm this booming Boston in our Monitor is doing the Christian Science Church, in New York and other places, but especially in New York. Tell Mr. Dodds that Mrs. Eddy strictly and lovingly enjoins him to avoid the aforesaid excess of civic laudation."

In 1909 there was a real chance the *Monitor* might have settled down into being merely a Boston daily paper. This would have been a tragic defeat. Mrs. Eddy made sure it did not happen.

There are very few bits of documentary instruction from Mrs. Eddy in the period after the *Monitor* was in operation. In one case, her humane distaste for slaughter of animals was combined with her zealous protection of the meaning of words, especially the words she had used in a vital context. In an undated note, which evidently was sent soon after Theodore Roosevelt had left the White House on March 4, 1909, and set forth for Africa, she said: "When you publish the notice of the President or the Peasant making a trip to find the Science of killing beasts you have vulgarized that term Science and deprived it of its true meaning. Never again leave such slip-shod writings in our Christian Science Monitor without their due explanation." Mrs. Eddy did not explicitly state disapproval of coverage of big-game hunting, although the *Monitor* has never looked with favor on blood sports and devotes little space indeed to such activities. But she said it should not elevate such things to a "Science" — without due explanation!

One more episode involving communication to and from Mrs. Eddy has much bearing on *Monitor* policy. There arose, in the *Monitor*'s early months, some feeling that perhaps it was "unscientific" to publish weather reports. Opinions and protests from Christian Scientists must have come in; after February 11, 1909, the weather reports were dropped. The question, seemingly minor, was really very important. It touched on a difficult point of religious application, and it affected a very significant part of the news. Therefore Mr. McLellan felt justified in taking it to Mrs. Eddy. If it had been possible to take similar problems to Mrs. Eddy in the years after 1910, a great many misconceptions about *Monitor* policy might have been avoided. In the middle years of the *Monitor*'s history, a number of needless restrictions grew up, only to be abolished when — in the late 1920's — there was a careful study made of the type of journalism Mrs. Eddy actually practiced and approved.

On March 30, 1910, Mr. McLellan wrote Mrs. Eddy to say:

A news feature which we dropped from the Monitor some time ago was the weather reports, and this has caused considerable complaint from business men, farmers, and others whose business (in belief) depends upon the weather. They have to make preparations in advance and they say that without these reports in the Monitor they are compelled to buy some other paper in order to get the weather news. There has been no other thing in connection with the Monitor that has provoked so much criticism as has the absence of these reports, and no other thing has retarded its circulation to the same extent. I am writing this letter asking whether we may not re-instate these reports, and shall be glad if I may have your advice.

Mrs. Eddy's secretary, Adam Dickey replied: "In reply to your letter of this date, in which you ask permission of Mrs. Eddy to publish the 'Weather Reports' in the Monitor, she wishes me to state that you may do so, provided they are published as *predictions*. I return a corrected proof endorsed by her." The proof, returned on the same day, bore Mrs. Eddy's handwritten signature and the changed heading from "The Weather" to "Weather Predictions."

The change was meaningful. Mrs. Eddy did not wish the *Monitor* to say that "The Weather" was positively and definitely what was published below. She wanted it to publish the "Weather Predictions" of the Weather Bureau. They were predictions only. They need not bind or impair man, responsive to God's law. Here once more, in addition to a position of religious principle, was another highly practical point. What the Weather Bureau announces is, after all, strictly a prediction, and how often does it turn out to be wrong! It was the height of journalistic accuracy to make this point, though with sufficient subtlety not to offend the hard-working meteorologists of the Weather Bureau. So, on April 1, 1910, the day after Mr. McLellan wrote Mrs. Eddy, reporting the weather predictions was resumed.

PART TWO

THE MONITOR GROWS

1908–1922

10

◆◆◆◆◆◆◆◆◆◆◆◆◆◆◆◆◆◆◆◆

Adventures of 1909

THE SUMMER of 1909 was a good time in which to learn by experience how to produce a strong newspaper. It was a good time to do this in Boston. For, just as soon as Congress had completed its revision of the tariff — mainly upward, to President Taft's profound disappointment — that genial gentleman joined his family at Beverly, Massachusetts. And the reporters for the young newspaper could keep track of the President's golf games at the Myopia Hunt Club, or follow the sailboat adventures of his young sons, or trail and interview the Cabinet members, Ambassadors, and business leaders who came to see him. To have a President right on your doorstep was excellent journalistic fortune.

But this was nothing in comparison to the story that was about to break. The *Monitor* has never claimed any prophetic powers. But on August 31, 1909, it published an editorial titled, "What News from Commander Peary?" It discussed the impending arrival back in Greenland of Commander Robert E. Peary's supply ship, the *Jeanie,* saying:

> Great interest is added to this matter by reason of the fact that we may hear of Commander Peary and of Dr. Frederick A. Cook, U.S.N., another polar explorer, at practically the same time or at even identically the same time. The latter has not been heard from for two years . . . It is within the domain of legitimate speculation at all events that we shall soon hear, and have good news from, both Dr. Cook and Commander Peary.

Then on September 1, Dr. Frederick A. Cook reported from the Shetland Islands (fraudulently, it turned out) that he had discovered the North Pole. On September 7, Commander (later Commodore) Peary announced from Indian Harbor, Labrador, that he had discovered the North Pole. It was the sensation of the year. Oddly enough, the wives of the two explorers were both at the coastal village of South Harpswell, Maine, though not together.

The *Monitor,* unlike some of its New York contemporaries, had not been able to subsidize either of these explorers, since they had set forth for the Pole before the paper was established. It probably would not have done so anyway. So it was in an admirably independent position to evaluate the claims of the two explorers. The evidence was very conflicting. It divided the scientific world. There were stout, authoritative supporters of Dr. Cook for many months to come. He was acclaimed by the King, scientists, and people of Denmark, to whose territories he first proceeded. This enthusiastic support from a nation highly knowledgeable about Arctic exploration gave a strong presumptive support to his claims.

The *Monitor* met this test of its judgment. At the very outset, having happily foreseen that the two explorers might turn up at the same time, the *Monitor* used very cautious language. In its news stories of September 2, 1909, it described simply what "purports to be the discovery of the North Pole by Dr. Frederick A. Cook." In the same issue it put its finger on the weak point in his claim — the extreme speed at which he said he had traversed the Arctic wastes. But the *Monitor* refused to condemn Dr. Cook until the facts were all in. It published objective reports of the praise that was showered upon him.

And its staff began to absorb what was one of its greatest operating rules: accuracy is of more importance to the *Monitor* than speed. The paper's staff can act quickly. It can get last-minute news into its columns as speedily as any paper, for its mechanical department is efficient, and its decision-making process is fast. But there must be reason for believing the news is accurate. At nearly all times, the paper has subscribed to two great worldwide news-gathering agencies. It can usually check one against the other, or against the reports of its own correspondents. If some news item is not capable of immediate checking, and has any element of doubt, it is either held up or properly qualifying language is introduced into its text.

So it was with the first stories about Dr. Cook. So it is with stories today. The *Monitor* is very proud of what it has published, but it is almost equally proud of what it has not published. The art of selection is perhaps the most important exercise of editorial judgment on any paper. Sensational newspapers scrambling competitively for circulation, sometimes rush into print with banner headlines over totally unconfirmed and sometimes false news.

The *Monitor* is always willing to wait or to qualify. This precept is manifestly one of the great sources of its reputation. It is one of the reasons why the files stand up in retrospect. At times, of course, the *Monitor* has been wrong. Sometimes it has accepted a general misconception when it might have known better. It makes no claim for infallibility. Some outstanding instances when its foot slipped will be presented in this account. It was prematurely optimistic — in the company of many other afternoon newspapers — on the day after the Titanic disaster. By next day it had caught up with the facts. Other cases will appear.

Of course, some cases of murky forecasting were from the lips of others quoted without commitment in *Monitor* columns.

Such a one, one of the great mis-estimates of the century, came on July 24, 1909, when the general manager of the American Motor Car Manufacturers Association firmly announced that the design of the motorcar had now been standardized. Future changes would lie only in the perfecting of details. If the good gentleman meant that cars would run on four wheels and gasoline, his prophecy could be defended. But quite a bit more than details has been changed!

In the *Monitor*'s early years there was much coverage of the burgeoning street railway transportation system. On September 23, 1909, the possibility of making a pleasure trip from Boston to Chicago by trolley was recorded. People thought interurban street railways had come to stay! But then, on July 26, the paper had an excellent report on Bleriot's flight across the English Channel and on July 1 the helicopter was foreshadowed. And on July 22 there was an appeal for American men to wear silk suits in the summertime, looking forward to the 1950's.

For several decades, the *Monitor* erred quite frequently on the side of excessive receptivity to new technical ideas, no matter how improbable. Perhaps this was a flaw. But in a period when the humanly improbable was becoming the technically demonstrable, month after month and year after year, perhaps receptivity was better than sterile cynicism. The *Monitor* would never have treated the Wright brothers the way the American press did when they first demonstrated heavier-than-aircraft flight at Kitty Hawk in 1903. The *Monitor* would have led the paper with the story.

Such interest, even starry-eyed, gave the *Monitor* many "firsts." Television, for instance, had its first rather visionary newspaper presentation in *Monitor* columns, on February 2, 1910, and its first careful presentation on May 1, 1924. But there were some other "firsts" which were hardly realistic. Such, on December 23, 1909, was the story that led the paper: an aircraft being fabricated by Boston men, a combination of monoplane, biplane, and helicopter which by 1911 would be able to cross the Atlantic in 48 to 50 hours! Printing such a story in serious prominence in 1909 certainly qualifies as being "prematurely right." More discrimination would have been wiser. Being so zealously on the side of progress, in the first decades of this century, meant publicizing practically anything. It hasn't been the same since atomic fission arrived. Nowadays the *Monitor* is much more skeptical. Robert C. Cowan, its natural science editor, a Master of Science from M.I.T., takes a long, hard look at the wonders of technology as they come along. But, fortunately, he is still capable of getting excited.

On August 16, 1909, came a front-page headline which might be read as a horrendous foretaste of a late-century disaster: " 'Reds' Are Rushing to Attack Boston By Land And Sea." Happily, it was only a war-game exercise.

When actual tragedy struck the year before, the *Monitor,* though but a few weeks old, was instant and outspoken in its coverage. On the morning of December 28, 1908, eight districts in southwestern Italy were laid waste by earthquake shocks. There was great damage and loss of life. The situation was fully covered. Charges that the *Monitor* publishes only "good" news, only cheerful or optimistic news, and refuses to recognize or print the dismaying or disastrous, is refuted by its coverage of half a century. The *Monitor* often seeks in its handling of disaster to emphasize the importance of relief work. In cases of disaster whose recurrence could be prevented, it tries to analyze causes and remedies.

Likewise the *Monitor* speedily in 1909 joined important local campaigns and crusades. During the latter part of the year there was a drive, of large magnitude, to build a new YMCA building in Boston, and others in the suburbs. The *Monitor* plunged enthusiastically into these civic enterprises, printing contribution coupons at the top of its front page for many successive days. It sought to be an effective local newspaper in plenty of other ways, having many columns of civic and community news every day. It gave particular attention to covering the affairs of other religious denominations, to give effective proof that its service was not confined to its own religious affiliation. No Boston newspaper today gives any more detailed coverage to community affairs than the *Monitor* did in 1909.

When business conditions continued to lag, toward the end of 1909 and early in 1910, the *Monitor* started a free employment bureau. It invited people to "send your want ad to The Christian Science Monitor Employment Bureau — It will be run free one week on the classified ad page. If you are looking for employment or for an employee, The Monitor offers you an opportunity to supply your need without the expense of advertising." For five years, the *Monitor* printed such advertisements in substantial volume, often averaging three solid pages of them. This was a large investment in good will. It was a major contribution to economic improvement in the community.

All through the final months of 1909 Boston was in the throes of a crucial mayoralty race. Then, as now, "reform" elements were trying to improve civic conditions. Boston in 1909 had not slipped as deep into machine politics and corruption as it did in the years following, but the signs were there to see. The eminent business leader, James J. Storrow, had been persuaded to run for mayor.

The outgoing mayor, George A. Hibbard, was running for re-election. The strongest opposition candidate was John F. Fitzgerald, the redoubtable "Honey Fitz," running among other things on the appeal of his mellifluous tenor rendition of "Sweet Adeline." Mr. Fitzgerald won re-election, having served as mayor from 1906 to 1907. In a way the mayoralty campaign of 1909–10 marked an historic ebbing of the tide. The old forces which had been dominant in Boston for so long, Anglo-Saxon, Protestant, wealthy, were waging one of their last contests for the occupancy of City Hall.

That is not to say that these elements do not even today have a considerable influence in civic affairs, especially when the City has to borrow money. And some "reform" administrations, usually disappointing, have been elected since 1910. But the race between the austere James J. Storrow and "Honey Fitz," with Mayor Hibbard splitting the old-guard vote, was one of the last fights that might have been won.

Meanwhile, the *Monitor* was intensely active in support of the "Boston 1915" plan, a concept for long-range civic improvement which did not achieve all its objectives but has had many echoes since, some of them fruitful. In short, the young newspaper sought at once to make itself an effective influence in the community.

The quality of its work was admitted and recognized and its staff began making an impression around town. But then as now, its role in Boston was more manifest in its integrity than in its circulation. The local circulation has considerably improved since 1909, but it has not yet become as strong as might have been expected. In 1909, one of the troubles was that the *Monitor* entered an even more crowded newspaper field than it encounters in the 1950's.

The Boston *Transcript* was still a powerful and responsible influence, a conservative, culturally rich, politically well connected, ably edited publication. It did well many things the *Monitor* was also committed to doing. The *Transcript* was very cautious in its journalistic techniques. It published no photographs in its pages until after 1908. In 1941, when the *Transcript* finally ceased to publish, the *Monitor* picked up a substantial part of its remaining circulation. The Boston *Post* was in 1908 approaching the largest morning newspaper circulation in the country, sensational and hard-hitting. Under General Charles H. Taylor, the Boston *Globe* was a strongly established, well-conducted newspaper with a deserved national reputation and a powerful hold on the New England hinterland. The Boston *Herald* was an eminent Republican Party organ, conservatively backed, just about to come under the editorship of Robert Lincoln O'Brien.

The Boston *Journal* had been a successful conservative publication, largely specializing in business affairs. By 1908 it was declining, and in 1917 it was sold to the *Herald*. The Boston *Traveler* was a lively and sensational afternoon daily, and in 1913 it became the afternoon publication of the *Herald*. The morning *Advertiser* and afternoon *Record* were jointly published. The *Advertiser,* once known as "the respectable daily," had also fallen on hard times. William Randolph Hearst had been publishing the Boston *American* since 1904. In 1917 he took over the *Sunday Advertiser* and in 1921 acquired the afternoon *Record.* So it will be seen that in 1908 the Boston pastures were crowded with hungry newspapers. In relative terms, despite the disappearance of many, they still are.

11

The *Monitor* and Its Community – An Anniversary

THUS, THE MONITOR took its place in one of the most crowded newspaper cities in the nation. To make great local headway in such a field, with the paper's special handicaps and somewhat limited appeal — human nature being what it is — would have been a commercial miracle. It could and speedily did achieve a *succès d'estime*. This gave it a local foothold, which it increased down the years.

A perceptive view of the *Monitor*'s relationship to its community is given in the recollections of Winthrop Pitt Tryon, who saw a streetcar card advertising the coming newspaper in early November, 1908, and applied at once to Mr. Dodds. He was then assistant to Philip Hale, respected music critic of the Boston *Herald*.

When Mr. Tryon told Mr. Hale that he had got a job with the new paper, he said: "Go ahead, boy, for as long as your paper lasts. I have seen these little things start up and go down before." Mr. Tryon had great opportunity before him, little known to Mr. Hale. He became the *Monitor*'s music critic in New York for many years, covering the growth of that city into one of the world's greatest musical centers.

Of 1908 Mr. Tryon writes: "Yes, that first year under Mr. McLellan and Mr. Dodds was a tough one. There were adverse views now and then inside, and there was opposition outside. But the excitement of getting out the paper and the enthusiasm of everybody on the staff for the Cause made the Publishing House sparkle. We were living in the last gasp of old literary Boston. The resistance to Christian Science which was so determined back in the 1880's survived, too, in some strength. Our 'enemies' had firm fibre. Nevertheless, they fought fairly. It was a lively moment."

Mr. Tryon adds: "Old Bostonians had their habits, and reading a daily newspaper with any such title as the Monitor bore was hardly one of them. But I happened to be in the current of Boston tradition myself, having passed the grind of one of its most exacting institutions, the Public Latin School; and of the things I learned there, one was that any great and liberal idea, regardless of the number of its immediate supporters, had a fair chance in the town and would ultimately be received." So, indeed, it proved to be.

Mr. Tryon, though retired, still prepares a weekly discussion of word derivations for the *Monitor,* "Words of Current Interest." At the age of seventy-seven he took up the study of Advanced Hebrew at Harvard University. At one point he was the only pupil in one of Professor Harry A. Wolfson's more abstruse courses.

Since the *Monitor* was seeking to be a national and an international newspaper, in many respects the first of its kind, it sought in every way to reach beyond the borders of Boston. Naturally it required national and international news sources. Prior to the first issue, the services of the newly established United Press Associations had been obtained. In 1909 the *Monitor* became a member of the Associated Press as well.

Many older and more famous papers did not have both great American news-gathering agencies at that time. The *Monitor* was the only one in New England. In addition, the *Monitor* engaged an experienced Washington correspondent, W. W. Jermane, to open its first news bureau there, and it began receiving an extensive file from New York.

In London, where announcement of the forthcoming newspaper had met with enthusiastic welcome among Christian Scientists, Frederick Dixon began at once to submit material and to have his staff — he was Committee on Publication for Great Britain — prepare additional material from the British daily and periodical press and other available sources. For some time this clipped material, which was used if at all with due credit, was rolled up and mailed in the form of what came to be called "the Boston sausage." From other capitals throughout the world excellent articles were obtained. But the development of the *Monitor*'s own corps of expert correspondents came later.

With a reasonably good product on their hands, the staff of the new paper needed readers. The first day's circulation was 82,500, an extremely good figure; but of course much of it was curiosity circulation, and on the second day the total dropped to 38,800. While this was a modest figure, it was a perfectly respectable start. At the same time, the circulation of *The Times* of London was under 40,000. The *Monitor*'s circulation must have been derived largely from Christian Scientists, plus a group of others in Boston and elsewhere who were interested in the journalistic experiment and who responded to the *Monitor*'s ideals and service.

Steady promotional efforts were undertaken on a wide scale. The *Monitor* has always had the advantage of efforts on its behalf by individual Christian Scientists and the circulation committees of branches of The Mother Church. Without this work, the paper never could have survived or been successful.

However, subscription to the newspaper has never been forced on Christian Scientists. Mrs. Eddy expressed a wish that they subscribe, saying in a letter of November 16, 1908: "My desire is that every Christian Scientist, and as many others as possible, subscribe for and read our daily newspaper." * Yet, as with other aspects of the Christian Science Church organization, the ultimate decision is left to the individual and no further pressure is applied. Thus the circulation of the *Monitor* has always been much less than the church membership. Within these terms Christian Scientists have always supported the paper loyally and eagerly. Without this sturdy backlog of support, the experiment of a national and international newspaper dedicated to the *Monitor's* ideals would have been dubious indeed.

The same support has made the *Monitor's* advertising revenue possible. The *Monitor* has always been a good advertising medium to those who have used it, or they would not have continued using it so faithfully down through the years. One of the earliest and largest advertisers, the Boston department store Jordan Marsh Company, was noticed most appreciatively by Mrs. Eddy. Observing that the firm had purchased a full-page advertisement, she asked her secretary to find out what the company had paid for it, and to convey to them her personal appreciation. The firm remains a half century later among the *Monitor's* steadiest advertisers. Such patronage, which extends to many parts of the world — and will be described more fully in Chapter 35 — was possible because *Monitor* subscribers in substantial volume patronize *Monitor* advertisers, a response which makes *Monitor* advertising valuable far beyond its circulation figure.

All these elements came into play during the paper's earliest months. A good start had been made: a worthy editorial and news product, a well-printed and organized paper, excellent advertising, an encouraging circulation, a vigorous promotion effort. But to survive and grow, the paper must multiply its achievements. A major opportunity came along with the end of the first year of publication. It was decided to publish an impressive anniversary issue. So on November 24, 1909, the staff produced a 96-page paper with a circulation of 250,000. This was almost as mammoth an undertaking as was the

* Mary Baker Eddy, *Miscellany,* 352:29.

production of the first edition after only three months of preparation from scratch. Few editions of American newspapers of that size had ever been printed. It was the largest newspaper many of its readers had ever seen. And it made a tremendous impression on the newspaper world. With the anniversary edition, the *Monitor* passed fully and totally into the professional class: its colleagues recognized its proficiency, and calculated that it had come to stay.

For instance, the Helena, Montana, *Daily Record* said: "No publication has been started in the United States in the last ten years which has so quickly attained a standing in the newspaper world as The Christian Science Monitor. In the first place it is a newspaper. The only indication that it is controlled by a religious sect is in the name . . . It is one of the few eastern newspapers which realizes the importance of the other parts of the country, and prints articles telling of the progress these other regions are making along every line. In the opinion of many, the Monitor approaches nearer to being a national newspaper than any other daily publication."

The Los Angeles *Herald* said: "It is a newspaper in every sense of the word, and in every sense of the word a competitor of other newspapers. It is thoroughly commercialized, and evidently has a shrewd business office and an able and intelligent advertising staff. Its special number is as good a special edition as any published by any of the 'great dailies.' "

The Peoria, Illinois, *Journal* said: "Started less than a year ago, The Christian Science Monitor has already achieved a phenomenal success. It has taken rank among the great papers of the country . . . It is a newspaper in every sense of the word, but it is a newspaper that is devoted to the uplift . . . The Christian Science Monitor may have been started more or less as an experiment but it is no longer such. It is a success and a big one."

These words brought cheer to those who were learning their new jobs in Boston. But they were more aware than their complimenting colleagues of the problems they had to solve every day, and of the big jobs that lay ahead before the *Monitor* could feel a sense of permanent achievement. It was remarkable that so good a job had been done so fast. But a great deal remained to be accomplished. Their purposes and their commitment were made very clear in an unsigned article which led the front page of the anniversary edition.

This article, like other articles, speeches, promotional advertisements, and leaflets takes its place in the quite extraordinary literature of analysis of purpose which has concerned the Monitor. In this whole literature of analysis, no statements are more valid and impressive than those made responsibly by the original staff while Mrs. Eddy was still keeping an active eye on its development and content. The first anniversary article thus takes on special importance and value.

The article is excusably proud: a 96-page edition with a circulation of a quarter of a million, six tons of copies shipped into England, proving that "a success can be made of a journal conducted along the lines laid down by the management of the Monitor."

"Why has this success been possible?" asks the article. Because of the mandate: "To injure no man, but to bless all mankind." Thus, says the article, "During the twelve months of its existence the Monitor has never, in newspaper parlance, 'gone after' anybody: it has done its best to aid a number of praiseworthy undertakings, and it hopes to be able to assist a great many more, in its own individual way, in coming years. It has gone out along an unbeaten track and has blazed its own trail. It hopes that it is only a pioneer along that trail, which it would be glad to see others following increasingly."

The article recognizes frankly that the problem of truly representing and reflecting the endeavors of mankind will not be solved in a day. The staff has learned as it went along. And it has found that "there is a large community of broad-minded men and women in the world who prefer to hear of a remarkable feat of railroad construction or a $1,000,000 gift to a university rather than of incitements to local strife or the dismal grist of the police courts."

It has taken time, the article affirms, "to acquaint the general public with the fact that The Christian Science Monitor is not a sectarian publication, but is conducted as a general newspaper."

In a declaration which was widely followed by representative spokesmen for American newspapers beginning in the 1930's, the article says: "The Monitor not only seeks to keep its readers informed of events all over the world, but to interpret those events in a way to show their relation to the great movements that are of service to the human race."

"Interpretive news" has been very much under discussion by American newspapermen for some years. Able speeches affirming the need to give readers more than the bare bones of the daily event have been made and are still being made by thoughtful editors. This was the *Monitor's* commitment from the beginning.

In one paragraph the first anniversary article gave a definition of its position toward crime and disaster which was the rule while Mrs. Eddy was still alive, but came to be somewhat misunderstood and misapplied in practice until it was rediscovered, re-emphasized, and repracticed from the late 1920's onward. Here is the paragraph:

> It is not to be understood that the Monitor has stooped to a censorship so narrow or opinionated as to render its new service inadequate, inefficient, or incomplete. Far from it. Whatever is of public importance or affects the public welfare, even though it be news of what is ordinarily reckoned as crime or disaster, is printed in the Monitor in completeness sufficient for information, but without unnecessary embellishment or sensational display. The emphasis, however, is reserved for the helpful, the constructive, the encouraging, not for their opposites.

Such unequivocal words gave the *Monitor* great freedom. "Whatever is of public importance . . . completeness sufficient for information . . ." — those phrases, it was discovered as time went on, offered a practical rule of operation. But their applicability was not adequately felt until the *Monitor* had gone through much more pioneering.

The anniversary article probably was written by Alexander

Dodds. It bears the touch of newspaper professionalism. Of course, it had the full support of Archibald McLellan, and he may have had much more than a nominal hand in its preparation. Probably it was a joint effort, following careful discussion. Proofs must have been cleared with Mrs. Eddy, as were all editorials and religious articles. Her own pride and gratitude at the 96-page anniversary edition, capped by the tributes from the newspaper profession and the public, must have been warm. She had carried through one more successful undertaking, against the advice of many friends, in the face of countless practical difficulties. She did, indeed, express her satisfaction freely.

Mere physical production of the anniversary edition was a triumph. The *Monitor*'s plant, only a year old, had already grown inadequate and soon had to be enlarged. The presswork was begun a week in advance; the paper was run in 12-page sections, two sections being completed at a time. The whole was assembled and stored in a big marquee tent pitched on land adjoining the Publishing House. There the completed sections awaited the printing of the November 24 news section and the dispatch of the assembled papers to the four ends of the earth.

A pleasant vignette of this newspaper adventure comes from Miss Mabel E. Burnside, who came as a worker in the subscriptions department in 1908 and retired in 1942. The 96-page paper, she recalls, was too large to wrap by mailing machines, and there was only one machine available with which to address the wrappers.

> This one and only machine [she writes] was operated in shifts, from 5 A.M. until midnight, in the endeavor to get the wrappers addressed in the shortest time possible, to meet the need for leaving the stencils free for daily use in the Mailing Room and to give opportunity for the necessary clerical work to be done on them.
>
> I had become one of the regular addressing workers as well as helping daily at the mailing machine when the paper came off the press. My choice of time on the anniversary wrappers was from 5 A.M. to 11 A.M. On one of the five o'clock mornings the drive belt of the machine broke. No regular mechanic would be available for

three hours. However, a call to the boiler room brought the night engineer to the rescue. Fortunately he was able to provide another belt.

As the great day approached, tables were assembled on the third floor, wrappers properly separated into towns, cities and states, with mail sack tags attached, mail sacks conveniently placed. The several sections of the paper were arranged so as to be readily combined, one each into a complete paper. A considerable part of the wrapping was done on this third floor by a group of volunteer workers from nearby churches, joyously interested in this first anniversary of "our Monitor."

During the work there was need for food, and the purchasing department, in the recollection of Luther P. Cudworth, then in charge, sent out for several hundred homemade sandwiches. Evidently they were of the afternoon tea variety. Anyway, Alexander Dodds coined a neat typographical phrase when he called them "single-leaded sandwiches."

Food does keep cropping up in the memories of those who were young and hungry in the salad days. Jean Edgar Taylor, who was a messenger in 1911, remembers that Samuel McCutcheon, the circulation manager, "brought in apples and pears, different fruit in season and gave it to everyone. He spread an air of inspiration that gave each one a greater desire to work harder than ever."

Mrs. Taylor also recalls that Mr. Dodds "was kind and helpful. He always had candy or fruit to give away. He helped each one to get a clearer insight of what the cause of Christian Science stood for, and was accomplishing in the world. Mr. McLellan was very informative and kind. He always inspired us to higher efforts, and he told us to go to school and equip ourselves to reach the high spots in business, for those who know the Truth are needed there."

Such memories indicate a great deal about the morale which helped bring the *Monitor* into being, and which made it an enthusiastic collective enterprise down through the years. The same intimate relationship between executives and staff has prevailed most of the time; it is certainly the case today. Any member of the staff feels entitled, and is encouraged, to talk over his problems with any executive, and many pleasant and useful hours are invested in this type of staff development.

Among the most recent activities along these lines are the *Monitor* editorial department's so-called "sandwich sessions" and "four o'clocks." At the sandwich sessions, held at noontime weekly, members of the editorial department, in rotation, meet in a pleasant room for discussion over sandwiches of "how to make a better *Monitor*." The department is divided into five groups, and every member of the staff, beginning with the greenest and eagerest copy boys or girls, has a chance once in five weeks to get off his chest in the presence of the editor — who also comments — anything he wishes to say about the improvement of the paper. Many very useful ideas and acute criticisms have resulted, along with a deep and genuine sense of participation. For the four o'clocks, which take place after the official work day has ended, a senior member of the staff is on hand, again over simple refreshments, to lead a discussion. The opportunity, particularly for younger staff members, to delve more deeply into professional problems, is as valuable for staff training and morale as it is for the generation of good ideas. Sometimes the talk is more general, ranging over the day's news. This, too, is helpful and spontaneous. And often it turns to the paper's job of leavening human thinking.

Thus, from 1908 to 1958, similar attitudes have knitted the staff together. They have had a large bearing on the quality of the newspaper itself.

12

Problems and Taboos

THE CHRISTIAN SCIENCE MONITOR during the two years of Mary Baker Eddy's direct observation was a free and forthright undertaking, as its declaration of policies on its first anniversary makes very clear. "Whatever is of public importance or affects the public welfare, even though it be news of what is ordinarily reckoned as crime or disaster . . ." is scope broad enough for any newspaper.

It was the kind of journalism Mrs. Eddy herself had practiced when she was editor of the *Journal.* It was the kind she supervised in the *Sentinel.* There was nothing squeamish or timid about those publications. From time to time they discussed the public events of the day, without affectation or distortion. Their attitude to other religions was broad, generous, and interested. They had few discernible stylistic inhibitions. They were candid, outspoken, and spiced with wit. And so was the *Monitor,* especially during its first two years.

It is quite evident that this strength, albeit combined with a good deal of experimentation, pioneering, and learning by trial, was possible in large measure because of the continual and tacit support of Mrs. Eddy's presence. If any controversial difficulty arose, it could be referred to her. Usually when this was done, a broadly liberal and supporting answer was forthcoming, without dogmatic taboos, but sometimes with wise cautionary directions.

On December 3, 1910, Mrs. Eddy passed on. Thereafter, such policy questions had to be settled without her help. Moreover, the sense of confidence which her presence had provided in the conduct of the *Monitor* was replaced by one of caution. This was entirely natural, perhaps inevitable. Christian Scientists believe profoundly in man's immortal and undying being, as the individualized image and likeness of God. They knew that Mrs. Eddy, in words of her own used by the First Reader, Judge Clifford P. Smith in The Mother Church on December 4, 1910, was "still with you on the field of battle, taking forward marches, broader and higher views, and with the hope that you will follow." * They knew that in her writings she had given them an imperishable leadership. And they knew that her newspaper was an integral part of her total church conception.

But, up to that hour, Mrs. Eddy had always been at hand. Christian Science had been discovered, had grown, had passed through severe trials, had established itself under the direct guidance of Mrs. Eddy. What would happen now to Christian Science must have been a question that arose challengingly in the thinking of many Christian Scientists, though their faith gave them reasons for believing that their cause would go forward just as before.

As it went forward, however, the question of policy decisions constantly arose. These were matters of almost hourly challenge in the production of a daily newspaper. What was in accord with basic *Monitor* standards? What wasn't? The natural tendency was to decide such questions on the side of caution and conservatism. When a serious doubt arose, the watchword

* Mary Baker Eddy, *Miscellaneous Writings,* 136:5–7.

tended to be "better not do it." In the atmosphere of 1911 or 1912, such reasoning would be the most natural thing in the world.

Of course this kind of caution did not come along all at once. Slowly and gradually the boldness which marked Mrs. Eddy's own journalism was replaced by a varying and indeterminate set of taboos which had a considerable effect on *Monitor* style and did not begin to melt away until the mid-1920's. The nature and extent of these taboos should not be exaggerated. They were very largely stylistic, and style is not a very important matter. They were counterbalanced by many steady elements of important professional growth. But they produced in the community and the world at large an impression, not altogether unjustified as far as style went, that the *Monitor* was "odd."

There were, in addition, simple but elusive problems in daily operation which built up taboos unnecessarily. The transitional situation is well described by a copy boy of that day, Volney D. Hurd, who has been since 1945 the *Monitor*'s able Paris correspondent. He began working for the paper as a youngster, in 1913. In the intimate atmosphere of the early days, writes Mr. Hurd, men like Mr. McLellan and Mr. Dodds had time to stop and talk with a starry-eyed young neophyte. Many of them still have the time, and it is time very well spent.

Anyway, as Mr. Hurd saw it, there were two causes for unnecessary inhibitions. One was what he describes as misapplied "sweetness and light." The other was the search by professional members of the staff, especially non-Christian Scientists, for definite rules which could be applied to all cases. Since most such rules cannot safely and wisely be generalized, the effort to broaden them led to unnecessary taboos.

The sweetness-and-light concept is illustrated by a ban Mr. Hurd found when he became radio editor in 1924 against referring to "jazz bands," which were somehow thought to be indecent, or to "ballroom dancing," for — he was told — "you know what that can lead to!" Mr. Hurd and many others, set about re-examining and challenging these concepts, and they were steadily cleared away in the 1920's.

Many non-Scientists on the staff, Mr. Hurd observed, sought written policies on everything. They did not understand that circumstances govern cases. When they got a ruling from some superior authority they would write it down and say: "At least we've got that one settled." Thus many reference points accumulated into an aggregation of editorial don'ts which, followed year by year, came to be accepted as traditional *Monitor* policy when they were nothing but overgeneralization of single cases. They had to be cleared away, and they were. Readers, far from protesting, welcomed the new freedom.

Mr. Hurd gives one very important aspect of the picture. Another aspect is that of Christian Scientists, in an excess of zeal, deciding "Mrs. Eddy would have wanted it this way," or "Mrs. Eddy would have wanted it that way," without ever taking the trouble to look up how Mrs. Eddy actually did it. When this reversion to first sources was undertaken, the kind of emancipation which began as Mr. Hurd describes it, was carried to an effective if gradual conclusion.

The practice by which Christian Scientists avoid flat, dogmatic rules and seek to work out each case on its own merits is not an easy one for operative journalism. It requires maturity, wisdom, and confidence. These elements came to the *Monitor*, in some cases returned to it, as the years went by.

Meantime, the taboos led, as Mr. Hurd writes, to considerable ridicule. Some of it was deserved. Some was apocryphal. The famous and widely published tale of the "passed-on mules" is myth. It has been alleged (the story still reposes in newspaper and magazine morgues, so when anybody wants to write a piece about the *Monitor* it tends to turn up) that during the First World War the *Monitor* described a battlefield as being littered with "passed-on mules." It is a piquant story. Happily, we know where it came from. As Mr. Hurd explained:

> In World War I we had to use anyone we could in Europe, often foreigners who knew so little English that they worked mostly from dictionaries. Much of Europe was blockaded, communication was mostly by mail in those days, particularly with a war on, and so we would get the most oddly assorted kinds of articles. They would

often be hand-written and not too legible, or badly typewritten on all kinds of paper.

It was one of these, apparently sent in by someone in a particularly difficult area behind the German lines, who was a Scientist. He wrote of the battlefield being littered with "passed-on horses." When the phrase came up the whole office was delighted and it was passed around from one person to another. Naturally, it was never considered for publication.

There are few *Monitor* taboos today. There is no word, except a profane or obscene one, that cannot be used in its proper context. In speaking of people, the *Monitor* prefers "passed on" to "died" because it more accurately describes what Christian Scientists believe happened.

The matter was accurately summarized by the Reverend Nathanael M. Guptill, in an article in the *Christian Century* for September 7, 1955. He wrote, on the subject of "death": "A Monitor writer will tell you: 'We use the word "death" but we use it when we want to say what the word means. Webster says that death means "extinction of life" and when this happens to a bill in Congress or a political movement we say so. We don't believe this happens to people; so we report the termination of the earthly residence of people in the news by saying that they have "passed on," which any Christian should admit is a more accurate description of what has happened.' " When the expression would be strained or awkward, we are free to use "dead" or "death." Mrs. Eddy did. The word is regularly used in her writings and in the Christian Science periodicals prior to 1910, whenever it was the accurate word.

There is another *Monitor* taboo or preference which might have brought us a lot of ridicule. For some reason it never has. As explained earlier, Christian Scientists do not use habit-forming stimulants, such as liquor and tobacco. So *The Christian Science Monitor* does not publicize or promote, even silently, these elements of servitude, however petty.

It does not publish photographs which show drinking scenes, and does not print pictures of pipes, cigars, cigarettes if this can be avoided. To print such pictures, though in an innocent and newsworthy context, seems to the paper to support and promote practices from which it would like to see men freed.

Christian Scientists do not interfere with the decisions of others in choosing whether or not to smoke or drink. There have been no Carrie Nations among them. Not to print pictures of drinking or smoking does not distort the news. So, in considering picture copy, *Monitor* editors select the picture without these elements. Moreover — and here, perhaps, the paper is open to some criticism — sometimes it has had one of its artists retouch a cigarette or a whiskey glass neatly out of the hands of some photographed person. It is a wonder the paper hasn't been caught at this and satirized. *The New Yorker* might have done it long ago.

It should be added, however, that all well-edited newspapers and magazines have their photographs retouched to some degree, just as portrait photographs are retouched. Insofar as the *Monitor* has retouched, it has cleaned up the picture, not sensationalized it. Often the job can be done by cropping. Furthermore, if it is a picture of historic importance, the paper will not retouch it for purposes of its own taboos. The *Monitor* has printed the famous Churchill cigar, notably at a conference with President Roosevelt in the White House in 1942.

There are three particular areas in which the *Monitor*'s news service may accurately be said to be incomplete. They should be frankly explained. First, is the matter of obituaries. The *Monitor* prints accounts of the deaths of persons in accordance with their news value. That is to say, it prints obituaries of prominent people. It does not print a large number of strictly local obituaries, as a Boston newspaper, nor does it print the paid death notices which appear in other newspapers. It tries to let readers know accurately of the passing of people in the news.

It prints rather more obituaries than would be published in, say, a nationally circulated news magazine. To this it adds the most newsworthy of the deaths in the New England area. The reason it does not publish extensive obituaries does indeed relate to its religious background. It simply does not want to make that much of death, though it will amply record the achievements of the person concerned. Christian Scientists wish to turn the attention of people to the thought of immortality, toward man's eternal, spiritual birthright of life. They are aware that news coverage of death is not skimped in other newspapers; to the *Monitor* is left the mission of emphasizing life, and life everlasting.

A second area which the *Monitor* scarcely touches at all is that of "society." To cover society news on a national scale would be technically very difficult, if not impossible. To do so locally means devoting a lot of space to material essentially trivial. The *Monitor* does cover organizational news, which is next door to social news, when it is sufficiently interesting. Women's clubs, benefits, lectures, garden tours, exhibits, and such are covered in the Boston area strictly on their news merit. Weddings and coming-out parties and similar social items are simply not covered. Again, it may be said that such events are fully covered in some other papers. And they are not of the essence of what well-informed readers need to know. Important marriages and parties of real news importance of course are covered.

The third area is that of medical news. As has been repeatedly emphasized, the *Monitor* wears its colors on its sleeve. It is *The* Christian Science *Monitor*. The church which owns the paper is committed to spiritual healing. It is a significant fact that the largest single professional group subscribing to the *Monitor*, as far as the paper's admittedly limited statistics on this point shed light, is the physicians. It is to be supposed that their thoughtful and dedicated approach to humanity and its well-being leads them to the *Monitor*. It is perhaps also true that their growing awareness of mental causation in disease, as evidenced in their study of psychosomatic medicine, also has led them to the *Monitor*.

But being committed to spiritual healing, and frankly proclaiming this fact, the *Monitor* is very conservative in its treatment of medical news. It prints only the most important and officially sponsored news of medical developments. It prints medical news that affects the general community, such as legislative actions or sanitary or hygienic decisions. It has printed a great deal, most of it very satisfactory to organized medicine, on the subject of socialized medicine, which the *Monitor* firmly opposes, although it has applauded voluntary alternatives such as insurance plans.

The type of medical news the *Monitor* does not print is, in effect, promotional medical news. Some such news is self-evidently excessive. But there remains an amount of news, perhaps not such a great quantity, which would be admitted under all the *Monitor*'s other news criteria were it not for the paper's commitment to spiritual healing. Of course it covers important news of illnesses, such as those of President Eisenhower, Sir Winston Churchill, and many others.

This restraint may have kept some news from some *Monitor* readers which as well-informed citizens they should have known. It has certainly kept from them a good deal of news that has been transitory, and has been superseded or contradicted by other news a little later. A certain amount of "wonder drug" publicity has been plainly overdrawn. And this restraint has kept *Monitor* readers from a state of mind which sometimes seems to border on fear or hysteria in the face of propaganda regarding an epidemic or the money-raising needs of some affliction. The *Monitor* takes a thoroughly respectful attitude toward the medical profession, as Mrs. Eddy always did. It appreciates the debt humanity owes to consecrated doctors and researchers. It feels that they, and the public, understand its reserves on the subject of medical news. It covered the Salk vaccine development carefully and regularly.

In peripheral areas, the *Monitor* co-operates with and supports community measures which have some medical elements. The paper, and the church organization in Boston, have always taken a helpful role in community fund raising. In recent years it has supported the American Red Cross, knowing this splendid organization does much disaster relief work and is by no means totally medical in its aid. Christian Scientists rigorously obey the law of the community concerning medical regulations, while they strive to obtain exemption from laws which interfere with the individual's conscientious right to choose his own methods of healing.

Down through the years, the *Monitor* has crusaded a good deal on behalf of the individual's right to choose his own form of therapy, which in the case of the Christian Scientist is a religious right protected by the Federal Constitution. The *Monitor* has resisted many forms of medical compulsion. It has fought against compulsory physical examinations, inoculations, and other forms of medical treatment that may be contrary to an individual's choice. Such, indeed, is part of its commitment to freedom. Many of these battles were won back in the 1920's. Religious exemption is now a fact in many areas.

There has run much basic reasonableness through all this crusading. Always the *Monitor* has recognized that the ultimate decision of the community must be obeyed; but it has insisted that the decision must be taken in a democratic manner, not by some kind of administrative fiat. It was some years ago — indeed, in the early 1940's on the issue of socialized medicine — that the *Monitor* last pressed a full-fledged crusade in the field of medical freedom. It has been clearly aligned against compulsory fluoridation of water supplies, but has largely left the crusading to local elements, covering such contests carefully and helpfully but without raising the issue to the pitch of fanaticism. It has not shared the views and arguments of some of the opponents of fluoridation.

The relationship between the *Monitor* and medicine has once or twice produced ironic and amusing situations. On a certain occasion, the editor was visited by a Boston lady of the old school, a charming and highly respected person whose late husband had been an eminent specialist in arthritis. She told the editor that she was currently honorary chairman of a national foundation on arthritis. She said that the medical specialists on her board of directors had assured her that arthritis was about 50 per cent mentally caused, and 50 per cent physically caused. Her plea was this: couldn't some kind of an alliance be perfected between her foundation and the *Monitor* by which the Christian Scientists would take care of the 50 per cent of mentally caused cases and the physicians would attend to the others.

The editor explained that he doubted if such a mixture of

functions and approaches would work, although he would be glad to forward her request to The Christian Science Board of Directors. He added as a personal view that the campaigns conducted by such foundations, moreover, often stirred up considerable fear, and hence might do more harm than good. The sturdily independent lady replied that she, too, had been troubled by the fear aspects of campaigns. Wouldn't the editor consent to go on an advisory board which would tell the foundation how to set up a campaign that would not foment fear!

Of course there are other *Monitor* taboos which are based on the paper's standard and well-understood desire to print only what is significant and important for the citizen to know rather than that which is simply trivial, sensational, and bizarre. Scandal, sex, and all that is tawdry and vile, will be published only when there is a useful and necessary social purpose involved. Quite often there is indeed such a social purpose. The *Monitor* never ignores such problems, but it seeks only to print what will help in their solution.

13

◇◇◇◇◇◇◇◇◇◇◇◇◇◇◇◇◇◇◇◇

Six Years of Progressive Experience

For six years the *Monitor* continued under its original top direction. Archibald McLellan remained as editor and Alexander Dodds as managing editor. Although the paper had speedily sprung to a respected and relatively mature position in the eyes of its contemporaries, it still needed to learn many elements of its new form of journalism, needed to develop by practice and experience, needed to strengthen its staff. Its local service was still relatively better than its national and worldwide coverage, even though in the latter areas it frequently ran important copy that escaped the attention of other newspapers.

The period was one of growth in capacity and performance. A good deal of shaking-down took place. News judgment matured. There had been times in the earliest years, as we have seen, when articles and pictures found their way to page one without adequate justification in terms of news or reader-interest. Such items were "wholesome" and that is about all that could be said for them. They were definitely the exception to the rule. But their presence did the *Monitor* harm in the eyes of its contemporaries and the discriminating public. While the basic fact is that the *Monitor* did remarkably well in a very short time, the corollary remains that its new standards of journalism contained professional pitfalls as well as opportunities. With unhappy seriousness, the *Monitor* published on January 17, 1910, a picture of a device for the concoction of early-morning tea. The machine should have come from the crayon of Rube Goldberg or Rowland Emmet. Since Christian Science disapproves addiction to tea and coffee and their advertisement is not accepted, the publication of this absurd device was doubly surprising. In February, 1910, a banal story about the Saugus, Massachusetts, High School alumni play was rewarded with a prominent spot on page one. This is better than a page-one story of some spectacular but meaningless crime or tragedy happening at the ends of the earth, with which sensational newspapers then and now embellished their front pages, but it did less than nothing to establish the *Monitor* as an expertly edited newspaper. There were other similar aberrations. They illustrate the absence of clear-cut news standards and judgments.

Certain other slips were more excusable. On January 13, 1910, the *Monitor* expressed its confidence in the future role of the horse, in rather too glowing terms. Under the head "Man's Friend, the Horse," the *Monitor* averred that as in the past automobiles would only make more work for horses. It said: "New conditions make new and increased demands on the horse. And so it will prove with the coming of the automobile. Those who say 'the horse must go' are quite right. He must keep on the go all the time. There is so much for him to do he can hardly find time to eat his oats and hay."

The *Monitor* continued its reporting of new inventions and technologies. As mentioned under the unbelievable date of February 2, 1910, it described "a new process called television." That fabulous word was indeed used! The device described would enable a person's voice and image to be seen afar. It would supplement the telephone. It was produced by a lamp, projecting through a lens on sixty-four cells of selenium, which produced an artificial retina. "All we need now," said the *Monitor* speaking of friendly communication at a distance, "is an artificial handshake." A few days later, on February 10, the paper had an interview with Thomas Edison describing a "perfect combination of phonograph and motion picture." In short, the talkies. This discovery would be "a great aid to the schoolroom." And, said Mr. Edison, "the moving pictures will be shown in their natural colors, will stand out from the screen in a natural manner, and will talk." Technicolor! 3-D!

These and many other notes throughout the early files, are a vivid reminder of how clearly but how long great ideas remain in human thinking before they are worked into practical operation. Item after item is "prophetic" as we look through the columns with the advantage of hindsight.

Sometimes the prophecy is simply expert analysis, which should be given due credit. Thus, in January, 1910, the *Monitor* forecast the choice of Charles Evans Hughes as a Republican Presidential nominee, and gave its opinion that quite probably he would also become a member of the Supreme Court. In January, 1912, speaking of the durbar at which King George V and Queen Mary were greeted by their imperial subjects in India, the *Monitor* said: "The just demands of the Indians for a larger share in the government of the country will eventually have to be satisfied." The paper also paid high tribute to Britain's contribution of order in India, making clear that without British control the subcontinent would have dissolved into chaotic rivalry and despotism. But it plainly forecast the day of ultimate independence — a position that was only a dream to most Indians at the time.

Brigadier General Hiram W. Chittenden, U.S. Army Ret., in 1910 wrote a series of articles on the problems of peace in which he envisaged the ultimate necessity of a world parliament, saying, "Unless civilization turns backward, this germ will grow and develop and bring forth its destined fruit in good season."

Of particular local interest to Boston in 1958, the *Monitor* carried in 1912 a story advocating the use of the Back Bay yards of the Boston and Albany Railroad for an important commercial purpose. This idea is coming to life in the late 1950's with the $150,000,000 project of the Prudential Life Insurance Company.

By 1912, the *Monitor*'s political coverage in the United States had become expert. In January of that year, it foreshadowed the probable nomination of Woodrow Wilson by the Democratic Convention at Baltimore six months later, while explaining the very complicated political tangles in both parties. It had published Mr. Wilson's picture on page one as early as July 1, 1909, before he became Governor of New Jersey. Its regular political articles, as 1912 wore on, gave the campaigns in all three parties shrewd and perceptive attention.

With Mrs. Eddy's condemnation of monopolies and the abuse of freedom running as an undercurrent through its editorial position, the *Monitor* on January 22 defended President Taft (and Theodore Roosevelt) from attacks of a conservative Democratic Senator in these words, which have an impressive topicality in the 1950's:

> To set up the man of straw of socialism and pound it is a convenient and melodramatic device of statesmen of a certain school nowadays; but it deceives no one who knows the genesis of the present social unrest or political agitation in the United States. Individualism both as a theory and a practice is too thoroughly interwoven into the fabric of American activities to have been lost from it during the past decade as a result of insurgency. What the American public really is concerned with is not socialism but social justice. President Taft is not worried about socialism, whether of the Marxian or Berger brand, nearly so much as he is about the disinclination of the strong to bear the burdens of the weak and the persistence of the few in the effort to exploit the many through special privileges granted by law or through monopolies in manufacturing and trade. The President's chief enemies now seem to be men high in authority in the worlds of finance and commerce who resent his impartial enforcement of law, who

would have discriminations in its enforcement, who would be a law unto themselves, that is, anarchists.

Buttressing its position regarding the contempt for law then shown by some financial leaders, and disagreeing also with the highhanded attitude being advocated by Theodore Roosevelt, the *Monitor* took Elihu Root as its authority and added: "Both Mr. Root and President Taft realize that for the preservation of society and for the securing of essential justice there must be major emphasis on principles of right applicable to all. No national 'hero' [e.g., Theodore Roosevelt] on the one hand, can with safety be permitted to determine who shall be prosecuted and who not; and, on the other hand, no magnate, however wizardlike his gifts in corporation consolidations and economies, can be exempted from obedience to law."

The editorial concluded by welcoming Mr. Root's "admission that altered social structure, modes of living, of industry and of commerce had created problems 'for the solution of which the old reliance upon the free action of individuals appears quite inadequate. In many directions the intervention of that organized control which we call government seems necessary to produce the same result of justice and right conduct which obtained through the attrition of individuals before the new conditions arose.' " Is Mr. Root a Socialist? asked the *Monitor.*

When it is considered that the *Monitor*'s readers included, as they do today, persons of all varieties of political and economic views, with a considerable number of them representing solid conservative elements in the community, it is remarkable that it could maintain so boldly progressive a position especially in an election year. But its position was not partisan, and it was certainly based soundly on the analyses Mrs. Eddy had given of the same problems. There may well have been pressures from readers, as there have been ever since, some pushing in one direction and some in another. But in 1912 the paper was able to maintain a forthright position.

This approach to grave social problems was shown in its

coverage of the Lawrence, Massachusetts, textile strike, in early 1912. Here, at the paper's very doorstep, was an industrial dispute of major magnitude combining many of the troublesome elements of that "year of radicalism," as the paper's Washington correspondent called it.

There have been many charges that American newspapers, especially in the earlier years of this century, did not cover labor disputes adequately. No such charge could be held against the *Monitor*'s copy on the Lawrence strike. There, mobs of foreign-born strikers had tried to rush into the woolen mills with weapons to drive out those who continued working; a dynamite plot was fabricated; large numbers of the strikers could not speak English; most of them joined the Industrial Workers of the World, whose redoubtable leader, William D. Hayward, came and took personal charge; other strike leaders were jailed and held without bail; Governor Eugene D. Foss had sent in the militia and at one point they had charged the workers with drawn bayonets.

Walter Cunningham, the diminutive reporter from Dundee who held many important spots on the staff down through the years, was sent to Lawrence for eyewitness coverage. He barely missed being clubbed by police when he found himself between marching strikers, headed by women, and police on horseback barring the road to the mill gates.

Despite these forbidding circumstances, the *Monitor,* in addition to publishing daily lead stories, ran nearly a page of analysis by Julius Moritzen, a special correspondent who visited Lawrence, interviewed leaders on both sides, and wrote a balanced and illuminating account, getting at the roots of the conflict.

So the *Monitor* concluded:

> The wage scale of the employees put over against the dividend rate of the mill owners inevitably calls on the one hand the problem of remuneration adequate to maintain life according to American standards, and on the other the legitimacy of income from investments legal in form but often representing no actual investment of wealth. Society is loath on the one hand to attempt to determine arbitrarily that labor never shall be paid less than a given sum, and

on the other hand to place a definite margin of profit to investments that are genuine. Yet the public conscience is alive to aspects of both these phases of the industrial problem as it never was before; and there is reason to believe that in the course of time a public policy will be worked out that will express a moral conviction.

The editorial added that "promoted" emigration from Europe for the sake of procuring cheap labor had gone on long enough. "With far too many of these workers who are thus disillusioned there comes either deliberate choice of a scale of living which is not tolerated by ordinary American communities or a resort to lawless methods of changing economic conditions."

These blunt words continued the commitment to freedom.

One opportunity for calling the paper's capacity to the attention of a concentrated group of important Americans came at the Republican National Convention, held in Chicago in 1912. The Convention was one of the most momentous in American history, since it marked the climax of the struggle between the Theodore Roosevelt Progressives and the Republican Old Guard for control of the G.O.P.

Never in American politics have passions been more intensely aroused, on both sides, than in the effort to seat — or to keep unseated — the disputed delegates who would have brought about the nomination of the Rough Rider. Most inopportunely for the Chicago newspapers, their pressmen went on strike just as the Convention approached. The Chicago Christian Science churches, alert to opportunity, suggested that the *Monitor* publish a special edition in Chicago during the Convention. In seventeen days — again a marvel of extemporization — all the staff and plant equipment necessary for the publication of a daily newspaper was assembled.

One of the first questions was where to get a press. This is not simple, for newspaper presses are made to order. Fortunately, the Goss Printing Press Company in Chicago, which made the original *Monitor* presses, had just overhauled a used press and it was ready to be shipped to the buyer. Arrangements were made to delay the shipment and let the *Monitor* use the press in Chicago for a week. As there were plenty of vacant buildings, a suitable place to issue the paper was quickly found at 1413 South Michigan Avenue.

There were yet the composing and stereotype departments to be equipped. A firm in Chicago dealing in secondhand printing machinery was visited. The proprietor happened to be a Christian Scientist, and naturally was interested in helping. What he could not supply from his stock he quickly obtained elsewhere. Even the Linotype machines became available.

"And here is an interesting point," writes Amos Weston, first foreman of the composing room. "Months before this, when the Monitor was putting in new equipment, it sold to a Chicago second-hand firm two used Linotypes. It was supposed that they had been disposed of long since, but no, there they were in the storehouse in the very crates in which they had left the Publishing Society in Boston.

"The Monitor avoided the labor trouble by paying the scale asked by the pressmen. As all departments of the Chicago dailies were idle, the pick of the skilled trades was available. The newsboys, of course, were delighted to have a Chicago paper to sell. Thus every need was supplied. It need hardly be added that the paper came out gloriously on the first day of the Convention. In circulation, in the amount of advertising carried, and in the good that was accomplished, this venture was an unqualified success."

Mr. McLellan and other top members of the staff went out to see the operation through to success. One of the copy readers who was there recalls today with pleasure the sight of the dignified and urbane Mr. McLellan bending excitedly over the stone on which the pages were made up as the editions went to press each day.

The impact this feat made on the newspaper and political worlds can readily be imagined. If there had been any doubt of the technical skill or professional virtuosity of *The Christian Science Monitor,* it was now dispelled. The paper had made a splash in a big puddle.

The *Monitor* did not endorse any of the three candidates in the ensuing turbulent campaign. It thought very highly of the special qualities of each of them. It had felt President Taft to be unduly criticized by fervent supporters of Theodore Roosevelt in the period from 1909 to 1912, and in this respect its view has been substantiated by the historians.

It had supported many of the progressive measures which Theodore Roosevelt had pushed through, particularly in connection with trust busting, in view of Mrs. Eddy's condemnation of monopolies and trusts. But it did not approve of his effort to get what virtually amounted to a third term, after his most explicit declaration on November 8, 1904, that he would not seek such a term. He said then: "Under no circumstances will I be a candidate for or accept another nomination."

When Theodore Roosevelt in February, 1912, announced his candidacy, the *Monitor* pointed out that he had placed his old supporters under a strain, and in expressing its doubts about multiple terms — beyond the traditional second term — questioned "the desirability of a nation coming to depend upon any man as a foreordained guide of national affairs."

This reluctance foreshadowed the *Monitor*'s position when another Roosevelt sought a third and then a fourth term. But in 1940, as in 1912, the *Monitor* was not silent about the important good things done by each Roosevelt, as well as the doubtful ones. Finally, in 1912, the *Monitor* had much appreciation for the statesmanlike qualities of the scholar in politics, Woodrow Wilson. Thus its attitude in the bitter three-cornered race of 1912 was thoroughly nonpartisan. The newspaper gained strength and respect for its role.

14

A New Editor

As TIME WENT ON, it became apparent that the *Monitor* could and should be raised to higher levels of journalistic competence. The divided function as between Archibald McLellan as editor and Alexander Dodds as managing editor had been an admirable solution for the founding period. Mr. McLellan's position on the Board of Directors gave the authority and support necessary within the church organization, while Mr. Dodds brought the technical capacity and drive needed to put together a new and complicated production operation. But the founding period drew to an end. The kind of leadership now needed was of a different nature.

A different solution was at hand, and had been for several years, but it had not been needed before. In June, 1914, the Directors offered the post of editor to Frederick Dixon of London. Mr. Dixon had been very closely related to the *Monitor* from the beginning. For a few months in 1908–9 he had held the title of associate editor, his name being carried in the paper's masthead along with those of Messrs. McLellan and Dodds.

Mr. Dixon had been an active Christian Scientist and a lively journalist for many years. He began writing for *Macmillan's Magazine* — on American subjects — in 1888. Soon thereafter he became interested in Christian Science. He joined The Mother Church in 1900 and a letter from him to Mrs. Eddy was published in the *Journal* in 1904. In 1906, Mr. Dixon was appointed head of the Christian Science Committee on Publication in London. As an impressive writer, he had long been favorably known to Mrs. Eddy.

So, on November 27, 1908 — just two days after the first *Monitor* appeared — Mrs. Eddy wrote to Archibald McLellan through her secretary Adam Dickey in these terms: "Mrs. Eddy wishes me to say to you, that taking entire control of the editorials in our daily newspaper in addition to your regular duties, is more than should be put upon you, and in order to relieve you of some responsibility our Leader wishes you to send for Mr. Frederick Dixon of London, England, to take charge of the editorial page of The Christian Science Monitor."

On December 11, 1908, Mr. Dixon arrived in Boston to take up his new duties. On January 21, 1909, Mrs. Eddy again wrote to Mr. McLellan, saying, "We have called Mr. Dixon from England to America: he was our star in England and he should be promoted to some office in America. He would make a splendid Editor but we do not want to change our present chief Editor. Please consider this matter and act wisely and justly."

Doubtless as a result of this note, Mr. Dixon was given the title Associate Editor and his name placed on the masthead with the other two. Now, though a great spirit of co-operation and dedication prevailed during these difficult operations, and Mrs. Eddy's officials were deeply responsive to her directions, it may be seen that Mr. McLellan was receiving an instruction putting his own status in some doubt. To be told that Mr. Dixon "would make a splendid Editor" must have required Mr. McLellan to rise to full heights of selflessness. Mr. Dodds, if he knew of the interchange, might well have been concerned also about his role.

These are but speculations and inferences. The external facts are that Mr. Dixon's work from the outset was prominently and effectively used in the *Monitor.* His ideas must have been helpful in the weeks following his arrival on December 11, 1908, as the paper found its feet. Many editorials in his distinctive style are to be found on the editorial page. Then, on April 24, 1909, Mrs. Eddy directed him to return to London, and he resigned for that purpose. His name dropped from the masthead on May 1, 1909.

Back in London, Mr. Dixon continued in the combined role of Committee on Publication and representative of the *Monitor.* In this capacity he did substantial work, organizing correspondence in much of the Eastern Hemisphere and writing freely himself. The task of collecting overseas news was delegated by the Boston office to London, where the material was gathered, partially edited, and forwarded to Boston. News dispatches, feature materials, and some editorials followed this procedure. A staff of sixteen or seventeen persons was organized in the London office by Mr. Dixon. The funds to support the operation were privately raised by Christian Scientists in London. Such an undertaking would have been possible only in the early stages of a venture in which zealous voluntary help was a large element. In due course it was professionalized. And during the entire period, the *Monitor* in Boston was subscribing to daily worldwide wire services.

There is no explicit word indicating why Mrs. Eddy sent Mr. Dixon back to London only a few months after he had been brought to Boston. The McLellan-Dodd combination could not have been expected to work too comfortably with the addition of Mr. Dixon. Moreover, there was important work for him to do in England, as he was told by Mrs. Eddy. Her secretary wrote Mr. Dixon on April 24, 1909: ". . . your opportunities for doing good are greater in your native land than they have been here. Our Leader trusts you will understand that this step is for your good, as well as for the advancement of our mutually beloved Cause."

By 1914, the situation had changed. It was becoming apparent that the Directors would have to relieve themselves of their departmental offices, such as Clerk of The Mother Church, Treasurer, etc., which they had held since the beginning. In November, 1917, these extra functions were all handed on to others. It would have seemed natural for Mr. McLellan to give up his responsibilities as editor of the *Monitor,* since he had so much else to do. In addition, the *Monitor* needed a full-time editor who could bring it the benefit of worldwide experience, high journalistic skill and capacity, cultural depth. Mr. Dodds, for all his flair and drive, did not have this breadth, and was an impetuous person. One of his friends said recently: "He was a big boy!" Under the guidance of another and wiser head, like Mr. McLellan's, these qualities were assets. But Mr. McLellan's guidance could not be full time. A situation that had worked admirably for six years was now ready to evolve into something else more suited to new conditions and needs.

In the meantime, Mr. Dixon had received honors and opportunities at the hands of the Christian Science church. In 1910 he and Mrs. Dixon had instruction in the Normal class of the Christian Science Board of Education, an opportunity open every three years to only thirty persons. He was thus qualified to become a teacher of Christian Science. To be a teacher meant that he could instruct one class a year of thirty students. In addition, in 1913 Mr. Dixon was elected President of The Mother Church by The Christian Science Board of Directors. The office, while a great honor, does not carry executive authority, and lasts a single year.

Here, then, was an eminent and honored Christian Scientist, a man who had been singled out with high praise several times by Mrs. Eddy, who was a skilled writer and student of manifest talent. To appoint him editor of the *Monitor* was clearly, in the eyes of the Directors in 1914, a real step in progress. So, for a considerable period of years it proved to be, though there are hints that Mr. McLellan felt some concern about resigning, and Mr. Dodds's appointment as managing editor was not renewed. He left the paper. At the meeting held on June 8,

1914, to announce Mr. Dixon's appointment, Mr. Dodds made an outspoken protest against it, in the presence of the Board of Directors and various members of the staff.

These small clouds did not darken Mr. Dixon's assumption of his post. Almost at once, however, he set out for Europe. One reason was an obligation to teach his class of students in London. But also he wished to take a swing around the diplomatic circuit in Europe, since war clouds already were dark and lowering. He and Mrs. Dixon were in Berlin in July, 1914, and just managed to get out on one of the last trains. He taught his class in London in August.

Back in Boston the staff did the best they could, with the original managing editor resigned and the incoming editor in Europe. Oscar Stevens, who had been assistant managing editor, held the fort and he writes: "Mr. Dixon was delayed for some weeks in getting back to the office. The weeks until he got back to his post were like trying to navigate by 'dead reckoning.' "

Mr. Dixon brought to Boston not only his knowledge of history and his writing capacity but his acquaintance with important public men. He was to be on intimate terms with Colonel Edward M. House, President Wilson's confidential assistant. Mr. Dixon appears in Colonel House's papers and letters as a kind of unofficial intermediary between the British and the American governments. When frank but delicate information needed to be obtained, Mr. Dixon could readily get it from British sources and provide it to Colonel House or President Wilson direct. He was fully convinced that the war with Germany was a matter of deepest principle, and he wanted the American influence to be cast on the right side, though the *Monitor* did not urge American entry until it was officially proposed by President Wilson in 1917. At the same time, he was a sophisticated European, and maintained journalistic relations with Count von Bernstorff, the German Ambassador to the United States, until just before the envoy was required to leave by the American government.

How deeply a newspaper editor should get into personal and private diplomacy is a question that can be disputed both ethically and practically. What Mr. Dixon did, however, was very much what the editors and most eminent foreign correspondents of *The Times* of London were doing through the nineteenth century and the first part of the twentieth. Mr. Dixon's tireless and shrewd involvement in diplomacy parallels no one's more than it does the activities of *The Times*'s Wickham Steed in Vienna, Berlin, Rome, and Paris. They were somewhat similar men. I know of no editor of a newspaper published in the United States in the years since 1914 who has had more extensive, continuous, and intimate contact with leading world statesmen. Only a few American foreign correspondents have in these years had comparable relationships. Many journalists have interviewed public men, but it has not been the way of American newspapermen to discuss world affairs in quite the same terms Mr. Dixon and his generation of British diplomatic specialists did. The ethics were those of British journalism of the period, especially of *The Times.*

Even if we wonder today whether an editor should be quite so deeply involved, there can be no doubt that Mr. Dixon's contacts paid big dividends in terms of information that could be used as the background for editorials, for the making of editorial policy, for gathering news throughout the world, and for enhancing *Monitor* prestige.

His personal papers are a mine of historic material. They include numerous records of talks with President Wilson, with former President Theodore Roosevelt, with Lord Grey of Falloden, Britain's Foreign Minister, with Lord Robert Cecil, with Sir Cecil Spring-Rice, Britain's wartime Ambassador to the United States, with Wellington Koo, the Chinese Ambassador, with Henry Morgenthau, Sr., American Ambassador to Turkey, who was rather pro-German in his sympathies before American entry into the war, and with numerous other personages.

The record is that of a very well-informed journalist who is also an intense partisan, with sharp views, all adding up to the support of Great Britain in the world war. Take the following *aide-mémoire* of February 1, 1915, as an example. Mr. Dixon wrote:

I had a long talk with the President. He was interested in getting at the point of view of England in the struggle, and admitted that his reports presented the fight now as between democracy and arbitrary power. I asked him what was going to happen to this country at the rate the Germans and the Irish were going with their plots. He said he thought that they would not dare go beyond a certain point, as there would be such a revulsion of feeling if they did.

I asked him if he realized that the guards had been taken off the American ships [*sic*] in New York harbor and in Boston. [Presumably this refers to American guards on German merchant ships voluntarily interned in American harbors.] He was tremendously surprised and made a note of it, and asked me why I said it. I said because I knew that they had been, and I thought that he would find out that they had been taken off at the instigation of the very people who wanted the ships at sea, and that if the ships did get to sea, there would be a little nest of "Alabama" claims. He asked me as soon as I left him to go and see Mr. McAdoo [the Secretary of the Treasury] and tell him about the Boston harbor, and also to see Mr. Peters [Andrew J. Peters, later Mayor of Boston but in 1915 Assistant Secretary of the Treasury in charge of customs], and that meantime he would communicate with them. That afternoon the guardships [*sic*] were put back in the Hudson, and the next day in the port of Boston.

I asked him what the position of the government was going to be towards the blockade, and towards the British part in it. He said he hardly knew what the British position really amounted to yet, but that if I would get him a memorandum on the subject, he would be deeply grateful, as he could only get one officially which did not amount to the same thing. I said that I thought I could get that all right, and on leaving him I drove up to the British Embassy, and got Rice [Sir Cecil Spring-Rice, the Ambassador] to dictate it to me, and then sealed it up and sent it in to him.

The fruits of this memorandum were apparent in Mr. Dixon's next visit to President Wilson, on March 8, 1915, of which he wrote:

I saw President Wilson again, and we covered most of the political situation once more. He told me that he was very much obliged for the memorandum, which had been exactly what he wanted, and that he saw through all the plots to force a row between the

United Kingdom and the United States, and would take care that they did not succeed. The difference between a quarrel with Germany and the quarrel — so far as there was a quarrel — with the United Kingdom was very marked, the one being on the subject of polemical questions with respect to the blockade, contraband, etc., and the other with regard to sheer acts of piracy on the high seas. The first could never lead to a real row and could be adjusted after the war, the other might very easily lead to actual hostilities, and could never, in any circumstances, be atoned for. Then I asked him if he knew of the smuggling of German sailors out of America, chiefly through the port of Boston, on Swedish ships, and I gave him the evidence I had on the subject. He said he knew it was going on, but the difficulty was in catching the people, and he asked me to go and see Mr. McAdoo again when I left him, and put the actual evidence in his hands for him to deal with. After I left him I went up and saw Mr. McAdoo and gave him the papers.

In the foregoing memorandum, we have an estimate by President Wilson as early as March, 1915, that the German submarine campaign "might very easily lead to actual hostilities." This is a noteworthy statement, only a few weeks after Germany laid down its submarine blockade around the British Isles, and two months before the sinking of the *Lusitania*. President Wilson's public utterances did not go nearly so far. On the contrary, he made his "too proud to fight" speech not long afterward. And we see Mr. Dixon sleuthing away at such matters as the ship guards in the Hudson and the German sailors being smuggled out of Boston.

Mr. Dixon was one of the important channels which kept pouring pro-British information and interpretations into the ears of the most responsible American officials. His visits to Colonel House were numerous, and through Colonel House he could always get facts and ideas to the President. As a close confidant of Lord Grey, the British Foreign Minister, he could be counted on as a useful channel for private and discreet interchanges of view. Such things often happened in European journalism. They were not customary in the United States.

Colonel House's tiger became a very real thing to Leslie Allen, who was chief of the *Monitor*'s New York Bureau during this period. He wrote: * "I almost got on speaking terms with the tiger rug in Colonel House's New York apartment. Mr. Dixon numbered House among the half dozen inside men he had to see every time he came over from Boston. I'd go up with Dixon, he'd go into an inner room with House, and I'd sit outside wondering why the tiger's open-mouthed snarl always singled me out so definitely."

In another interview, this time with Secretary of State Lansing, Mr. Dixon defended Sir Cecil Spring-Rice against the attacks of those in Britain and America who wished him to be replaced by someone like Lord Balfour or Lord Bryce. He minced no words: his expression was indiscreet, not to say intemperate. Perhaps this open character of his opinions made him useful to the statesmen who usually got mealymouthed double talk from official sources.

Secretary Lansing had proposed Lord Balfour or Lord Bryce as British Ambassador to Washington. Said Mr. Dixon:

I asked him [Lansing] if he really knew anything about Balfour when he made such a proposal as that. He said no, only just in a general way. I said Balfour is a man of over seventy, tenacious of his opinion beyond words, charming when he chooses to be charming, but with the sting of a rattlesnake when he doesn't. A man who puts pure intellectualism before everything else in the world, and who is the most adroit wielder of phrases, with a view to making those for whose intellectual attainments he has a contempt sorry for themselves. I said if that is the sort of man you want to have as ambassador here, I have a strong suspicion your last state will be worse, a good deal, than the first. Anyway I do not think you could get him for the simple reason that he would not come away as he is too old.

As for Lord Bryce, he has made a reputation as an ambassador here. When men have made their reputations and then have come back for a second time, they almost invariably unmake them. To begin with, they all think they have nothing to learn from anybody, and that they all know more than anybody else . . . Anyway, I do not believe that there is any chance whatever of Grey replacing Spring-Rice. I said that I would talk to him about it if

* In *The American Press,* June 1933.

he liked. He said he wished that I would, without involving him. From inquiries I have since made I am perfectly sure that the malicious statements let out by Harmsworth [Lord Northcliffe], in London, have been picked up in Washington, by Bernstorff, with a view to making mischief, and that the whole thing over here has been engineered from the German Embassy.

As it turned out, Sir Edward Grey did not replace Spring-Rice. But in December, 1916, he was himself succeeded by Lord Balfour as Foreign Minister, and Balfour came to the United States on a war mission in 1917. During that visit, Lord Northcliffe himself wangled an appointment to Washington from Prime Minister Lloyd George. This episode is vividly described in Lord Beaverbrook's *Men and Power,* published in 1957, in which he quotes Mr. Dixon. For the editor, though he might describe Lord Balfour in the terms he used with Secretary Lansing, was nevertheless on intimate correspondence terms with him and wrote: "Whatever induced the Government to send Lord Northcliffe here? May I explain hastily that this is not a question to which I expect an answer. It is merely a horrified note of exclamation. I thought everybody knew that the gentleman was regarded here as the British Mr. Hearst . . . The fact is, if I may so say, that I should think a man less a persona grata it would have been difficult to find, nor is it very wise surely to have as a government representative, in any way, a man with a journalistic claque always rubbing the skin off its hands, in its exertions." *

After his talk with Secretary Lansing on February 22, 1916, Mr. Dixon had an equally remarkable discussion with Count von Bernstorff, and with Mr. Wellington Koo, the Chinese Ambassador. It was a noteworthy day of interviews, which few journalists could have equaled.

On April 3, 1916, we find Mr. Dixon dining with Henry Morgenthau, Sr. Unabashed by the relationship of host and guest, Mr. Dixon describes the scene thus:

A girl who was there, who told him she was a pro-ally, asked him

* Dixon to Balfour, June 22, 1917, Lloyd George Papers, quoted in William Beaverbrook, *Men and Power* (New York, 1957).

what he was. He told her he was a neutral but that I was an Englishman and would sympathize with her. She asked me if he really was a neutral. I said yes, I thought he really was because as far as I knew neutral was a synonym for extreme partisan, at which he laughed. There is no question that he holds a strong brief for Germany, and that he is out to head the most dangerous pro-German propaganda imaginable. After dinner we had a long talk in his study, and after he had laid out the situation to me at great length, I took the wind out of his sails, and made him jump sideways like a cat, by saying how extraordinarily he had managed to arrive at the same conclusions as Bernstorff, because Bernstorff had talked to me in almost the identical words a fortnight ago, when I saw him in Washington. If, I said to him, there was a curtain between us, I should have thought it was Bernstorff.

Such conversation, if we are to accept Mr. Dixon's memorandum as literal, and he was a practiced journalist, was sharp to the point of impertinence, overlaid with sarcasm.

The burden of Henry Morgenthau's talk was that Germany was very strong, and growing in strength every day. "All this was not very important on the surface, and might pass for bad information," says Mr. Dixon. "At the same time, I made certain it was not bad information, but a deliberate attempt to make me believe in a condition of things contrary to the truth, and possibly to pass that along." (Germany in April, 1916, may not have been as strong as Mr. Morgenthau said. But it was certainly not weak, and its relative strength may well have been growing.)

Mr. Morgenthau then suggested President Wilson should send an intermediary to talk to the Allied governments. "Then I began to see what was coming," said Mr. Dixon. "Obviously the ambassador in Constantinople [Mr. Morgenthau] was the man for this important job. I said, if Mr. Wilson knows what he is doing when it comes to that, he will use an Englishman and not an American, that is if he wants to be successful. I think that startled him a little. I said there are any number who could be found if it was advisable. What I wanted to see was whether the American was himself, and I am absolutely convinced it was."

All sorts of meaning can be read into both sides of this conversation. If Mr. Morgenthau was proposing himself as an intermediary, then Mr. Dixon was with equal absence of self-consciousness suggesting himself as a better choice. It is sobering to speculate what would have happened if the United States had mediated successfully in 1916 and brought about a negotiated peace between the European combatants.

Germany's immediate role in Eastern Europe and the Middle East would have been increased, and it would have retained an overseas empire. The Russian Revolution might have been evolutionary. The losses of blood and treasure in both Britain and France would have been far less debilitating. German inflation might not have led to Hitler and parliamentary government under the Hohenzollerns might have evolved responsibly. The United States would not have gone through the emotional and physical experience of participation in world war, hence its reaction of withdrawal might not have been so severe.

And, of course, all these if's may be quite wrong. A stronger Germany might have led to dominance and an ultimately bigger and tougher war. To most Americans at the time, and perhaps to most of them today — not to mention most British and French people — a negotiated peace leading to considerable triumph for the Central Powers was unacceptable and dangerous. At the perspective of forty-five years, we are less sure today. It is hard to see how any consequences could have been more difficult than those that have ensued.

Discussing German submarine warfare, Mr. Morgenthau said: "I tell you, and I know, there will be no break [between Germany and the United States]. The difficulty . . . will be to carry on until November. Once the elections are over and Wilson is returned, we can swallow any number of insults . . . We will swallow anything to keep out of the war, and unless the Germans should prove utterly crazy — which I don't imagine — they will not do anything from which we cannot find a way to escape." This was poor prophecy.

Then Mr. Morgenthau forecast that Charles Evans Hughes, the only man he thought could beat President Wilson, would be kept from the nomination by Theodore Roosevelt, who would be nominated but would not have united Republican support, and Wilson would be re-elected.

Mr. Dixon suggested that the trouble would be in electing a Democratic Congress. Morgenthau said:

"You have put your finger on the sore spot. What made you say it?" Then he looked at me and said: "Young man, how far dare I go with you, for you seem to know a good deal?" I said you can go as far as you choose and no further. "Well," he said, "the whole of the Democratic energies are to be concentrated on carrying the House. We are sure of the Senate. We believe we can carry Wilson against Roosevelt, and that it will be made impossible for Hughes to stand. If we can carry Congress, he said, with a majority of forty, we are safe, and then nothing any of them can do will draw us into a war. We are not going to fight."

Crane [Charles Richard Crane, former United States Minister to China] warned me before I saw him that Morgenthau's head had been turned by his success in Turkey and there may be something of this in it. I wanted to see how far it was safe to go with him. I said: "What would you do if you were Mr. Hughes?" He said: "I would wait until 1920 until Wilson is out of the way." Then he said, "Speaking as a citizen and not as a Democrat, nothing can keep a Republican out then." I said, "Why?" Of course I knew why.

He said, "Because there is nobody in the Democratic party that can take Wilson's place." I said, "Will there not be in 1920?" He said, "I think not." I said, "What about Mr. Lansing?" He said, "Well, I never thought of him. He might." Then I played my card. I said, "What about yourself?" He took it like a trout, and shook my hand with both of his, and said it was impossible because he was a Jew. I think I landed the fish all right, but it was not a pretty episode for a man I really thought a great deal of, at one time.

It is tempting to go on quoting from the Dixon memoranda indefinitely, for they are filled with material as interesting as it is historically pertinent. One talk he had with Theodore Roosevelt on April 12, 1916, graphically reveals the position of the former President on the war issues and domestic politics.

With typical Theodore Roosevelt exaggeration, he told Mr. Dixon that

> Wilson had discredited the United States in the eyes of the governments of the world in a way which it would take a half century to undo. The failure to protest against the invasion of Belgium had been the first downward step, and it had been followed by a series of positively degrading episodes . . . He would give anything to have the settling of the affair and the restoring of American credit before it was too late . . .
>
> In Mexico Wilson had permitted things to go from bad to worse, and he was approaching a condition of things when he would either have to fight or to run. With respect to Europe, things could not be much worse. The United States had not a single friend on the other side, and he did not see how she could have a friend on either side. She had shown no regard for the lives of her own citizens, so she was not likely to show much regard for the lives of other citizens.
>
> His own program if he came into power, and whether or not he came into power, would be to try to restore the soul of the United States. To him preparedness was not merely preparedness for war, though that was an inevitable issue, and by preparedness for war he meant not an army on the present lines, but universal military service, in other words, a nation in arms. That, however, was quite the minor side of it.
>
> The real preparedness was the restoration of the country's soul. The country had got to learn to recover its ideals. It had got to learn to give itself to the state in support of its liberties and ideals. It had got to learn to brag less, and not to make promises which it was not prepared to fulfill. It had made promises in the past, such as Belgium, and then it had run away from them. All this and the piling up of wealth was sapping the moral stamina of the country today. The day had come when it was necessary to force the country to see this, even though it should, for the moment, turn down the man who attempted to force it to open its eyes.

Here was a good summary of Theodore Roosevelt's intense views and the position he was to take during the early months of 1916. The phrase that the country "had got to learn to give itself to the state" shows how narrow is the borderline between the position of the fire-breathing patriot, like the Rough Rider, and the Fascist who also urges the individual to give himself to the state. Of course in 1916, in the midst of war profiteering without risk or sacrifice, which Roosevelt saw all about him, it is understandable that he should urge a higher concept of the individual's duty. He went on to say, in the Dixon interview:

"I do not know what my chances of election are, and I do not care. When I was in Cuba it twice fell to my lot to lead charges in the field. I never stopped to ask myself whether I should get through or not. I perfectly well knew that if I stopped to ask myself that question, — and nobody knows this better than you do, you know it better than I do, — that if I stopped to ask that, I should have admitted an inability to get through, should probably have failed. When I gave the order to advance, I said to myself now I am going to do the best job I can. I don't care what happens, I am simply going to do the best I can do. Consequently I got through in each case. I am going to fight the present election in exactly the same way. I am going to do the best I know how for the ideals which are my own. As to whether I get through or not, will not count for a second. I am telling you all this, he said, because I have talked to you before; I know that I can trust you absolutely not to give it away in connection with me. You can, of course, and you will, use it if you want to, but not as coming from me direct."

This was Theodore Roosevelt the adept in press relations. It had long been his custom to confide freely in newspapermen, although there was nothing particularly confidential in what he told Mr. Dixon on this occasion, and then if it turned out inconveniently afterwards for the views to be attributed to him he could always deny them. Thus the Ananias Club came into being — the Washington correspondents who had been the beneficiaries of Theodore Roosevelt's confidence, only to have the views repudiated and themselves nominated by him to the nonexistent Ananias Club.

Roosevelt did not win his charge in 1916. He did not come close. Charles Evans Hughes was nominated. And Theodore Roosevelt loyally campaigned for him. My own first political memory is of a campaign speech by Theodore Roosevelt at the Lewiston, Maine, City Hall in the fall of 1916. I was twelve years old. I watched Theodore Roosevelt drive up in an open car, waving his broad-brimmed campaign hat and baring his sensational teeth. In his speech, attacking President Wilson, he reiterated with immense sarcasm: "He kept us out of war," but the thesis was not that we should have been at war, but that we were actually involved, and deeply. It was an ingenious blending of Roosevelt's convictions and the campaign needs of the Republican ticket.

15

The Paper Evolves

THE MONITOR as Frederick Dixon took over had many merits. It had made remarkable progress during its brief life. But it plainly needed many of the elements which a journalist of high intellectual stature and world view could give it. It also needed some technical improvement. Its make-up was not as smooth and orderly as it could be. Its front page and inside pages were choppy, with too many very short stories and too little editorial integration. It was just what a strong, earnest, lively, breathless, relatively youthful newspaperman from Pittsburgh would make it, modified by the deep ideals and restraints inherent in the *Monitor* and controlled by the overall editorship of Mr. McLellan and the decisions of the Board of Directors. Despite its advantages, some elements were lacking. In many cultural aspects the *Monitor* was a trifle amateurish, folksy, scrapbookish. While its assiduous cultivation of the local Boston field had much merit, its local preoccupation was being overdone. The paper was often parochial. It needed its sights lifted.

This is precisely what Mr. Dixon was able to contribute. But it must also be said that he, too, overdid his specialties. Just as the paper as produced by Mr. Dodds under Mr. McLellan's guidance was a little too spotty and intense, so the paper as produced by Mr. Dixon was too subdued and bland. And the new editor's own editorials and articles, while possessed of a brilliant literary style and an almost overwhelming erudition, were sometimes just too rich a mixture for a general readership. Moderation was called for. The paper badly needed the continuous guiding hand of the Board of Directors, applied under the provisions of the Church Manual. Increasingly, even from 1914 forward, this guidance was attenuated and it was missing altogether from 1919 to 1922. All this will appear as the narrative unfolds.

For the years between 1908 and 1921, it seems to me that the *Monitor* was at its best around 1915. At that time it retained a good deal of the dynamics of Pittsburgh blended with the smoothness and cultural depth of London.

The breadth and boldness of *Monitor* thinking is shown in an editorial of December 3, 1913, on the annual meeting of the National Civic Federation. The questions to be discussed foreshadowed the major economic problems of the mid-century. Asked the *Monitor:* What shall be the size of the industrial corporation of the future? What is the difference between restraint of competition and restraint of trade? How can competition be prevented from reaching the destructive point? Should a manufacturer be permitted to fix retail prices? Is price-cutting a benefit to the public? Is fixing or limiting output by farmers permissible? Are agreements between organizations of working men and organizations of employers a violation of the Sherman Act? If illegal, should they be made legal? Should there be an interstate trade commission with power to pass upon trade agreements? Should large corporations be compelled or permitted to take out a federal license, their acts to be supervised by this commission?

If any editorial writer of 1958 compiles a list of questions as pertinent forty-odd years from now as these questions are today, he can be proud of himself. But the *Monitor* went on to give its own general view, saying: "We are leaving the competitive for the combination system — humanity is breaking the last ties between individualism and collectivism — but there is this difference in the situation from any that has existed in the past: mankind is conscious of the change, is alert to it, and is striving in every way possible to accelerate it and to adjust humanity to it." This would be pretty strong doctrine even in 1958. Just what did they mean, "humanity is breaking the last ties between individualism and collectivism"? Just how collective did they think we were getting? From every context, it is of course perfectly clear that the *Monitor* was not talking about a kind of collectivism remotely resembling Marxism or socialism, but rather a form of social responsibility enforced by law whenever required. It was an age of combinations, throughout the business world, and they had to be regulated against the evils of monopoly. Unrestrained competition, of the tooth-and-claw sort, was indeed passing out. The *Monitor* saw the signs of basic economic change with great clarity, and sought to safeguard the essential elements of freedom.

Such was the paper at the end of 1913. While it had plenty of international news, it is clear that its surpassing interest was in the development of sound progress in the United States, coupled with the maintenance of peace.

It was lively and interesting, presenting subjects most likely to be uppermost in the concern of thoughtful Americans. But it is perhaps fair to say that it was not a distinguished paper, in the sense of having articles unique and outstanding in their authority, written and processed with the maturity and style of the best in Old World journalism.

A typical editorial page of 1914, after Mr. Dixon had taken over, was on December 3. It was led by "The Case of India." Here the writer, in straightforward fashion, praised India's loyalty toward Great Britain in the European war, especially after war was declared against Turkey, the country dominated by the spiritual head of Islam, since many millions of Indians were Muslims. The *Monitor* foresaw the result of the war on Indian self-government, saying: "It is inevitable that one result of the present struggle will be an increasing willingness to delegate to Indians the government of their native country, and a gradual trend of Indian politics to a condition of autonomy within the British Empire." But it added: "This is a consummation which it would be absurd to precipitate too soon. A people unused to self-government cannot be trained to it in the twinkling of an eye. The duty of British statesmanship, therefore, will be neither to hurry nor restrict the necessary progress but to carry out a gradual devolution of authority for the benefit of India alone." This wisdom was well ahead of its time.

Another editorial correctly maintained that the great bulk of the Wilson reform program had already been enacted. It said: "Measures regulating business in one way or another have been numerous during the last ten years. Almost a continuous sitting of Congress since Woodrow Wilson's induction into office has taken the action called for by the progressive proposals of the present administration. There is little to be done now beyond perfecting the legislation enacted and putting into operation the regulatory machinery provided for in the new laws. Prudence calls loudly for a pause in the progressive program until the legislation already placed upon the statute books shall have had an opportunity of proving its value to the country."

This was, in fact, the result, although more nearly caused by the emergence of engrossing wartime problems than through a glut of progressive legislation. There was still unfinished business, some of which did not come up again until 1933. And then, after little more than four years of lawmaking, by 1937 or 1938, there came another pause while the country, in the *Monitor*'s words of 1914, had a chance of proving the value of the new laws.

The *Monitor* of late 1914 under Mr. Dixon had already felt the effect of a more cosmopolitan viewpoint and a more restrained attitude toward purely local news, headlines, and display. But the changes were all matters of degree. Some of them might have come about through natural development and progressive thinking, whoever had been editor. There was nothing drastic or revolutionary about the changes, as has often happened in other newspapers when there was a change in editorship. Moreover, the twelvemonth beween December, 1913, and December, 1914, had been filled with profound change and shock. Many Americans had felt with President Wilson in his message to Congress in 1913 that a period of settled peace would continue. The Balkan wars were a long way off. But to have all of Europe, and dominions and possessions in all corners of the globe, go to war, and to have American ships stopped and searched and American citizens lost through sinking of other ships at sea, suddenly brought the United States into the kind of world in which we have lived ever since. There was a lot of coming-of-age in these months, and a good deal of it was reflected in the columns of the *Monitor* regardless of the change in editorship. The *Monitor* had also come of age. It was dropping off some of the gaucherie of its extreme youth. In the process, it was also foreshadowing the loss of some of its vigor.

The trend is still further apparent in 1915. The paper's leading editorial on November 5, 1915, the aftermath of the defeats of women's suffrage in several key states, was entitled "The Franchise Candle." There's always a tomorrow, it told both the proponents and opponents of suffrage, though the editorial put it: "Il y a toujours un demain." It described the inevitability of a true cause, recalling the Protestant martyr Latimer's deathless remark to his fellow martyr, Ridley, outside the walls of Balliol College, Oxford, as the flames leaped upward around their stakes: "Be of good cheer, Master Ridley, we shall this day light such a candle, by God's grace, in England as I trust shall never be put out." So, said the *Monitor,* had the suffragists, and the day would come "when the world will be just as surprised that cannibalism should ever have been a possibility, as that the suffrage should have been refused to women."

Why was it refused? asked the *Monitor,* answering: "This is merely the blind human manifestation of the struggle which began in the world on the day when the writer of what is known as the Elohistic document of Genesis declared, 'So God created man in his own image, in the image of God created he him; male and female created he them.' The writer of that sentence lighted the candle of equality without question. It has been burning in the world ever since, and will continue to burn until there is no material universe for it to light. Several centuries have been spent in the effort to put it out. It is burning today, not because it was the saying of a human being, a human being who quite possibly hardly understood its full significance, but because it is a statement of Principle."

It was in such rousing periods, with such fervor and conviction, interlaced with such a rich mixture of allusion, that the Monitor's leading editorials appeared for many years.

The editorial page, on December 1, 1915, led with a smasher on "Religious Freedom in Peru." Opening with reference to Francisco Pizarro, Diego de Almagro, and "the priest Luque" — few but the readers of William Hickling Prescott's *Conquest of Peru* would have identified the latter two — it praises the recent decision to permit freedom of worship. It pointed out that though, in 1913, only one-third of the children of school age were actually in school, out of those who did manage to get an education came the demand for liberation. "Yet out of the schools," the editorial said, "and through the universities, such as they were, emerged a small group of thinkers and scholars who were determined not to rest until the sunlight should disperse the fog that had settled upon the Peruvian intellect." And so the editorial hailed Peru's emergence.

To the staff, Mr. Dixon was an impressive figure. Walter W. Cunningham writes: "Mr. Dixon had a rare perception and an intuitive sense that was almost poetic in that he seemed to be ahead of the times. I remember in the early stages of World War I when a group of our German readers challenged his attitude on the war, which was definitely pro-British, he answered them in this way: 'This is not a war between the British and the Germans. It is a question of right and wrong. We are for the right.' From this position he never yielded an inch."

Mr. Cunningham stresses another particular perception of Mr. Dixon's. At a time when Britain itself was linked in alliance with Japan, he was aware of its expansive tendencies. According to Mr. Cunningham: "Mr. Dixon kept a close eye upon Japan. He early discerned its intention to dominate Asia and annex islands, large and small, in the southern Pacific. He saw it plant its foot firmly in China, and felt the readers of the *Monitor* ought not only to be apprised of what Japan was doing but to be constantly reminded of it. So Mr. Dixon instructed me to run a one-column map, on page 1, showing the Japanese pincer grip of the Shantung peninsula, and he instructed me to run the map on page 1 as frequently as possible —, at least whenever it was appropriate to do so. He believed that though the map was small the constant repetition would greatly enhance its effect."

Volney D. Hurd says of Mr. Dixon: "His big effort was to get the Monitor out of straight American news writing into something different, to permit the paper to play its proper role. It was Dixon who developed the correct sense of interpretation through establishing the background to events instead of merely trying to write everything on a 'sweet' basis as a means of 'interpretation.' "

A graphic picture of the paper's daily operation, as he saw it, is painted by Mr. Hurd.

In those days [he recalls] we had a seven column paper and no ads on pages two or three, which were devoted exclusively to foreign news. Thus you would find 14 columns of this news, which came in by mail. The cable material was on Page 1 and at least half the space was given to it. Thus a total of around 18 columns [equivalent of 20 columns today] of foreign news had to be handled every day and Walter Cunningham was given the whole job to do. He had no copy desk. I opened up the stuff, stamped it with all the "special to" and other editing aids needed so as to leave him only the text editing to do. But he had to write the heads also and it then went straight to the composing room carried by yours truly. Walter was an extremely fast, tough, and dynamic little Scot. He had to be to do that job.

I had to read the entire 18 columns for errors which was also quite a chore. In addition I did the research and dug out maps for him to keep his time free purely for editing.

Survey of the *Monitor*'s columns during the years when this skeletonized regime prevailed — from 1915 to 1918 — shows it replete with war summaries, dispatches, and up-to-the-minute attention to an immense panorama of news. By 1918 another extremely able journalist, Henry J. Sowerby, was added to the foreign department, and a little later Frank Shovelier, who could read in nine different languages, was brought in from the proof room as another assistant. Mr. Sowerby, incidentally, graduate of Oxford University, had rowed in the same college boat with the Red Dean of Canterbury (the Very Reverend Hewlett Johnson, D.D.). During the Second World War, still a pillar of the *Monitor*'s foreign department (though in the meantime he had been off the staff and turned his hand to farming in North Prescott, Massachusetts), Mr. Sowerby wrote practically all of the *Monitor*'s war summaries, which were published on page one — usually in the lead position — under the signature "By The Christian Science Monitor's War Editor." He did a brilliant job of condensation, interpretation, and analysis.

During the Dixon period, in particular, the *Monitor* attracted to its staff a galaxy of extraordinary individuals, some of them more colorful than expert in newspaper skills. Sir Henry Japp, an engineer who had drafted plans for a tunnel across the English Channel, came to Boston with a strong desire to break into journalism, and was set to work on the foreign desk. Later he was transferred to the London office. He left the paper when Mr. Dixon did.

With Sir Henry, Mr. Cunningham had the services of Howard Buchanan, a former captain in the British army who had written a vivid personal war diary, and Thomas W. Wilby, also an author. The most spectacular figure of all also worked for Mr. Cunningham, although a bit later. This was Demarest Lloyd, a man of wealth and a stockholder in the Chicago *Tribune*. Mr. Lloyd, as a *Monitor* reporter, went on assignments in a Rolls-Royce driven by chauffeur. Perhaps only

Lucius Beebe, in his heyday for the New York *Herald Tribune*, ever matched Demarest Lloyd for motorized elegance. He worked in London for a time, and developed a liking for a certain hair cream only to be obtained in a particular barber shop in the Burlington Arcade. He had a secretary in the *Monitor*'s London office send him impressive quantities of the stuff after he had left the *Monitor* and was living in his mansion in Dupont Circle, Washington. Once as a favor I brought him back a few bottles by hand. It must have been wonderful hair cream. The *Monitor* has had no reporters since — or I believe, before — who went on assignments in such style. It was said, falsely, that the Rolls-Royce was gold-plated.

In terms of make-up and display, the paper in 1918 had struck an all-time level of conservatism. On many days, not a single photograph appeared in its pages, and there were not many line drawings. There were rarely heads of more than one column in size from cover to cover. Even "The Home Forum," which had clung to attractive multi-column feature heads to the last, was now down to single-column heads.

Even upon the stirring events of Armistice Day, November 11, 1918, and in the exciting period just before and after, multi-column heads were kept to a minimum that could have been matched in the United States only by such papers as the Kansas City *Star* and the Cincinnati *Enquirer*, which affected single-column heads for long years. In the extra edition published after normal deadlines on November 11 (the *Monitor* had become a morning paper earlier in 1918 in order to conserve newsprint and cut down on editions, and so remained until 1922), the front page permitted itself only a three-column two-line head in the middle of the page, in 36-point type, with a single bank.

Instead of merely recording the Armistice, the paper with proper journalistic attention to the developing news featured the Armistice terms which had been announced by President Wilson to Congress in a special session at noon. It stressed the occupation of the Rhine River crossings, for the occupation of some part of Germany was of the essence of the hope to teach the German people a lesson. Throughout all the rest of the

Armistice Day extra, no more than single-column headlines were permitted, except that a page on "The House of Hohenzollern" was under a banner line. This page is a spectacular tour de force of historical writing. The front page, incidentally, recaptured some of the make-up symmetry which had been striking in early *Monitors.* It was perfectly balanced in a way that few editions had been for a number of years.

But after the Armistice excitement was over, the paper reverted to its extreme conservatism. Troubled by the stormy political tides, the editorial page on December 4, 1918, gave its first attention to the President and the Congress, deploring the attacks on him in the Senate, and affirming: "The nation is with the President. From the moment when he expressed the spirit of its people and cast the lot of the Republic with the democracies of the world, it has never wavered in its devotion. He has spoken as has no other man in many years what is in the thought, heart, and conscience of the United States. He goes to the Peace Conference with the full faith and confidence of the great mass of his fellow citizens."

16

The Crisis

THE IMPACT of Frederick Dixon on *The Christian Science Monitor* had been great. He enjoyed much prestige within the church organization. As well, he was a journalist of high capacity and positive ideas. He and Mrs. Dixon were a team. Both came to the office — Mrs. Dixon nearly every day — and carried on their duties with intense concentration and seriousness.

Mr. Dixon was given a degree of supervision over the advertising department and other parts of the paper not normally considered within the editorial purview. His own statement of his position is that he felt a new man and an Englishman as editor of the *Monitor* would have difficulties, but that he agreed to the appointment on condition that "I should have complete control of the paper, and that at all times should be at liberty to apply to the Board [of Directors] itself for advice and help. In agreeing to this the Directors requested me to settle all financial and business questions with the Board of Trustees."

Even in 1914, it would seem clear that Mr. Dixon's authority was too great for safety, and would have led to some kind of revision even if the legal dispute had not sprung up. The great strength of *The Christian Science Monitor* down through the years, as far as policy making and administration are concerned, has been the combining of wisdom and experience through the various boards and individuals concerned. Never except for the brief period in reference, has it been dominated by a single individual.

The Board of Directors strive continually to fulfill their duty, expressed in the Church Manual, to see that the paper is "ably edited and kept abreast of the times." This terse phrase reveals again Mrs. Eddy's wisdom and constitutional skill. The words "ably edited" give the Directors authority over appointment of the top editors. "Abreast of the times" is a wonderful injunction and authorization for progress. It opens the way to whatever constructive developments and evolutionary steps in the production, editing, and management of newspapers may come along. The *Monitor* staff, as well as the Board of Directors, therefore are under constant orders to investigate and develop whatever will keep the *Monitor* in the van of journalistic progress. It is a permanent "research and development" requirement.

Under these provisions, the editor of the *Monitor* is constantly responsive to the basic authoritative conclusions of the Board of Directors. To say, as Mr. Dixon does, that he stipulated he "should be at liberty to apply to the board itself for advice and help" is putting the cart well before the horse, although these relationships may not have been as clearly understood in 1914 as they were by 1922 and have been ever since. The editor must be responsive to the Board for orders, not simply free to apply to it for advice. Mr. Dixon's concept was embodied in a letter he wrote the Board upon first receiving his appointment in June, 1914. He was reappointed annually.

Speaking as one who has worked in this relationship for seventeen years (for four years with the title of managing editor and thirteen as editor, though throughout as the chief editorial executive) I can say that the relationship is as constructive as it is comfortable. Some newspaper editors have demanded a free hand from the proprietors of their publication — a free hand, that is, until the day the proprietors become dissatisfied and demand the editor's resignation. Such a relationship is carried out on many papers. It would be extremely undesirable in the *Monitor*. Indeed, it would not work at all. The *Monitor* can never be a personal organ and succeed. Collective responsibility, as defined by the Church Manual, is a vital safeguard and a strength. The close contact maintained between the editor and the Directors — involving, sometimes, almost daily contact and checking — insures stability, force, and courage.

Mr. Dixon approached his job in the personal sense, and his attitude toward the Directors, as revealed in his memorandum, was not responsive but demanding. He was at all times a personal editor. In this role he accomplished a great deal, but in the end it helped to lead to tragedy — for him as well as for the *Monitor* and the whole Christian Science movement, even though in the end strength and permanent guarantees emerged.

As the world war ended, *Monitor* circulation was at an all-time high over previous figures. Its staff was strong and increasingly experienced, and its editors had retained through the critical years a confidential and influential relationship with the men of decision in two continents. These must have seemed very hopeful elements. There was ample reason to expect that the paper would move briskly forward in the intense and controversial period of peace making. It was a thrilling moment, with Woodrow Wilson stirring the hearts of war-weary humanity as he went to the Versailles Peace Conference and the multitudes acclaimed him and his eloquent words. The world had been made safe for democracy and the war to end wars had been won.

For the nations it was soon to turn into a period of disillusionment, political conflict, greed, jealousy, and shortsightedness. For the *Monitor,* and for the whole Christian Science movement, it was to be a testing time, from which ultimately great strength emerged. As a result of the grave legal conflict over the authority of the Church Manual to guide and control the activities of the Christian Science organization, the *Monitor's* capacity to function effectively was for a period to be seriously diminished. In addition, some of the directions in which the paper had been led were open to question. An austere newspaper, lacking many of the elements that make journalism effective and dynamic, was not the kind of publication Mrs. Eddy had founded and supervised for two years.

Even had there been no litigation over the control of the Christian Science Publishing Society, it is likely that substantial changes would have been made in the operation of the paper. Perhaps, as was done in 1927, it might have been put into the hands of an editorial board. There were signs that some such arrangement would have been worked out.

But such a revision was thrust off the scene by the legal conflict over the authority of the Church Manual. On March 25, 1919, the Board of Trustees of the Publishing Society filed a bill of equity in the Massachusetts Supreme Judicial Court. The defendants were The Christian Science Board of Directors.

In the bill of equity, the Trustees requested the Court to restrain and enjoin the Directors from taking any further action to remove from office one of the Trustees, Lamont Rowlands, or to compel the resignation of either of the other Trustees, Herbert W. Eustace and David B. Ogden. On the same day, the Court issued an ad interim injunction restraining the defendant Directors from taking such action, and in other ways from interfering with the business of the Publishing Society, until such time as the whole matter was adjudicated.

Thus, by order of the Court the control of the Publishing Society, including the *Monitor,* was placed entirely in the hands of the Trustees until the conclusion of the case. The final decision did not come until November 23, 1921, and legal formalities were not cleared away until January 28, 1922. During the intervening period, the *Monitor* suffered severely. Its circulation, which at the end of the war had been 123,080 dropped to 20,939 because loyal Christian Scientists felt they could not support publications issued by a disloyal Board of Trustees.

The staff was decimated. Many of them, including experienced and responsible departmental editors, resigned. Some of them returned when the litigation was over. A core of workers, feeling that the *Monitor* must not be permitted to collapse altogether and that they were not involved personally in the issue under litigation, remained at their posts. But they were not able to keep the paper up to its basic standards.

The shock of the experience on the paper was severe, and the rebuilding job of great magnitude, but the settlement of the issue was a major long-term gain, both for the paper and for the Christian Science movement. It has been a real and indispensable factor of stability down through the years. So clear were the issues, and so decisively were they settled by the decision of the Massachusetts Supreme Judicial Court, that trouble of similar nature has never recurred.

The misconception which led to the litigation had begun to cast a shadow on the *Monitor* several years before. Mr. Dixon's own character and point of view were part of the problem. He had, as has been seen, a vivid sense of himself as a personal editor. While he was willing to consult with the Directors, and in fact was given instructions by them from time to time, he insisted that "editing of the periodicals is the editor's demonstration." His journalistic and public views were sharp and dogmatic, admitting of little latitude for the honest divergences of others. The way in which he laid down the law to Presidents and Foreign Ministers and Secretaries of State was certainly no greater than the way in which he laid down the law in the office, and even to the Board of Directors on occasion.

Furthermore, in addition to being a journalist, Mr. Dixon was also what may be called a theologian. He frequently wrote religious articles for the other Christian Science periodicals, and many of the unsigned religious articles published daily in the *Monitor*. As recounted, he had been President of The Mother Church; he was a teacher of Christian Science, and therefore held a position of great respect and responsibility within the church structure. Although such eminence may seem to have been an advantage, it was not altogether so. It combined in Mr. Dixon personally a sense of authority and justification that did not comport with the actual distribution of responsibility and power under the Church Manual. And sometimes there would be differences of view over the interpretation of Christian Science.

One such dispute concerned a set of religious articles by Mr. Dixon, published on the *Monitor*'s "Home Forum," then combined into a pamphlet, and sent out contrary to the request of the Directors.

The divergence broadened to cover the respective duties of the two boards under the Deed of Trust of January 25, 1898, and under the Church Manual. In the Deed of Trust, Mrs. Eddy placed the Publishing Society in the hands of a Board of Trustees. But she also provided that the power of removal of any of the Trustees (literally, the creation of vacancies) should be vested in the First Members of the church and in the Board of Directors. In 1901 Mrs. Eddy proposed and the First Members adopted a bylaw providing that business hitherto transacted by the First Members should be done by the Board of Directors. Thus the First Members, who had become Executive members in 1903, ceased to have any power. They were disbanded in 1908. In addition, the specific power of declaring vacancies among the Trustees was vested by bylaw exclusively in the Board of Directors.

The references to the First Members were the basis of the Trustees' claim that their rights under the Deed of Trust took precedence over the Manual. The fact that the First Members no longer existed as a church group released the Trustees, they contended, from the Directors' power of removal. This would have meant that the plain provisions of the Manual were nugatory and the church itself would have been under divided or no authority.

The issue was also complicated by a question over the Directors' power to remove one of their own number. On March 17, 1919, the Directors voted to remove from office John V. Dittemore, who had been a Director since 1909. He had been a highly contentious and unruly member of the Board for some time. The resolutions of dismissal specified many grounds on which he had violated the Church Manual. He resisted, brought suit, which was finally decided in favor of the integrity of the Manual and of the Directors' responsibilities and powers under it. Had the Directors been unable to remove one of their own number for misconduct, it is easy to see that their authority over the church affairs would have been nullified.

For a time Mr. Dixon seemed to play a mediatory role between the Boards. This fitted in with the position of the Directors, save Mr. Dittemore, for they strove long and patiently to resolve the dispute without acrimony and without going into the courts. They did not initiate the legal action, but tried for months to bring the Trustees to see that the Church Manual must be supreme. During the earlier stages, preceding Mr. Dittemore's dismissal as a Director, he would confuse the situation by personal interventions with Mr. Dixon and others.

Mr. Dixon was deeply dedicated to the *Monitor*. He wanted to bring it through the storms safe and sound. One day in late 1918 or early 1919, he returned to his office after a long conference with the Directors. His secretary, Miss Irene Armstrong, records: "He said to me, in a very tense, strained and serious voice: 'You have two groups, each convinced that it is right, and each diametrically opposed to the other on this issue.' And he illustrated the position by placing one hand in the palm of the other at right angles: 'both like adamant.' Then he added: 'And we are going to carry the Monitor through this without it being in the least affected.' "

Miss Armstrong gives her conviction that "no one who worked with Mr. Dixon at that time and during the succeeding days [this was just prior to the filing of the bill of equity] could doubt his sincerity, his determination to maintain the paper's standards, his loyalty to the job of editing as he saw it. In the beginning he would confer first with the Board of Directors, then come back and be in the Trustees' room with Mr. Eustace, Mr. Ogden, and Mr. Rowlands. He believed all were sincerely trying to live up to what they believed Mrs. Eddy's instructions were."

It is noteworthy that Mr. Dixon, who felt so strongly that the issues between the Allied Powers and Germany, from the earliest days of the First World War, were issues of right and wrong, should not have felt the distinction of right and wrong in the issue of maintenance of the Church Manual.

His ultimate decision in casting his lot entirely with the Trustees and against the Directors may have been influenced in no small measure by his belief that there was a "great conspiracy" to oust him from control of the *Monitor,* and that members of the staff were involved. In the event of the Directors' victory, even had he taken his stand with them, or somehow remained neutral (and he had told Mr. Morgenthau that neutrality was partisanship!) his authority on the paper might well have been greatly modified. Thus he had a definite personal motive, which may or may not have been decisive or conscious, in aligning himself against the *Manual.*

The situation by which Mr. Dixon's position was called into question came about in this way. No sooner was the war over than Mr. and Mrs. Dixon went to London. There Mr. Dixon taught his class of students of Christian Science in January, 1919, refreshed his contacts with leading British statesmen, and attended the crucial Versailles Conference. Before he left, he knew that trouble was brewing in Boston. But he did not suspect that there was also trouble concerning the *Monitor*'s editorship.

When he got back on February 11, in his own account: "I discovered that something curious was going on in the office. Flinn, whom I had always looked to as one of my great helps [John J. Flinn had been chief editorial writer since the paper's establishment] was silent and morose . . . In addition to this, Warner, who had always kept up a warm correspondence with me from Washington, had become perfectly silent."

On March 22, still according to Mr. Dixon's own account, Miss Cora Rigby, a member of the *Monitor*'s Washington staff and an experienced newspaperwoman who later became chief of the Washington Bureau, came to Boston to tell him that

Charles D. Warner, then chief of that bureau, had been in Boston and returned with a tale that Mr. Dixon was to be replaced by an editorial board. She said that Mr. Warner had appeared before the Board of Directors, and that other members of the staff had been called in by the Board, and that all had given their impressions and criticisms concerning the *Monitor*'s well-being under Mr. Dixon.

When Mr. Dixon talked to the Board of Directors, he says they told him the charges against him had largely been managed by Mr. Dittemore, and they frankly described to him the conferences with staff members they had held. Mr. Dixon then talked to Mr. Flinn, who immediately offered his resignation and indicated his disagreement with many of the ways in which Mr. Dixon had been editing the paper. The editor then sent for Mr. Warner, who also admitted his contacts with the Directors and his belief that an editorial board was to be established. Mr. Dixon talked with two other staff members, one of whom admitted his criticisms to the Directors, and later resigned to return after the litigation. The other had no criticisms, but suggestions for improvement if desired.

This whole sorry mess, for which there is only ex parte documentation, is readily enough clarified by a study of the files of the *Monitor*. The paper had progressively been led away from many of its more sprightly aspects. It had taken on the coloration of the staider London press. It had virtually ceased to cover local news effectively. Its headlines were gray and dull, its make-up was uninspired, it had cut down the use of photographs drastically. Its foreign dispatches were inordinately long, and sometimes dull. Some of these regrettable deficiencies came from the severe newsprint cuts of 1918. For the paper of 1915–16 under Mr. Dixon was better than the paper of 1918–19. But certainly not all of them resulted from war conditions. Mr. Dixon's great journalistic interest was in the diplomatic chronicle. The *Monitor* had become something of the sort. Its emphasis on historic details and obscure problems, many of them of minor significance, had become excessive.

Mr. Dixon was ever a brilliant writer and man of affairs.

But his very long editorials were often too positive and opinionated. Amid the notes of genuine insight and prophetic judgment there were occasions when he saw things quite wrongly. Journalistic writing is subject to unusual hazards. Circumstances will change. But the wise and responsible journalist will not permit himself to publish, as Mr. Dixon did of the League of Nations ratification battle on May 1, 1919: "Careful observers expect ratification sentiment to be clearly in the majority. There is no need to worry about the league."

There can have been few editorialists of the half century who included in their editorials such a perfectly fantastic wealth of historical, geographic, mythological, and literary reference. His erudition and power of recall were stupendous. Miss Armstrong, the secretary to whom many editorials and articles were dictated, insists that Mr. Dixon never looked up anything in a reference book. And yet, in the checking that I have given his references (I have read a very substantial number of Mr. Dixon's editorials and articles, but it would be the labor of Hercules to check his sources) I have found few indeed that were manifestly inaccurate or misremembered. Of many of his opinions, hindsight reveals about the degree of error that would be expected. And there is that constant dogmatism and positiveness. But on many important points, Mr. Dixon was triumphantly right.

In giving samples from Mr. Dixon's writing, it is difficult to know where to begin and where to end. One of his most readable articles is that perfectly rollicking page about the rise and fall of the House of Hohenzollern, published on November 11, 1918. Among many other things, Mr. Dixon tells the famous Carlylean story of the great Kaiser, Sigismund Super-Grammaticam. Sigismund, at Constance, was making a speech in Latin, and used the words "nefanda schisma." This dismayed a cardinal standing nearby, who remarked: "Domine, schisma est generis neutrius." ("Your Majesty, schisma is neuter!") To which the autocratic Sigismund replied, "Ego sum Rex Romanus, et super grammaticam." ("I am King of the Romans, and so above grammar.")

There is likewise the story of Frederick William of Prussia, who economized on everything else but spent freely for his Potsdam Giants. "Not a country in the world but was ransacked for these knock-kneed giants. The bazaars of Aleppo, the cabins along the Irish bogs, the streets of Madrid or Stockholm, were searched for any man who could see over his neighbor's head," said the article. And these giants made up a battalion paying tribute to the mad whimsy of one of the Hohenzollerns. So ran a page of astute historical tracery.

Without plunging into quotation of inordinate length, it is difficult to illustrate Mr. Dixon's overwhelming erudition. But here is one example. On November 13, 1916, a few days after President Wilson had squeezed back into office over Charles Evans Hughes, Arabia was proclaimed a separate kingdom and the Grand Shereef of Mecca its first sovereign. Thus the modern kingdom of Saudi Arabia came into being. Petroleum had not yet been discovered in Arabia, and Mr. Dixon did not foresee it, but his editorial on "The Grand Shereef" began with this paragraph:

> From the Queen of Sheba to Muhammad, from Muhammad to Albuquerque, from Albuquerque to the day the British came to Aden is a story of almost three thousand years, but it has passed over Arabia, and left it very much as it was on the day when the Queen of Sheba "came to Jerusalem with a very great train, with camels that bare spices, and very much gold, and precious stones." It might, it is true, puzzle the Grand Shereef, today, to find the gold and the precious stones, unless amongst the treasures of the Holy Places, those insatiable collectors the Ottoman Turks have seen to that all right, but there is even now the encampment in the desert, there are droves of camels yet round Muscat, whilst, as for the spices, myrrh is still extracted from the trees round Suda, and balm drawn from those in the mountains over Safra.

Of course, it might have puzzled some of Mr. Dixon's readers to know what Albuquerque has to do with all this, and Mr. Dixon didn't bother to explain. (It was not the same Albuquerque for whom New Mexico's metropolis was named.) But all of them, puzzled or not, could savor the richness of prose like this:

> In the streets of Mecca and Medina . . . the silent Arabs come and go, the Holy Carpet sets out on its annual procession, the balm shrubs and the myrrh trees thrive where the oases make their green ribbons in the desert, and, behind the savage rock mountain walls, the silent wastes of sand roll their vast seas into the interior. Here, then, in the streets of Mecca, by the well Zemzen, where the Arabs love to think Hagar came with her little Ishmael, is the famed and holy stone, toward which every evening, at sunset, from where the throne of Solomon thrusts its head high above the Indus shore to where the white houses of Fez cast their lengthening shadows, the Muhammadan turns his face and bows his head.

And so on — for 1000 or 1500 words of rich, purple prose — historically exact, literarily rich, politically shrewd. It was extraordinary journalism.

How did Mr. Dixon develop this lore? Whence came his flair for journalism, which he only practiced in Britain to the extent of writing magazine articles? By profession, before he entered the full-time service of Christian Science as practitioner and official in London, he was a bank clerk. One of his old associates remembers him in a branch bank not far from Regent Street, in London. He had not attended Oxford or Cambridge, but had been at a famous old public school, Sherborne, which he left in 1875.

His free hours from the prosaic tasks of bank clerking, still in the recollection of his old associate, he spent reading, usually in the rich and famous round reading room of the British Museum. He read voraciously, delving chiefly into history, and he remembered all of it. To this abundant and pertinent lore, he added a capacity of free and vigorous writing, and an incessant curiosity in public affairs. That he maintained such contacts with public men can be attributed both to the prestige which the *Monitor* had already gained and his own power of analysis and address.

He contributed much to the *Monitor,* hampered it to the degree that he inhibited its local and American coverage and dulled its techniques and dynamics. The great tragedy was that in the legal issue which became acute in 1919, he did not see the constitutional importance of the control of the Christian Science movement by the Church Manual, which establishes the ultimate authority of the Board of Directors.

The Supreme Judicial Court of Massachusetts, which did see these issues clearly, thus not only affirmed the rule of law within the Christian Science organization, but helped the *Monitor* emerge from a period which led it close to the doors of collapse. With the issue settled and the crisis surmounted, the paper could proceed speedily to restoration and new strengths.

17

The Church Resumes Control

ONE DAY IN EARLY 1921, Mrs. Willis J. Abbot was busying herself with her normal duties in her New York house when the telephone rang. It was her husband. His tone had the calm of a man about to tell something big.

"I have news for you, dear," he said. "What do you suppose happened today?"

"I don't know," she replied, ready — as a true newspaperman's wife — for anything. "Are we going to Europe?"

"No," replied Mr. Abbot. "I've just been offered the editorship of *The Christian Science Monitor*."

"Well!" exclaimed Mrs. Abbot. "You didn't take it, did you?"

Pause. Slight embarrassment.

"Oh!" said Mr. Abbot, "what newspaperman in the world wouldn't be proud to be editor of *The Christian Science Monitor!*"

Mrs. Abbot, who was herself an earnest Christian Scientist, had of course known of the legal dispute then unsettled between the Directors of The Mother Church and the Trustees of the Publishing Society. Furthermore, she was thoroughly devoted to New York and the thought of living in Boston came as quite a surprise to her.

She had time to get used to it. The Directors were not in a position to install Mr. Abbot as editor until January 28, 1922. Only then were legal formalities completed by which control of The Christian Science Publishing Society was returned to the Directors. But on November 23, 1921, the Supreme Judicial Court of Massachusetts had handed down the historic decision which gave complete legal authority to the Church Manual as the governing constitution of the movement. Thus was the Manual recognized "as law by law," as Mrs. Eddy had foreseen it would be. From that day forth, the Directors were able to bring Mr. Abbot to Boston and prepare for the time when they should resume control of the publications.

They had been preparing, as a matter of fact, for many months before, being confident that the ultimate decision of the Supreme Court would uphold the Manual, and seeking to be ready to fulfill their trust without delay when the hour came.

In the months thus afforded for preparation, Mr. Abbot was able to survey and analyze the challenging task that lay ahead of him, and to assist in recruiting a staff to replace the many who had left the *Monitor* not to return, or those few who while remaining had so aligned themselves with the disloyal Trustees as to be untrustworthy of future employment. Many who did remain, keeping themselves free from the controversy and simply seeking to preserve the *Monitor* during the grim period, were gratefully retained in employment.

But acceptance of Frederick Dixon's resignation was a foregone conclusion, along with those of the three Trustees and various others who had occupied authoritative posts and had deliberately compromised themselves. Mr. Dixon went to New York, and with John R. Watts, who had been manager of the Publishing Society, founded a weekly called the *Interna-*

tional Interpreter. Mr. Dixon continued some of his active contacts with public men, but the new publication was not a success. He and Mrs. Dixon submitted their resignation from The Mother Church on November 5, 1923, and Mr. Dixon passed away on November 24, 1923. Thus ended a relationship and a human life which had both magnificence and tragedy.

Willis John Abbot, who came to the *Monitor*'s helm that day in January, 1922, was one of the most widely experienced of American newspapermen. He, too, had an extensive personal acquaintance with nearly all Americans in high political life, and many others besides. He had worked in responsible newspaper positions in Chicago, New York, Washington, and other cities. Much of his newspaper career had been in the service of William Randolph Hearst, and from time to time he had taken leave of regular newspaper work to serve as an official in political campaigns.

He was a grandson of John S. C. Abbott (the family name is spelled both with and without the second *t*), a grand-nephew of Jacob Abbott, and nephew of Lyman Abbott, all distinguished American men of letters and the cloth. He began newspaper work as a young man of twenty-one in New Orleans. The story of his attempt to persuade Jefferson Davis, retired President of the Confederacy, to give him an interview on the subject of General U. S. Grant, is a newspaper classic. So are many other of his professional exploits.

In the manner of late-nineteenth-century journalism, Mr. Abbot worked in many cities and on many newspapers. Along the way he found time to write many "drum-and-trumpet" books for juveniles, leading with *Blue Jackets of '61*. Among two-score volumes, his most widely circulated book was *Panama and the Canal in Picture and Prose*. His autobiography, *Watching the World Go By*, is filled with colorful and important political lore.

Fascinated by the operation of American politics, Mr. Abbot had managed his friend Henry George's campaign for mayor of New York in 1895 and never lost interest in George's single-tax proposals. He directed the press bureau in William

Jennings Bryan's Presidential campaigns in 1900 and 1908. His description of Bryan's famous "cross of gold" speech is a moving eyewitness picture of a great episode in American history.

Mr. Abbot had entered Hearst service as editor of the New York *American* in 1896. After serving on other papers, not always with Mr. Hearst, he resigned because he could not support Hearst policies at the time of the sinking of the *Lusitania* in 1915. Thereafter he wrote for and was associate editor of newspapers and magazines in Washington and New York, until the day came when the *Monitor* needed a new editor.

Willis Abbot brought new elements which rounded out and enhanced the *Monitor*'s equipment. The general respect which the paper had achieved from its earliest years had fallen under a severe strain during the litigation period. Its circulation had dropped to 17,500. This pitiful token was, of course, far from enough to earn adequate revenues either from subscribers or from advertisers.

But, more fundamentally, the paper's basic independence and strength had been hurt by the internecine strife within the church organization. If the church behind the *Monitor* was to be riven by dispute, then the *Monitor* itself was vulnerable and weak. In actual fact, the moral authority and prudent vigor of operation which the *Monitor* normally enjoys, through the Church Manual and the control by the Directors, had been missing. It had not been an authentic product, possessed of its real selfhood, during the years of usurped control. Naturally, therefore, it could not serve and impress the world as once it had done.

The choice of Mr. Abbot by the Directors was most timely. Foreseeing the return of the paper to their hands, they had been surveying the field of available Christian Scientists who were newspapermen. There were some prominent Christian Scientists — one was a member of The Christian Science Board of Lecturership — who had been working newspapermen some years before. The Directors deliberately looked for a person who was first all an eminent American newspaperman. Judge Clifford P. Smith, the manager of the Committees on

Publication, had known Mr. Abbot in his role as newspaper editor in Washington and New York. The Committee on Publication in New York, Dr. Albert Field Gilmore, who was himself about to become editor of *The Christian Science Journal, Sentinel,* and *Herald,* asked Mr. Abbot to drop over to his office on that morning in early 1921. James A. Neal, a member of the Board of Directors, had come from Boston to talk with Mr. Abbot. Apparently the Directors already had looked over Mr. Abbot's qualifications with care. Mr. Neal was authorized to ask him at once if he would be interested in the job.

When the appointment was announced, it signaled to the world of journalism and public affairs that the *Monitor* had been placed in experienced professional hands. Had the Directors chosen the course of 1908 and appointed an eminent churchman, such as a member of their own board, as was Mr. McLellan in 1908, or a member of the Board of Lectureship, they would have announced to the world that the *Monitor* was being placed in what might be called churchly hands. Such a decision might have been expected after the Massachusetts Supreme Judicial Court had returned the control more closely to the inner body of the church.

This was another important turning point. In 1908 it would have been possible for the *Monitor* to have become strictly a church organ, aiming solely to serve Christian Scientists. But by careful design it was made, in Mr. McLellan's words, "a real newspaper." As the years went by, its news and editorial policies might have taken on a more denominational cast. They did not. Care was taken to prevent it. Oddly enough, the period in which special religious viewpoints and theses were most assiduously presented was precisely in the period where control was not in the hands of the church's Directors. The kind of editorials which were stopped, evidently by Mrs. Eddy's orders, in early 1909, were getting into the paper with some frequency in 1919. News and editorial policies which directly violated Mrs. Eddy's instructions in other respects were to be exemplified in the paper in the litigation years. Disobedience was in the saddle.

But all this ended with the Court decision. And again the Board of Directors prevented the *Monitor* from slipping into the role of a limited denominational voice. Mr. Abbot was known far and wide as a professional newsman — a newspaperman's newspaperman.

In 1912, suffering from two years of serious ill-health, Mr. Abbot had turned for healing to Christian Science and was speedily free of the trouble, which, he says, "had made my life miserable." The healing also regenerated his human experience, turning him to more constructive journalistic channels, as an assiduous student of Christian Science. Mr. Abbot's appointment was hailed in professional and public circles as eminently appropriate. It gave *The Christian Science Monitor* a professional status it had never hitherto enjoyed.

His earliest task was staff rebuilding. Only a faithful nucleus had remained. Among them, however, were steady and experienced veterans who have always done their best to keep the paper on an even keel and have done the spade work, day in and day out, which has always met its basic responsibilities.

For example, there was Frank L. Perrin, who had been an editorial writer since 1916 and became chief editorial writer in 1922. He was executive editor (the equivalent of managing editor) and a member of the editorial board from 1929 to 1934. Mr. Perrin, who retired in 1946, had had a rich experience in what almost might be called frontier law and journalism. He was graduated from the University of Wisconsin, practiced law in Wisconsin, and became editor of the Chippewa Falls, Wisconsin, *Herald* and the Reno, Nevada, *Gazette*. Later he was on the staff of the St. Louis *Globe-Democrat* and the St. Louis *Star*. He was one of a long line of Westerners to come to the *Monitor,* bringing it an authentic sense of the mountains and the wide horizons, which it never lost altogether, even in its most intense periods of preoccupation with international affairs.

Paul S. Deland became city editor again. Other key men who kept right on getting the *Monitor* to press were George

M. R. Holmes, the sports editor from the beginning until 1940, Arthur Stubbs, an able and genial news editor and copy reader who became head of the universal copy desk, and numerous others.

Veterans who had felt conscientiously impelled to leave the paper during the litigation came flocking back. They included the original financial editor, Forrest Price; the production manager, Amos Weston, who had been original foreman of the composing room; John Phillips, the original news editor; and many others.

During the litigation, the paper's executive editor — replacing the function of managing editor — had been Oscar L. Stevens, another of the pioneer group. But he left late in 1921. In his place, Charles Messer Stow was appointed executive editor. He was an experienced, able, urbane newspaper veteran who had been on the staff since 1912. However, Mr. Stow only remained with the *Monitor* for about two years thereafter. His place was taken by one of the 1922 recruits, a man who was to play a large part in the paper's development for the following eighteen years, Roland R. Harrison. He had been for nineteen years in newspaper work in New York City, serving as day city editor and night city editor of the New York *Herald.*

Thus the most important editorial posts were filled. Similarly, of course, the Trustees and manager of the Publishing Society were replaced, as were the advertising, production, and circulation managers, and the editors of the *Sentinel* and *Journal.* The new Trustees were Fred M. Lamson, William P. McKenzie, and James E. Patton. Mr. McKenzie will be remembered as a member of the Board of Trustees when the *Monitor* was established, as, indeed, he had been when the Board itself was established in 1898. Mr. Lamson and Mr. Patton were men of wide business and financial experience. Mr. Lamson had been a vice-president of the Old Colony Trust Company of Boston, and Mr. Patton had been General Officer of the Pittsburgh Plate Glass Company, as well as president of several corporations. Charles E. Jarvis, who had been corresponding secretary of the Board of Directors and Clerk of The Mother Church, was appointed manager of the Publishing Society.

The role of the Trustees and manager in restoring the *Monitor* was of vital importance. Substantial sums had to be expended in order to restore the paper's staff and re-establish its usefulness. The editorial department was not the only need. To restore the paper's revenues from advertising and circulation was as essential to its survival as to its utility.

There had been a breach between the paper and the overwhelming part of the Christian Science movement. The loyal and enthusiastic co-operation of branch churches all over the world had to be organized. The work of these churches and their committees in support of *Monitor* circulation and advertising, which the Trustees and manager worked to evoke, was an essential element in the speedy recovery of the paper. Thus the months following February, 1922, were another great testing time.

The new advertising manager was Norman S. Rose, a thoroughly seasoned and skillful member of the George Batten Co., later Batten, Barton, Durstine & Osborne advertising agency.

Though the editorships of the *Journal* and *Sentinel* are not directly connected with the *Monitor,* Mr. Dixon and Gustavus Swift Paine of the *Monitor* had been given temporary appointments in this capacity during the latter days of the litigation. With the restaffing, a strong group came to direct the periodicals. Dr. Albert Field Gilmore, the New York Committee on Publication, was elected editor. Later, he became a Trustee of the Publishing Society, and a member of the Monitor Editorial Board. He wrote many articles, series, and book reviews for the *Monitor.* As associate editors, Mrs. Ella W. Hoag of New York, a student of Mrs. Eddy, and Duncan Sinclair of Glasgow, Scotland, a member of the science faculty of Glasgow Academy for many years, were elected.

Altogether a very experienced and impressive group were brought into the posts which effected the well-being of the *Monitor.* There was a deep sense of relief, gratitude, and enthusiasm throughout the staff and among Christian Scientists everywhere. All was at hand for a major forward movement.

Under Mr. Abbot's editorship, and with the support of the entire Christian Science movement, the *Monitor*'s circulation began steadily to return to its pre-First World War figures, and ultimately to excel them. By 1924, only two years after the paper had been returned to loyal hands, its circulation again exceeded 100,000. At the end of the decade, it had reached 130,000. It was a steady and sure restoration.

Without delay, in 1922, Mr. Abbot and his colleagues set about the task of rebuilding the *Monitor,* rethinking its purposes, enlarging its utility. New bureau chiefs and correspondents were required in many parts of the world. Miss Cora Rigby was appointed in charge of the Washington Bureau, which had had a rather disturbed career. In London, John Sidney Braithwaite was put in charge of the European Bureau. Already, in Paris, the *Monitor* had acquired the services of Sisley Huddleston, who was an old hand at continental journalism, having been Paris correspondent for *The Times* of London during Lord Northcliffe's ownership, and of the *Westminster Gazette* under one of Britain's editorial titans, J. A. Spender.

As had been the case from the beginning, much autonomy was given the London Bureau for some years in organizing coverage of the European Continent and the British Commonwealth. Mr. Braithwaite was a man of affairs, though not himself a journalist. He did not write articles, but organized an able office in London and established correspondents throughout the continent. In 1923 Mr. Abbot himself went to Europe and surveyed the *Monitor* staff. Later, in 1925, he wrote a noteworthy series of interviews with European leaders.

As Mr. Abbot took over there was a definite feeling, on the staff and outside, that the coverage had previously had too much of an Old World cast. Mr. Abbot did not seek to impose a set of preconceived opinions upon the staff he inherited, but to work things out co-operatively with them. He was not a dictator, but a modest and even-tempered person, with a sincere respect for the *Monitor*'s previous achievement and its personnel. He knew how to obtain the good will and genuine support of a staff. Indeed, he had moved into many a newspaper office before, and knew the pitfalls facing the cocksure intruder.

In 1922, as Mr. Abbot and the new manager and Board of Trustees stepped into their offices, vast tasks of rebuilding had yet to be done. The tasks which lay ahead were as great as the opportunities.

18

◇◇◇◇◇◇◇◇◇◇◇◇◇◇◇◇◇◇◇◇

Problems of Transition

ALTHOUGH THE CHANGEOVER in control of the *Monitor* seemed smooth, it was nevertheless profound. The settlement of the suit in equity had lifted a great burden from the entire Christian Science field. It brought an enthusiasm and freedom back to the *Monitor* which it had not known for a long time.

Even before the actual litigation broke out, there had been for years serious disagreements between the Trustees and the Directors, often involving the editing of the various publications. It is altogether remarkable that so effective a newspaper was produced under the conditions which had prevailed for such a length of time. Only in Mr. Dixon's first year or two in Boston can an unflawed relationship of confidence have prevailed. And just before that period, in the months of 1914 which led to Mr. Dodds's departure, there was growing criticism and uncertainty preceding the changes.

It is quite apparent that the dedication to idealism and the unselfish service and support which stand behind the *Monitor* are much greater than individuals. The concepts and practices of the *Monitor* were able to survive and even to flourish in the midst of a great deal of human misunderstanding and confusion, and despite persons and personalities. That is the only explanation of the persistence of its values, through various misadventures.

But with the issue of January 31, 1922, the *Monitor* brightened up. The gray, dreary monotony which had prevailed with increasing intensity for half a decade began to lift at once.

The incoming Trustees had been appointed by Mr. Justice Crosby of the Massachusetts Supreme Judicial Court on Saturday, January 28. Since the *Monitor* was then temporarily a morning paper, the issue which had to be completed on Sunday evening, January 29, bearing the date of January 30, was published under the old trusteeship and editor. But on Monday, January 30, the new group took charge.

The results are immediately manifest in the columns of the newspaper they published under date of January 31. An announcement in a deep two-column box tells of the change. It begins with these words: "For two years The Christian Science Monitor and the other periodicals issued by The Christian Science Publishing Society have been deprived of that intimate and life-giving association with The Mother Church which was contemplated by our beloved Leader, Mary Baker Eddy, and for the maintenance of which she made explicit provision in the Church Manual.

"This situation has been corrected by the very wise and far-reaching decree of the Supreme Judicial Court . . . This decree not only recognizes the firm and unshakable character of the foundation upon which the Christian Science movement was built but marks a notable advance in the interpretation of law in the spirit of progress and humanity . . .

"In now resuming their lawful control of The Christian Science Monitor, and other periodicals, The Christian Science Board of Directors desires to thank the field which, with substantial unanimity and in no uncertain way, has condemned the effort to sever those publications from their association with

The Mother Church as formulated by Mrs. Eddy. Plans are already perfected for making The Christian Science Monitor more fully correspond with Mrs. Eddy's purpose that it should be a 'daily *NEWS*paper,' and to give a more complete demonstration of her wish that 'The object of the Monitor is to injure no man, but to bless all mankind.' " The statement then announced the appointment of the various news editors and manager, beginning with Mr. Abbot.

The announcement was followed by an editorial reprinted from the Boston *Herald*. The editorial, speaking with the objectivity of an outside newspaper which had covered the case zealously and sometimes with what seemed to be criticism of the Directors' position, declared the issue to be "whether the design of Mary Baker Eddy to key all the activities of the organization to the church, was to be defeated by a construction of the deed of trust to the Publishing Society, which would declare practically independent a most important branch of the denominational activities. And in that broader issue was locked the extension, if not the maintenance in its present strength, of the cause she initiated.

"The controversy was not any less serious because it was not one between factions in the body of the church following. There was no schism; there was no cleavage; there was substantial and very nearly complete union in the great mass of believers, which was not weakened in the presence of a disturbance raised by the small official group in the Publishing Society."

The *Herald* concluded: "To the extent that there is recognition of the service of the Christian Science Church as a power for good in the community, there will be congratulation to its members on their victory. To the extent that there is tolerance of faith and belief and sympathy for sincerity in devotion to it, there will be relief that this church has not found its fundamental reliance torn from under it.

"Legal students of the future will, we can believe, be directed to the careful phrasing of the Supreme Court's decision in this suit for guidance as to the effect in judicial treatment of even so sacred and binding an instrument as a deed of trust, in that it seeks full light in all possible sources of contribution and that it places its insistence upon the intent of the maker of the trust against the microscopic examination of the written terms. We are not sure but the painstaking discussion of this case in the clear language of Chief Justice Rugg does not mark another and a notable instance of the broadening to human considerations of the whole process of legal interpretation."

This, then, was the community atmosphere in which the *Monitor* resumed its role. And the community soon saw that the paper was to revive its effective local coverage, which had been so sturdy an element of its earlier years. The first front page of the restored regime carried an interesting story from Providence, Rhode Island. A few days later, the outbreak of a serious textile strike throughout New England found the story in lead position, under a three-column head and with a two-column "Textile Strike Situation" box set in larger than normal body type in double-column measure.

These technical details, and many others, show the swift and uninhibited return of the paper to forthright journalistic practices. Nothing is more striking in this renaissance than the use of pictures, which have remained ever since an important part of the *Monitor*'s journalism. In the fourth issue under Mr. Abbot, the editorial page blossomed out for the first time with an editorial-page cartoon. The cartoon occupied the two central columns of the page's four columns, which meant that it was of smashing size (larger than is thought necessary at present by the *Monitor* and by most other newspapers) and it was in excellent style. It showed the four leading delegates marching proudly out of the global chambers of the Washington Arms Limitations Conference, brandishing their mops and brooms, with the caption: "The Housecleaning Brigade Departs." The cartoon is signed Sturges, one of the relatively few times up to that date that the *Monitor*'s greatly talented artist Dwight C. Sturges was permitted to sign a drawing. With his skill at portraiture, the cartoon catches amiable likenesses of Messrs. Hughes, Briand, Balfour, and Kato.

Throughout the paper, pictures — both photographs and

drawings — reminded readers of the paper of 1914 and earlier. And double-column heads on all the news and feature pages took away the look of endless columns stretching up and down, side by side, an unrelieved gray mass from cover to cover.

By a happy coincidence the lead editorial of February 1, the first lead on public affairs since the restoration, hammered away at the need for a more liberal and intelligent, workable economic policy — an issue at which the *Monitor* had been busy since its earliest days. The editorial rings with the force of Mr. Abbot's practiced hand at political writing. It begins somewhat astringently: "It is no reflection upon President Harding's grasp of the tariff — a subject which has always been at the very base of the policy of his party — to say that his recommendations upon this vexed question are thus far a little vague and possibly a little confusing."

The editorial went on to support the President's proposal of a tariff commission with real authority to apply flexible rates. The *Monitor* had been in favor of such a tariff commission ever since the Payne-Aldrich tariff was worked out under President Taft, with the hope that a genuine tariff commission would be created. For over a decade the paper had hammered away at this need. It continued to do so until the authority to vary duties in accordance with changing economic conditions, and to further a more efficient flow of world trade, was created under the Reciprocal Trade Act of 1933.

In the 1922 editorial, without hesitation in plunging into highly controversial areas, the paper said: "Very much of the difficulty which the President finds in reconciling the ancient protective policy of his party with the new financial and economic conditions which the outcome of the World War has forced upon the United States would be very largely removed if the enormous inter-allied debts, which compel a steady interest payment of six hundred million dollars a year, were all cancelled or at the very least deferred for a prolonged period of reconstruction."

The same page — perhaps it was the first one for which Mr. Abbot was able to write personally — contains another editorial which reflects an important change of emphasis. Ever since Mr.

Dixon had become editor, he had criticized the policies and positions of Japan with particular acerbity. Among the many subjects on which he held strong and uncompromising views, this was one of the most acute. He felt Japan's aggressions on the Asian mainland should be exposed at every opportunity. And the *Monitor* had done so. There was much justification for this position, and especially for criticism of Japan's occupation of the Shantung Peninsula and its "twenty-one demands" on China during the world war.

But the *Monitor* in the years between 1916 and the end of 1921 carried matters to an extreme. In an editorial on January 27, possibly the last *Monitor* editorial from Mr. Dixon's pen, the paper said: "In plain English, the Japanese want to hand over Shantung with a halter around its neck, the end of which they propose to tie to a diplomatic post in Tokyo. But has anybody ever heard of the English wanting a traffic manager at Amiens or Trent, or the Americans demanding to make a loan to the Alsace-Lorraine railroads, whether they want it or not? Has anybody ever heard of the British making any claim on the mines at Lens, or the Americans demanding compensation for the Briey basin? Why, then, should pressure be put upon the Chinese to compensate the Japanese for the thoroughly selfish claims which they, alone among the nations engaged in the great war, have made?"

Less than one week later, the editorial control having changed, the *Monitor* — in what may have been the first editorial written by Mr. Abbot — under the head "Understanding Japan" said: "With Japan at the very heart and center of most of the oriental tangles we must see that Island Empire's position with the eyes of Tokio [even the spelling had changed!], as well as of Washington, if we are to be of any true aid in the untangling . . . If we are to do permanent and mutually advantageous business with her, if we are to assist the world by first assisting her to a better stand before it, we must appreciate where she finds herself, and therefore follow her arguments with an honest appraisal of their true worth . . . Better than ever before do we realize Nippon's economic needs and the not less than unique industrial riddle her government is called upon to solve."

The editorial was far from uncritical of Japan and its policies. But it urged the west, Americans particularly, not "to hold to the idea that no good can come out of the Tokio Nazareth." It was a constructive and healing editorial, without sting, condemnation, dogmatism. The *Monitor* had returned to its true mission.

With the aim of making it a *NEWS*paper, page three — which had been a feature page with light essays and columns on it for some years — was put back into the mainstream of the news. The columns which had run there were transferred to "The Home Forum." Anonymity began to slip away also. By-lines began to reappear in the paper during the first week of the new regime. It would still be many years before by-lines were regularly used over staff-written news stories, but their number gradually increased from 1922 onward.

The paper's revived interest in local affairs required a city room staff, which had severely declined, but even with the minimum corps of reporters available in early 1922 stories began to pour into the paper. On February 10, the paper ran a story describing as an immediate necessity, a new state's prison, to replace the monstrous old Bastille at Charlestown. It was at this prison, still unreplaced, that I was to have the unexpected privilege of helping to end a rebellion and siege on a dark January night over a quarter of a century afterward. And on February 13, the paper had a cut and story on Mayor James Michael Curley. He had first been chronicled in its columns during a vigorous reform election fight in 1909. He was one of the candidates for the City Council whom the *Monitor* did not support. On February 13, 1922, after having been a morning paper since mid-1918, the *Monitor* returned to its traditional afternoon deadlines, which it has maintained ever since.

The switch to a morning paper had been explained on grounds that it would permit combining of all editions, resulting in savings both in newsprint and money. However, there were real advantages which have always weighed in favor of afternoon publication. For one thing, an afternoon paper can be produced by daytime work, by both editorial and mechanical staffs, which is generally more efficient, somewhat more economical, and more pleasant for the staff. It does not require Sunday work, which is less than desirable in a newspaper published by a religious organization in a building adjacent to a church.

News from Europe happens with a five-hour time start, so that dispatches from the Eastern Hemisphere reach Boston advantageously for daytime publication. And for shipment of papers to points west, trains leave Boston during the daytime rather than at night, and get to western points more quickly than if they were available for shipment from 9 P.M. or midnight onward. Thus there was no hesitation in 1922 in converting back to afternoon publication without delay and there was general satisfaction at the result.

The *Monitor*'s rebuilding began at a kind of turning point in post-First World War history. With the defeat in the American Senate of Woodrow Wilson's plan for membership in the League of Nations, with the manifold disillusionments of the Versailles Treaty, with the impossible demands for reparations made of Germany, with acute disagreements brewing up not simply between the United States and its late Allies, but between Britain and France likewise, with continued Japanese expansionism in China, it was quite apparent that the world was heading for serious trouble if the trend was not halted. Thus the paper's rejuvenation, as 1922 began, could not have been more timely.

◇

PART THREE

THE MONITOR'S MATURITY

1922–1945

◇

19

◇◇◇◇◇◇◇◇◇◇◇◇◇◇◇◇◇◇◇◇

Problems of Peace

TO THE MONITOR, as to the world, the Washington arms conference of 1921–22 gave badly needed inspiration and encouragement. It helped lift the general disillusionment accompanying American rejection of membership in the League of Nations and the sordid political scrambles of nations old and new, European and Asian, in the years after 1919. The conference was the first ray of hope in a world all the more gloomy because its expectations had risen so high in late 1918 and early 1919.

So the *Monitor* covered the Washington conference with great diligence. Very little in American journalism of that period was more penetrating than the studies of the principal statesmen at the conference which it ran on page one during the opening weeks. The opening dispatch on President Harding, published the day before the conference convened, told of the anonymous author's contact with him before and after his election. Once, sitting informally on the edge of a bed while campaign typewriters clattered in an adjacent room, Senator Harding had been "sincerely confident of victory and refreshingly devoid of excitement."

"Mr. Harding," continued the dispatch, "does not possess the volcanic energy of Roosevelt, nor the calm doctrinairism of Mr. Wilson, but he has brought off the Limitation Congress after all, and, to the disgust of the Bernhardis and the armor barons, he is going to make a success of it." Despite the generally unfavorable verdict of history on President Harding, these were accurate words. Even now, the Washington Arms Limitation Conference and the Far Eastern agreements that were a part of it stand as a hopeful contribution to world stabilization and economy, though but one step and an inadequate one.

The conference opened on Saturday, November 12. The *Monitor* as a morning newspaper could only print preliminary dispatches, and it had no Sunday paper. Hence when Monday, November 14, came, it had to catch up with the tremendous sensation made by Secretary of State Charles E. Hughes' opening proposals of drastic naval armament cuts. Its front-page dispatches connected Mr. Hughes' proposals with the results of the Paris Peace Conference, saying: "The Paris Peace Conference sought to prevent wars indirectly by the machinery of the League of Nations. The Washington Conference is to strive to prevent them directly by making it impossible for them to begin."

On the same page was an analysis of Secretary Hughes, again based on close personal contact. "As you sit in the great chair by his desk in the State Department, and listen to him discoursing on affairs from China to Peru, you cannot fail to be struck by his mastery of his facts, and the certainty of his judgment." The author recalls a revealing episode of five years before: "When he was running against Mr. Wilson for the presidency, I asked one of the astutest leaders of the Democratic Party whether he was afraid of him or not. 'That depends,' was the reply, 'If he takes the election into his own hands, yes; I have seen him campaign before. But if he lets the machine interfere, no; they will wreck him, in a sea of crocodile tears.' After the election I reminded the prophet of his prophecy. 'Oh,' he laughed, 'that was easy. He let the machine interfere.' " Mr. Hughes failed to get the Republican nomination in 1920, the article continues, because of "political and industrial reaction." President Harding then disregarded the reaction and made Mr. Hughes his Secretary of State. Thus is revealed the behind-the-scene nature of the *Monitor*'s political information and the independence of its views.

This inside position was revealed even more fully in the article on November 16 on Arthur James Balfour, Britain's Foreign Secretary and head of its delegation. It discussed Mr. Balfour in very sophisticated terms, referring to a talk which the writer had with British Prime Minister David Lloyd George, "one day in Downing Street," when the Prime Minister said enigmatically: "If ever you want an Ambassador to the Amalekites, choose Mr. Balfour." The article graphically brought out Mr. Balfour's qualities of parliamentary finesse, his intellectual profundity, and ended: "There never was anyone in the world less akin to the 'jolly bankholiday everyday young man.' Life to Mr. Balfour is a metaphysical problem, a glorified x forever demanding solution, the opportunity to know. That is why it is so embarrassing to the gentlemen who do the biographies for the newspapers, and who cannot understand that x, to use the word they so honor, is just as intriguing in the Foreign Office as in the cathedral, in the laboratory as in the theater."

Turning a few days later to Elihu Root, the former Secretary of State who was also a member of the American delegation, the writer felt that Mr. Root had not played a larger part in American affairs because of "the dormant suspicion of great ability which seems to haunt all democracies." People who say that, adds the writer, "say that it is the jealousy of the mediocre, but it is probably rather some instructive dread of the general on the black horse."

"There is a certain intellectual exclusiveness about Mr. Root which is probably the secret of the mystery: he is nearer John Hay than Mr. Roosevelt. Talk to him, as he sits in his library, without the restraint of office, and you might wonder 'that one small head should carry all he knew,' and mind you, it is not the things Main Street knows, though probably he knows them, too.

"The real key to Mr. Root's public life is that, like all great thinkers, he is an individualist. Now sometimes the individualist is ready to sink the individual in party, and in such case the earth and the fullness thereof may be his . . . This did not Mr. Root, and so when he came athwart his party on the Hay-Pauncefote treaty, he could not possibly see it their way, any more than he was able to see the League of Nations their way. Perhaps such a man has no business in a party. But if that is so, then so much the worse for the party."

Finally, said the article: "Look at Mr. Root and what do you see? A gentleman of altogether exceptional ability, gifted with an inability to see other than as he sees. This does not necessarily mean that a man is right, but it does mean that an opinion formed after careful consideration of the evidence is a valuable opinion, and one which it is naturally not easy to change. A Lloyd George jumps from opinion to opinion like a grasshopper animated by intuitions. And Elihu Root is something of a great rock in a thirsty land."

It will be seen that these articles were highly personal, opinionated, and brilliant. To call the British Prime Minister a "grasshopper animated by intuitions" is a scintillating phrase of political journalism.

In any event, a fourth character sketch published on November 21, the longest of the series, was devoted to Aristide Briand. In the light of M. Briand's later career as a peacemaker between France and Germany, it takes on double interest. It analyzes with great skill M. Briand's capacity to remain outside party lines, but to return to power whenever the country needed him. "It is necessary to defend him for his own reputation," says the *Monitor,* referring to M. Briand's label of opportunist. This view of M. Briand, it says, is unjust. "To keep his end up he has indeed to possess plenty of parliamentary craft, but that is by no means all he possesses. Time after time he has pulled his country out of difficulties and anyone who has followed his recent career must have been struck with the way in which for the first time since the armistice France is becoming practical and practicing a policy of conciliation. France is forgetting her hates and her fears. She is no longer talking night and morning of fresh invasions of Germany, of dislocation of Germany. She is sitting down quietly to talk with Germany and to frame a common scheme of mutual trust and cooperation. Nobody but Briand could have accomplished this . . ."

The article is replete with insights. As the head of a party of one, it says M. Briand has the advantage of standing outside all groups and parties and combinations, and "rides them as a circus-rider may ride four or five horses." He began as a youthful extremist, a Socialist, and "he made fiery speeches with all the simplicity of youthful ardor. This denotes at least that his sympathies are generous, and his sympathies have not altered since those early days, although he has learned moderation and knows that there can be no efficacity in a sudden change of the system of society. He is today prudent, safe, and sound but he still preserves a touch of that fine faith — for it is a fine faith even though it may express itself in unwise words — that characterized his youthful efforts to revolutionize the world."

One of the secrets of M. Briand's political success, concludes the article, is his silence when in opposition. He does not write articles or make speeches. "He relapses into silence," the *Monitor* said, "and it is perhaps his studied silence, which more than the eloquent diatribes of other men, has brought him back time after time to power. He is one of the most remarkable orators in France, with the voice of a violoncello, but if he can, as the French say, charm Parliament, if he can lull suspicions and antagonisms to sleep, if his speech is silver, his silence is often golden."

Again the verdict of history has agreed strongly with this view of M. Briand. In the years following 1922, his role as a peacemaker became dominant. Even in Geneva, where his violoncello voice so often charmed the statesmen of the world while I was a correspondent there, it was also true that his silences were just as eloquent.

Still another article, on Sir Robert Borden, Canadian war-time leader, revealed an intimacy of knowledge: "It was in the winter of 1914 that I first met Sir Robert Borden. The snow was deep in the grounds of the old Parliament House, and it was as cold as it can be in Ottawa. I had come to Ottawa to talk to him about political conditions, for the war was making great demands on the press, and safe information was as valuable as the writer of Proverbs claimed rubies to be. Seated opposite to him in his office I learned how kind and generous he could be in his desire to help, a desire which has only deepened through the intervening years. Sir Robert had gone into the war for the sake of humanity, and he was already resolving those broad and unselfish schemes for uniting all Canada in the effort; schemes which perhaps only his own disinterestedness could have made so entirely successful . . . He built up an ideal of leadership which will not be lightly forgotten by his countrymen."

Once more, this is a position with which history heartily accords.

A few years before, the *Monitor*'s London correspondent, Algernon Hervey-Bathurst, had been told by Lord Beaverbrook that Sir Robert Borden was a careful reader of the *Monitor*, clipping, marking, and saving its articles.

The *Monitor*'s coverage of the Washington conference was, of course, far from limited to such studies of leadership. Its regular daily dispatches were expert, and made use of novel as well as obvious sources. The paper was especially interested in the economic consequences of the conference. But its deepest concern, alongside the basic task of stopping the building race in naval armament, was the solution of problems of the Pacific. It sturdily supported the fabric of treaties that emerged from the conference.

The transition of control of the *Monitor*, which took place in the very midst of the conference, made no difference to the zeal and effectiveness of its coverage. The editorial position over Japan changed, in emphasis at least. Intense personal editorializing, both on the editorial page and in special articles, disappeared. Otherwise, the paper's commitment to careful coverage of international affairs grew not one whit less. Rather, the coverage became broader as it became less personal.

Soon the Permanent Court of International Justice held its inaugural session at The Hague, and all the hopes in the justiciable settlement of international disputes which Americans had cherished in the years before the world war sprang again to the fore. The *Monitor* was a fervent supporter of American membership in the World Court. When President Harding proposed American adherence, it did everything it could to support the step. But once again the isolationist forces in the Senate were too strong, and the same epithets and bitterness filled the air which had marked the League of Nations fight.

Patiently the *Monitor* emphasized the role the United States must play in peace making and preserving. Its voice helped to support the Administration in such steps as it was able to take. In particular, the *Monitor* emphasized the American involvement in the debts and reparations discussions. In an editorial urging American participation in the Genoa Conference, which had been called to consider economic and financial problems arising in the peace making, the *Monitor* said:

> The United States has never — whatever theorists may urge — enjoyed splendid isolation. It had hardly passed from the stage of a loose confederation to that of a nation when its growing foreign commerce dragged it into the Napoleonic wars, and the only time since 1812 when it was wholly free from foreign problems were those when it was almost equally devoid of world trade.
>
> If there were ever a time when a conventual retirement from the world were possible to the United States that time is not now. No nation, more than any man, can be sufficient unto itself. No man was ever enriched by withholding his meed from the general service, nor impoverished by giving freely of the best that is in him for the general good. That is as true of nations as it is of individuals.
>
> It is in the firm conviction of the truth of this proposition that The Christian Science Monitor urges upon the people of the United States the worldly wisdom and the Christian duty of participating in all conferences designed to bring stability to Europe. The Washington Conference was a beginning that revived a hope which

languished in the world after the repudiation of all that had been done at Paris. Let not Washington in turn be followed by a new withdrawal from the plain duties of the day.

This was unequivocal language. It was apparent that the *Monitor*'s editorial voice was newly firm and confident, and more capable of speaking directly "to the people of the United States" than it had been before. Indeed, the policy advocated in this editorial went substantially beyond the positions advocated in the recently preceding years. But it was not followed by the American government, which in March, 1922, declined to participate in the Genoa Conference.

To attest its right to speak "to the people of the United States," the paper gave its news attention more effectively to their problems. And it broadened its interests. Thus on February 20, the major story on page one, with picture, was of the appointment of Judge Kenesaw Mountain Landis to be baseball commissioner. It was the first story dealing with sports to appear on the front page for some time. And, to demonstrate its new freedom to cover the news, the paper led page one on February 21 with the story of the wreck of the Army dirigible *Roma*. Again, it was back in the early days — when Mrs. Eddy was observing the paper in person — that similar treatment of great disasters was to be found. The inhibitions of the years from 1914 to 1922 were by no means all gone, but they were beginning to be peeled away.

On March 3, 1922, as the Harding Administration ended its first year in office, long before the scandals which wrecked it came to light, the *Monitor* analyzed the first year. It recalled that just a century before, the Administration of President James Monroe had started out as an "era of good feelings," and ended in debacle.

Prophetically it asked, would the same thing happen again? And it said: "President Harding approaches the beginning of his second year with the nation turning from the most generous and unlimited approbation toward an attitude at least of criticism and doubt . . . People are beginning to ask whether he is capable of handling the tools which under the Constitution are given him for the purpose of accomplishing these ends. They charge against him the unquestioned failures of Congress, and the elements of dissatisfaction and revolt arising in that body and becoming visible throughout the political organization of the United States are a sufficient warning that more force, more determination, more self-assertion in the presidency are likely to be needed if the collapse of the era of good feeling of a century ago is not to be repeated in 1924."

The *Monitor*'s apprehensions were shown to be only too well founded, though in a manner which it could not have foreseen fully in 1922.

A little later in 1922, Britain gave independence to Egypt, and the *Monitor* analyzed the terms of Britain's new relationship to empire in words once more prophetic and farseeing. It said: "Great Britain stands for empire and liberty; stands for empire as a means for liberty. Nor does she forget the corollary: without liberty there can be no empire. Freedom is the first condition for survival of empire, and so of the preservation of every actual and potential good which an empire can confer upon civilization. Force, other than in the service of freedom, spells disruption. The living empire must be increasingly free and increasingly cooperative. Under force it must harden into a brittle structure which would break into fragments with slight external pressure, whereas the strongest pressure from without could only increase the toughness and elasticity of a voluntary union and association in support of mutual interest and a common political doctrine."

However, the *Monitor* was not blind to Britain's unfinished imperial business. Mahatma Gandhi's nonviolence movement was in full operation, and in March he was arrested.

Gandhism [said the *Monitor* editorially] is no longer a personal creed, but a great popular movement in India. As Gandhi goes to prison he leaves with his followers the same message that his lieutenants who preceded him had reiterated: Abandon violence, all ye who would enter into true liberty!

It is shortsighted to imagine that the great reforms in India in the past few years, reforms that point directly toward autonomy and home rule, and since 1915 toward a real self-sufficiency for a reconstituted India, will go for naught because of a few cases of callous or even (as at Amritsar) of criminal ineptitude. England has an endless capacity for exasperation, but she has a parallel profound capacity for learning from her own mistakes. She can make, as in South Africa and as lately in Ireland, a vital surrender seem like a moral victory.

Among the recent instances of her aptitude for exasperation, it must be admitted now that the tour of the Prince of Wales has turned out to be singularly unfortunate at this time. It is no one's fault, least of all the gallant and well-intentioned Prince's. But the spectacle of innocuous royalty passing through an India at grips with such terrible realities as we see in the contributing causes of Gandhi's arrest, flaunted in the faces of serious Indians a symbol of irritating complacency which only increases their bitterness. India is not a succession of hunting-grounds and reception marquees, but a modern statesman's first-class problem. The approach to this problem is not one that royalty, even in the best Victorian tradition, can usefully make.

This is strong, independent journalism. Considering that the *Monitor* had many British readers, many of whom had little sympathy for Gandhi and his nonresistance movement, and profound belief in the institution and efficacy of royalty, the *Monitor*'s position was challenging. It is a position which has been reinforced by the verdict of history. It is quite possible the editorial was contributed by one who for many years was extraordinary helpful in the *Monitor*'s world-visioned utility: Philip Kerr, later Marquess of Lothian. As a thoughtful Christian Scientist, Lord Lothian took a great interest in the *Monitor* and often wrote for its columns, later with many signed articles. For years he wrote a regular editorial-page column, "The Diary of a Political Pilgrim." In the 1930's he was chairman of the British delegation to the Round Table Conference, which did the key planning that later led to Indian independence, and his authority on Indian matters appears in the foregoing editorial. In 1939 he became British Ambassador to the United States.

20

Rebuilding a Staff

It was manifest, as the new regime went ahead with the *Monitor*, that major staff strengthening was necessary. A number of experienced staff members had left with the return of the paper to the Directors. The recruitment of a staff in the years when the litigation overhung the paper had been far from normal. Some who had gone to war had not returned.

Two sensible processes were at once employed. For the long-range rebuilding of the staff, promising young people were hired and put into training. For immediate needs, special dispatches and articles were obtained from experienced journalists. Some of the recruits of that period are still with the paper. Many have gone to other fields of journalism.

Two young reporters who began at once to pull useful editorial oars were Richard Lee Strout and Stanley High. Mr. Strout, then a young man just out of Harvard, had gone to Sheffield, England, to gain reportorial experience at the working level on a British provincial newspaper. On his return to the United States he was hired by the *Monitor,* worked on its Boston staff for three and one half years, and then was transferred to Washington, where he has remained ever since.

Mr. Strout was then and is now a tireless reporter, with an impressive literary style and a sharp eye for color and human interest. One of his earliest identified articles was an editorial-page piece, "Random Interviews," printed on October 16, 1923. It recounts talks with Eugene Debs, William E. Borah, and Joseph Conrad, surely a trio of very interesting and very different human beings. Senator Borah remained one of Mr. Strout's favorite characters to the very end, and many were the confidential talks they had in Washington. Sometimes they met in Rock Creek Park at the Washington Zoo, which both enjoyed. No correspondent now writing in Washington has been for a longer period a closer observer of the United States Senate than Mr. Strout.

Stanley High, who came to the *Monitor* in 1923, was then a young theological student at Boston University and an active participant in youth movements. He went to China, and wrote a book about it when doing so was only a degree less adventurous than it was in 1957 and 1958. For the *Monitor,* he did many useful jobs. In 1923 he was assigned to cover the trip of Britain's recently retired Prime Minister David Lloyd George as he traversed the United States. Later he did a series of articles from the Soviet Union, with relatively little naïveté and more than a few insights.

Mr. High left the *Monitor* to go actively into Methodist Church work, and held a pastorate in Darien, Connecticut. But his heart was in journalism and public affairs. He is one of the few men, surely, who have written speeches for Presidents or Presidential candidates of opposite political parties in sequence. He did this for Franklin Roosevelt in 1936 and Thomas E. Dewey in 1944 and 1948, and for Dwight D. Eisenhower in 1952. Later he became a senior editor of the *Reader's Digest.*

These young men, and many others over several decades, were members of what they liked to call the Deland School of Journalism. They all worked under the tutelage of Paul S. Deland, for most of this period city editor of the *Monitor*, and hence in charge of the training of its cubs.

Others in the same rigorous school were Roscoe Drummond, who made a large contribution to the paper which will be set forth in its proper sequence, and myself. An alumna of the Deland School was Margaret Lee Runbeck, later a popular novelist and magazine feature writer.

All of us were subjected to a kind but uncompromising course of sprouts. Mr. Deland's pedagogy, as it impressed me, was in three parts: (1) the tradition and commitment of the Monitor itself; (2) the use of words; and (3) the development of ideas. As a pioneer member of the paper's staff, Mr. Deland was deeply imbued with its obligation to "turn the news right side up," as he often said.

Thus, instead of permitting neophyte reporters to emphasize the aspects which other newspapers would feature in covering situations — conflict, passion, shock, and such things — Mr. Deland would require them to seek out elements of genuine and long-range significance. His system of value judgments was filled with integrity: stories must have social importance, lasting meaning.

Furthermore, a reporter had sometimes the obligation to protect a public man from misstatement or rash impulse. We must seek out his meaning and reflect it truly. More than once as a young reporter I have turned in an interview to Mr. Deland, only to have him bounce it right back to me with the comment: "I expect the man said what you have quoted, but that isn't what he meant." Then he would explain the viewpoint and commitment of the public figure, which I would recognize as valid. I would go back to the interviewee to get a better quotation, or put his real meaning into indirect discourse.

Invariably this scrupulous care produced gratitude and respect from the public man, who saw that the *Monitor* was striving to get penetratingly into his thinking and to present it accurately. Such journalism was not merely careful, it had a profound responsibility to real meanings and, indeed, to history. Perhaps that is another reason why the *Monitor*'s columns stand up so well in retrospect many decades later.

Mr. Deland's insistence on the exactness and precision of words was one of the greatest of his lessons. So simple a newspaper cliché as "Jones declared" taught an illustrative point. "Never use the verb 'declare,'" Mr. Deland insisted, "unless the man made what can accurately be called a declaration. If he just 'said' it, then use the verb 'say.'" He taught us the difference between "say" and "declare" and "affirm" and all the other verbs one can use in quoting a public statement. We could not use these words loosely. Every single word had to have meaning.

Stern discipline is absolutely necessary to inexperienced writers. They must learn the value of words, the individuality of each one of them. Mr. Deland taught us that no two words ever mean exactly the same. It was our job as writers to make sure we found just the correct word for every usage. He made us rewrite our copy time and time again. The *Monitor* has always sought to publish a brisk, newsy paper, but it has never been the abject slave of the clock. The kind of copy Mr. Deland made us rewrite time after time was usually copy unrelated to a daily event. It was often exclusive to the *Monitor*.

I can remember many a dreary trudge back to my desk after Mr. Deland had bluntly torn my copy to figurative shreds. At first I was more than a little frightened of him. His uncompromising words made me quake within, but did me a world of good. Roscoe Drummond, now a widely syndicated national columnist, recalls that more than one night he resolved to quit his job the following morning, so sensitive was he under the tight Deland harness. But quit he never did, and the time soon came when Mr. Deland made him his assistant and imposed full confidence in him. That was an important point: when you had worked your way through the Deland School of Journalism the diploma was friendship and confidence.

The *Monitor* had another inspiring journalism teacher who will be discussed more fully when he enters the story in sequence, Charles E. Gratke, for many years foreign editor, who was lost with the planeload of American journalists returning from Indonesia in July, 1949.

Few other factors are more important in the development of the *Monitor* as it evolved from the 1920's to the 1950's than the training of expert and deeply grounded staff members. In the first decade of the paper's history everything had to be done from scratch. There was no pattern of *Monitor* journalism. All concepts and practices had to be worked out. Some had to be discarded. Men whose training had been in very different schools had much to unlearn. Sometimes they did not go far enough. Sometimes they went too far in this process. Then, with the litigation, there came such a turnover of staff that the process of maturing and training almost had to begin all over again. The unbroken line of Mr. Deland's teaching was of double advantage. And as the 1920's advanced into the 1930's, the men and women of the staff began to come into their own. Confidence and skill replaced experimentation. The men were separated from the boys. The true professionals with an expert capacity to practice real *Monitor* journalism replaced the incompetents, the time-servers, or the merely zealous.

In 1922 this process of new staff recruitment was only beginning. It would bear great fruitage in time, but the paper had to be published every day. It had to be improved. Therefore the sensible expedient was adopted of buying copy from trained journalists who for one reason or another, were not available as staff correspondents, but who could provide first-rate copy without delay.

By-lines of distinction began to appear in the paper's columns within a few weeks after the new control was installed. One of the first was that of Frederick William Wile, writing from Washington. Mr. Wile was then connected with the eminent Philadelphia *Public Ledger* syndicate. His first few articles, which included special interpretive news dispatches and a roundup Washington column, were credited to the *Public Ledger* syndicate. But soon an arrangement was made to obtain them exclusively. For seven years, until 1929, Mr. Wile supplemented the work of the *Monitor*'s own Washington Bureau. He was a thoroughly experienced and competent correspondent, both in Europe and America. He had been in Berlin working for Lord Northcliffe's *Daily Mail* when the First World War broke out. Since he was an American citizen he could remain there for a considerable period, though Lord Northcliffe was double-dyed anathema to the Germans. After his *Monitor* service, Mr. Wile became a pioneer radio commentator for the Columbia Broadcasting System. For some years, his talks were very widely followed in American homes. He might be called a pre-Murrow Murrow. Two more different human beings can scarcely be imagined.

On July 16, 1923, writing from Wyoming during a cross-country political survey which overlapped President Harding's ill-fated journey across the continent, to Alaska, and back to San Francisco, where he died, Mr. Wile wrote what seems to be the *Monitor*'s first interpretive discussion of the Teapot Dome oil leases. The situation had only barely emerged into the news. Reports of the leases had come to attention in early 1922, had been stoutly defended by President Harding, and had been taken for granted by nearly everybody. It was eighteen months before the painstaking investigation conducted by Senator Thomas J. Walsh of Montana began to uncover the scandals. Not until October 25, 1923, did the Walsh hearings begin.

Mr. Wile wrote:

The Wyomingites would like very much to have heard from President Harding on the Teapot Dome oil affair. A few heart-to-heart remarks on that subject would have come straight home to them . . . Unless present indications are deceptive, the Teapot Dome affair is going to cause the Republican Party trouble in 1924. It may even rise up to bother so invulnerable a candidate as Senator Warren, who generally is regarded unbeatable in the state in which he arrived a poor lad nearly 60 years ago, and which has honored him time and again with every office in its gift. Mr. Warren concedes that conditions are "serious" for the Republican

Party, though he radiates confidence that the Harding visitation has done wonders in rehabilitating Republican fortunes. Wyoming ranks as the fifth oil-producing state in the United States.

Read in retrospect, these words do not seem at all remarkable. But they were written three months before Senator Walsh was to call former Secretary of the Interior Albert B. Fall to the stand, and when he did, as Mark Sullivan reports in volume six of *Our Times,* page 293, "the impression Fall made on his hearers was distinctly favorable . . . The despatches that went out to the country intimated that Walsh was on a preposterously false trail." So Mr. Wile's sharp nose for news had detected something wrong in the state of Wyoming, and passed it on to his *Monitor* readers.

To cover the burgeoning field of aeronautics, the *Monitor* turned to a neighbor at Massachusetts Institute of Technology, Professor Edward P. Warner. He wrote a weekly column on aviation from 1923 to 1926, when he became the first Assistant Secretary of Commerce for Air, under Calvin Coolidge. His contribution to the development of commercial aviation was very great, both in the *Monitor* and in the Department of Commerce.

Even before the *Monitor*'s staff needs of 1922 became apparent, it had been using experienced journalists on a space or retainer basis. One of the most reliable and productive of these was Crawfurd Price. He had worked in the Balkans for *The Times* of London, but had returned to Britain as the result — it would seem — of a coup in walnuts. Whether this also resulted in his parting company with *The Times* is not clarified in the massive six-volume history of the "Thunderer."

It appears, as Walter Cunningham remembers the situation, that Mr. Price observed the failure of the walnut crop in Eastern Europe, where he was stationed, and proceeded to invest heavily in Spanish walnuts. If he did not corner the European market he did well enough in that direction. With his tidy earnings, he retired to London, where he bought a hotel or two, and kept his journalistic hand in practice by writing for the *Monitor* and others. His work as it appears in the paper's columns for nine years, is sober and competent. Originally he was to cover the Versailles Conference for the *Monitor,* but found it was more than he could swing. So he turned the job over to another British journalist who was to have a much longer connection with the paper: Sisley Huddleston.

Mr. Huddleston wrote for the *Monitor,* usually from Paris, from 1919 to 1939. He, too, was connected with a Liberal British newspaper, being also Paris correspondent for the *Westminster Gazette,* and later for Lord Northcliffe's *Times.* Such doubling-up prevailed in *Monitor* experience only for a brief time. Soon *Monitor* staff correspondents wrote for no other daily newspapers and had no other staff connections. Sisley Huddleston's daily newspaper writing became exclusive to the *Monitor* in 1924.

Mr. Huddleston is one of the most colorful and perhaps cryptic characters in the history of latter-day journalism. He was a Yorkshireman, but he left his native shores early, and in Paris became more Bohemian than the Parisians, in the best Left Bank manner. He lived on the Boulevard Raspail, he wore an artist's flowing Windsor tie, and broad-brimmed stiff black hat. His mustache and goatee, uncompromisingly red in hue, added to the artistic impression, as did his given name Sisley, for the French painter. He was portly, he carried an ivory or gold-headed cane, and he knew everyone — political or artistic — in Paris.

Perhaps his most sensational journalistic coup was an unacknowledged interview with Lloyd George on March 31, 1919, in which the British statesman, then at the Versailles Conference, preached the doctrine of a sensible and moderate peace with Germany. The interview created a sensation, and was followed by a telegram signed by no less than 370 M.P.'s demanding a more punitive peace settlement. The dispatch, which was more or less confirmed by Mr. Lloyd George a few years later, proved that at the very time of the peace making two of the big four, Lloyd George and Wilson, knew that an impossible and harmful treaty was being drafted. Mr. Huddleston's skill in obtaining this information from Lloyd George shows how well informed and well connected he was at the peace conference. Few other correspondents for newspapers published in the United States, at least, had closer sources of information. The interview also adds a footnote to the grim history of Versailles which is of some importance.

For the next fifteen years, Sisley Huddleston served the *Monitor* skillfully. But his later career reveals the cryptic side to his character. And it casts something of a cloud over much of his relationship to the *Monitor*. At all times he was a thoroughly workmanlike writer. He wrote with flair and dash, not hesitating to introduce the first personal pronoun in the British manner, and to splash the colors of the diplomatic world in which he mingled.

Where the sometimes naïve hopes of the *Monitor* could have been importantly balanced and rectified by cautions from Mr. Huddleston, it got very little. At times he seems to have been writing to please what he thought to be the *Monitor*'s policy. His copy had more virtuosity than virtue in it. And for a number of years nobody in an authoritative position on the *Monitor* did anything about it.

At the core of Mr. Huddleston's thinking was a profound distrust of the whole concept of collective security. He did not believe in the effort to enforce peace. He condemned the power of public opinion and of democratic elements in the conduct of foreign relations. The fearful carnage of the First World War, during which he was in France, though incapacitated from military service himself, seems to have bitten deeply into his consciousness.

Then, in the first postwar period, he was close enough to the political leaders of all principal countries to see their feet of clay. He had nostalgia for earlier modes of diplomacy. But, as he explains clearly in his autobiography, *In My Time*, published only in 1938 when his relationship to the *Monitor* was about at an end, his idea for the solution of the problem of peace lay in "the education of a cosmopolitan elite." *

He called for "recognition of the mischievousness of Conferences and all forms of public demonstration and disputation

* P. 402.

on foreign affairs, and their abandonment. This sort of claptrap demogogic diplomacy has, whether practised in or out of the League, been one of the most sinister agents of self-seeking politicians, fire-eating Imperialists, sadistic belli-pacifists, revolutionary Communists who would plunge the world into a bath of blood, frenetic 'antis' and muddleheaded reformers." *

Huddleston copy did not leave readers with an altogether false picture of European problems. The overwhelming part of it was objective enough reporting. A vast amount of information was communicated to readers by Sisley Huddleston with great ability. The *Monitor* need not be ashamed for printing almost everything he wrote for it. It was far better than much other correspondence of the period; but at its heart lay a concept that rejected nearly everything he was reporting and turned toward sinister models.

Ultimately, the weakness in Mr. Huddleston's world outlook came to the surface. He could not conceal it in his writings, it took him off the *Monitor* staff, and led him into political exile.

In the later 1930's into Mr. Huddleston's writing there began to creep notes of admiration for the Fascist dictators of Europe — Mussolini, Franco, and even Hitler. He spoke sympathetically of the need for strong-arm government in France. His criticism of the efforts to curb Hitler was outspoken. In short, Mr. Huddleston began to write like a full-fledged Fascist. The *Monitor* could not print this sort of copy.

Already in 1930, the *Monitor* had attenuated Mr. Huddleston's correspondence with the paper, sending a staff correspondent and bureau chief to Paris, and using only general dispatches from Mr. Huddleston. So it was an amicable matter to terminate his connection with the *Monitor*. He was busy with magazine and book writing. During the Second World War, he chose to remain in Vichy and Monaco, broadcasting on the Nazi-controlled Vichy radio, calling upon his British countrymen to refrain from bombing French targets, and singing the praises of Marshal Pétain's government.

* *In My Time,* p. 399.

When the war was over, he sought the *Monitor*'s help in transferring himself and his assets from Monaco to Switzerland. Despite his record, which was fully publicized at the time, Mr. Huddleston was able to find a respectable American publisher for a postwar book summarizing his reflections on the diplomacy of the century. In at least one American magazine of wide circulation, his opinions were praised.

If I seem to have written with some feeling on the Huddleston episode, it is simply because I believe so earnestly that he and one or two other persons who were trusted by the paper might have enhanced their considerable services to it by words of warning in time. Before his Fascist later days, Mr. Huddleston knew many pitfalls which the *Monitor* could have avoided. Happily it did skirt most of them, but not all.

All this was far ahead and unforeseen in 1922–23. In those years and for long afterward, Mr. Huddleston provided *Monitor* readers with a sophisticated, extensive, knowledgeable, and intelligent flow of copy. A larger content of integrity would have made it invulnerable. Happily, as time went on, the *Monitor* developed correspondents whom it could trust, whose deepest commitments were not ambiguous, and whose dedication to *Monitor* ideals was deep and genuine.

In the galaxy of trained professionals, the experience with Sisley Huddleston is virtually unique. Another important British acquisition in October, 1923, was the weekly "A British Onlooker's Diary" by H. W. Massingham, which continued until 1924. Mr. Massingham had been from 1907 to 1923 editor of the London weekly the *Nation*, and he had been editor of the *Star* and the *Daily Chronicle*. He was a sage observer of firmly Liberal view, one of the pillars of early-century British journalism.

At just about this time, when the Liberal Party was beginning its tragic decline after centuries of eminence, from Whig days onward, a number of London dailies formerly published in the Liberal interest were consolidated and vanished. Several first-rate journalists looked around for other connections, and a number of them began to write occasionally for the *Monitor*.

One of them, Hugh Spender — brother of the more famous J. A. Spender and Harold Spender — came on the paper's staff, first in London and later in Geneva.

My own first overseas assignment was in 1926 as an assistant to Mr. Spender in Geneva. He was an experienced but rather fluttery gentleman, exceedingly kind to a very green cub. I was in Geneva during vacations from Oxford University, where I was a Rhodes Scholar. I happened to be an undergraduate at Hugh Spender's old college, Oriel. Nobody had given Mr. Spender any particular instructions in *Monitor* journalism. He usually wrote competent dispatches in the British newspaper style. They well illustrated the gap between the *Monitor* neophytes — of whom I was one — and the non-Monitor veterans to whom the paper turned in the early 1920's.

Among those who were swiftly recruited in 1922 to give the paper strength and seasoning, the average quotient of capacity and integrity was very high. And the realism came as well. For instance, H. W. Massingham never hesitated to express his doubts about the ways in which peace making was being pursued in the early 1920's. Sometimes his doubts were not shared by the paper.

Thus, on November 1, 1923, the Massingham column on the editorial page expresses the feeling that the Reparations Conference about to be held was bound to be a failure. The *Monitor* printed the Massingham column, but on the same page printed an editorial taking issue with it. The editorial turned out to be right. Indeed, the successions of financial revision which the Reparations Conference started, became the only sound form of revisionism in the period between the wars.

A literary star from an entirely different galaxy began to write for the *Monitor* in 1923. It was V. S. Pritchett, who later became one of the most eminent British critics and a novelist of some distinction. The *Monitor* may fairly claim to have discovered Mr. Pritchett and brought him first, as a very young writer, to the attention of a wide audience. He began to write charming sketches of Ireland. Later he went to Spain, and if his travels there are not recorded in prose of the quality of George Borrow they are fairly close to it. Mr. Pritchett later included bitter satiric sketches of Christian Scientists in at least one of his novels. But his work which the *Monitor* published stands there in the files, delicious and talented writing, giving promise of the lofty literary figure who was to emerge.

Use of such literary sketches as those of V. S. Pritchett were the least of the *Monitor*'s attention to the arts. Contributors to "The Home Forum," which in the 1920's settled into something like its present form with a daily light essay in the best literary tradition, were of a consistently high order.

At all times throughout the half century, the *Monitor* has kept up its steady interest in all the arts. At all times it has had eminent theatrical and musical critics on its own staff, writing full time. Ernest C. Sherburne, whose youthful adventures in The Christian Science Publishing Society from 1898 on have already been mentioned, kept a wise and discriminating eye on the theatre for a quarter of a century, and then edited the *Monitor*'s weekly magazine section for a decade. I have gone with "Sherb" to the dressing rooms of some of the most eminent stars to pay our respects, and there to observe the affection and regard with which they hailed him.

The *Monitor*'s critics have been as complete individualists as their colleagues everywhere. "Sherb" was a kindly critic, whose attitude toward stage and life was generous and mellow. But his taste never yielded to compromise even when his dissents were expressed in quiet key or by omission. He was a constructive critic in the best sense of the term. Also in New York, previously referred to as one of the *Monitor*'s pioneers, was music critic Winthrop Pitt Tryon. He is a man of vast learning, and his criticism, like his prose style, is distinctive and authoritative.

On the Boston staff, most of the time as arts editor, was Leslie A. Sloper. He supervised the other critics' work and himself covered an immense field. In addition to scrutinizing and managing the criticism from New York, London, and other world capitals, he also reviewed plays in Boston and the

Boston Symphony Orchestra concerts, and supervised the *Monitor*'s book reviewing! He even wrote, for seven years, a delightful column called "A Bookman's Holiday."

Leslie Sloper was a critic's critic, and a pungent and forceful wielder of the analytical pen. He said frankly what he did not like, with clinical directness. As a result, though his judgment was constantly respected and his criticisms — especially of plays — sometimes led to constructive and successful revisions, in the tryout city of Boston, he was not especially popular with managements.

So it was at the Boston Symphony concerts, which he reviewed for twenty-seven years. Sometimes Leslie's candor outraged sentimentalists when he spoke with critical freedom of their favorite popular singer. Once a widely admired radio singer gave a recital in Symphony Hall. It was admitted by those who knew that this tenor's voice did not begin to compare with that of concert artists. Mr. Sloper said so. And the office was swamped next day by admirers of the popular singer, some of them with considerable influence and authority. The critic had to be defended against his critics.

The nature of critical responsibilities is not something that laymen, and laywomen, always understand. But the *Monitor* has found that there are ways of maintaining high critical standards without egregiously offending sensibilities. Mr. Sloper was a better critic than he was a diplomat. His work gave the paper lofty artistic standards, and he was a trojan for production. How he ever did so much is astonishing. He passed on in what one of his fellow critics described as just the way a critic should go, quietly, without a murmur, in his seat on the aisle at the Boston Opera House. At his side was his brilliant wife Margaret Lloyd, who then and now furnishes the *Monitor* with some of the most expert dance criticism in America. Mrs. Sloper has singlehandedly kept the *Monitor* at the forefront of dance reportage for over two decades. This is one of the possibly minor distinctions of which it is very proud.

Since this summary of arts criticism in the *Monitor* has ranged from the 1920's well up to the present, it is timely to speak of the remarkable individual who has covered the British theatre for the *Monitor* since the early 1930's. Harold Hobson's life story is a romance which he will perhaps publish someday.

He was born of parents in the most modest of circumstances at Sheffield, England, laid low with a paralytic attack when a small child, healed by Christian Science before he went to school, and learned to read at his mother's knee from the novels of Sir Walter Scott, which were almost their only books. His is a success story more typically associated with the New World.

As a small boy, seriously deformed, walking only with a stick and a trick of carrying his hand in his trouser pocket to pull his game leg along, Harold first applied for admittance to a school in Sheffield. The school was far above his parents' station and finances. At first rejected, then accepted, he went sailing through school. He became the first of its graduates to go either to Oxford or Cambridge. Attracted to Oriel College, Oxford, because of Thomas Hardy's Jude the Obscure (who made a similar appeal to an Oxford Provost) Harold was again rejected and then accepted.

His successful Oxford career opened new vistas to him, expecially of the magic world behind the footlights. So he went to London and knocked on the *Monitor*'s door. Again rejected, he was permitted to submit copy at space rates. Soon he wrote so much which couldn't be turned down that it was cheaper to put him on salary! From that time forth, early in the 1930's, Harold Hobson has made a name for himself, first in the British theatre and then on the Continent. In addition to his *Monitor* post, he has been for several years chief theatre critic of the *Sunday Times* of London, succeeding James Agate.

Harold Hobson's writing for the *Monitor* for a quarter of a century has brought the flavor of London's rich and abundant theatre to a worldwide audience. Latterly he has made a serious study of the French theatre, and writes about it with authority. He has busily published books of criticism. His views are original, flavored with historical and literary lore and spiced with wit.

21

Turmoil of Politics

THE DEATH OF Warren G. Harding in the Palace Hotel in San Francisco, on August 2, 1923, gave the *Monitor* a test which it passed with flying colors. He was the first President to pass on in public office since the *Monitor* had been established.

Some who have written about the *Monitor* on the basis of inadequate research, have said that "death never appears in its columns." This has never been so. There are few persons, if any, of genuine importance during the half century whose deaths have not been reported in the *Monitor,* although with restraint.

But in the case of President Harding, there was simply straight journalistic coverage. The front-page full-width banner headline read: HARDING PASSES ON — COOLIDGE IS PRESIDENT. The middle three columns were filled with a singularly sympathetic and gracious portrait of the handsome President. The leading story, from San Francisco, told in straightforward terms of the President's passing. A two-column box recorded the achievements of the Harding Administration. At the opposite side of the page, in columns one and two, was a balancing two-column box giving the outstanding details in the career of Calvin Coolidge. Beneath was the dramatic story from Plymouth, Vermont, telling how Calvin Coolidge took the oath of office under kerosene lamps, at the hand of his father, John C. Coolidge.

Today, impressed as we are with the subsequent revelations of the Teapot Dome Scandal and President Harding's personal weaknesses, it is difficult to conceive the affection and respect with which he was held at the time of his death. He was a well-loved President. He had brought "normalcy" to a country which had just gone through the intense emotional struggle of America's First World War and first global peace making. His public acts and his speeches, up to the time of his passing, had contained elements of evident magnanimity. Seldom has the verdict of public opinion been so sharply reversed as it was during the following year.

Even in the light of all that is known today, the Harding Administration was not without its achievements. When unemotional historians assess it, they find such major virtues as: the choice of Charles E. Hughes as Secretary of State and unswerving support for him in the Washington Arms Limitation Conference; the choice of Herbert Hoover as Secretary of Commerce, with the many vigorous policies he instituted in trying to bring American business into the modern world of social responsibility; the choice of the elder Henry Wallace as Secretary of Agriculture, in an effort to meet the problems of the American farm on a moderately progressive basis. President Harding also strove diligently to bring the United States into the World Court. He brought pressure unremittingly on "Big Steel" until by his persuasion the industry changed to the eight-hour day from the twelve-hour day, with its "stretchouts" every two weeks of twenty-four hours' continuous employment.

The achievement of the eight-hour day was an illustration of the best in Warren G. Harding. He did not bully the industry leaders, did not assail inhuman working conditions in their plants, but invited 41 of them to dinner at the White House. There he set before them the case for a reduction in hours. What Mark Sullivan calls his "good-natured insistence" won. On August 2, the very day of the President's passing, Judge Elbert H. Gary, head of the United States Steel Corporation and president of the American Iron and Steel Institute, announced that elimination of the twelve-hour day would begin at once.

Warren Harding also instituted the federal budget system, and appointed Charles G. Dawes, later Vice-President, as budget director. This was one of the most notable steps of the century in improving the orderliness and economy of the federal government. President Harding stood firm against the demands for a soldier's bonus. He enforced the prohibition amendment as diligently as possible.

But for the oil stains of Teapot Dome, and the "cronies" who catered to the genial Ohioan's weaknesses, President Harding would have left an impressive record. His stock was high in 1923. But the *Monitor* nevertheless found on August 3 some elements to deplore. They were the very elements which were later shown to have been President Harding's undoing.

After an opening paragraph referring to the international and national issues which were "seething and seeking new forms and outlets" the paper's front-page dispatch said:

> He brought to this stupendous task no proportionate equipment of tried and proved statesmanship. He did face it with a touching humility, an expressed desire to learn, and a yearning to do the right thing for all the people. Those who saw him from time to time at close range, watched his mental processes and his political and official acts, observed Mr. Harding groping for the right move, listening to the counsel of trusted friends . . .
>
> Mr. Harding was swayed by personal influences to a large degree in many instances, but that he was able to adopt a comparatively independent line at times is what many persons who knew him well had not expected . . . President Harding was comparatively happy in his political family. There were divergences within the Cabinet. It could not be otherwise with men of such varying caliber and experiences, but so far as the country knew they were all loyal to

their chief. . . . Mr. Harding's genial kindness to persons of all degrees was one of his strongest characteristics. It began with his staunch friends, which sometimes led him to appoint friends to high places to which they were not suited . . .

The failures of President Harding were due to mistaken actions based on good impulses but unguarded by sufficient wisdom and information. In part he was the victim, as many a one before him, of circumstances with which he had no more to do than any other citizen in the country. He typified a system and it was the system which was condemned. His successes were due to honesty and good intention and favoring winds.

In the face of whatever was known in August, 1923, this is an estimate with which few historians will quarrel. It is fair, even in the light of all that is known today. In the entire dispatch, there was no mawkishness or fulsomeness.

On the editorial page, and repeatedly for many weeks afterward, the *Monitor* argued for a reassessment of the duties of the Presidency so they would not bear so heavily on the individual. But of course Calvin Coolidge, the Massachusetts neighbor who moved so unexpectedly into the White House, saw to it that the cares of state did not grind down the President. His attitude suited many at the time; it has not received the approval of history, and properly so. Furthermore, some of the cares which beset Warren Harding, and may have laid him low, were cares of his own making compounded by the venality of some of his friends.

With Calvin Coolidge the *Monitor* had been on very good terms for many years. The new President had been especially fond of the *Monitor*'s Massachusetts State House correspondent, Rush T. Jones. This delightful and — in many ways — typical old-time newspaperman was a great comfort to "Silent Cal" in some of his moments of relentless taciturnity. Soon after the new President entered the White House, Rush wrote for the *Monitor* the story of the Saturday afternoon when Governor Coolidge had summoned him to his little back rooms at Boston's Adams House for the express purpose of listening to him talk. Rush wrote:

"Come in," called the Coolidge voice when I knocked, as the Governor himself opened the door, hand extended, and a smile, for which he appeared to be sorry immediately afterward, flitted over his composed face.

Then Calvin Coolidge looked at me and I looked at him. I haven't any idea how long this lasted, but I began to feel that something ought to be done and Mr. Coolidge didn't look as though he intended to do it. I grew desperate and began to talk. Mr. Coolidge listened. In all my life I never had a better or more willing listener. He didn't do a thing but listen . . . This lasted for about 15 minutes. I was doing all I could and more, too, but the Governor wouldn't open his mouth to save the country, and things grew worse. Finally, wiping my brow, I said:

"Well, Governor, I think I'd better go."

"What's your hurry?" asked Mr. Coolidge, finding his voice at last. "I'm enjoying myself and I hope you are." Again the smile for which he seemed sorry.

So I sank back upon the chair, thinking that he might help matters by doing a little talking himself. The serious shrewd blue eyes turned to me again but the drooping mouth closed and stayed closed. The Governor was listening again . . . I don't have any idea what I talked about during the second 15 minutes of my "visit." Guess it must have been politics. The Governor listened and I talked for the second period and clear through. I had to stop — make a break for it this time.

"Really, I think I should be going, Governor," I said. "I must not take any more of your time." And I reached for my hat.

"Sent for you, didn't I?" asked the Governor placidly and evenly, rocking to and fro as though for the rest of the day. "It's Saturday afternoon. Nothing to do."

Another 15 minutes dragged along, the Governor listening and I talking . . . He sat there just as he had 45 minutes before, gazing intently at me and listening to every word, with no change of expression. Since that day I have never believed an interview I have read with Calvin Coolidge.

Oh yes! Frank W. Stearns came to see the Governor with a dinner invitation at the Touraine just as the third quarter hour of this "visit" came to a close and I bowed myself out. When I left, Mr. Coolidge was looking at Mr. Stearns, who was doing the talking.

Rush Jones's tour of duty at the Massachusetts State House came to an end almost exactly two years later under circumstances involving the present writer. I joined the *Monitor* as a cub reporter in the summer of 1925, and was making my way through the Deland School of Journalism, with ups and downs, when Rush Jones became involved with a "gentleman from the *Transcript*" who was that dignified journal's State House correspondent.

I never knew what caused the incident. Rush was gentle, though not of tongue, diminutive, and elderly by that time. The "gentleman from the *Transcript*" was none of these. And he was also inclined to break the Volstead Act. Anyway, the day came when, incensed for some reason with the sometimes sharp-tongued Rush, he implanted on the *Monitor* man's eye a most impressive "shiner." The *Monitor*'s city editor felt that a good State House man should not be exposed to this kind of hazard, so he transferred Rush to a less vulnerable beat (it was Mr. Curley's City Hall) and sent me to the State House. I was somewhat larger than the "gentleman from the *Transcript*" and not given to raillery with my elders. We never had any trouble at all. I enjoyed the State House very much.

The paper's perspicacity and wit are agreeably shown in these remarks from a leading editorial on July 18, 1923. The editorial was called "Give Magnus Johnson a Chance." It was a plea for kindness toward the rugged dirt-farmer, glass-blower, and all-round homespun character who had defeated Minnesota's regular Republican candidate for the Senate, running on the Farmer-Labor ticket.

Said the editorial:

> The newly elected United States Senator from Minnesota is admittedly illiterate. But that does not prove him either incompetent or unfit. The value of the literacy test, even as applied to immigrants, is coming to be doubted. Would you use it to judge the worth of a senator? — well, Henry Cabot Lodge is, perhaps, the best educated of that group of worthies, and look at him! Mr. Magnus Johnson is said to have a loud, coarse voice, the perfect product of his early trade as a glassblower. The Senate may suffer

aesthetically from the exercise of so clarion a note, but the country as a whole will rather feel that it is the things which are whispered, rather than those which are shouted, in that dignified chamber, that are apt to cause trouble. Conspirators don't shout. If Minnesota's new Senator is ungrammatical at the top of his voice, he may do less harm than some of his colleagues whose voices are seldom heard outside the cloak room.

Recalling the conditions which for decades had produced agrarian radicalism in the United States, the *Monitor* continued:

Now some force — economic, political, or what not — has brought the farmer today very near to ruin. We say without hesitation or equivocation that the gravest question confronting the United States today is the distress of the farming community. At the present cost of labor and supplies, the farmer cannot earn a living. Day by day the facts showing his condition appear in the press, and at the very time the farmer is suffering because of the low prices obtained for what he has to sell, the rest of the world suffers from the high prices of farm products. Magnus Johnson, like Shipstead before him, incarnates the farmers' attempted answer to this problem. He represents the protests and the hopes of that great body of producers upon whom rests the prosperity and even the existence of the Nation. He is not to be dismissed flippantly. He is a figure to be treated with respect, because of the convictions and the justifiable revolt which he typifies.

Few newspapers published on the Atlantic seaboard would have expressed such fervent and cogent sympathy with the farmer's plight. It illustrates the way in which the *Monitor* during most of its fifty years, has had a deep understanding of the problems of the great continent. Many of its staff, like Mr. Abbot, who seems clearly to have written this editorial, had been brought up or lived many years in the middle West, often on farms. They could feel in their deepest emotions the plight and the importance of the farm.

Few items more vividly signal the changing times than this one printed on July 1, 1925. Frank A. Goodwin, Registrar of Motor Vehicles in Massachusetts, vehemently declared that a speed limit of thirty-five miles an hour is impossible! "It would never work in Massachusetts," said Mr. Goodwin. "In fact, it is my opinion that it will never work anywhere. There are many automobiles which, while perfectly safe at a normal, sane rate of speed, become a positive menace at 35 miles an hour!"

One of the delights in reading old newspaper files is to come upon the trail of national and world-famous figures long before they emerged upon the great stage. The traces of greatness are already there, though only the most perceptive can see them. Thus, on November 16, 1923, the *Monitor* had an informative special dispatch from New Hampshire, reporting the rival candidacies for the governorship of that state of Major John G. Winant and Major Frank Knox. Their familiar, earnest but youthful faces stand out from the page. And the story refers to their qualities in ways which reveal, to those thoughtful enough to know, that they were men who would make their mark.

Each man, of course, played a significant part first in national politics and later in the Second World War. Governor Winant was given serious consideration by Republican leaders when they were looking for a Presidential nominee for 1936. He destroyed his chances with a singularly ill-prepared speech in New York in late 1935, and the way was open for Alf M. Landon. Oddly enough, Frank Knox — by then transplanted to Chicago — was one of Governor Landon's rivals for the 1936 nomination and became his running mate. Then in 1941, Governor Winant became President Roosevelt's Ambassador to the Court of St. James, and Winston Churchill's companion as he traveled the blitzed quarters of London. In the same year, Colonel Knox became President Roosevelt's Secretary of the Navy, and aided selflessly and nonpolitically in the war effort.

22

The *Monitor's* Own Peace Plan

THE MONITOR FIRST PUBLISHED a picture of Adolf Hitler on its front page on November 9, 1923. It was on the morning after the beer hall putsch in Munich that the major story on page one, and a single-column drawing, were devoted to the man who was to dominate so much of the news two decades later.

This was not the *Monitor*'s first interest in Hitler. On October 3, 1923, it had published an exclusive interview with him, in which the brutal character of his political ideas was plainly recorded. Hitler said: "If I had been at the head of the Government, the Ruhr district [which France had just reoccupied] would have been burned down as Moscow was burned by the Russians. France would never have found a single tree or a bridge there. Since the Ruhr district no longer belongs to us today, it should vanish from the face of the earth."

Hitler's voice, wrote the correspondent, almost rose to a shout in excitement. Outlining his political hopes, he said:

"What has been possible in Italy also is possible in Germany, where the German people, given a Mussolini, would fall down on their knees before him and worship him more than Mussolini has been worshipped in Italy."

The correspondent used his eyes, and wrote: "An anteroom of his office was filled with men of military age who show unmistakable signs of service during the World War. His headquarters resemble a hive of swarming bees . . . Herr Hitler has a potential armed strength which is not to be regarded lightly."

Thus were *Monitor* readers warned of his plans and danger almost a decade before Hitler seized power. It was an extraordinarily foresighted interview. It proved to be timely also. Just a week later, Hitler sought to seize power in Munich. The failure of his putsch was recorded in the leading story on page one, and Dwight Sturges shrewdly caught the fanatical pomposity of the Austrian paperhanger in his portrait. The *Monitor*'s news comment recalled Hitler's statement that he was ready to use force, and that the German people would fall at the feet of a Fascist dictator.

By coincidence, the same November 9, 1923, *Monitor* that reports the Hitler putsch also carries a signed article by Winston Churchill. He was recently out of office, with the fall of the Lloyd George government, and he was filling in the odd hours with journalism. His article was a witty and severe attack on H. G. Wells's socialist plans for the merging of the British Empire into a world federation.

That the two men — Churchill and Hitler — who faced one another in the great crisis of 1940 should have faced each other in the *Monitor*'s columns in 1923 is another of history's small ironies. Sir Winston Churchill has appeared, I am sure, more steadily in the columns of the *Monitor,* and of most other newspapers in the world, down through the half century than any other individual. He was in the news every single year of the entire period. The only other well-known person now living who approaches this record is Herbert Hoover.

There were persons prominent in Boston whose appearance in the news also covers the entire period. One of them, of course, is James Michael Curley.

Norbert Wiener, the cybernetics genius, still very busy at Massachusetts Institute of Technology, and H. V. Kaltenborn, then a prominent Harvard undergraduate, were among those who made the front page in the first weeks. Henry L. Stimson was also eminently in the news beginning in 1909. Among the college athletes on the *Monitor*'s pages in 1908 there are men now rounding out their careers in business. One such, whose prowess as a track star — complete with picture — appeared in the first weeks is William M. Rand, subsequently president of the Monsanto Chemical Company and now a director of the John Hancock Mutual Life Insurance Company and numerous other companies.

On November 15, 1923, the entries closed on Edward W. Bok's great peace plan competition. He had offered a prize of $100,000 for the most practical peace proposal and enormous interest had been aroused. The *Monitor* submitted no entry, but on the day the lists closed it presented its own peace plan. This was the proposal of a constitutional amendment to "take the profits out of war." This is the text of the proposed amendment: "In the event of a declaration of war, the property, equally with the persons, lives, and liberties of all citizens shall be subject to conscription for the defense of the Nation, and it shall be the duty of the President to propose and of Congress to enact the legislation necessary to give effect to this amendment."

The idea that economic motives were the chief causes of war was very persuasive in the early years of the century, and substantially up to 1939. There was reason enough to believe that economic rivalries between imperial Germany and other powers had led to the war of 1914–18. But the case was pushed farther. It was charged, and believed, that because munitions makers and other elements in heavy industry derived great profits from war they also fomented wars.

Big business, and notably the steel, shipbuilding, chemical, and explosives industries were profoundly unpopular in the first quarter of the century. They were regarded as monopolistic. They employed a great deal of unskilled immigrant labor at low rates and sometimes with wretched conditions of working and living. It was the same in many countries. The Krupps in Germany, the Schneider-Creusots and Comité des Forges in France, and similar heavy industrial enterprises elsewhere had great power over political parties and governments. Their economic strength was vast. Theodore Roosevelt, William Jennings Bryan, the pamphleteers, "muckraking" journalists, and humanitarians of the United States attributed a vast part of the nations' internal and international problems to the "merchants of death."

One of the most striking proofs of the changing economic and social climate in the United States is the almost total disappearance of such concepts. Big business is not necessarily popular in the United States, and a period of economic suffering and unemployment might change the climate again, but there is nothing like the criticism — and hatred — of economic power in 1958 that there was up to about 1940. The enlarged power of organized labor, the various reforms enacted into law, and the increased sense of social responsibility held by business itself have changed the climate.

But as far as the "merchants of death" are concerned, very few people today believe that wars are caused by munitions makers. It became apparent in the late 1930's that the threat to peace which came from Adolf Hitler was only secondarily supported by the ironmongers at the Economic Club in Düsseldorf. Nor was peace endangered especially by the heavy industrial leaders of the United States (who would have been conscripted under the *Monitor*'s amendment) or of Britain, or France. Rather, the dangers came from a deep-seated and fanatical dream of domination, feeding on Germany's hard times and grievances.

In 1958, the war dangers which the world faces do not arise because any capitalists are going to make profits out of war, but because a group of rulers who control two great Communist nations, and dominate a few satellites, seek to extend their hegemony over other nations and peoples. Certain economic motives are plainly involved in all this, it is true. But a constitutional amendment conscripting the property of American citizens is not faintly related to the present problem of war deterrence. Governments no longer have to act to make it "total" war. If the tragedy of major war comes, it is widely recognized that it will be "total" war in a more comprehensive sense than ever, and that nobody will profit.

But in 1923, as for many years before and a decade and a half afterward, the idea of "taking the profits out of war" had wide appeal and persuasiveness. It was not necessarily unsound, in the terms which existed in 1923, and for years after. It meant that the United States, at least, would have clean hands in any war. There would have been no gigantic war profits and no profiteers among Americans.

By the time war actually did come, in 1939, excess profits taxes and high, graduated income taxes had seen to it that there were no war profiteers in the old sense. Men did not necessarily make more money out of war than they could make out of a normally expanding economy. In either case, the building up of great fortunes in the nineteenth- and early twentieth-century manner was no longer possible. Moreover, the war powers granted to the American President and the emergency agencies of government made it possible to utilize for defense purposes any part of the American economy that might be needed.

In short, the actual results envisaged in the *Monitor* peace plan — namely, rendering property and economic sinews as conscriptable as people — substantially came into operation. And the long-range purpose of the plan, to make sure that greed did not motivate war as far as the United States was concerned, was removed by the magnification of war to the level of totality.

In 1923, however, the *Monitor* peace plan was not only good journalism but good sense and good civics. It started many people thinking harder than ever about the motivation for war. It served its historic purpose. And it helped greatly to bring the *Monitor* to the attention of the nation and the world.

The *Monitor* peace plan had been devised by Mr. Abbot. It was advanced and promoted by him with untiring zeal. His connections with public men helped to evoke the very favorable support for the plan which came from wide circles. The

THE CHRISTIAN SCIENCE MONITOR

AN INTERNATIONAL DAILY NEWSPAPER

BOSTON, FRIDAY, AUGUST 3, 1923—VOL. XV, NO. 210

[H]ARDING PASSES ON—COOLIDGE IS PRESIDENT

COOLIDGE TAKES OATH [B]Y THE LIGHT OF OIL LAMP AS THIRTIETH PRESIDENT

[Oath] Administered by His Father in Vermont [Fa]rmhouse While Neighbors Look On—New Executive Starts at Once for Capital

Calvin Coolidge—Public Servant

Reared in Plymouth, Vt.; worked on father's farm and [att]ended school in village of Black River, later in St. Johns[bur]y Academy.

Entered Amherst College in 1891, graduating in 1895.

Began study of law in Northampton, Mass., and was [ad]mitted to the bar on July 2, 1897.

City councilor, Northampton, 1899 and 1900; city [sol]icitor, 1900, 1901.

Member of Massachusetts House of Representatives, [190]7 and 1908.

Mayor of Northampton, 1910 and 1911.

Member of Massachusetts Senate, 1912 to 1915; president [of] Senate, 1914 and 1915.

Lieutenant-Governor, 1916, 1917, 1918; Governor, [191]9, 1920.

Nominated as Republican candidate for Vice-President [at] Chicago, June, 1920; elected on Nov. 2, 1920.

[PLY]MOUTH, Vt., Aug. 3 (AP)—Calvin Coolidge became President [of the U]nited States at 2:47 a. m. today, eastern standard time, when [he took] the oath of office in the living room of his father's farmhouse [in the li]ttle mountain village where he was born.

Warren Gamaliel Harding

WARREN G. HARDING'S LAST PLEA WAS FOR MORE OF CHRIST SPIRIT

Tolerant Executive's Final Official Words Invoked the Wayshower's Humility—Speech Read in Los Angeles

COOLIDGES' STEPS TO WHITE HOUSE

New President and Wife Will Prove Adaptable to White House Environment

ATTENDANTS HAD ISSUED OPTIMISTIC STATEMENTS FOLLOWING HOPEFUL DAY

Mrs. Harding Was Reading To Husband When Change Came—Body To Be Taken To Washington for Ceremonies

President Harding's Achievements

Washington Conference on Limitation of Armament. United States took bold position and important treaties were evolved.

Peace re-established with Germany and Austria. Army of occupation withdrawn.

Declaration in favor of American participation in World Court.

Treaty with the Republic of Colombia ratified, settling long-standing dispute.

Budget system established and the Government enabled to carry on its business with greater efficiency and economy.

Extension of credit to farmers.

Firm stand on enforcement of prohibition laws.

Regulation of immigration by modified restriction.

Settlement of British war debt; also that of Finland, with Czechoslovakia and Jugoslavia in prospect.

Influence extended in Central and South America.

SAN FRANCISCO, Aug. 3 (AP)—Warren G. Harding, twenty-ninth President of the United States, passed away at the Palace Hotel here last night. The late President's body will be sent to Washington tonight. Mr. Harding had been confined to his room less than a week. He passed on after having served his country as President for nearly two and one-half years.

Warren G. Harding Became President in Midst of After-War Problems; Worked His Way on Weekly Newspaper as Boy

THE CHRISTIAN SCIENCE MONITOR

AN INTERNATIONAL DAILY NEWSPAPER

BOSTON, FRIDAY, NOVEMBER 9, 1923—VOL. XV, NO. 292

DRY AGENTS SEIZE 14 BIG BREWERIES IN PENNSYLVANIA

Liquor Interests Taken by Surprise as 50 Officers Sweep Through State

Mr. Haynes Moves to Put Padlock on Plants Which Will Close Them for 365 Days

Russian Steamer Brings Wheat and Coal to Italy

INCIPIENT DISORDER IN MEXICO QUELLED

General Strike Designed to React Favorably to Señor de la Huerta Nipped

Leaders of the Bavarian Revolt

Adolf Hitler — Gen. von Ludendorff

WARLESS WORLD IS OBJECTIVE OF 2,800,000 AMERICAN WOMEN

Club Leaders "Show the Way" at San Francisco Institute—Hate, Ignorance and Fear Must Go, They Declare

BAVARIAN COUP D'ETAT SUDDENLY COLLAPSES AS STATE FORCES CAPTURE REVOLT LEADERS

Bavarian Coup Disturbs All Elements in Austria

General von Ludendorff and Adolf Hitler Captured After Barricading Themselves in Ministry of War—Former Police Chief Placed Under Arrest

Federal Government Makes Good Its Threat to Sever Relations With Bavaria Until Normal Conditions Restored—Economic Retaliation Planned

FRANCE AMAZED AT MILITARY MOVE OF HITLER FACTION

Question Mooted of Possible Fighting Between Republic and Reich

BRITAIN WIPES OFF SOME £500,000,000

Two striking front pages of the 1920's: a President passes, a Dictator appears.

3
No2

European Bureau, before London office, 1930. Front row, left to right: Cherry Ekman, Stockholm; Paul Cremona, Rome; John Sidney Braithwaite, Managing Representative for Europe; J. Roscoe Drummond, European Editorial Manager; Sisley Huddleston, Paris; William Henry Chamberlin, Moscow; Reuben H. Markham, The Balkans. Second row, left to right: Floris Canté, The Netherlands; Colonel M. P. Kennard, London; Frank E. Stevens, Bucharest; R. Maillard Stead, London; Phyllis Lovell, London; Peter Lyne, London; A. Godfrey Lias, London; Reginald Calvert, Madrid; Everard Coates, London; J. Emlyn Williams, Berlin; Howard Siepen, Berlin; Erwin D. Canham, Geneva; Lewis Rex Miller, Paris; Robert S. Allen, Washington.

Delivery trucks poised.

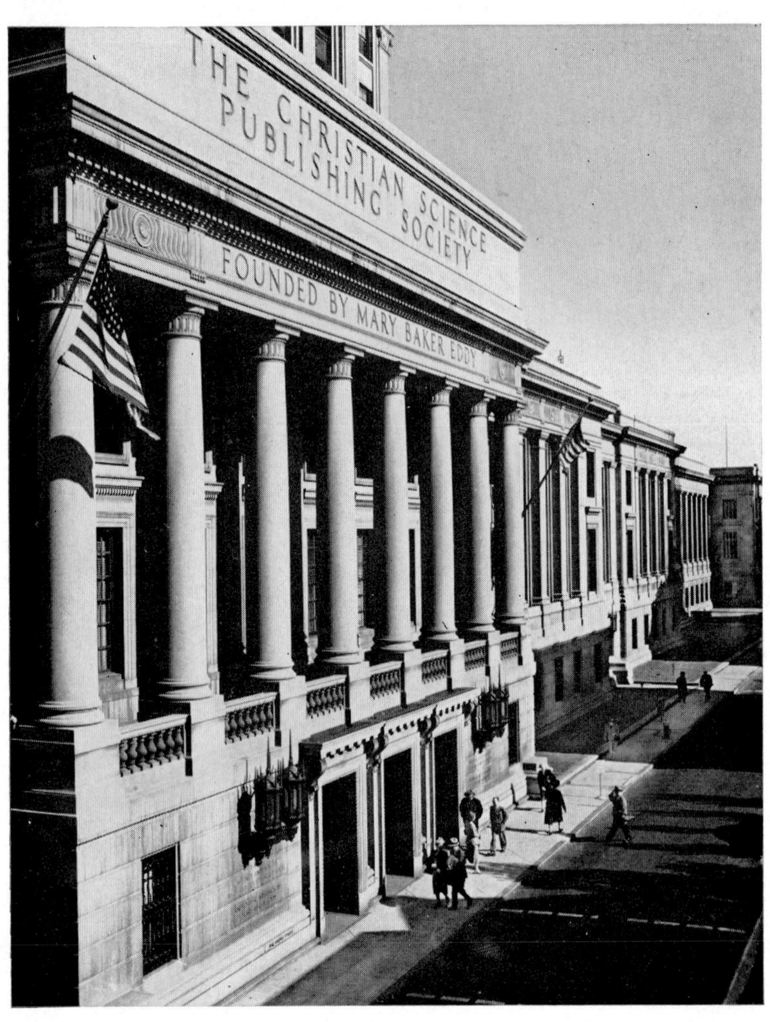

Christian Science Publishing Society building, completed in 1934.

Mapparium in Publishing House.

Lincoln by *Monitor*'s great artist,
Dwight C. Sturges.

Early political cartoon by Mr. Sturges and typical cartoon by Paul R. Carmack.

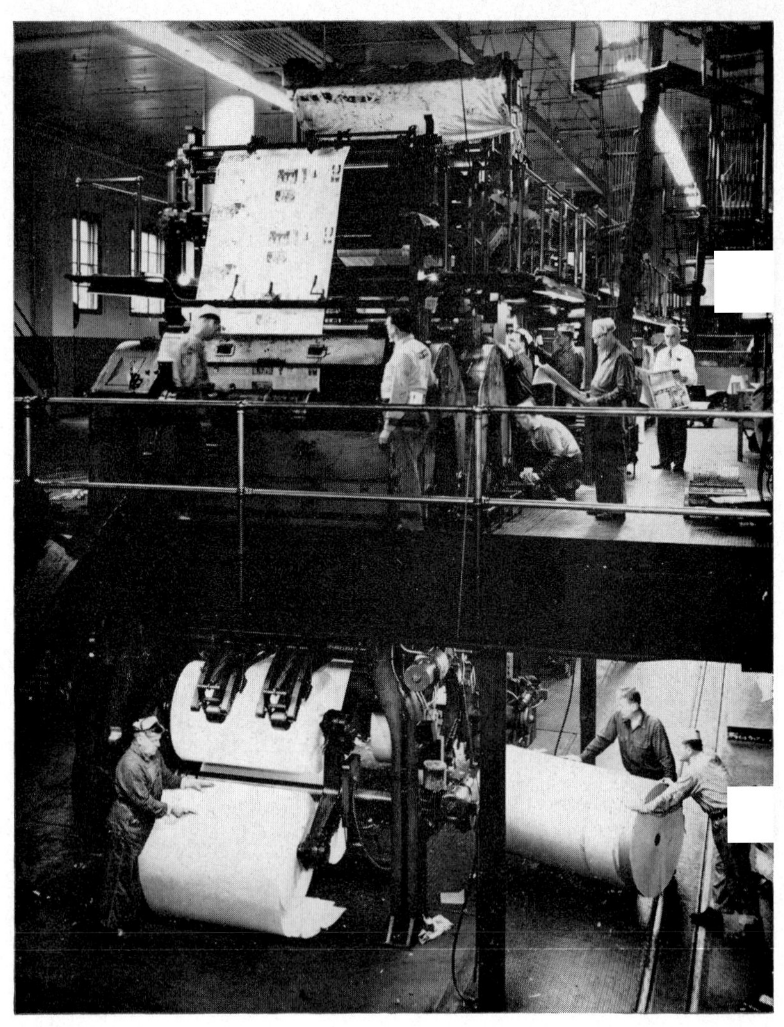

Monitor's modern Hoe presses at work.

Quaint little figures who have marched across *Monitor* pages.

Monitor war correspondents: William P. Stringer in North Africa; Gordon Walker returning from a bombing flight over Wake Island; Edmund Stevens during Egyptian Campaign; Joseph G. Harrison aboard a Greek battleship, 1945, with evzone aide-de-camp to Archbishop Damaskino.

Gordon Walker with Marine Raiders and native aides, New Georgia, 1942. Mr. Walker is second from left, front row.

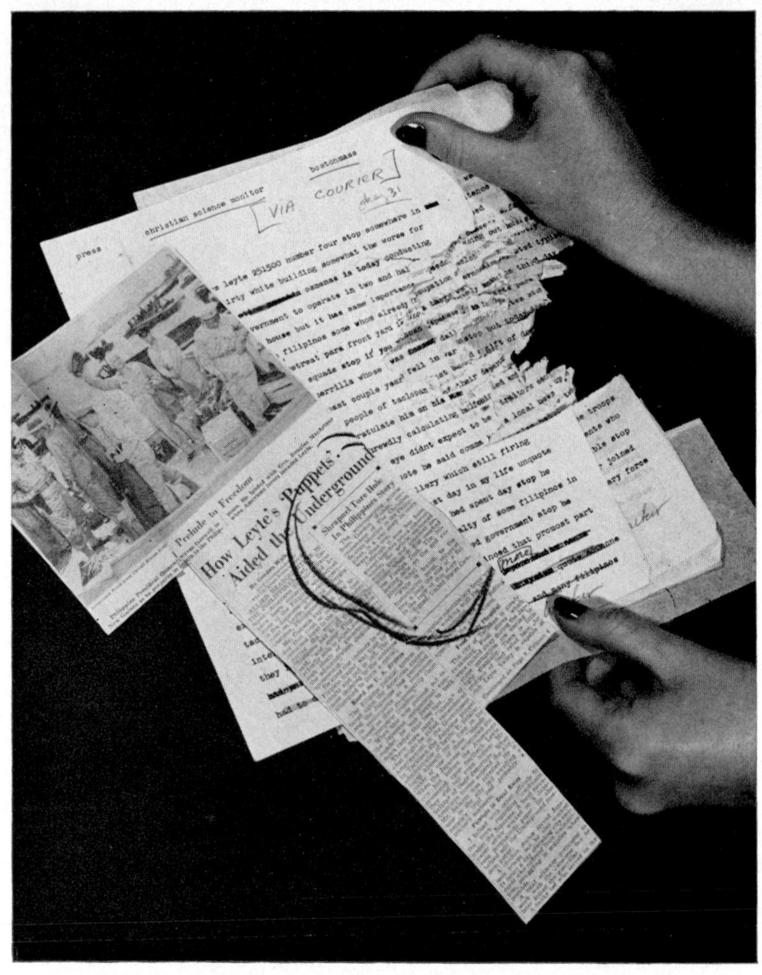

Mr. Walker's copy, shredded by shrapnel.

THE CHRISTIAN SCIENCE MONITOR

AN INTERNATIONAL DAILY NEWSPAPER

BOSTON, WEDNESDAY, AUGUST 15, 1945 — ATLANTIC EDITION

The World at Peace

shall beat their swords into plowshares,
and their spears into pruninghooks;
nation shall not lift up sword against nation,
neither shall they learn war any more.
Isaiah 2:4

Gasoline and Fuel Oil Ration Ends; U.S. Industry Geared to Peacetime

Allies Prepare To Occupy Japan

By a Staff Writer of The Christian Science Monitor

Continued on Page 4, Column 5

'Cease Fire' Ends War in Pacific

By the War Editor of The Christian Science Monitor

Continued on Page 6, Column 2

Master Reconversion Plan Unveiled by Government

WASHINGTON, Aug. 15—The rationing of gasoline, canned fruits and vegetables, fuel oil, and oil stoves was ended today by the Office of Price Administration.

Rationing continues for meats, fats, oils, butter, sugar, shoes, and tires "until military cutbacks and increased production bring civilian supplies more nearly in balance with civilian demand."

"Right now," said Price Administrator Chester Bowles, "it's impossible to estimate" when other items will be released, but "it certainly cannot come too soon as far as we are concerned."

By Neal Stanford

WASHINGTON, Aug. 15—As the gigantic American war economy shuddered with the command "Reverse engines," the Administration unveiled today its master reconversion program bull's-eyed straight toward a peacetime production surpassing anything in history.

A fact-jammed 31-page cover-all report from John W. Snyder, Director of Reconversion, became the cover-all charter by which the Government hopes to map the way, bridge the war-to-peace transition, and avoid permanent dislocation.

War-contract cancellations reaching $35,000,000,000 within a few weeks, and temporary unemployment rising to 8,000,000 jobless before next spring, are the fundamental shocks which require expert handling by Government in collaboration with industry, the Snyder report warned.

Even as the War Department was announcing contract cancellations which would total $23,000,000,000 in a year, the reconversion charter was propounding that "only a peacetime production, vastly expanded over anything this or any other nation has ever seen," will provide jobs for all and a rising standard of living.

Immediate Steps Planned

Mr. Snyder announced these immediate steps in the nation's task of shaping weapons into the plowshares and production of peace:

1. The Army's vast munitions procurement program is being cut immediately "by 94 to 100 per cent." The tremendous food procurement for the Army will be cut "as fast as demobilization will permit." Navy reductions will be smaller and more gradual.

2. At least 7,000,000 men will be demobilized from the armed forces within the next year. The Army's demobilization rate will climb in several months from its current 170,000 a month to 500,000. The Navy will demobilize some personnel now, but must await determination of its future role and police duties before taking drastic action.

3. Many wartime production and distribution controls will be removed at once. Some must remain in force to expedite production, break bottlenecks, thwart inventory hoarding, and maintain economic stabilization. The Director of Reconversion and the War Production Board agree heartily on this.

4. Rationing of scarce commodities must continue, but restrictions on others will be lifted immediately. Transportation controls must continue—rail travel may become

Continued on Page 5, Column 5

Fireworks Flare in Hub; Dual Holiday Proclaimed

By Everett M. Smith

Continued on Page 7, Column 3

Exit Thor: Now the Tasks of Peace

U. S. Molds Dynamic Pattern Based on Global Co-operation

By Roscoe Drummond

Staff Correspondent of The Christian Science Monitor

WASHINGTON, Aug. 15—Once more the world is at peace and once more we have an opportunity to keep it.

This time the end of the war finds the United States putting its total influence—its political, economic and military as well as moral influence—behind the peace.

This may well be the difference which can spell success for World Peace II. That after this "one world" has suffered the travail of two vast wars and a total of at least 33,000,000 military casualties in one generation, the United States is joining the peace, not seceding from it; is placing its maximum power behind creating a good peace and securing it.

This time the timetable of peace-making has outpaced the timetable of war-making, and now the abrupt climax to the fighting in the Pacific finds the beginnings of the peace already well advanced.

Peace Must Be Dynamic

The new league of United Nations has been framed and its 50-nation interim commission is already at work in London.

The pattern of the war settlements in Europe, laid down at the Potsdam Conference, is being slowly but steadily realized.

The essential outlines of the war settlements in the Pacific, partly established by the Cairo declarations, are already visible.

The cessation of destructive hostilities does not guarantee the beginning of constructive peace, and World Peace II shows signs of being neither Utopian nor easy nor automatic.

For peace is dynamic, not static, and whether we keep world Peace II or throw it away depends on how the United Nations use it.

For its part the United States has, there is reason to

Continued on Page 3, Column 1

World Faces New Challenge To Reshape Mental Concepts

By Henry Sowerby

Staff Writer of The Christian Science Monitor

The war is ended. The victory is ours. The heroic work of our young men who fought has been accomplished. The greatest evil that has ever menaced the entire human race has been beaten down. An orgy of destruction such as has never before stained the annals of the nations is a thing of the past.

World War I was called Armageddon. There is no name in the vocabulary vast enough to embrace these six years of conflict—infinitely more ravaging in their drain on men and resources, in their destructiveness and in their shattering effect upon the faith and hopes of humanity.

After World War I we looked for the voice to thunder: "It is done!" It never came.

Road to Freedom

Today as the "tumult and the shouting dies," and the "captains and the kings depart," we know it is not yet done. The Four Freedoms have yet to be established and protected. The prayer of all hearts is:

"Lord God of Hosts, be with us yet
Lest we forget, lest we forget!"

Today we know, as we did not in 1919, that victory has brought us, not an end to the struggle, but only the right and the responsibility to resolve the chaos that remains in our own way—the opportunity to set humanity on a better road to faith and harmony.

We have learned since 1918 that victory does not of itself leave democracy strong. In this war we carried no glittering emblems of a war "to end war," or a war "to make the world safe for democracy." Millions of young men who went out to fight in Europe and the Far East understood the call without slogans. They knew that the evil menacing all our concepts of freedom and justice must be destroyed, or democracy must go under.

We are in no mood to boast of our military victory. We

Continued on Page 4, Column 1

Supreme Allied Commander

Gen. Douglas MacArthur

One of history's great front pages.

Diplomatic whirl vividly sketched by Emil Weiss: President Eisenhower and UN Secretary General Hammarskjold; Dean Acheson, Ernest Bevin, Robert Schuman.

American delegation at UN General Assembly, 1949. Erwin D. Canham in back row, center. Front row, left to right: Mrs. Eleanor Roosevelt, Philip C. Jessup, John Foster Dulles, Warren R. Austin, Dean Acheson.

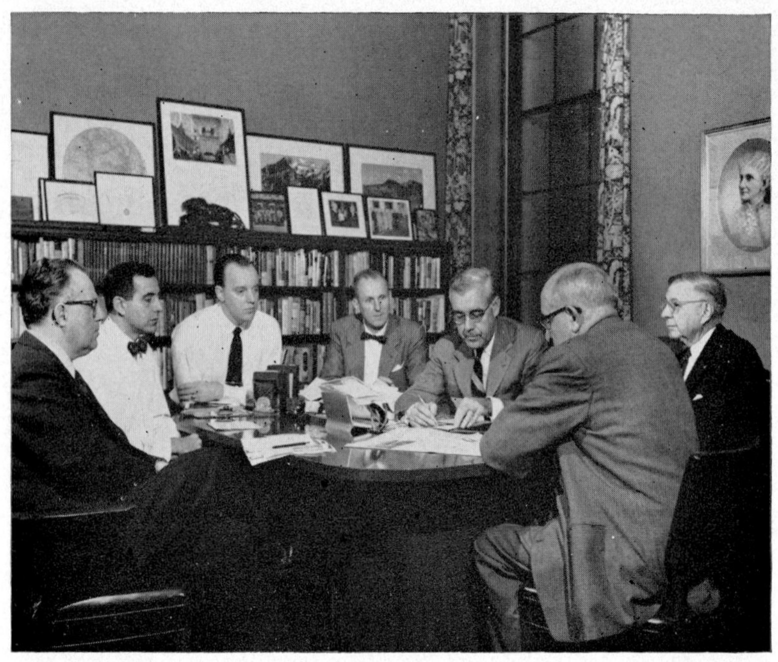

News conference, left to right: Joseph G. Harrison, Overseas News Editor; R. R. Brunn, American News Editor; Robert C. Bergenheim, New England News Editor; Saville R. Davis, Managing Editor; Erwin D. Canham, Editor; Harry N. Hazeldine, Copy Desk Head; Paul S. Deland, Associate Editor.

plan was very timely, for it brought the *Monitor* strikingly and constructively to the attention of the nation and the world as the paper was rebuilding its standing and prestige. The plan helped greatly in the restoration of the paper's circulation. Many leaders of government and public opinion acclaimed the proposal in the days following its publication. President Coolidge cagily indicated "agreement in principle."

Herbert Hoover, Secretary of Commerce, said: "The more evident it is that the whole Nation will be put in the storm and made to bear its share of the sacrifice, the less likely we are to go to war." Secretary of Navy Wilbur gave warm support. Bernard M. Baruch, with the experience of the War Mobilization Board keen in his memory, was an articulate supporter. Many military leaders expressed earnest agreement. Five different measures to achieve the objectives of the plan were introduced in Congress.

Many Senators were warm in their support. The American Legion made the plan one of its major planks. Such labor leaders as John L. Lewis said, "Proper concern for home and country should cause all citizens to approve the amendment." Officials of various peace movements were enthusiastically in support.

There were many voices in opposition, however, and the *Monitor* printed their views as well. Thus, Fred I. Kent, then vice-president of the Bankers Trust Company, said the constitutional amendment would be "a very terrible mistake," and did so under a double-column head on the *Monitor*'s front page, augmented by his picture.

His reasons, though published at very considerable length, are not very clear. They boil down to the natural conviction for a banker that private capital should be left alone. That there should be, he said, as little governmental interference with business and finance as possible was as important in wartime as in peace.

It is likely that Mr. Kent's arguments helped the *Monitor*'s plan rather than hindered it, and that the paper's freedom in publishing plenty of opposition to its ideas gained it popular and professional respect. On the editorial page in the same issue, the *Monitor* tartly took issue with Mr. Kent, describing him as a "capitalist."

Justifying its proposal, the *Monitor* said:

> Primarily it is the purpose of this paper to make the very idea of war so hateful, so repugnant, so terrifying to the very class that heretofore has looked with the utmost complacency upon it, that it will take the lead in opposing it. As a financier of eminence, Mr. Kent is undoubtedly aware that there was a very considerable element in the United States who regretted the end of the war because it meant the end of profits. We believe that if the end of profits be decreed before war shall be declared, the end of war will be brought before its beginning.
>
> And we would finally like to inquire just whence came the capital which prosecuted the last war, and which this eminent banker threatens would be driven to cover in the event of another war. Did not the greater part of it come from the savings of the people? Did not the people buy Liberty bonds at par? And just what proportion of those Liberty bonds are now in possession of the financiers who later acquired them, not at par, but at a very heavy reduction? It comes with bad grace from a leader of finance to threaten the hasty retreat of Capital when called upon to support the Nation in time of war. What happened to individuals who sought to evade their military duties is a matter of history. Would the same punitive methods be inapplicable to evaders of the draft of capital?

This is rather stern stuff. And it indicates just how radical the *Monitor* peace plan actually was. It indicates further that in 1923, as for some years thereafter, it was still open season on "capital." By the mid-century, a newspaper of moderation and balance did not speak this way to the bankers, because the bankers did not justify such language. In 1923, and for some fifteen years afterward, a great part of America was still debt-conscious, still in debt.

The *Monitor* in 1923 was still speaking in the climate of William Jennings Bryan's "Cross of Gold." Undoubtedly, Willis Abbot, who stood at Bryan's elbow when he made that historic speech, wrote this very editorial.

Something of this same concept that purse strings could be an incentive or a deterrent to war was picturesquely expressed in the paper as early as 1912. Not long before the Balkan wars broke out, in a considerably overoptimistic forecast, a dispatch from London said: "The fact is that today in the Balkans men do not rush so light-heartedly into war as they did when a soldier's equipment was a powder flask and a bag of bullets. The bourses of Sophia and Belgrade may not be so sensitive as those of Vienna and St. Petersburg but they are sensitive enough. The web of commerce has spun itself from Dulcigno to Kustendje, and the pax mercatoria is to be found in every thread of it."

Here, indeed, was the other side of the coin from the *Monitor*'s peace proposals. Here the correspondent was assuming that the merchants of the Balkans would deter their governments from rushing into war, since wars were so expensive. The concept of the "pax mercatoria" is one which found little effect in 1914 or 1939. But in 1912, after a century troubled only by relatively minor wars, it was a persuasive thesis.

The *Monitor*'s interest in peace planning was far from limited to its own proposals for "taking the profits out of war." As official American standoffishness toward the League of Nations diminished, and the United States took more and more active part in various League activities, the *Monitor* covered each step. It was particularly interested in the control of world production and trade in narcotics, and followed the League conferences and committees which sought to curb the nefarious trade.

The paper saw in the early 1920's that economic revision of the Versailles Treaty was essential. It urged the scaling down of reparations schedules and war debt payments, seeing the fiscal folly of unbalancing world trade and weakening the western European nations upon which a stable peace largely depended.

The *Monitor* was naturally much interested in the proposals which culminated in the Kellogg-Briand Pact for the Outlawry of War. It felt that here was a practical and hopeful method by which the United States could re-enter world peace making and administering, but on a basis of long-range idealism. However, the *Monitor*'s attitude toward the Pact of Paris was not naïve.

A lucid analysis of the problem was published on its editorial page as early as April 27, 1928, while the Pact was still being negotiated. The author was the Marquess of Lothian, writing his regular column, "The Diary of a Political Pilgrim."

> War occurs [he wrote] because there is a dispute in which opinion on both sides is so set that it will not yield to ordinary diplomatic methods. If war is to be prevented it will clearly be because both sides allow the intervention of some impartial element into the discussion, whose duty it shall be to sift the facts, and make proposals for settlement which are sufficiently fair and just for the reasonable elements on each side to accept them rather than go to war.
>
> What all thinking Europe is asking, therefore, is whether Mr. Kellogg's note implies that the United States is willing to include in his proposed treaties practical methods of conciliation and arbitration, as the members of the League have done. Unless it is willing to do so, a mere abstract declaration outlawing war as an instrument of national policy is not, in its opinion, likely to have much practical effect in preventing war. The negotiations which now happily seem likely to take place between the great powers about the Briand-Kellogg proposals ought surely to elucidate this question.

Here was a blunt and realistic statement of the situation which is as valid thirty years later as it was in 1928. Thus *Monitor* readers were told the essential terms for the practical preservation of peace. Here the lofty idealism of the movement to "outlaw" war was harnessed to the need of timely and effective conciliation and arbitration of disputes. And so, although the *Monitor* supported and applauded the conclusion of the Pact of Paris in August, 1928, it steadily affirmed that closer American co-operation with the machinery to settle disputes was needed.

The *Monitor* had covered the abortive naval limitation negotiations in Geneva in 1927 with care, observing with concern the strain and misunderstanding between Britain and the United States which were expressed there. The activities at that conference of William B. Shearer, a lobbyist for American armament interests, which were later investigated by the

United States Senate, helped to convince the paper that the armament makers were obstructing the path to peace, and that its own proposals to conscript the wealth were on the right track.

The same viewpoint emerged with even greater vigor in the 1930's, when Republican Senator Gerald P. Nye of North Dakota, carried out his investigation of the munitions industry, and the Neutrality Act was passed, seeking to insulate the United States from economic involvement in war. The *Monitor* at first supported the Neutrality Act, though always with careful reservations. As chief of the paper's Washington Bureau, I obtained early and confidential information about the Neutrality Act, and wrote many dispatches about the State Department's plans to refrain from arming other people's wars. I did not cover the Senate hearings, and thus it was that I never happened to meet Alger Hiss, who as secretary of the Nye Committee conducted the investigations. It was from these investigations that the phrase "merchants of death" arose. The *Monitor*'s long espousal of the conscript-the-wealth plan shows it was not of Communist or fellow-traveler origin, however much men like Hiss may have pressed and distorted the issue in its later years.

While the Neutrality Act helped to prevent American resources from being heavily engaged in the Spanish Civil War, it did not prevent the emotional involvement of the American people, on both sides. Since Nazi-Fascist support was pouring into Spain on behalf of the Franco forces, and Communist support for the Spanish republicans, the inefficacy of this law was rather evident. Then when the Neutrality Act did not curb the flow of American scrap iron and other war sinews to Japan, Americans again felt it was seriously imperfect. With its repeal, after the outbreak of world war, the last element of belief had been removed that the United States could somehow keep the peace by curbing the flow of armaments. Finally, the new tax laws and the totality of modern war completely swept away the thesis of war prevention by drafting the wealth or curbing the war profiteers. War's new dimensions presented an essentially new problem.

23

Lenin and MacDonald

NOT MANY MONITOR front pages contained at one time three more important and different news stories than did the issue of January 22, 1924. Nikolai Lenin's death was announced, and a two-column drawing and news dispatch concerning him dominated the center of the page. In the right-hand lead was the story of the British Labor Party taking the reins of government for the first time in history. And also prominently displayed was the subpoena the Senate Public Lands Committee had issued to Albert B. Fall, former Secretary of the Interior, demanding that he explain the source of the $100,000 with which he had improved his New Mexico ranch. This was the biggest news break in the Teapot Dome story to date. A little earlier, on January 16, Senator Thomas J. Walsh had returned from Florida, where his private cross-examination of Edward B. McLean, publisher of the Washington *Post* and the Cincinnati *Enquirer,* had provided the unmistakable lead that ultimately placed Mr. Fall in prison.

Throughout the half century, the *Monitor* has been aware of the increasing importance of Russia. Part of this awareness stems from Mrs. Eddy's own prescience. In 1905, immediately upon the conclusion of the Russo-Japanese war, in a message to the Boston *Globe,* she referred to the Douma in Russia as "no uncertain ray of dawn." * She recognized in this effort to work out the beginning of democratic reforms, in the midst of tsarist autocracy, a highly important, historic step. Referring to adverse experiences such as the defeat Russia had suffered, she continued: "Through the wholesome chastisements of Love, nations are helped onward towards justice, righteousness, and peace."

The *Monitor,* from its inception, kept up an intent watch on the progress of constitutional reform in Russia. Its readers were also informed of the backwardness of the tsarist imperial government, the plight of its peasants, the pogroms which afflicted its many Jews, the aspirations for autonomy or independence of the national groups around its fringes, especially in Poland, Czechoslovakia, and the Baltic states. The Russian penetration of Finland to the Swedish frontier was described in early 1914.

Russia's expansive tendencies were also identified, especially its efforts to dominate Persia and find a way to the warm water of the Persian Gulf, as well as the open ports of the Dardanelles and the Aegean. Its role in supporting Serbian nationalism was chronicled. The relation of Russian imperialism in Persia, and Italian expansion in North Africa, to the possibility of a Muslim "holy war" was graphically described in January 1912.

On May 6, 1914, the paper did not hesitate, in a discussion of Russian threats to Persia, to assert that "Russian bureaucratic government and all that it entails is the last word in legislative and executive evil." So *Monitor* readers were prepared for the worst. And these same elements of bureaucratic evil were detected and described in the turbulent decades that followed the Soviet revolution.

* *Miscellany,* 282:9

While the *Monitor,* like almost everyone, felt the massive Russian armies would give a better account of themselves in 1914 than they were actually able to do, it was not long before the elements of weakness in the tsarist system were very apparent. Thenceforward the paper intensified its interest in all elements which might reform and liberalize the corruption and decay of St. Petersburg, and eliminate the influences by which Prussianism had undermined Russian integrity and independence. The paper's correspondents and editorial writers clearly depicted the vicious influences of the monk Rasputin.

In the weeks and months that followed, the revolution was ably covered. The *Monitor* had a resident special correspondent in St. Petersburg and many dispatches from expert observers who were in and out of the Russian capital during the revolution and in the weeks that followed. Hopes sprang high with the initial triumph of moderate forces and the effort to install parliamentary democracy. But *Monitor* readers were told of the grave difficulties in the way, and the depth of corruption which must be reformed. The possibility of a more violent revolution was clearly recognized.

Throughout this period, the paper had the great advantage of many special articles by Professor Samuel N. Harper of the University of Chicago. He was one of the world's great authorities on Russia and frequently wrote from that country. His dispatches penetrated more deeply and with greater historical context than much of the excited journalism of the period.

In *The Decision to Intervene,* the second volume of his distinguished chronicle of Soviet-American relations, George F. Kennan describes Professor Harper as "a central point of contact and liaison for almost all the major American elements interested in the Russian problem . . . In 1918, in particular, he played — with his manifold connections and his taste for operating on the fringes, rather than at the center, of all streams of activity — a role that could have been played by no one else in the effort to unify the various elements of American opinion concerning Russia and to channel them into a single effort."

Mr. Kennan points out that Professor Harper's articles in the *Monitor* "cautiously, and with evidence of some torture of spirit, pleaded generally for economic aid and moral support to the Russian people as a matter of first priority, admitting — more and more freely as time went on — that if a few soldiers were necessary to assure the proper distribution of these expressions of friendship, they could of course be sent for that purpose." Be that as it may, the *Monitor* was no out-and-out supporter of Allied intervention in Russia.

The *Monitor* pulled no punches in reporting the barbarisms of the Bolshevik regime. It covered and analyzed the American military experiences in Siberia, followed the mixed fortunes of the various White Russian armies, but expressed no great sympathy with these adventurous efforts to overthrow the Moscow regime. It did not go as far as those Americans — like William C. Bullitt, Raymond Robins, and others — who felt it was a mistake not to maintain closer and more friendly relations with the revolutionaries.

After the Washington Arms Limitation Conference, a resurgence of American interest in the world led also to new questions about relations with the Soviet Union. While the *Monitor* never excused or failed to report the excesses and evils of the Bolshevik government, it never joined the hysterical hue and cry which depicted it as an instant and alarming menace to American democracy in the years 1919–23. It reported the A. Mitchell Palmer investigations and prosecutions of alleged sedition. It did not defend Communist sympathizers in the United States but it was able to distinguish between actual Communist infiltration or native radicalism, the lineal heir of the Populists and the early labor agitators, or socialism of the Debs or Berger brand. It remained calm during the days of fanaticism.

This was the period when Senators William E. Borah and Burton K. Wheeler and various others were urging recognition of the Soviet government, after appropriate negotiation and adjustment of the claims between Washington and Moscow. Their efforts were futile. By 1933, when President Roosevelt's Administration actually recognized the Soviet Union, the

Monitor approved but had not been urging the necessity of the action.

By 1933, indeed, the *Monitor*'s opposition to the Stalinist regime was inevitably greater than it had been in 1924. In the years between, of course, the concessions Lenin had initiated with the New Economic Policy in 1921 had been wiped out. The forced liquidation of the kulaks, with the famine which killed millions of Soviet citizens, had been reported in the *Monitor*. The anti-God crusades of the regime had been frankly described.

In 1922 the *Monitor* began accepting articles from the Soviet Union by William Henry Chamberlin, and in November, 1923, engaged him as its permanent correspondent in Moscow. Mr. Chamberlin has candidly admitted in his book *The Confessions of an Individualist* that he was initially bemused by the Soviet system. He says:

> My first two trips to Russia [in 1922–23, during which he wrote little for the *Monitor*] left me, on balance, a Communist sympathizer, although with a good many more doubts and reservations than I had felt before leaving America. I still remember a little shamefacedly some of my naive first messages to the Monitor from Moscow, especially one in which I rashly accepted the word of a walrus-mustached Commissar for Justice that there were only two hundred political prisoners in Russia, and that these were lodged pretty comfortably in places where the climate, in the euphemistic words of the Commissar, "was clear although cold." But continued residence in the Soviet Union was a good cure for credulity. Some time in 1924 the last traces of partisanship slipped away, and I no longer experienced even an unconscious desire to report developments from the standpoint of an apologist.*

Any excess of sympathy for the Soviet experiment which may have entered Mr. Chamberlin's *Monitor* copy could have lasted only over a period of months, certainly less than a year. A study of the articles he wrote during that period do reveal a few instances of apologia. These were relatively minor. Most of them in rereading sound like little more than an excess

* Toronto, 1940, p. 88.

of caution. As soon as Mr. Chamberlin's eyes were opened, in 1924, he developed into a more and more penetrating observer and critic. He was a careful student of the revolution, an assiduous researcher in Russian history, culture, and art. His books on the Soviet Union are standard authorities on the subject. When he left Russia, in 1934, he wrote for the *Monitor* a searching and scathing series of articles which were among the earliest and best analyses of Stalinism. The material was the basis of Mr. Chamberlin's well-known book *Russia's Iron Age.*

In 1924, when Lenin died, the *Monitor*'s dispatches from Moscow and its editorials did not foresee the rise of Stalin. On the whole, the coverage estimated that since policy under Lenin had been moderating for over two years, this tendency would continue. And the editorials were much too generous at the outset. Thus on January 22, 1924, an editorial on Lenin's passing said:

> . . . Lenin . . . was instrumental in directing Russian policies to the center of that stream where, now it may be said those policies are being carried on more by the force of the stream itself, than because of the power of any individual leader or group of leaders. When he secured the adoption of the New Economic Policy, Lenin, perhaps against his own desires but certainly in line with demands that could not be ignored, made possible the commencement of orderly development in Russia. That development, whoever may be Lenin's successor as President of the Council of People's Commissaries, is likely to continue because it is an expression of the will of the newly articulate masses of the Russian people themselves.

H. W. Massingham, the *Monitor*'s experienced British columnist, too, thought the Soviet System was changing, and wrote that there was "a genuine public opinion arising in Russia whose ultimate expression will be a demand for a free press and a free party, and neither the unpopular F. C. Zinovieff nor the doubtful and ambitious Leon Trotsky, who oppose it, is in favor. There is ground for hope that there will be a quick resort to a form of democratic government."

The editorial and Mr. Massingham's opinion may well stand as a warning to those in mid-century who believe the Soviet Union is in an inevitable evolution toward a more responsive and reasonable regime, again perhaps under the impulse of "the will of the Russian people." The *Monitor* in 1924 failed to foresee Joseph Stalin and the forces he was able to amass and apply.

In the next day's paper, January 23, 1924, the *Monitor* carried Stalin's picture on its front page, together with those of Zinovieff and Kameneff. But its Moscow cable, presumably from Mr. Chamberlin, said: "In view of the crushing defeat of Mr. Trotsky's partisans at the party conference [Stalin had led the attack on Trotsky, the *Monitor* reported on the previous day] it seems unlikely that any individual will inherit the authority of Mr. Lenin. The present group leading the majority of the central committees [Stalin, Kameneff, Zinovieff] seems firmly entrenched in control of the party and the Government." Perhaps it was asking too much for either correspondent or editorial writer to read the signs any more accurately. But we can remember the same possibility of misjudgment today and always.

Of course the *Monitor* was not alone in thinking the Soviet government in 1924 was in process of evolution toward democracy. This was also the conviction of the British Labor government. And many others, repelled by the extreme fanaticism of those who saw Bolsheviks behind every hedge, went too far in their effort to see good in the regime. The *Monitor* position, taking it as a whole during this period, was not so extreme as the quotation just given would indicate.

In a very interesting editorial titled "Two Opposite Extremes of Socialism," the paper on February 7 compared Lenin and Ramsay MacDonald. Its definition of socialism rings with the dissatisfaction with the economic order of the early years of the century:

> Socialism is the conscious protest against the industrial serfdom of the many and the arbitrary exercise of economic power by the few, which has been one of the products of the industrial revolu-

tion and the growth of modern capitalism. It sees in the poverty of the masses and the excessive wealth of the few, in the chronic liability to unemployment and bad housing which besets the poor, in the vehemence of the modern commercial competition and the widespread passion for piling up material wealth, evils of society which are due to the social system itself — to the system of permitting the unrestricted ownership of land and industrial property in private hands. It believes that these evils can only be remedied by some form of collective ownership and management. On this fundamental point Lenin and MacDonald would agree. On the question of how their ideal was to be attained they have been as the poles apart.

The editorial explained that Lenin believed in "dictatorship of the party of the Communists, exercised ruthlessly and without any form of genuine popular control, in the interests of the revolution." Lenin, said the *Monitor,* "has imposed his ideals on Russia at a fearful cost, in suffering, in terrorism, in the destruction of independence and freedom of thought, in the interruption of democratic progress."

Despite these clear expressions of the evils in communism, the preceding definition of socialism and its aims is one which by 1958 would be profoundly modified. In the intervening years capitalism, especially as developed in the United States in the 1930's, 1940's, and 1950's, has wiped out many of its arbitrary and selfish elements. Socialism, especially as developed in the Soviet Union, has become even more clearly the dictatorship of a favored and privileged group, ruthlessly seeking to crush those who stand in its way.

That the *Monitor* was able to proclaim such a definition in its leading editorial was another proof of its trenchant independence. As the Methodist organ, *Zion's Herald,* said, it stood almost alone among American newspapers, and it was courageous. But of course the *Monitor* had itself no slightest taint of socialism or sympathy for socialism. It understood the causes that produced socialism, whether British or Russian, but its own remedy for these conditions was "more freedom," just as Mrs. Eddy had said. At all times it supported and does support the capitalistic system, but it believed — as succeeding events proved to be the fact — that capitalism was capable of removing its taints of plutocracy and reducing its materialism and selfishness. A free economic order based upon private ownership, genuine competition, a minimum of governmental regulation, and opportunity for fullest development of the individual were the elements the *Monitor* always supported.

The wishfulness expressed in some *Monitor* dispatches from Moscow and editorials of the 1924 period was soon replaced by a greater degree of realism. When, twenty years later, the Soviet government was a military ally of the United States, the *Monitor* had learned its lesson. It never descended into the naïveté of Soviet-worship. The true nature of the Stalinist system, exposed in full barbarity in the deliberate starvation of millions of Russians between 1929 and 1933, and shown in the perfidy of the Moscow-Berlin alliance of 1939, was never out of the *Monitor*'s sight. It recognized the heroism of Russia's patriotic resistance against the Nazi hordes, and it supported full military co-operation. It never again was deluded into believing that the Communist government was, or was becoming, a form of democratic government.

24

Coolidge, Hoover, and Al Smith

WITH AN EDITOR who had himself had a lively, career in American politics, it was natural that the *Monitor* in the 1920's should take an intensified interest in the sharp and emotional political issues confronting the people. By 1924 the complex mixture was presented of prohibition, Tammany Hall, extreme progressivism, and — for an abundance of good measure — the question of a Roman Catholic Presidential nominee.

Willis Abbot, sniffing the 1924 nominating conventions with the zest of a tried political war horse, made arrangements for a special *Monitor* edition of 30,000 copies to leave the presses at midnight in Boston and be transported to New York for early morning delivery each day. He did not know, when the decision was made, that the embattled Democrats at Madison Square Garden would carry their bitter conflict to 103 ballots. Nor could he foresee exactly how intense and emotional the struggle would be.

But the *Monitor* was ready. For two years, as has been mentioned, it had been receiving dispatches from Washington from the shrewd political pen of Frederick William Wile. Mr. Wile had not only detected the scent of oil in Wyoming well ahead of his professional colleagues. He also analyzed and forecast accurately the nominations of both major parties in 1924, many weeks and months before the event.

To announce the certain renomination of President Coolidge was no feat. But Mr. Wile also foresaw the availability and likelihood of Charles Gates Dawes as his running mate. On April 11, and again on April 19, Mr. Wile put forward the Coolidge-Dawes ticket! As early as February 6 he had forecast the Coolidge nomination, had said Senator La Follette would be nominated by a third party, and had mentioned John W. Davis as a possible Democratic nominee. He kept on referring to Mr. Davis from time to time, and even suggested the possibility of Governor Charles W. Bryan of Nebraska (Brother Charlie) as Vice-Presidential nominee. Finally, on June 23, when the situation to many others was as murky as possible, Mr. Wile wrote that two things were certain: the Ku Klux Klan issue would split the Convention, and that a dark horse would be nominated for President. "This observer's definite conviction," he said in his second paragraph, "is that the nominee will be John W. Davis, of West Virginia."

Such political prescience was matched by Mr. Wile's alertness in other fields. When the *Monitor* inaugurated a radio page, on May 1, 1924, Mr. Wile had a story from Washington on it in which he forecast television, saying "seeing as well as hearing is an imminent possibility." Again, the observation falls into the category of premature rightness. On May 6, 1924, Mr. Wile had a reference to Christian A. Herter of Massachusetts in his column. Mr. Herter was just resigning as a young assistant to Herbert Hoover, the Secretary of Commerce. Let us not pretend that Mr. Wile foresaw the Herter career in Congress, in the Massachusetts State House, and in the State Department!

The *Monitor* had strong attitudes in the 1924 political strife. Up to that year, at least, Calvin Coolidge stood as a rather independent Republican. He had been nominated for the Vice-Presidency against the wishes of the party bosses in 1920. He had fought against the stand-pat leaders in Congress. His legislative proposals were relatively progressive. In the congressional session just preceding the 1924 nominations, he had made 38 proposals, many of them attractive and forward-looking, but only three were enacted. Against his opposition, Congress passed the Japanese exclusion act, the soldier's bonus, and a tax reduction bill.

His more fervent supporters at the Cleveland Convention in 1924 were the more liberal Republicans, though of course not the insurgents who later went along with Senator La Follette. Indeed, the La Follette strength included the left-wing extremists, with some outright Communist sympathizers among them. The *Monitor* exposed Communist activities at the "Progressive" convention at St. Paul which was dominated by William Z. Foster, then and now an active Communist leader.

At Cleveland, however, Mr. Wile wrote: "The elimination of the Senate oligarchy which prevailed at Chicago four years ago is the overwhelming, outstanding feature of this convention." Mr. Abbot, too, felt that the eclipse of the Old Guard was notable. He could not resist a reminder of recent Teapot Dome history. A clergyman who opened one session with prayer had concluded with the phrase "lest we forget!" Mr. Abbot added: "One of the chief needs of this campaign will be to make the people forget."

The paper's sympathies at the Democratic Convention were plainly against the antiprohibition, Tammany candidate, Alfred E. Smith, and with William G. McAdoo, his opponent. The situation was that Mr. McAdoo started with a substantial majority of the delegates, but not the two-thirds then required by Democratic rules. He could get no further. Nor could Governor Smith. The party split, and deep wounds were created.

At once the *Monitor* saw the import of these events and Mr. Abbot wrote: "Two weeks ago in Cleveland, it did not seem to practical political observers that the ticket there nominated would have any chance of success." Only "a radical blunder by the Democrats in New York" could save it. But, said Mr. Abbot as the Madison Square Garden convention opened, it would now be seen "whether that blunder is not about to be committed." So it proved to be.

Yet, with all its opposition to the Smith candidacy, the *Monitor* wrote of the speech in which he was nominated by Franklin Delano Roosevelt, appearing on one of the first occasions following his illness: "His speech was earnest, dignified, and worthy of any cause."

When, finally John W. Davis was nominated, the *Monitor* praised his character and record warmly. It did not take a sharply partisan role during the actual campaign. Even had it felt a great deal was at stake, there was no need. The Democratic split and the La Follette candidacy so divided the opposition that President Coolidge had no trouble at all in winning election.

In 1928, many of the same issues recurred. Again the *Monitor*'s viewpoint was very largely influenced by the prohibition issue. And it had grave doubts, which it expressed cautiously and discreetly, concerning the possibility of a conflict of loyalties between church and state if a Roman Catholic were elected President.

It is important to make this issue very clear. Mrs. Eddy had enjoined the officials of her church and the editors of her publications that they must hold at all times an attitude of love and respect for other religions.

In her message on the occasion of the dedication of the extension of The Mother Church, June 10, 1906, Mrs. Eddy wrote: "A genuine Christian Scientist loves Protestant and Catholic, D.D. and M.D., — loves all who love God, good; and he loves his enemies."

She had issued a remarkable statement, "On the Death of Pope Leo XIII, July 20, 1903," in these words:

> The sad, sudden announcement of the decease of Pope Leo XIII, touches the heart and will move the pen of millions. The intellectual, moral, and religious energy of this illustrious pontiff have

animated the Church of Rome for one quarter of a century. The august ruler of two hundred and fifty million human beings has now passed through the shadow of death into the great forever. The court of the Vatican mourns him; his relatives shed "the unavailing tear." He is the loved and lost of many millions. I sympathize with those who mourn, but rejoice in knowing our dear God comforts such with the blessed assurance that life is not lost; its influence remains in the minds of men, and divine Love holds its substance safe in the certainty of immortality. "In him was life; and the life was the light of men." (John 1:4)*

These statements reflected Mrs. Eddy's views toward another religion. The *Monitor*'s position in regard to other churches, and the convictions of their adherents, was precisely the same, as it is today. But its position regarding the attitude of any church that would seek to dominate government or intervene improperly in politics is a quite different issue. It has never hesitated to speak out against such aggression. It is profoundly committed to the separation of church and state. It believes in public school education, although it does not question the right of any religious group to form its own schools or to give religious instruction therein. But it believes such religious groups must finance their own schools, rather than call on the taxpayer for assistance, whether overt or covert.

And in the case of an individual Roman Catholic like Alfred E. Smith, when nominated for the office of American President, the *Monitor* joined many others in raising the question of possibly divided loyalties. The *Monitor* never made common cause with the extremists on this issue. It did not support or endorse the attitudes of the Ku Klux Klan in 1924, but condemned them. In general it left the distressing and emotion-ridden arguing of the problem to others, since it did not wish to give offense unnecessarily. But it felt Americans should face honestly and frankly the problem of divided loyalties.

However, the *Monitor*'s doubts about Al Smith as he contended for the Democratic nomination in 1924 and when he ran against Herbert Hoover in 1928 were by no means based solely on the questions of church and state. He was the prod-

* *Miscellany*, 294:22.

uct of Tammany Hall, embodying — it may be thought fairly or unfairly — all that was most unwholesome in boss politics in the United States. And he was the very spearhead of the wet crusade to repeal national prohibition.

Here the *Monitor*'s convictions were touched to the quick, since Christian Scientists are total abstainers. They regard intoxicants as among the most serious of social evils. Like a vast majority of other Americans in the first two decades of the century, they felt the unrestrained liquor trade was deeply injuring American life. It was the age of the saloon. The tragedies which the liquor traffic produced in the lives of Americans were to be seen on every hand. Then followed the enactment of prohibitory laws, in state after state, until finally the Eighteenth Amendment was law of the land.

During all this period, the *Monitor* shared and reflected the views of many trusted American leaders in political and civic life, and of many responsible newspapers. It refused to believe prohibition could not be enforced. It had no sympathy for the "jazz age" hysteria of the 1920's. The speak-easy and the hip flask, bathtub gin and mountain dew all repelled its social and its law-abiding instincts.

Few newspapers can have given any cause as unswerving, zealous, and well-documented support as the *Monitor* gave prohibition. It ran series after series, explaining social and economic benefits and exploring better methods of enforcement.

And so, when a spokesman for repeal came forward like Al Smith, the *Monitor* was naturally predisposed against him. As if these negative factors were not enough, Herbert Hoover's public record was enormously impressive to the paper. His international experience, his triumphant service as Secretary of Commerce, the kind of progressivism for which in 1928 he was the symbol, all made him the paper's natural preference. It is no wonder, therefore, that the degree of detachment which it had maintained in each Presidential election since its establishment should be cast overboard in 1928.

By this time, the *Monitor*'s own staff writers had gained

more professional maturity, and were able to handle the political writing without difficulty. Mr. Wile's writing tapered off. The Washington Bureau was getting stronger. In New York, Chicago, and California there were bureaus with able writers. The paper's staff was becoming more effective than it had ever been.

And in 1927 an important organizational change took place. The office of editor-in-chief was broadened into an Editorial Board of four members. Mr. Abbot remained as one of the Board's members, with the title of Contributing Editor. The other three members were Roland R. Harrison, who had come to the paper after important New York newspaper experience, in 1922; Frank L. Perrin, who had been chief editorial writer since 1922 and on the staff since 1916; and Charles E. Heitman, who had been associate editor since 1926, but who in 1927 became manager of the Publishing Society.

Why was the single editorship changed to an Editorial Board? The simple explanation, tersely mentioned by Mr. Abbot in "Watching the World Go By," is that in the Christian Science organization the preference was for collective responsibility. This is but a partial explanation. It is true that there are various examples of collective organization through the church structure. And in realistic fact, policy making on the *Monitor* has nearly always been collective, as it is at present. Except during the litigation period, it has never been the vehicle for a single individual's views. Even then, moderating influences existed from 1914 to 1919. At other times when the paper was under an individual editor, in the years 1908–14, 1922–27, and 1939 to the present, he has been steadily responsible to the Board of Directors, and in close contact with others whose wisdom and experience have been of pertinent value.

So the change from Mr. Abbot to an Editorial Board made collective responsibility formal and organic, as well as operative. Such a method had been under discussion since at least 1918. Prior to establishing the Editorial Board, the Directors had called to Boston Mr. Heitman, a New Yorker of wide experience in business affairs, who was also a practitioner and teacher of Christian Science. Mr. Heitman was at first made associate editor of the *Monitor*. He began an intensive and careful study of the paper's needs, resources, and policies.

Meantime, Roland R. Harrison had become executive editor in 1924, succeeding Mr. Stow. His long professional experience and his dedicated insights into Christian Science journalism soon began to make themselves felt. All these factors came together in 1927. So the Directors combined in the Editorial Board the qualities represented by Mr. Abbot as editor, Mr. Heitman as business manager, Mr. Harrison as executive editor, and Mr. Perrin as chief editorial writer. Here collective responsibility was knit into an organic group, and with various changes in membership, it proceeded to operate the paper for a dozen years. Once more, the procedure met the needs of the hour. Under the Editorial Board, the *Monitor* grew steadily. It brought the paper through the severe problems of the depression, meeting newly challenging versions of old political and economic problems. It greatly modernized the *Monitor,* leading it effectively into its second quarter century.

25

◇◇◇◇◇◇◇◇◇◇◇◇◇◇◇◇◇◇◇◇

The Bull Market and "*Monitor* Form"

IN THE LATE 1920's, under the newly established Editorial Board, an experienced business management, and steadily more expert advertising and circulation departments, the *Monitor* increased its revenues and firmed its financial base.

The years 1928 and 1929 were for the paper, as for the United States, a period of confidence and exuberance. The great bull market was far from the chief source of the *Monitor*'s hopes. To the contrary, the paper foresaw at an early date and persistently warned against the dangers of stock speculation. But the election of Herbert Hoover, the Kellogg-Briand Pact, the agreement on naval armament limitation between President Hoover and British Prime Minister MacDonald, and the general prosperity which prevailed and was not at first destroyed by the stock price collapses of October 1929, all motivated the paper's hopes and expectations.

Then, as the depression set in and deepened, the paper asked searching questions, not only of the national government and of its relations with other nations, but concerning its own news and editorial policies. There was a careful and critical review of the paper's operations in 1932–33 which resulted in important liberalization of its policies and broadening of its horizons.

But in 1928, world affairs were at their most encouraging pitch since 1919. The paper reflected hopes and ideals for progress toward more stable peace and sounder economy. Nevertheless, it detected and pointed out both in news and editorial columns that there were grave dangers going uncorrected.

As early as May 14, 1928, the *Monitor* proclaimed the fatal weakness of the bull market. In an exclusive interview with Professor Gustav Cassel of the University of Stockholm, a world-renowned authority, published on the front page, it quoted him as saying: "Speculation has gone beyond the limits of reason. Securities as a whole are out of line with their true values and a few securities are greatly overpriced. This the people should know. They should be told that the chances of losing on a stock exchange are far greater than those of winning, and it is the province of the newspapers to tell them."

The Federal Reserve System, powerful though it was, could not hold speculative enthusiasm within bounds, Professor Cassel felt. "The thought of the people must be changed," he affirmed. He added, "The gold standard cannot be any longer relied upon as an objective standard, automatically guaranteeing the stability of our money." And he said that those who object to a managed currency "should combat other forms of unnecessary governmental control of trade."

Not content with printing this warning and giving it strong display, the *Monitor* followed with interviews from American and European banking and financial leaders. On May 17, it found Chicago bankers agreeing that stock prices were too high and anticipating a recession. One of them, David R. Forgan of the National Bank of the Republic, said, "When the public takes the bit in its teeth you cannot stop the runaway until something disastrous happens."

On May 18, Professor O. M. W. Sprague, of the Harvard

School of Business Administration, told the *Monitor* that the Federal Reserve Bank could correct the existing situation, but that the press and public also could help. He urged a rise in the rediscount rate, though he preferred a direct curb on security loans. It might be asked, said Professor Sprague, "why worry if speculators are wiped out?" He answered by pinpointing the danger that collapse of the security market might lead to "general recession of business with a sacrifice of prosperity in all lines from agriculture to retail selling."

There could hardly have been more explicit warning. On the same day, the *Monitor* ran an editorial titled "Lambs Beware" in which it drove home to its readers the warnings it had been printing from high authority. There were few dissenting voices among the leaders the paper chose to interview, although it ran briefly the persistently optimistic statements of Professor Irving Fisher, of Yale University, and of some industrial leaders who could not read the signs. On May 19, it had a statement from W. Randolph Burgess, then assistant Federal Reserve Agent for New York, emphasizing the warning against speculative loans and too great increase in credit. As Undersecretary of the Treasury in the Eisenhower Administration, Mr. Burgess was one of the chief architects of the program to curb another inflation in the 1950's, through management of the huge public debt.

The *Monitor* kept on raising its voice against the mesmeric rush of speculation. Its readers, insofar as they heeded its words, could have been amply protected when the debacle struck. On September 5, 1929, two days after the market reached its apex, it carried Roger Babson's famous words on its front page: "Sooner or later there is a crash coming and it may be a terrific one. This does not mean selling all that you have but it does mean paying up your loans and avoiding margin speculation."

In addition, the paper had pointed out for years that high American tariffs and insistence on repayment of the war debts in cash were creating a gravely unbalanced world economic situation which could be no more than mitigated by the flow of American private investments abroad. On August 16, 1929, again on the front page, it quoted Professor T. E. Gregory of the London School of Economics, saying: "The recent upward development of stock prices in New York simply means that America is asserting her old role of disturber of the economic peace of the world." This warning was echoed by Robert B. Warren of the Federal Reserve Board and Case, Pomeroy & Company, and by Herbert Feis, the economist who was soon to play an important role in the State Department.

For the *Monitor* to give such prominence to these prophets of doom is all the more remarkable and responsible in view of the fact that Christian Science thinking is basically optimistic. It is expectant of good, as part of God's harmonious plan. But Christian Science, adequately and accurately applied, aims never to be blindly optimistic nor heedless to factors of danger.

"To injure no man, but to bless all mankind," the *Monitor*'s basic role as defined by its Founder, has always tacitly but most genuinely included the role of warning. The very best kind of blessing may often be the exposure of evil and the prevision and prevention of dangers. The worst kind of injury may be the failure to sound a note of warning in time.

In words fully applicable to this phase of the *Monitor*'s role, Mrs. Eddy wrote in *Science and Health:* * "Many are willing to open the eyes of the people to the power of good resident in divine Mind, but they are not so willing to point out the evil in human thought, and expose evil's hidden mental ways of accomplishing iniquity.

"Why this backwardness, since exposure is necessary to ensure the avoidance of the evil? . . . Who is telling mankind of the foe in ambush? Is the informer one who sees the foe? If so, listen and be wise. Escape from evil, and designate those as unfaithful stewards who have seen the danger and yet have given no warning."

The *Monitor* certainly risked the displeasure of more than a few of its readers when it warned of the dangers of a stock market crash. And it was facing sharply divided financial opinion. Many eminent leaders, particularly in the banking and business fields, thought it was virtually treasonable to

* P. 570.

imply that disaster might be impending. But the *Monitor* knew it must not become an unfaithful steward and it went ahead, in this as in later and perhaps graver crises, risking displeasure of some in order to help awaken and save the many.

Its role was not a strident one. The *Monitor* was not a Cassandra, constantly proclaiming doom. It hoped to energize the necessary measures to bring speculation under control and steady the national economy. Its motives were entirely therapeutic, not — like those of some prophets of disaster — sensational and sadistic. Though it frequently gave top emphasis to the warnings, the general tone of its columns reflected the vigor and confidence of the national economy in 1928 and 1929. It was not selling prosperity short, but urging self-control and public awakening which would have been more effective therapy than anything the Federal Reserve Board or the Treasury could have done.

When, in September, 1929, the market began to slide downward, the paper recorded the daily events and the warnings, and on Black Thursday, October 24, and still blacker Tuesday, October 29, it gave vigorous page-one prominence to the catastrophic market breaks. Editorially, on October 25, it discussed "The Mirage of Easy Wealth," and on October 30 it urged Americans to learn a lesson from the stock market. The paper pulled no punches in its reports of what had happened. Like virtually all others, it hoped the collapse in the market would contribute to a more salutary economy. It felt there were many measures that might be taken which would check a widespread depression. It had long realized, and pointed out, that agriculture's place in the economy was severely undervalued. For years it had urged effective measures to stabilize farm prices and maintain farm credit. It had explored and endorsed programs to balance farm production with consuming capacity.

The verdict of historians on Herbert Hoover remains highly controversial. But the more objective and least doctrinaire among them have pointed out that the strengths in the Hoover program to combat the depression considerably outweighed the weaknesses. They emphasize that he had to face implacable political opposition at first financed by elements in big business, the Raskob–du Pont–General Motors interest. Later the opposition extended to all the Democrats who were unwilling to support remedial measures until they returned to power in 1932, and to more extreme left-wing elements.

The *Monitor* gave President Hoover unswerving support, though it sometimes urged him to go farther than he felt it possible to go. It had no sympathy with the Raskob-directed smear campaign against him. The program President Hoover sought to develop in the years 1930–32, and which the *Monitor* supported, included many of the policies that were readily enacted, though somewhat modified and accompanied by more experimental measures, when the New Deal came into power. The program the President laid before Congress in late 1931, favored by the *Monitor*, included an expanded public works program, home loan banks, regulation of the stock exchange, laws to regulate the irresponsible policies of state banks, authority to liquify the frozen assets of shutdown banks, expansion of Federal Reserve credits, revision of the bankruptcy laws, appropriation of new funds to continue the Farm Marketing Board's support of agricultural prices, the appropriation of $300 million for direct relief, and the raising of the income-tax rate on the upper brackets.

The *Monitor* strenuously opposed the Hawley-Smoot Tariff, which raised the average duties from 33 per cent to 40 per cent. It opposed special-privilege increases and reminded readers that a higher tariff would make the war debts harder to pay. It conducted and on July 30, 1929, published a poll of newspapers showing heavy opposition to the Smoot-Hawley bill. Repeatedly it urged more concern for the consumer. Finally, on June 5, 1930, it urged President Hoover to veto the Smoot-Hawley bill.

When in June of 1931 President Hoover persuaded other governments to join him in declaring a year's moratorium on intergovernmental payments, the *Monitor* was heartily in support of the move.

Whatever criticisms may be made with validity of President Hoover's policies, it cannot be denied that the opposition to his program was bitterly partisan and obstructionist. One of history's frustrating ifs is to speculate on how much sooner national and world recovery might have come if Mr. Hoover had been able to secure nonpartisan support and carry out his program from the outset. That, of course, is what the *Monitor* favored.

It could not join in the chorus of condemnation of the President from partisan quarters, from doctrinaire, and left-wing sources, and to some degree from the extreme right-wing in big business. Nor would the *Monitor* join those who criticized Mr. Hoover because of his inhibitions of personality or political finesse. Like everyone who has ever worked closely with Mr. Hoover, the *Monitor* saw the constructive, warm, and humanitarian sides of his character. It did not consider his extreme shyness a reason to condemn his policies. One of his associates has remarked, "Mr. Hoover has a multitude of enemies but no ex-friends," and the *Monitor* was among the friends.

Professor Leland Baldwin, from whose *Recent American History* this quotation is taken writes: * "Hoover has been maligned unjustly as callous, reactionary, inept, and even stupid. His policies may or may not have been shortsighted and mistaken, but it is evident that he always kept before him a zeal for promoting human welfare and with this as a guide and principle never flagged nor deviated. His shortcomings — if these be such — lay in too great a faith in human reasonableness and in too great a faith that the economic forces which had made us great must continue to operate. He was an old-fashioned liberal who believed in local responsibility and preferred voluntary association to imposed controls. He believed in democracy and its precious diversities."

All these qualities endeared President Hoover to the *Monitor*. The paper inevitably resisted the unfair, destroying tactics used against him. Combined with these elements of opposition there was once more arrayed the power of the big city boss-ridden machines, and the full force of the movement to repeal prohibition. It is no wonder that the paper gave the Hoover Administration unswerving support, and that when

* Rindge, N.H., 1954, p. 182.

the 1932 election came along it continued to endorse him. Like Walter Lippmann and various others who knew Franklin D. Roosevelt well — or thought they did — it was not greatly impressed in advance by his strength and stability of character, and it feared his alliance with the wets and the bosses.

The full import of President Roosevelt's social and economic program and the real meaning of the New Deal were scarcely visible in the 1932 campaign. Nothing stood out more in that campaign than Mr. Roosevelt's pledge to cut federal spending and balance the budget. Yet when Mr. Roosevelt made his famous speech at the Commonwealth Club in San Francisco, September 24, 1932, hinting at the scope of his program, its import was at once detected and described by Mr. Strout, covering his campaign tour.

The *Monitor*'s editorial and news policies were precise and positive during the years when preventive measures might have averted or mitigated world depression, and might have preserved peace. On crucial points its voice was unmistakable: it crusaded early and often for the relief of American farmers from a grossly unbalanced price structure and an intolerable burden of debt; it analyzed and specified the measures that might have curbed stock market excesses; it hammered away at the importance of relieving the blockade of international debt and opening the channels of trade by lower tariff policies; it favored early and extensive revision of the unfair and unenforceable elements in the Versailles peace settlements; it advocated closer and more constant American co-operation in the enforcement of peace; it pressed for more active limitation and reduction of armaments.

But in all this, its reiterated program was to dig deep into the causes of wars, conflicts, economic unbalance. Its remedies were in the main the steps which hindsight now commends as the most likely to have been effective. To record these facts is not to pretend any sort of infallibility. The *Monitor* was capable of misreading the signs of the times, though its inherent safeguards of moderation and reasonableness protected it from many mistakes. Had its proposals for constructive and remedial action been followed in time, the world might have been a very different place. The *Monitor* did not often prophesy doom, because it was persistently urging the kind of action that would — or might — have prevented disaster. Hence, in retrospect, it can be criticized for not spelling out more forcefully the consequences of not taking remedial action. The thesis of the inevitability of disaster is not congenial to the *Monitor,* since its constant preoccupation is with the measures which need to be and can be taken to avoid disaster. The record reveals an unwillingness to surrender to disaster at any time, and an urge to salvage, to improve, to prevent.

Such attitudes have turned inward to the organization and planning of the newspaper, as well as outward to the world. In a sense, the *Monitor*'s first quarter century — though replete with extraordinary journalistic accomplishment from the very beginning — was a shaking-down period. The tenure of its top editorial executives was relatively brief, though of Methuselahn length compared with the jittery editorial turnover in some famous publishing groups. The first editorial team on the *Monitor* held office for six years, 1908–14. The second lasted eight years, 1914–22. The third prevailed from 1922 to 1927. The fourth, the Editorial Board, extended to twelve years. Followed the brief period November 1939 to January 1941, when Roland R. Harrison was administrative editor and I was his second in command. Ever since then the same editorial hands have been in charge. It will be seen, therefore, that stability of operation increased in the 1920's and has prevailed ever since.

This fact has resulted in the *Monitor* staff's learning its job more effectively, though with a constant interest in internal improvement. Thus it was that in the early 1930's, as the end of the paper's first quarter century approached, friends both on and off the staff carried out a careful re-examination of its purposes and performance.

The need for re-examination stemmed from several sources. Advertising and circulation revenues had been reasonably satisfactory in the 1920's. But earnings felt the effects of the depression, in common with all other elements in the national and world economy. Deeper than problems of revenue and circulation, it was seen that the *Monitor* should do a better job. Such an accomplishment, it was realized, would lead to better revenues. So all concerned put their heads together.

A "Fact Finding Committee" was set up by the Board of Directors. Its chairman was Dr. Albert F. Gilmore, a former editor of the *Christian Science Sentinel* and *Journal,* and then a member of the Board of Trustees of the Publishing Society, as well as of the Monitor Editorial Board. Associated with him were Messrs. Abbot, Harrison, and Perrin of the Editorial Board, Norman S. Rose, the advertising manager; Colonel Herbert A. Johnson, the circulation manager; Rufus Steele, a long-experienced author then writing a lively daily column in the *Monitor;* and the Marquess of Lothian.

A great deal of the spark of the inquiry was furnished by the two members who were most nearly outsiders to the staff: Lord Lothian and Mr. Steele. They were talented and remarkable men, deeply interested in the *Monitor*'s progress, and widely experienced in world affairs. Both were earnest Christian Scientists. Lord Lothian, as Philip Kerr, had been a member of the "Milner Kindergarten" which set up the self-governing statute of the Union of South Africa and helped liquidate the Boer War. He had been private secretary to David Lloyd George during the First World War, when his experiences were challenging and informative. Later he became Secretary to the Rhodes Trust; he handled the Round Table Conference which eased the strains with Mahatma Gandhi as India was pressing toward independence in the early 1930's; and in 1939 he became British Ambassador to the United States. He was intimately acquainted with the United States, as he was with all parts of the English-speaking world.

Lord Lothian had begun to write for the *Monitor* in the early 1920's, giving its editorial page a uniquely informed and experienced analysis of world affairs. More deeply, Lord Lothian's thoughtful interest in Christian Science persuaded him that its teachings held a great message for mankind which must animate the attitudes of the *Monitor* though they would not find overt expression in its columns beyond the daily religious article and rare general references in editorials.

Rufus Steele brought a lifetime of successful, energetic magazine writing to the *Monitor* in 1931, augmented by his own interest in Christian Science. He felt the paper should be freed from some of the inhibitions that had crept into its news and editorial policies since the earlier days. Above all, he believed there was no subject — crime, disaster, or otherwise — which the paper could not treat effectively as part of its editorial mission. He felt there should be a style, which he called "*Monitor* form," in which the paper would delve into any and all social problems.

The Fact Finding Committee went into all phases of the paper's editorial operation with zeal. Among its specific concerns was the fact that local circulation, in Boston and New England, was at disappointingly low levels. If the paper could not reach a satisfactory number of readers at its own doorstep, it asked, how could it expect to spread sufficiently throughout the world?

As a result of the committee's deliberations, three important actions were taken: (1) the local editions were revitalized with strong coverage, gathered by an enlarged and strengthened staff; (2) the paper's stylistic sights were lifted and many old limitations were stricken away; (3) a weekly magazine section was established, printed in rotogravure, containing vigorous articles from world-renowned authorities, effective feature material, and one article seeking especially to bring to bear Christian Science thinking on world affairs.

The magazine section resulted in particular from the thinking and urging of a group of British readers led by Lord Lothian. The group included Viscount and Viscountess Astor, who were also longstanding students of Christian Science with an especial interest and concern in world affairs, and other persons of wide experience and distinction. They felt a magazine section, oriented especially to world problems, would add dignity and prestige to the paper, which as a daily newspaper unavoidably reached its British and other overseas readers late, and contained a substantial amount of domestic American material of varying interest to overseas readers. Meetings were held in London with enthusiastic discussion of the project.

Of the three great forward steps projected by the Fact Finding Committee, two were a return to earlier, dynamic days. The paper had begun in 1908 with an extensive and effective local coverage, and again in 1922 had sought to restore a vital relationship to the New England community. But for various reasons — Mr. Dixon's worldwide orientation being one, and economy in the 1920's another — the local effort had each time been cut back to a mere token.

Likewise, the restoration of an uninhibited capacity to tackle unsavory news was a return to the earliest days. The *Monitor* during the years when Mrs. Eddy was carefully following its growth had none of the taboos that crept in during later years. Nor had the religious periodicals published from 1883 onward any timorousness in attacking delicate problems, or any squeamishness of style in treating them. But the taboos had grown up; they needed to be swept away. Progress had already begun in the late 1920's — Mr. Hurd's story of getting mention of jazz bands into the paper is typical of other quaint stylistic concepts and liberations.

In 1933, with the cordial approval, support, and co-operation of both the Board of Directors and the Board of Trustees, the *Monitor* set forth to produce an outstanding local edition, to tackle any and all news that the well-informed citizen would need to read, and to produce an excellent weekly magazine section.

In other respects, 1933 was a period of progress and growth. The paper's twenty-fifth anniversary, falling in November, provided a bench mark for analysis and challenge. At the same time, a tremendous new Publishing House was under construction. And it was a period of ferment and change. The Roosevelt Administration in Washington was taking stirring measures to cope with the depression. The *Monitor* supported many of them, especially those which had been long a part of its editorial commitment, and had in fact been foreshadowed by earlier administrations as longstanding needs.

26

◇◇◇◇◇◇◇◇◇◇◇◇◇◇◇◇◇◇◇◇◇

Years of Solid Progress

As THE 1930's advanced, evidences of unified and intelligent thinking became readily apparent in the pages of the *Monitor*. For the first time, a substantial number of newspaper men and women who had "grown up with the *Monitor*" were reaching the point of professional competence and genuine skill. The nature and meaning of *Monitor* journalism was perceived and applied with new craftsmanship. The paper, in short, had come of age.

In Boston, as well as all over the world, the paper's staff had new abilities, not just based on professional service with other publications, not simply rooted in idealism and zeal, but deriving from actual and protracted experience in *Monitor* journalism itself. This new generation of *Monitor* craftsmen might have come a decade sooner if there had not been the two experiences of discontinuity: the break-off of the McLellan-Dodds regime in 1914, and — much more severe — the litigation culminating Mr. Dixon's overpowering personal editorship.

Somehow, during the late 1920's and early 1930's the people, the ideas, the experience, and the leadership all came together. Despite the paper's amazingly precocious youth, it was only in the 1930's that it began to prove its full stature. It was a "team" success. The two basic Boards — the Board of Directors and the Board of Trustees — gave full, perceptive, and generous support. They were deeply interested in the paper's welfare and devoted a great deal of time to its improvement. The Monitor Editorial Board was a strong and diversified collective executive and its individual members both worked together and did their specific jobs with skill. At other levels, the paper was enriched by the accumulating experience of its staff and the arrival of new talent.

Though Mr. Abbot's role as editor-in-chief was broadened into the Editorial Board in 1927, both before and after that event he gave the staff a stimulating and productive example. His own writing, whether in editorials, his regular signed column, his dispatches from political conventions or other important meetings, his interviews with leading figures throughout the nation and the world, or his book reviews, was an exciting illustration of lively journalism. His experience and sagacity in the background of American government, his wide and intimate acquaintance with public men brought the paper very large elements of realism. His counsel on the Editorial Board drew from a lifetime of diversified newspaper operations to assist the *Monitor* in developing new modes and strengths. From his appointment in 1922 to his passing in 1934, Mr. Abbot gave unstintingly of his knowledge.

Not the least valuable of Mr. Abbot's many undertakings were his interviews. Possibly the most remarkable of these was with Benito Mussolini, in January of 1928. Here Mr. Abbot sought to understand and record the reasoning and motivation of fascism. He talked with Mussolini in the dictator's awesome great office in the Palazzo Venezia. Though Mr. Abbot questioned the effect of fascism on Italian liberties, his interview was published as a pamphlet by the Italian Embassy in Washington and distributed far and wide. With the same generous detachment Mr. Abbot interviewed Viscount

Cecil, Dr. Gustav Stresemann, President Masaryk, Dr. Beneš, and many others. Similarly, he talked with many outstanding Americans and recorded their views in ample scope: Cyrus H. K. Curtis, the great publisher, Judge Elbert H. Gary, chairman of the board of the U.S. Steel Corporation, and many others were represented.

Mr. Abbot helped greatly to professionalize the *Monitor* staff, to bring it into the mainstream of American journalism. He was a founder and officer of the American Society of Newspaper Editors, and helped decisively in shaping its Code of Ethics. He fought constantly for clean and responsible newspapers. The effect of such a man on the young fellows growing up on the *Monitor* in the 1920's can readily be imagined. It meant to them that their paper was not "peculiar," their editor was a recognized leader in the profession. The gleam in his eyes, the neat little goatee on his chin, his tweeds, his easy kindness and sophistication composed a personality which charmed and inspired the eager young cubs. And, if one of the cubs may add a personal note, the sight of Mr. Abbot's gracious wife and handsome collie dog waiting in the car in which they would all drive home, composed a picture of just what a cub thought an editor should be!

Saville Davis, who was a cub reporter toward the end of Mr. Abbot's period, recalls being met by the editor in the corridor one day. Mr. Abbot looked with interest at the new face, remembering no doubt just how a young fellow feels when he meets the boss, and said: "Don't let anybody fool you. There's only one title a man would want on any newspaper, and that's the title of reporter."

This note of professional wisdom remains a *Monitor* proverb.

Roland R. Harrison, who had moved from executive editor of the *Monitor* to become manager of the Publishing Society in 1929, retained in the business office his deep interest in news and editorial affairs. Finally, in 1939, he returned to the editorial department as its chief executive, with the title of administrative editor. Mr. Harrison's combination of long newspaper experience in New York and dedication to the *Monitor*'s particular role, made him a tower of strength. He directed the publication of the handsome and informative special editions which marked the paper's twenty-fifth anniversary. He had the mammoth job of directing the planning and erection of the new Publishing House. All this took place during depression and limited-recovery years, when advertising and circulation revenues were hard to increase. Thus he worked under constant pressure for economies. Nevertheless, he and the staff, with the support of the Boards, frequently lifted their sights in experiments and enlargements of the paper's scope and operations — all of which cost money.

Mr. Harrison was a person of medium stature, and in his years on the *Monitor* his tightly curled hair was gray, his cheeks were pink, and his bright eyes held a twinkle. He was kindness and patience personified with junior members of the staff. His thinking constantly ranged over new projects and techniques, though certain fundamentals of his journalistic youth remained fixed points with him. Thus for instance, he rather regretted the steady increase of by-lines in the paper and would have preferred a return to the anonymity of his greatly admired New York *Herald*. Though Mr. Harrison's basic convictions were relatively conservative, he was exceedingly fair-minded and always ready to see the merits of a good case.

Indeed, Mr. Harrison was imbued not only with a deeply idealistic devotion to the paper's purposes, but an incessant practical interest in improving its techniques. It would be hard to say whether the newspaperman or the idealist was dominant in his make-up: both were vividly illustrated to his associates every day. When he talked a problem over with a staff member, his ideas would be illuminated with spiritual motivation. Such direction was inspiring to the maturing editorial staff, which turned the corner from experimentation to confidence during his years of executive responsibility. Year in and year out, through his long service on the Monitor Editorial Board, Mr. Harrison exerted great influence on the paper's progress.

He loved to walk out to the composing room just as the most difficult editions were going to press. There he would stand, dressed in dignified dark blue with stiffly starched white linen, his hands clasped behind his back, his eyes sparkling, sniffing the heady scent of printer's ink and watching the swift mechanical processes that mean so much to the born-and-bred newspaperman.

Most effectively teamed with Mr. Harrison, from 1933 to 1939 as executive editor of the *Monitor* and member of the Editorial Board, was Roscoe Drummond. To him must go a substantial share of the credit for the steady improvement of the paper in the late 1920's and during the 1930's. Mr. Drummond's journalistic genius hardly needs to be explained, since he is at present very active as Washington columnist for the New York *Herald Tribune* and 140 other newspapers, as well as a special adviser to the *Herald Tribune* management. He writes a frequent exclusive column for the *Monitor* itself, and is an old and welcome friend and associate of its staff.

I may as well confess that I cannot write about Mr. Drummond with much detachment, since Mr. Drummond and I came to the *Monitor* as cub reporters at nearly the same time (Mr. Drummond in 1924, I in 1925), and we have remained very close friends and colleagues during our professional careers. When, in 1939, the responsible Boards decided to switch the jobs of Mr. Drummond and me, making him chief of the *Monitor*'s Washington Bureau and me general news editor, later managing editor, our friendship was undisturbed.

Mr. Drummond weathered this abrupt change with the utmost equanimity. What on the surface was a demotion proved to be an open door to large service to the paper as a writer. He plunged into the Washington job with such enthusiasm and skill that very shortly he became a leader of the professional corps there. His resignation from the *Monitor* in 1953, after more long years of able and dedicated service, was entirely amicable. It was motivated by his desire and opportunity to reach a numerically larger audience.

But we are getting ahead of the story. Mr. Drummond soon progressed from cub reporter in 1924 to assistant to Mr. Harrison when he was executive editor, from 1927 to 1929. In 1929 Mr. Drummond became chief editorial writer for a brief period, in 1930 went to London as European editorial manager, and in 1933 returned to Boston as executive editor. While still in London, he had taken part with Lord Lothian and others in the study of *Monitor* problems which led particularly to the establishment of the magazine section.

Upon Mr. Drummond's return to Boston in 1933, he was given the job of carrying out the recommendations of the Fact Finding Committee. An engrossing first task, irrelevant to the long-range improvement of the paper, was to get out the twenty-fifth anniversary edition. This "Progress Edition" was composed of six daily rotogravure sections with the regular paper. It was an admirable review of the state of the world, and of the Monitor. It commemorated not only the anniversary, but the construction of the new Publishing House and the fiftieth anniversary of the Publishing Society itself. The issues included much historical data of the paper's founding and early years, but their chief focus was forward. One of its features was a symposium from outstanding world leaders on "What Does the World Most Need Today?" Each day for a week the paper reprinted in facsimile two pages from its initial edition of November 25, 1908, so that a complete copy of the historic first number was provided.

Though the production of the anniversary edition was a mammoth task, it was as nothing compared to the establishment of the magazine section, the activation of a strong local edition, and the freeing of the entire paper from old inhibitions and taboos. Mr. Drummond and the rest of the growing, strengthening staff set about the jobs with enthusiasm.

The magazine was a major achievement. Its editorship was placed in the hands of Lewis Rex Miller, who had been the paper's correspondent in Paris since 1929 and Geneva since 1932. Mr. Miller is a Kansan, who had been educated at Harvard and Oxford Universities, had taught six years at Harvard, and was a foreign service officer for the Commerce Department before joining the *Monitor* staff in 1929. His cosmopolitan background well fitted him for the task of producing a magazine especially designed to have a cosmopolitan touch. Authoritative articles by world leaders, strong and attractive pictorial features, lighter articles of human interest, book reviews, and an interpretive article with special religious undercurrents were the chief content of the handsome new product.

Prime ministers and cabinet members, senators and members of Parliament, diplomats, high-ranking Army and Navy officers, scholars and men of letters, all contributed to the magazine and made its contents in these earliest years a kind of *Who's Who* of the world.

Mr. Miller was transferred to California in 1936, where he became Pacific Coast correspondent for the *Monitor.* He left the paper in 1940, and has continued to have a distinguished career as foreign information officer, university teacher, writer, and radio and television speaker. He was succeeded by Ernest C. Sherburne, who edited the magazine imaginatively until 1943.

Following Mr. Sherburne, Walter W. Cunningham took over the magazine from 1943 to 1950. His earlier career has also been described. He retired from the *Monitor* in 1953, but continues to lead an active professional life. The fourth and last editor of the magazine was John Beaufort, who is now the *Monitor*'s dramatic critic in New York.

By virtue of producing the magazine in the rotogravure process, it was possible to give its art and typography the bright colors and accuracy in detail which escape letterpress. Thus the magazine was clearly a de luxe job, impressive, rich, and dignified. For almost two decades it added strength and depth to the paper. Many of its articles were notable expressions of policy and opinion by responsible public men. One of the most noteworthy was a heroic statement of Japanese liberalism and conciliation by Viscount Saito, who had been Japanese Prime Minister but was out of office. Soon after the *Monitor* article was published, Viscount Saito was assassinated by military nationalist fanatics because of his liberal views.

The magazine section's first art editor, Mrs. Frances Davis, set high standards for selection and reproduction of noteworthy illustrations. The composition, layout, and general quality of the magazine's art have never been excelled in any American newspaper. From 1934 to 1949, the magazine was produced by outside rotogravure firms, first in New York and then in Louisville. But in 1949, since the *Monitor* had installed its own Hoe Color-Convertible Presses, the printing of the magazine was transferred from rotogravure to letterpress, and to the *Monitor*'s own plant. The change marked a notable shift: from being a magazine-type product, on extra-quality paper, it now became more akin to the supplement of a daily newspaper, on newsprint. The *Monitor*'s own color-printing facilities were and are of the highest newspaper standard, but the work is of a different genre than rotogravure, and does not pretend to achieve the same gloss or precision. However, there was one great gain. The magazine could now be produced on almost newspaper deadlines, instead of two weeks to a month in advance.

But experience in producing the magazine in more nearly newspaper form, though once a week, led inevitably to another logical step. Instead of being produced only once weekly, its contents were separated and added to each day's paper, with the magazine material occupying the first page of the second section. Thus each day's issue of the *Monitor* was comparable to each other day's. A premium issue was not being produced once a week.

The ultimate distribution of magazine material through each day of the week was the result of a rather important fundamental awareness which had not been so clear in 1933–34. It was recalled that *The Christian Science Monitor,* as established by Mrs. Eddy, is a daily newspaper, not a weekly. Down through the years, from time to time, well-wishers have proposed that the *Monitor* should publish a weekly, or should convert itself into a weekly. It was reasoned that a publication with so much background material, such high cultural standards, and reaching most of its readers later than the day of publication, was more than many readers could absorb six times weekly. Its relationship to its public, these friends claimed, was more like that of a weekly. So, said some of them, why not turn the paper into a weekly, or at least add a weekly to the daily. The publication of weeklies by *The Times* of London, the Manchester *Guardian,* and other papers, was recalled. The conversion and consequent success of David Lawrence's *United States News* from a daily in newspaper size to a weekly in magazine format was used as an example.

Such arguments ignore the fact that Mrs. Eddy set up a *daily* newspaper, and that to convert to a weekly or to emphasize a weekly issue would be to violate the terms of her trust. Unwittingly the magazine section, set up so splendidly and successfully in 1934, did in fact draw from the daily paper some of the support it should have received. It attracted new readers and friends as well. It is an experience which is remembered without any regret, but with pride. Yet from the experience those responsible for the paper have learned the basic lesson that its mission is daily, and that the daily task must never be blurred or adulterated. Moreover, from a strictly practical point of view, one subscriber to the daily newspaper would be worth six subscribers to the weekly magazine. Additionally, the discontinuance of the magazine section in 1949 was also motivated by the decision not to accept one-day subscriptions to the paper. This meant that readers were no longer able to take only the Saturday paper, with its premium contents. As a result, subscriptions were spread more evenly throughout the week. Today, the six-days-a-week *Monitor* is made as nearly complete as possible, containing the depth values associated with a magazine as well as its basic news values. Anybody who picks up any copy of the *Monitor* can count on a complete and representative product.

Another important lesson was learned through the magazine experience. As has been noted, at the outset it contained one article in which religious thinking was directly applied and expressed in discussing some political, economic, or social problem. Some of these articles were much appreciated. Such a one was "Clipping the Wings of Fear" by Rufus Steele. But in time it was seen that these articles, like some editorials and articles prior to April, 1909, were giving the paper an excessively religious and denominational aspect. The articles themselves suffered from the defect of not being totally religious or totally secular. They were often neither one thing nor another, and they took on the disadvantages of compromise and mixture.

It was seen that religious thinking can and should underlie anything and everything in the *Monitor*. Copy can be motivated, illuminated, and inspired by deep convictions and insights, but it must not be preachment or proselytizing.

The revival of the *Monitor*'s strong local coverage, which began in 1934 also, has never been suspended. From that day to this, the paper has maintained a group of able reporters and has given prominence to important local news. The first city editor under the new dispensation in 1934 was Volney D. Hurd, whose recollections of earlier days have been quoted. Mr. Hurd, since 1944 the paper's correspondent in Paris, is an original and ingenious thinker. He organized, trained, and continuously stimulated a group of young men and women who were competent then but have since grown into first-line editors and correspondents. They include: the paper's present managing editor, Saville R. Davis; its present overseas news editor, Joseph G. Harrison; the chief of its Washington Bureau, William H. Stringer; the chief of the London Bureau, Henry S. Hayward.

Among the many others were Neal Stanford, now the *Monitor*'s diplomatic correspondent in Washington; Nate White, its business and financial editor; John Beaufort, its New York dramatic critic; and two men who have since made eminent careers for themselves elsewhere — Robert R. Mullen, a public relations consultant in Washington who handled General Eisenhower's press relations just before his nomination for the Presidency in 1952, and Roland Sawyer, special assistant to the board of directors of the Export-Import Bank. Working for Mr. Hurd in the 1930's, they had fine experience in lively, careful, interpretive newswriting.

Prior to becoming city editor, Mr. Hurd had held the exciting job of radio and aviation editor, during the most stirring pioneer days of these two lusty infants. He had himself been an aviator during the First World War. Throughout the 1920's, and later, he guided into the *Monitor*'s columns a steady flow of ahead-of-the-minute, well-informed news about the growth of radio and the spreading of airlines. He was himself an able broadcaster. In 1930, he devised the practical plan of developing a script, "The Monitor Views the News," which was mailed to no less than 400 radio stations throughout the United States eager to get such excellent copy. It was a fine plan which was ultimately outdated only by the growth of radio networks. To prepare this script, and double on the city staff, Mr. Hurd had the able group of writers mentioned above.

Through such experience, "*Monitor* form" — the freeing of the paper from false inhibitions and stylistic taboos — was quietly but seriously getting under way. The taboos had not grown up overnight; they were not removed overnight. It simply had to be realized, in daily operation and practice, that there was no subject of public importance in the news, however much it might turn on crime or disaster, which could not be treated effectively and helpfully in the *Monitor*. The test of social significance is the only genuine test that needs to be applied. Items which are only scandalous and trivial are merely ignored. There must be a valid social reason for printing anything. The reason must be as apparent as possible. In every case, all efforts must be made to give the story depth and significance beyond the bare news.

A graphic illustration is the Greenlease kidnaping and murder, in Kansas City in 1953. A more loathsome murder could scarcely be imagined. On the day the murder was discovered, when sensational newspapers splashed enormous headlines across their columns, the *Monitor* did not touch the story. This was in 1953. Perhaps today, in 1958, the paper would run a brief item on the first day, with the understanding that a meaningful follow-up would soon come. On the second day, the paper's special correspondent in Kansas City, not a *Monitor*-trained staff man at all, but a very capable newspaperman responsive to the direction of the *Monitor*'s American news desk, sent in a splendid discussion in depth of the social conditions which had formed the criminals. It was an exceedingly helpful story, a realistic sociologist's analysis of a problem society needs to solve. When it was published, nobody wrote the paper to protest. The value of the coverage was apparent.

There has been a favorable response whenever the *Monitor*'s crime articles clearly indicated their motivation. When, on an interim basis, the paper has simply but briefly recorded the criminal event, there have been some inquiries and protests. Then it has been necessary to tell such readers that the paper was providing information which it hoped and planned to supplement with analysis that would perform a social purpose. In addition, it has been explained that the paper considers it necessary to tell readers anything they need to know in order to be adequately informed for their civic duties. This does not extend to mere trivia.

There were many pioneers, in the 1920's and 1930's, who helped lead the paper from the sterility that had grown up since the early days, and was at its height in 1922. At a working level, writers like Volney Hurd protested against such taboos as those on jazz. At the level of the management and the Board of Directors, men like Charles E. Heitman had studies of early *Monitors* made, to prove the degrees of freedom which then prevailed and were the paper's real birthright. Brilliant writers and idealists like Rufus Steele argued — as he did vigorously on the Fact Finding Committee — that the paper must be freed from unnecessary inhibitions, and proved their point by writing bold copy illustrating the new "*Monitor* Form."

Mr. Steele's column, "The March of the Nations," ran from 1931 to his passing in 1935. It was a straightforward news-interpretation column, displayed in short paragraphs right down column one of page one. It did not pontificate in the manner of the "deep" thinkers, or peep through keyholes like the gossips. It was a very difficult column to write, for it required a sure touch on a wide gamut of subjects. Its interpretation was of course a form of editorializing, and it had pitfalls. The short paragraphs Mr. Steele wrote could not contain the carefully reasoned qualifications of editorials themselves. Sometimes they were oversimplified. And after Mr. Steele was gone, his successor — though a talented staff member, Henry Edison Williams — was not able to maintain the adequate standard. Few persons could have done so.

The late 1920's and 1930's also saw the development and

stabilization of national coverage, amid the stirring issues of the depression and the New Deal.

The paper's Washington Bureau is a good focus. Its history reflects the uncertainties of the early years. The first Bureau chief was not a full-time staff member but a writer for other papers also, W. W. Jermane. He ran the operation from 1909 to 1915. The second Bureau chief was a staff member, R. Eddy Mathews, serving only briefly. He was succeeded by Charles D. Warner, from 1915 to 1919. Mr. Warner, as the dispatches in the *Monitor* and his private correspondence with Mr. Dixon show, was a capable writer and digger. His contacts, on behalf of Mr. Dixon and the paper alike, were on a confidential basis with persons in the highest authority. Then Mr. Warner and Mr. Dixon had their falling out, as described earlier, and Thomas Dawson and A. J. Montgomery temporarily filled in. Mr. Montgomery, a forceful Scots journalist, left the *Monitor* to conduct the public relations activities of the American Automobile Association until 1955.

Mr. Montgomery was succeeded by another of the unique people who have served the paper down through the years. This was Miss Cora Rigby. She was one of the great pioneers in women's journalism. Daughter of a judge in Columbus, Ohio, and thus exposed to much political talk, this slip of a girl — she never stood much over five feet — began writing a daily column which one of the Columbus newspapers was glad to print. When the news leaked out that the column was written by a girl, Judge Rigby marched right down to the newspaper office and hustled his daughter straight home, enjoining her mother to take better care of her. But next day Cora was back with another column of political comment. Presently she began to be *paid* for her writing. Soon she found an unoccupied desk in the newspaper office — and she was in business!

For fifteen years, Miss Rigby was on the staff of the New York *Herald*, doing all the regular newsroom jobs. Then she moved to the *Monitor*'s Washington office. She was one of the earliest women members of the capital press corps. It took courage and poise in those days for a woman to do what was regarded as a man's job. But Miss Rigby paved the way for a great army of her sisters. She was popular everywhere, and had entree to most offices. She founded the Women's National Press Club, of which she was president for years. Her male colleagues in Washington bore her in highest esteem: I know, for I was first introduced by her to the leaders in the press corps there on my first venture in capital journalism. I saw the respect and affection with which she was accepted everywhere.

By the late 1920's Miss Rigby found herself presiding over a restless stable of young and aggressive reporters. The State Department and other international affairs were being covered by Drew Pearson, although not on a staff basis. Mr. Pearson had not yet become the "inside story" columnist and controversialist. He was rather more under the influence of his Quaker and academic background in those days. In fact, he was just off the faculty of the University of Pennsylvania and Columbia University, and had traveled widely as a free-lance journalist. His *Monitor* articles were thoroughly competent coverage of the Washington diplomatic scene.

Meantime, Robert S. Allen, later Mr. Pearson's colleague in books and a widely syndicated column, had come on as a staff correspondent in the *Monitor*'s Washington Bureau. In those days, too, Bob Allen was not the slashing behind-the-scenes muckraker which he proudly became. The copy he wrote about Herbert Hoover, for instance, in the Presidential campaign of 1928 could hardly have been more favorable.

Bob Allen succeeded Cora Rigby as chief of the Bureau after she passed on in 1930. He ran the office until 1932. On the one hand, he was sending the *Monitor* an unrelieved flow of favorable coverage of the Hoover Administration. On the other hand, he was writing the book *Washington Merry-Go-Round* with Drew Pearson, which was a scathing indictment of the Hoover Administration. The book was published anonymously. Rumor began to flow that Bob Allen was one of the authors. Soon it was revealed that he and Mr. Pearson were indeed the authors. Mr. Allen was discharged by the *Monitor*. The *Washington Merry-Go-Round* was in violent conflict with the *Monitor*'s editorial convictions, style, and attitude to public problems. It was in utter contradiction with the writing of the *Monitor*'s Washington Bureau chief in the paper's columns.

I succeeded Mr. Allen as chief of the Washington Bureau. Our relationships were always most friendly both before and after the Merry-Go-Round incident. Yet I have long felt the *Monitor* should have had a balanced and careful statement of the Hoover Administration's difficulties in the years 1929–33. But a re-survey of its columns now, and comparison with objective and uncommitted historical writing which today analyzes the period, shows that the file is not at all bad. It certainly lacks an adequate statement of President Hoover's problems of personality and political finesse. This would have been difficult to present in the *Monitor,* although the problem was measurably solved in describing the limitations of the Eisenhower Administration when troubles of a dissimilar but comparable nature came into being.

Under Bob Allen in the Washington Bureau were Richard L. Strout, Joseph C. Harsch, and Mary Hornaday. They had all also served under Miss Rigby. Miss Hornaday and Messrs. Strout and Harsch, who composed the Bureau when I was sent to Washington, are persons of great professional talent. Miss Hornaday covered the fabulous activities of Mrs. Franklin D. Roosevelt with skill and objectivity. She specialized in agrarian and social welfare problems. After a notable service in Europe at the end of the Second World War, when she covered relief work among the starving and distressed populations, and a period in charge of Pacific Coast coverage for the *Monitor,* Miss Hornaday was placed in the New York Bureau. She has specialized in the multifarious international life and news that flows in and out of New York. For extended periods, she has covered the United Nations.

Dick Strout is a correspondent of truly extraordinary talent. There have been few craftsmen working on any American newspaper to compare with him. From the Senate press gallery to Presidential conventions, from a first passenger flight across the United States to the D-Day invasion, he has covered the greatest events of thirty-five years for the *Monitor.* His writing is one of his greatest distinctions: well-trimmed, vividly descriptive, perceptive. His first job on the *Monitor,* the afternoon he was being tried out in 1921, was to cut somebody else's copy. He wrote in his diary at the time: "I was told to cut it 1/3. That was pie to me. I have cut my own stuff and revised and revamped it till I am an expert." This candid entry was, as a matter of fact, true of Dick's writing technique.

His personal political thinking has reversed the usual evolution. As a young cub in Washington, he fiercely resented the prying reporters' questions of Warren G. Harding, standing there at his press conference in his plus fours looking the perfect picture of a President. He was "my President," wrote Mr. Strout recently, and he carried this hero worship over to Calvin Coolidge and Herbert Hoover right through the 1932 campaign. Then his thinking began to respond to the progressive content of the New Deal, and as the years have gone by he has become more and more liberal. But this has never warped or hampered his independent and objective journalistic skill. He covers a story with clinical dispassion, writing with warmth and perception but without bias.

Of a very different journalistic school is Joseph C. Harsch. Joe came to the *Monitor* as a cub, just out of Williams College and Cambridge University, without newspaper training. He plunged into his job with great zest. It will encourage young writers to know that when I was in charge of the Washington Bureau, I had to require Joe Harsch to rewrite his copy, time after patient time, until his style acquired maturity and depth. They were hours well spent. Mr. Harsch became one of the great columnists and observers of the international scene. After the decade of the 1930's in the Washington Bureau, he spread out into radio and later television, but always maintaining a close connection with the *Monitor* and writing extensively and regularly for its columns.

These are samples of the young people who came of age on the *Monitor* as it turned its first quarter century. They made the 1930's a decade of solid, progressive growth.

The paper's ideas were also deepening and broadening. In domestic policy, after having supported Herbert Hoover for re-election in 1932, and enthusiastically backing his proposals for recovery right up to March 4, 1933, it found merit in some of President Roosevelt's initial proposals. It echoed the incoming executive's ringing dictum that "All we have to fear is fear itself." But it gave only modified support to the American departure from the gold standard and the efforts to manage the currency. The verdict of history also shares many of these reservations.

The fact that the *Monitor* found so much to support in President Roosevelt's program, both foreign and domestic, after having opposed his election, puzzled and disturbed some of its readers. They were intensely partisan. And they were opposed to the New Deal and all its works. The *Monitor* was not and never has been partisan in the sense of adherence to a single political party. Its reasons for supporting Mr. Hoover in 1928 and 1932 were essentially nonpartisan. They were based on fundamentals in government which took on, in the *Monitor's* eyes at least, the stature of moral issues. The question of prohibition was one of them.

But, as the prohibition issue was thrust aside by the decisive repeal of the Eighteenth Amendment, and as President Roosevelt put forward a dynamic recovery program, and as he advanced more and more into the field of world co-operation, the *Monitor* found many things to commend.

The role of an independent, nonpartisan newspaper is a very difficult one. Few of its readers are themselves nonpartisan. So the independent paper seems bound to displease or offend one group of its readers or another, whatever decision it takes. The only alternatives would be to be partisan, which would be impossible for a newspaper owned and motivated as the *Monitor,* or to take no positions whatever, which would be to evade its plain duty to help its readers reach well-informed decisions.

During the years from President Roosevelt's inauguration in 1933 until the electoral campaign of 1936, the *Monitor* gave his program a measure of carefully qualified support. Its position was once more very close to what careful students of the period have now decided is a reasonable historical judgment.

In one notable respect, however, the paper took a position which remains very controversial, pleasing conservatives but displeasing others, and scarcely in conformity with what might be called the verdict of history. Certainly it was greatly out of step with the verdict of the American people at the time. In 1936 it finally supported the election of Alf M. Landon, the Republican nominee for the Presidency.

This position may be described as more nearly a partisan decision than any other the paper has ever taken. In 1932 there were issues which transcended party politics. In 1940, when the paper also opposed President Roosevelt, the question of a third term had arisen. The *Monitor* felt very deeply that the two-term tradition should not be violated. It supported the subsequent constitutional amendment which made this obligatory. But in 1936 the case against the re-election of President Roosevelt rested on elements such as deficit spending, which the *Monitor* vigorously opposed, the increase in centralized federal power, and the degree of social experiment which the New Deal had pressed. These and other factors combined for the *Monitor* to represent an actual threat to free government. It foresaw and warned of an attack on the Supreme Court, which it accurately feared President Roosevelt would carry out. It objected to a managed economy, to extensive controls over business, to the restrictionist aspects of N.R.A. and A.A.A. The paper felt that the individualism and self-reliance of citizens was at stake. All these genuine and sincere considerations led it to a political position at deep variance with the decision of the polls, where President Roosevelt carried every state but Maine and Vermont.

The result led to a good deal of self-analysis by the paper and those responsible for its conduct. They gave deeper consideration to the thinking which had led so many Americans to so one-sided a verdict. *Monitor* support for many Roosevelt programs continued. But when, within a few months, the President produced his court-packing plan the *Monitor* resisted it and was gratified when Congress — with the apparent support of public opinion — refused to follow the President. The *Monitor* was not distressed when the personnel of the Supreme

Court began to alter in a natural and constitutional fashion, and Chief Justice Hughes led the way to an adjustment between progressive legislation and constitutional interpretations.

In short, those responsible for *Monitor* editorial policy, and that means the Board of Directors in the last analysis, sought throughout to base decisions on the most conscientious and prayerful consideration of that which is fundamentally right. Ordinary partisan politics took no part in this decision-making. Even when the results seemed to be politically motivated, the fact remains that the questions asked and answered by the Board were always questions going back to the fundamentals of human freedom and the rights of man. What the Board considered to be moral issues — and properly viewed they certainly were — remained ultimately decisive. If the result seemed to be partisanship, this was a misconception the paper strove to remove. Yet always, on political issues where human thinking was, naturally, widely and emotionally divergent, there remained a serious and continuing problem of misunderstanding.

27

The Second World War Comes

ON MARCH 18, 1933, a much respected teacher and practitioner of Christian Science in Berlin wrote to the Board of Directors in Boston: "What we have been going through these last weeks was a revolution. It was so splendidly organized that it was a bloodless revolution. Let us hope, that it will bring a new era of cleanliness, order, God-fearing, and work for the workless. What would have become of Europe, if Germany had come under Bolshevism? It needed a strong hand to prevent this catastrophe. And Hitler seemed to have it."

This was a mild statement of the way in which many of the numerous Christian Scientists in Germany at first felt about the coming to power of Adolf Hitler. And so for a number of years they tried with earnestness, with desperation, sometimes with anguish to persuade *The Christian Science Monitor* to support and praise the Hitler movement.

Rarely has any newspaper been exposed to such sincere, protracted, and impelling appeals to change its policy. The pressure was particularly strong on the Board of Directors, who were not only ultimately responsible for the editorial policy of the *Monitor,* but were also guiding and directing the affairs of the church. Naturally they did not wish to offend or drive out any significant part of the 64 Christian Science churches and societies and 166 not-yet-recognized groups then existing in Germany.

Christian Science in Germany had a relatively long background. It was established in the 1890's and had experienced remarkable growth. The strain on German Christian Scientists during the First World War had been severe enough. The *Monitor* had been outspoken in its sympathy for the Allied cause and critical of German imperial ambitions from the outbreak of that war. Though it had striven to prevent the coming of war in 1914, and had urged various reasonable ways in which the legitimate national objectives of the Central Powers might be adjusted to the French-British-Russian position, it had never hesitated to pin the chief responsibility for aggression on Hohenzollern expansionism.

German Christian Scientists suffered patiently through this earlier period, during which the motives of their nation were condemned by the newspaper and in effect by the leadership of their church. It was always pointed out, of course, that the *Monitor* was never condemning the German people, all possessed of the inalienable birthright of God's individual man, and that its attitudes went beyond nationalism to fundamental spiritual values. And at all times, the utmost loving consideration was shown toward people, as such, and toward the proper aspirations of a German nation, as well as all other nations.

All these basic considerations, however, could not fully assuage the hurt pride of many Germans. Also it may be said, with the complete detachment of time and history, that the *Monitor* sometimes took on the emotional and national coloration of American or British viewpoints. Such responsibility for not avoiding the First World War as may have lain to British imperial and commercial rivalries, or to French, Russian, or Serbian excesses and failures, was not pointed out at the time. The Germans reasonably enough felt that all the blame was not on one side, but that the faults of one side alone were being exposed and excoriated. The *Monitor* was not altogether free from wartime hysteria and susceptibility to propaganda when feelings and events were at their most intense.

With this background of defeat and national humiliation, the Germans went into the frustrating decade of the 1920's. Among the Christian Scientists there, who were predominantly of the solid and respectable middle class, many suffered severely in the inflation early in that decade. They observed inflation-profiteers around them also, and their resentment against the newly rich was not entirely curbed. The Weimar Republic had only a limited appeal to them. I remember living with just such a family in Göttingen in 1928–29, during my student days, and being astonished that gentle, sweet, upright middle-class folk should have such bitterness toward the Reichstag and the other elements of parliamentary democracy. They were ripe for the Führer.

So when Hitler took power in early 1933, and before, a considerable number of perfectly honest and admirable Christian Scientists in Germany resented and tried to change the *Monitor*'s attitude toward him. Most of these people were politically unsophisticated. They had had very little experience of representative republican government. They were in very severe economic difficulties. Bolshevism was in fact beating at their doors. In their view, Jews in Germany had benefited greatly during the years of inflation, and other Jews had been moving steadily into Germany from Eastern Europe. They had a passionate longing to see their national pride and discipline restored. Many of these aspirations were honorable and noble.

Such good people, naïve and upright, refused to believe the worst of the Nazi movement until it struck themselves and their own church. Even then, some were prepared to blame the repressive measures to the critical attitude the *Monitor* had always held. This was a misconception, but not an entirely unnatural one.

There were other German Christian Scientists, of course, who saw clearly and with a heavy heart what was happening in their beloved country. They tried hard to avoid the impending tragedy. However, they were not political conspirators. Few if any of them were in public life. Their kind of martyrdom was not that which plants bombs. They strove to maintain objectivity and detachment toward the political scene and to persuade their fellow Christian Scientists not to denounce "Boston" in a wave of shocked self-pity. The constructive role of those who helped keep Christian Science alive and vigorous in Germany was of inestimable value.

Nevertheless, the *Monitor* — and the Board of Directors — was the target for continuous and increasingly urgent appeals to refrain from criticizing Hitler. That the paper was able to maintain a clear vision and a real independence from the earliest impact of this flood of appeals to the last is a noteworthy achievement. The paper continuously saw National Socialism as dictatorship with heavy overtones of racial and religious hatred and nationalistic aggression.

The situation was compounded by the fact that the *Monitor* had always been sympathetic with Germany's criticisms of the Versailles Treaty. It felt the reparations clauses were largely unworkable, and it believed Germany had the right to full restoration of national sovereignty. The *Monitor* supported a reasonable peace treaty at the time that document was drafted in 1918, and it was in favor of peaceful, agreed revision right through the 1920's.

There were many elements in German life which appealed greatly to the *Monitor*, and predisposed it to support Germany just as far as it could. The people whose letters, telegrams, and personal visits hammered at Boston's doors during the 1930's were also trustworthy and appealing people.

Nor were they all Germans. Christian Science lecturers, American and British, were visiting Germany in a regular flow during these years. They came in contact with the aroused

German Christian Scientists, and without exception returned reports urging patience and consideration for the Germans themselves. Almost without exception, these reports recommended that the *Monitor* should blunt and muffle its criticisms of Hitler.

The recommendations, impressive and sincere as they were, simply were not followed. The Board of Directors permitted, in fact, they required the *Monitor* staff to report events in Germany accurately, but without needless offense. The farthest the *Monitor* went to cover the indignant convictions of many of its readers in Germany was to publish some of them as "letters to the editor," and to avoid unnecessary provocation. On April 15, 1933, for example, the paper printed a collection of such letters. They were significant letters to Christian Scientists because it was clearly evident that they came from eminent members of the church, though none was identified by name. One was described as "a Lecturer" and another as "a Teacher," which were indications of authority to Christian Scientists. In an accompanying editorial, the paper urged understanding of the Germans, though it pointed out that the reports from its readers were from persons "who may not have been in position to view the entire situation."

The paper's regular news columns made it clear that those who wrote so sympathetically of Hitler were under the spell of wishful thinking, and were overlooking brutal facts. The paper's staff used every precaution to avoid giving needless offense. It sought to make allowance for the long-standing grievances of the Germans and the deep-seated and emotional motivation of their thinking. It printed only what was absolutely essential to keep the record straight.

From the very moment of Hitler's advent to power, there was danger that Christian Science would be suppressed in Germany. Its followers there, with eager and continuous support from the United States and Great Britain, tried to avert the evil day by every proper means. In September, 1933, on behalf of the Board of Directors in Boston, a group of Christian Scientists composed of Viscount Astor, J. S. Braithwaite, managing representative for Europe of the Christian Science Publishing Society, and Charles W. J. Tennant, district manager of the Christian Science Committees on Publication for Great Britain and Ireland, went to Berlin to try to stop the arrest and persecution of Christian Scientists, which had already begun in Thuringia. They obtained an official interview with Wilhelm Frick, Minister of the Interior, and Lord Astor had a forty-minute personal talk with Hitler.

Upon assurance — which could have gone without saying — that the Christian Science churches did not and would not engage in Marxist propaganda, Herr Frick promised them freedom of worship. There was no mention of the *Monitor*, the absolute freedom of which could not be compromised. But the Frick promise was only a temporary barricade. In 1941, after various lesser interferences, the work of the churches was absolutely forbidden; the churches and reading rooms were closed, books were confiscated, practitioners curbed, and many Christian Scientists were arrested and persecuted in various ways. There is much evidence that the *Monitor*'s independent but fair-minded attitude delayed this onslaught rather than brought it about. The Nazis' stated grievance against Christian Science in an official impeachment published in 1938, was that it was "international," that its headquarters were in the United States, and that it taught doctrines of world peace, understanding, and brotherhood. Individual Christian Scientists under persecution had many heroic experiences. Their faith and devotion to their religion remained nobly and actively alive during the trials of the Second World War, and when Hitler had fallen and peace was again restored they resumed their rightful role of religious freedom.

These troubles did not diminish the *Monitor*'s careful coverage of German events, and its outspoken comment upon them. It had maintained staff correspondents in Berlin since the paper's earlier days. In 1931 one of its ablest staff members and later overseas news editor, Charles E. Gratke was sent to Berlin. He covered the latter days of Hitler's drive to power. The *Monitor* coverage of this drive began with what was certainly one of the first interviews published with the Austrian paperhanger, on October 3, 1923. In May, 1933, Roscoe Drummond was recalled from London to Boston, where he was needed for the sweeping improvements of the paper then under way, and Mr. Gratke replaced him as editorial manager for Europe.

At this point, Emlyn Williams (not the actor-playwright) took over full charge of the Berlin file, in which he had collaborated previously. Thereafter — from 1933 to the present, with the exception of the actual war years — Mr. Williams held the fort in Germany. Much of the time it was a rugged assignment. Mr. Williams had to live through the atmosphere of hate and stress which permeated Germany during the Nazi years, no small trial to a sensitive and conscientious man. As a British subject, he was also sometimes the object for special attack. Living conditions were often difficult. And for the Nazi period, Mr. Williams had a great deal of work to do for the church as well as the paper. On occasion, he was the best available intermediary in the effort to preserve Christian Science in Germany. His services in this respect are particularly noteworthy and faithful, since he is not himself a Christian Scientist, but a Presbyterian. No ardent member of the church could have given more diligent and perceptive service than Mr. Williams has always done.

Mr. Williams understood, and wrote about, the causes for Germany's Nazi mesmerism. He had the deepest sympathy and affection for the German people. He respected all that was good in their way of life and thought. From his coverage, readers got a moderate, responsible, careful, nonsensational picture of the period.

Thus the *Monitor*, like other free newspapers in the United States and Western Europe, gave full warning of the massing war clouds. The *Monitor*'s attitude was never that of appeasement; but it was always imbued with the motive to try in every way to avoid war. The concept of inevitability was not accepted in these years, any more than it had been before 1914, but always the *Monitor* recognized the possibility of war, pointed to the danger, and sought persistently to find ways of removing the causes. In the case of Germany, from the hour of the Versailles Treaty on, it strove for just and fair settlements.

But the *Monitor* could not compromise with the facts, nor its best understanding of them. There was another and lesser test of its fortitude at the time of British Prime Minister Neville Chamberlain's agreement at Munich. The *Monitor* could not agree that "peace in our time" had been assured. It believed that appeasement of evil could do no good. It pointed out the delusive nature of the agreements, and the dire blow that had been struck against Czechoslovakia. Again a considerable number of the paper's readers, this time in Great Britain and France, felt the paper was wrong. They protested with vehemence. They would accept no criticism of Mr. Chamberlain, or of M. Daladier, France's Premier, no intimation that Munich had perhaps done nothing more than buy some time. Again the paper stuck to its convictions, and urged a redoubling of vigilance against false confidence and security after Munich.

Since mention has been made of the Marquess of Lothian and Viscount Astor, both devoted Christian Scientists, it should be added that neither of these men ever tried to get the *Monitor* to follow a path of appeasement toward Hitler. When in the mid 1930's a then-Communist writer (Claud Cockburn, as set forth by himself in *A Discord of Trumpets*) hung the phrase "Cliveden Set" around Lord Astor and some of his friends — from the name of the Astors' famous country estate — there have been those who attributed pro-appeasement or pro-Hitler views to Lord Astor himself and his close associate, Lord Lothian. Some of those who spent weekends at Cliveden may well have been appeasers. The German Ambassador, like the American Ambassador, was there. But from the point of view of the *Monitor* and speaking as one who was in touch with both these men over a considerable period of years, I can affirm that neither Lord Astor nor Lord Lothian was ever bemused by pro-Nazi sentiments or false appeasements.

It is true that both men sought to explore Hitler's thinking and policies, in the 1930's and well before war clouds were really lowering, to find out what might be the bases of peaceful adjustment between Britain and Germany. This was an urgent patriotic task. It was highest statesmanship. But in everything that Lord Lothian wrote for the *Monitor,* he was clear-sighted and realistic about the impossibility of appeasing evil. Lord Astor did not often write for the *Monitor,* but in what he did, and in the contacts I had with him, and in his known public views, it is clear that he was seeking an acceptable and honorable basis for genuine peace, not appeasement.

When the Second World War broke out, the *Monitor* experienced a third great wave of reader-protest, this time from Americans. It was stronger than either of the others. It was from neutralists, nationalists, and isolationists in the United States who objected to the *Monitor*'s view of the issues of the war. Among those who protested were a considerable number of German-Americans, whose feelings — like those of their kinfolk in Europe — had been distressed ever since 1914. But there were also many sincere Americans who hoped to shield their country from another holocaust. They were prepared to see Europe fight out its conflicts, persuaded that "Fortress America" could be protected from involvement. And in the congeries of opposition were many whose justifiable antipathy for and fear of communism heavily outweighed all other considerations in their thinking. Eminent Americans like Charles A. Lindbergh and Herbert Hoover — not to mention John Foster Dulles — held the neutralist view. Indeed, the overwhelming national viewpoint in September, 1939, was sympathy with the Allies, but a desire to avoid involvement.

Thus again the *Monitor* was subjected to pressures. Again it did not yield, under the firm decision of the Board of Directors that moral issues of deepest significance were at stake. In an "Editorial Letter" to readers published on May 16, 1940, just after the "phony war" or "sitz krieg" of the previous winter had turned into serious conflict, as France was falling, and the Battle of Britain was soon to begin, the *Monitor* said: "Some of you have written that you do not feel a newspaper founded out of a great love for all humanity should 'take sides' in the conflict. However, it is that very love for humanity which compels this newspaper to take sides, not against any nation or group of nations in and of themselves, but against the evils which are attempting to destroy the very basis of civilization."

The editorial pointed out the paper's long commitment to revision of the Versailles Treaty, its sympathy with the plight of the German people, its work for years to bring about a more Christian attitude toward them. But it affirmed: "The issues have become far bigger than any question of colonies or of righting the injustices of the Versailles Treaty. There is at stake the right to live the Christianity upon which men's lives must be based, else they perish. The challenge to Christianity is being made on more than one front, but in this period it appears to be receiving its chief impetus by an attempt to overthrow the Nazarene's love-inspiring doctrines through the forceful application of hatred-breeding Nazi dogmas. For the brotherhood of man is openly scorned. Worship of person and state are given precedence over worship of God. The rights of peoples and nations to freedom of speech, religion, and self-government are denied. Unjustified, unprovoked attacks have been made on innocent countries and peoples, and their morale weakened through instigated treachery."

The editorial concluded: "Much as it deplores war, The Christian Science Monitor realizes that at this moment the Allies have no choice but to defend themselves and friendly smaller nations by military force, and that in so doing they are upholding democratic rights of people everywhere."

Such uncompromising sentiments helped to meet the doubts of Americans who felt the United States could remain aloof. They were given graphic reinforcement by the swift fall of Norway, Denmark, the Netherlands, Belgium, and France, and the clear threat to Britain. Panzer divisions, dive bombers, and paratroopers, as well as new and powerful submarine fleets, made it plain that Nazi aggression might well leap the oceans. The idea of Fortress America seemed less and less plausible.

At no time did *Monitor* policy deviate or waver. Protests from some of its American readers continued, and were met by other editorials. In early 1941 the paper said: "Something very much bigger than Britain or America must win the tremendous struggle now going on. There must be a victory won, in the interests of all the world, for the idea of freedom under law, of security from aggression, of adjustment by peaceful means."

Typical of many letters from readers was this from Hollywood, California: "I attended a meeting of Americans last night and the question arose as to whether The Christian Science Monitor was pro-American or pro-British and the unanimous opinion seemed to be that it was pro-British." The paper replied, in an editorial on June 7, 1941, in words which well summed up its credo:

> The Christian Science Monitor is not partial to any nation as such, but is pro-humanity. Long before Great Britain became involved in the present world crisis, the Monitor took its stand for humanity, civilization, Christianity, and law and order, against the inhumanity, barbarism, anti-Christianity, and international anarchy finding expression in the aggressive actions of the totalitarian nations. In its office as monitor, this newspaper issued a resounding warning each time the aggressor evil lifted its hydra head. Vigorous was the Monitor's opposition as step by step, ten years ago in Manchuria, then in Ethiopia, Czechoslovakia, Austria, Poland, Finland, Norway, Denmark, Holland, Belgium, France, this foe to world brotherhood swept on, trampling under feet men's rights to free speech, religion, self-government, and throwing its mantle of darkness over the light of liberty.

During this period, the *Monitor* was well represented in Berlin. In 1939, upon the declaration of war between Britain and Germany, Emlyn Williams had to leave the country. His services were later put to good use by his government as an expert on Czechoslovakia. He was able to write dispatches from London for the *Monitor,* under a pseudonym, throughout the war. They were singularly well informed. Part of the time he was available as a war correspondent.

To replace Mr. Williams, the *Monitor* sent Joseph C. Harsch first to Rome and then to Berlin. He had been in Europe on leave of absence from his *Monitor* job in Washington, working for Myron C. Taylor in the Intergovernmental Refugee Commission. He was delighted to get back into reportorial harness and was glad to remain in Germany until well in 1941. Again, it was not easy reporting for the *Monitor* from Berlin, since the paper's sympathies were self-evident. Mr. Harsch did it with great skill and perception, and wrote a book about it, *Pattern of Conquest.* He steadily warned world readers of Germany's aggressive intentions, its careful preparations, and the strength of its regime.

As early as March, 1941, he foresaw and warned of Hitler's plan to invade the Soviet Union, which did not begin until June 22, 1941. I remember greeting Mr. Harsch on his return from Berlin, in the late winter of 1941, and taking him for a bite of good American food at the South Station restaurant in Boston. Mr. Harsch wanted an oyster stew and apple pie with ice cream. As we sat eating, he remarked that only a few weeks before, he had been heating his hands in warm water in his Berlin lodgings so that he could type his dispatches.

28

◆◆◆◆◆◆◆◆◆◆◆◆◆◆◆◆◆◆◆◆

Covering the Second World War

ONE DAY EARLY in the Second World War a certain British general thought it would be a good idea if war correspondents, as well as troops, were toughened up and conditioned for the experiences they might encounter. So he issued orders to his press officer to see that the correspondents assigned to his command accompanied a group going on an all-night field exercise. Next morning he asked the press officer how they got along. The officer replied: "Oh, none of them made it except a correspondent for *The Christian Science Monitor*, and that doesn't count."

The correspondent was Ronald Maillard Stead. The press officer knew whereof he spoke. Ronnie Stead was not only a veteran sports writer but a veteran athlete. He played football, cricket, ran cross-country, and in the late 1950's he played polo. He even rode a bicycle. That is really another story: Ronnie had never ridden a bicycle seriously in his life, but in 1939 agreed to do so from Land's End to John o'Groat's to see if he could make it in ten days. He did, though he finished somewhat worn in spots.

Mr. Stead was one of the men who covered the fighting fronts for the *Monitor*. There had been no such professional corps for the paper during the First World War. Its dispatches then came from the wire services, and were supplemented by articles from various resident special correspondents. None of them were war correspondents as such. In the second war, almost from the outset, correspondents were accredited and wrote hot, vivid, eyewitness reports. Actually, in many countries the war came to the people, and the front was everywhere. Correspondents didn't need accreditation by military authorities.

The first *Monitor* correspondent to cover fighting in the Second World War was Edmund Stevens. He turned up in the *Monitor*'s London office one day in 1939, a young American born in Denver and graduated from Columbia University who had spent much of his youth in Italy. Thus he began early his notable linguistic training. After Columbia, he had gone to Moscow and worked for the Cunard Steamship Company, in the days — odd as this may seem — when it was useful for a steamship company to have representation in the Soviet Union. But his heart was in newspapering. So he knocked at the *Monitor*'s door to say he was soon to visit the Baltic States of Estonia, Lithuania, and Latvia. He inquired if the paper could use some copy from these infrequently visited nations.

Mallory Browne, then in charge in London, asked the blond, pink-cheeked young American to send in his copy. The paper would consider it. Soon cracking-good stories began coming from the Baltic states, which were speedily to fall into the maw of Soviet conquest.

Ed Stevens spoke first-rate Russian and was married to a Russian girl. By 1939 he had extricated her with greatest difficulty from the Soviet Union and taken her to the United States, where she began the process of becoming an American citizen. Permission to get Mrs. Stevens out of Russia was one of the good deeds performed by Ambassador Joseph P. Davies and his generous-hearted wife. At one of their diplomatic parties, which the handsome young Stevenses attended, Ambassador Davies put an arm around each of the young people and walked them over to Soviet Foreign Minister Litvinov. "Max," he said, "I want you to give this dear little girl a visa so she can go and see her husband's folks and homeland. Do it as a favor for me, old boy, right away tomorrow morning." The amazing thing is that Litvinov did.

In 1939, with Mrs. Stevens and their eldest son, Edmund Junior, safely in the United States, Edmund was free to roam the fighting fronts. That he certainly did. He watched the Russian garrisons enter the little nations along the Baltic's eastern shore, and the Baltic Germans depart under Hitler's orders. His Baltic States dispatches to the *Monitor* are full of spoken and unspoken pathos. They begin on October 4, 1939, when Moscow was still promising neutrality to its little neighbors. They end a few weeks later as the Russians use Estonia as one of their jumping-off places to attack Finland. He wrote other Baltic articles in 1940 when full Soviet absorption of these tragic nations took place.

Ed Stevens' mastery of Russian was extremely useful on the Finnish front. He talked with many Soviet prisoners, establishing that some of them were hastily conscripted farmers — mere cannon fodder, ill-equipped, ill-clad, ill-armed — while others were well-trained soldiers. One of his most poignant dispatches was the translation he made of a Soviet wife's letters to her fallen husband, telling in Tolstoian fashion of her misery and anguish at home.

After a season of heroic fighting in the arctic dark, with General Winter the only ally the Finns had, they were forced to surrender. Another graphic Stevens dispatch tells how peace and cruel punishment came to Helsinki. With scarcely time to catch his breath, Ed went to Stockholm and Oslo, watching and covering the Nazis invasion of the Norwegian capital. He was the last correspondent to leave Oslo as the Nazi tyranny began, and the first to break the story of the pro-Nazi fifth columns — the Quislings — who weakened the Norwegian nation from within. His copy from Norway was crisp and graphic, from the first-day story, which began "Norway fights while Oslo falls," and the second-day story, whose lead said "The streets of Oslo today echo the tread of German hob-nailed boots," to the dispatch six days later opening, "I have just arrived at this little Swedish frontier town . . . Oslo is still virtually completely cut off from the outside world. But its isolation is not alone the story of German conquests. It is a story of German-engineered treachery . . ."

Thus in a few short months, the young American steamship clerk had covered three campaigns with consummate skill! Back in Stockholm, he decided to head for the Balkans. By some legerdemain he got a transit visa through the Soviet Union, though a few months before he had been writing outspoken copy about the Russian attacks on Finland and the Baltic States.

In those tense spring days of 1940, he made his way from Moscow to Bucharest on a slow postal train stopping at every station. The troops were moving. All express trains were canceled. His fellow passengers were tremendously excited to hear that Ed had covered the Finnish war, about which they had been permitted to learn very little.

An artillery colonel asked him, "What did the Finns think of our forces?" Ed replied, in the words of Finnish General Wallenius, "The Russian soldiers are brave, the underofficers excellent, the commanding staff mediocre, and the generals rotten." The colonel's smiling commentary was, "Very neatly put."

On the last few miles up to the Rumanian frontier, he rode in a "Potemkin" (artificially impressive) train, a neat and handsome little affair with one shiny locomotive, an immaculate, freshly painted mail car, and day coach with plush seats, cretonne curtains, and potted begonias in each compartment! All to overawe a few Rumanian frontier guards!

In Rumania, Ed was adroitly poised — with no time wasted — to cover the Soviet occupation of Bessarabia. Thence he went to Bulgaria, Greece, and Albania, covering the plucky and successful Greek resistance to Italian invasion. Here, again, he saw much front-line action in the mountains of Albania. From Greece he shuttled back to Rumania, covering the tremendous buildup of German troops in the Balkans ready to march down into Greece and north and east into the Soviet Union. From Rumania he wrote in the lead to his dispatch on June 28, 1940: "Again by the will of a dictator the tears of new thousands have been added to the river of sorrow that flows through Europe."

Thence he proceeded through Turkey and Syria to Egypt, the Sudan, Eritrea, and Ethiopia. Here he covered then Lieutenant Colonel Orde Wingate's push up to Addis Ababa through the valleys and over the burning deserts of Italy's latest and most disgraceful African empire — the aggression on which the League of Nations foundered in 1936. On April 5, 1941, Ed interviewed the little bearded man who had made his pathetic appeal to the League Assembly. His story began: "In a pleasant ravine on the long banks of a winding brook where broadtopped acacia trees offer concealment alike from the burning equatorial sun and the prying eyes of enemy planes, the Emperor of Ethiopia and Lion of the Tribe of Judah has pitched his camp."

On the way, Ed found his boyhood Italian convenient. The black-bearded Colonel Wingate, who was later lost in Burma, had a very small force, scarcely fifty Europeans, but with Sudanese and Ethiopian support. He was making his way steadily along, taking Italian strong points as he went.

Ed Stevens' contribution to the campaign is described in *Gideon Goes to War: The Story of Major-General Orde C. Wingate,* by Leonard Mosley. He writes: "Most of Wingate's successes in Ethiopia were the result of bluff and ingenuity rather than the clash of arms. After he had captured Debra Markos, he found that the telephone line to Addis Ababa was still open, and called in Edmund Stevens, The Christian Science Monitor war correspondent, who spoke excellent Italian. Stevens called up each fort down the line and pretended great panic, shouting that a great enemy force was on its way; and all the enemy strongholds along the Blue Nile obligingly evacuated."

Scarcely a month after Edmund Stevens had sat with the Emperor of Ethiopia under the acacia trees, he was having an exclusive interview with General Jan Christiaan Smuts, the Prime Minister of the Union of South Africa, at Cape Town. He was on his way back to the United States for his first visit to the *Monitor* office, where he was greeted with the most earnest congratulations.

Next he returned to North Africa and covered General Sir Bernard Montgomery's Eighth Army as it chased Field Marshal Rommel across Africa, to Tripoli. It was a rigorous and exciting assignment. In between times, he accompanied Winston Churchill's flying visit to Moscow, and Wendell Willkie's quick tour through the Middle East.

Mr. Stevens was returned to Moscow as a correspondent in 1943, and dived into the campaigns in the Ukraine, around Leningrad, and on the Karelian Peninsula when the Russians again defeated the Finns. He must be one of very few correspondents who covered the two Russo-Finnish wars, on different sides each time.

Other *Monitor* correspondents were having similar adventures on all the fighting fronts, sending back to Boston the most accurate account of the fighting they could get through the censorships. They were under basic *Monitor* instructions — not just to seek out "hometown boys" and interview them, not simply to highlight victories, not to emphasize American undertakings to the detriment of Allies, not to overwrite or soup-it-up.

Their job was to give an authentic picture of war and its meaning, not solely its adventures. And so, the adventures as such tended to be played down, the significance was emphasized. Thus Mr. Stevens, and all the others, were constantly keeping the long-range meaning in view and writing about it. At very early stages Mr. Stevens, to mention only one, was pointing out the dangers of misunderstandings between the British and Americans in North Africa; between Americans and Russians in Moscow; between Poles and Russians in Eastern Europe.

But the adventures were inevitable, and many *Monitor* men

had them. One was Ronald Stead, whose prowess at all-night hikes has been mentioned. Right after Dunkirk he went into uniform with a typewriter as a weapon. His first assignment was the Battle of Britain, and he covered it not only in the streets of London but at R.A.F. airfields, on bombing raids.

He even went beyond the ports. Mr. Stead was the first representative of the combined American press to go into action with Britain's then new military arm, the commandos, on a surprise Continental raid. He went in with the attack near Le Touquet in June, 1942, and described graphically Britain's tough commandos who kept the Germans jittery all along the invasion coast. Mr. Stead's boat was caught on a sandbar as they left the French coast and was pinpointed by Nazi searchlights and hit by machine-gun fire. After a tense few minutes, it got off without serious damage.

In November, 1942, he covered the British and American landings in North Africa, going ashore with the central task force at Oran, Algeria. He was flown to Casablanca to attend the famous press conference given by President Roosevelt and Prime Minister Churchill. On the way his transport plane accidentally flew over Spanish Morocco and was fired upon by the Spanish — perhaps the only overtly belligerent act performed by them during the war — and a correspondent on the plane was lost. When King George VI came to visit the Allied forces in North Africa, and in Malta, Mr. Stead was chosen to represent the combined American press and his dispatches were distributed by the Office of War Information.

Later in 1943, Mr. Stead went to Sicily and Italy with the Allied forces, and was on the Anzio and Nettuno beachheads during the grim battle for their control. Then he flew with paratroopers when they invaded southern France. His story told of one soldier who said to him, as the correspondent stood up to adjust his cumbersome flak suit, "Take my seat, buddy, I'll be getting out soon!"

Then he followed the Allied forces up the Rhone Valley and ultimately into Germany, writing at an early stage, "The hardest thing about reporting the war in this zone of action is finding it." He caught up with it before long, and on November 22 wrote in his lead from Metz, "I am in this historic fortress city today with American infantrymen who are engaged in crushing the last German resistance. This has proved a tough job . . ."

In a few days he, and they, were in Germany. When he saw the United States Ninth Army cross the Rhine he wrote: "It was a 'pushover.' And the pushover was something terrific . . . As I am writing this, with the shells of our artillery batteries rushing overhead to crash upon German communications and rear positions, the first light of another beautiful spring day discloses the build-up of a new Allied bridge-head busily in progress."

A little later he spoke of high-speed Allied gains, saying: "An earthquake . . . is what it is as irresistible forces hurl the cracked German defense walls asunder and Nazi bastions of the Reich totter to their fall amid smoke, flames, and dust." Then came the day when he got to the Elbe, along a road not hitherto used by Allied troops, and saw the fraternal greetings of the American and Russian troops. Ronnie himself crossed the Elbe precariously in a racing shell, rowed by two husky Russian officers. Unlike some other correspondents, he did not fall in.

Few weeks had elapsed before Mr. Stead was writing from London: "One can almost hear the sigh of relief that is going up as a result of the British Government's decision to double the release rate for military demobilization." So it was also in the United States. But not so in the Soviet Union!

Russian troops were not demobilized for many a long day; indeed not until their political missions had been achieved and they were replaced by other Russian troops.

Ronnie was ever a man of resource. Once, when the United States Fifth Army was fighting its way into Rome, he wasn't heard from for a few days. Not understanding, Foreign Editor Gratke cabled. Mr. Stead cabled back: "Sorry, but I lost my pajamas." Appropriate expressions of bewilderment were cabled in return. Ronnie answered: "But my notes were in them." Mr. Stead had been out of his billet in an abandoned house when the bomb fell.

29

The Train to Tokyo

MONITOR STAFF CORRESPONDENTS were eyewitnesses to the start and the finish of the war in the Pacific.

On December 7, 1941, Joseph C. Harsch and Anne, his wife, were awakened in their hotel at Waikiki Beach, Honolulu, by the crump of bombs made familiar to him by long months in Berlin. Joe was on his way to Southeast Asia for the *Monitor*. Anne had gone along as far as Hawaii for the trip. Joe told Anne that somebody was putting on a good imitation. They went to the beach for their morning swim, assuming it was a practice maneuver by the Navy. Soon they saw a freighter off-shore begin to list. Then they knew it was a Japanese surprise attack: that Pearl Harbor was being bombed.

The next few days were frustrating to a newsman. Joe had a tremendous story and the authorities wouldn't let him file it. Only on December 12 did his vivid eyewitness story reach Boston.

The end of the war was witnessed by Gordon Walker. He had followed General MacArthur's campaigns for almost three years, from Australia and Guadalcanal to Tokyo. With a colleague, Gordon was the first American to set foot in Tokyo after the end of hostilities. He and Frank Robertson, who has written many able dispatches for the *Monitor* from Asia in postwar years, landed at Atsugi Airport, went to Yokohama, where American troops were in occupation, and simply climbed on one of the electric trains that go between Yokohama and Tokyo.

Wearing their war correspondents' uniforms, they were stared at with awe and bewilderment by the Japanese passengers, including some soldiers. In Tokyo they walked around the center of the city, and finally strode into the Imperial Hotel, where they demanded and consumed a five-course dinner at the expense of the Japanese Imperial Government. They went to Radio Tokyo, looking for Tokyo Rose, the Japanese-American girl who had broadcast to American GI's during the dreary fight up the islands, but were told she was temporarily indisposed. They had scores of fascinating conversations with Japanese civilians, officials, and — of course — newsmen. It was an incredible day. It was also the beginning of Gordon Walker's distinguished coverage of Japanese domestic affairs, which still continues. For a man who had taken part in twelve amphibious landings, who had dropped with Marine paratroopers behind Japanese lines and lived there for many days, who had watched and wept at the deeply moving scene when American internees were rescued in Santo Tomás University in Manila, it was a great climax.

Between these events Gordon crammed a lot of war coverage. His work on the *Monitor* had begun as copy boy. He had really learned his trade as clerk and rewrite man on the foreign desk under Charles Gratke. Young, slender, finely drawn, Gordon was a Hollywood type-cast for the idealized picture of a war correspondent. There was romance, too. He met and married a charming Australian girl who had been employed in the *Monitor*'s Sydney bureau.

Few men saw more war than Gordon, or more adventurously.

Along the way, he was elected an honorary member of the 4th Marine Raider Battalion. He had gone in to New Georgia, in the Solomons, in the initial landing in June, 1943. Then he went with the Marine Raiders on a thirty-five-mile trek through hip-deep swamp, neck-high rivers, jungles, and mountains to the capture of Viru Harbor. The Marines, with Gordon along, put up a terrific battle against Japanese snipers, and nature. They were often surrounded by Japanese. At one point, Gordon threw away his dispatch case, beside the trail. He had all he could carry, for he clung to his trusty portable typewriter. When he and his Marines reached Viru a few days later, they recovered the very dispatch case — now filled with Japanese maps.

Getting stories out was almost as hard as getting in. In New Georgia Gordon persuaded native canoemen to paddle him and his copy for ten hours under cover of darkness, eluding Japanese all along the shore, until they reached Rendova. The copy traveled: by war canoe to Rendova, by Higgins boat to another advanced base, by jeep along beach, by another Higgins boat to troop lighter, and so on until it reached the wire office over 1500 miles away!

Gordon was in on the massive amphibious assault of Bougainville. He went in with the detachment of Marine raiders whose mission was to capture the main Japanese bivouac. After describing the heavy fire that cut the foliage over their heads as they crawled through the marshy jungle, Gordon wrote with grave understatement: "It was none too safe an operation." As if the point needed proving, he added: "At one time, I crept into a foxhole behind a beach breastwork mounted with two raiders comprising the point of our column. We could hear the Japanese chattering on the other side barely 10 feet away."

Gordon's battlefront copy, like that of other *Monitor* correspondents, was often written graphically but without affectation or exaggeration. It had none of the jazzed-up elements which usually came from correspondents far behind the front line or beachheads. It gained its power from the deeply exciting events it was describing. It was genuinely and consistently understated.

On another occasion, in Leyte, a story describing the brave Filipino underground reached Boston with this explanation from the censor: "While in transit to the transmission point, shrapnel tore a hole the size of a fist in this story." I have the original copy of the story before me as I write; there is a picture of it following page 232.

As well as Gordon Walker in the Pacific area for the *Monitor* was John Beaufort, who had been — and now is — the *Monitor*'s New York dramatic and film critic. He began with the occupation of Adak and Kiska in the Aleutians, and went all the rest of the way to Tokyo. He landed on Makin Island in the Gilberts with the 65th Infantry Division, and covered the advance to Tarawa and the Marshalls. He landed at Kwajalein Atoll with the Marines, saw naval battles in the Philippines Sea, accompanied the landings on Okinawa, and covered the invasion of Ie Shima and Iwo Jima.

On Guam, John's instinct for the drama came out. He preserved for posterity the lyrics of a song by which two young Guamians kept up their courage during the Japanese invasion. It went, in lyrics not so much worse than some of Tin Pan Alley's most typical:

Oh, Uncle Sam, dear Uncle Sam,
Won't you please come back to Guam?
Our life is in danger, you better come,
Just come and kill those Japanese on Guam.
Oh, Uncle Sam, dear Uncle Sam,
Won't you please come back to Guam?

It takes genius only heard on today's popular radio to rhyme Guam with Sam in one line and with come in another.

John Beaufort was sitting in the sun in front of a Japanese dugout with Ernie Pyle, on Okinawa, on the day when that beloved correspondent was killed. "Like the GI's who were paying for Ie Shima," wrote John, "Ernie proved once again that there is no minor operation for those who don't come back. A correspondent who had covered many of the great events of this war, he was killed on an island which will be best known because he was killed there."

After the surrender, John — like Gordon Walker — stayed in Japan. There the two *Monitor* correspondents made contact with Japanese Christian Scientists and got from them vivid and frank accounts of life in the beleaguered islands during the war. They also learned, and wrote, the inside stories of abortive efforts to end the war at an earlier time. They had intimate and well-informed contact with the groups striving to set up government in Japan under the occupation forces.

Back in the European theater, Volney D. Hurd had gone to France at the end of 1944. He exchanged a radio commentator's post for that of war correspondent. Mr. Hurd's name was well known in occupied Europe. He had been broadcasting news and comment by shortwave radio since the war began.

Since the early 1930's the *Monitor* had co-operated with station WRUL, operated by the World Wide Broadcasting Foundation, in sending basically educational programs overseas. The station was noncommercial, and since it was both nongovernmental and established in Boston, the *Monitor* was glad to help as a public service. In the early war years and after the Nazis had overrun much of Europe, the shortwave broadcasts of what came to be called Radio Boston were very meaningful and precious to continental Europeans. Mr. Hurd gave a nightly newscast, and his wide-ranging, ingenious interpretations brought hope and thought-provoking, freely speculating discussion to many millions.

In 1943, the *Monitor* agreed to permit its correspondents to take part in nightly news roundups from the various fighting fronts and overseas capitals on the Mutual Broadcasting Network. First Volney Hurd, and later Saville R. Davis, was commentator and integrator of these overseas broadcasts, speaking from Boston. It was a very good operation.

The broadcasts included many notable news beats and adventures, but none more thrilling than those given by Gordon Walker on April 23 and 27, 1944. On the first occasion, representing the combined press and radio, he told of General MacArthur's forces making a surprise landing at Hollandia-Aitape on the north coast of New Guinea. His broadcast of April 27 was believed by the Mutual Broadcasting Corporation to be the first made by any correspondent in the Pacific area during battle. Sometimes radio dissemination was quicker and more available than cable. Regular dispatches were often delayed. It was a means both of keeping in touch with correspondents and performing a wide service for the American public.

It was from this kind of operation that Volney Hurd went to France. As an amateur strategist, Volney wrote penetratingly of the over-all war planning, particularly of the relation of air and land tactics. He went in to many advanced air bases, and did a mission with the 365th Fighter Group of the 9th Air Force over the "drop area" and down flak alley, protecting a bridgehead opened by combined land and airborne Allied forces. He wrote very early of the role of radar. Mr. Hurd was one of the correspondents going into liberated Paris, and soon reopened the *Monitor* bureau there.

Mallory Browne, as European editorial manager, directed the staff from London during six years of war. He had been the paper's Paris correspondent from 1932 to 1938, and reporter in Boston from 1929. Mr. Browne left the *Monitor* in 1945 to join the *New York Times.* He is now a Foreign Service Officer for the United States Department of State. He, too, saw a lot of the European war. He covered the sitz-krieg, toured the Maginot Line from the French side. When Sumner Welles came to Europe as a last-minute envoy of the American government, seeking a war settlement, Mr. Browne traveled with him.

Two years and two months later, Mallory directed the *Monitor*'s staff in the Normandy invasions, went in himself, chased the drive inland, saw the breakthrough at Caen, and finally the liberation of Paris, his old headquarters. Before these campaigns, Mallory had sailed with coastal convoys, saw service with the British Navy, the American Air Force and Army in France, the United States First Army in Germany, and Field Marshal Montgomery's forces on the continent. He was the first correspondent accredited to United States Forces in Europe — SHAEF — and alternated between its London and Paris headquarters.

While Mallory Browne, like the *Monitor*'s other correspondents, kept up diligent and alert coverage of the fighting fronts and the war situations, what was often their most important and revealing writing was done in two rather different contexts. All of them wrote regular articles under the title "Correspondent's Diary" and all of them wrote for a recurrent series, "Inside the War." Both these undertakings gave the war situation depth and vividness. Each of the correspondents told what he was doing, what the ordinary life of people was like, how they were seeking to preserve the values for which they were fighting.

"Inside the War" was an effort on the part of each correspondent to dig into the very deepest, most essential elements of the situation, on a long-range basis. The Boston office called upon each one of them to withdraw himself mentally from the immediate situation, and take the longest, hardest look possible at the total picture. This turned out to be a very fruitful enterprise. It produced splendid copy. It was the essence of *Monitor* journalism. Furthermore, the paper kept its eye on peace planning at all times.

Already in 1939, even as the war was breaking out, the *Monitor* began presenting careful studies of the possible terms of peace. By 1942, a few months after United States entry into the war, it ran its most notable series, "The World We Want." This was a careful exploration of the ultimate foundations for peace, written by outstanding world leaders. Americans, Europeans, and Asians joined in the study. From the beginning of the war until its end, the *Monitor* accepted the responsibility of helping to prepare the terms of peaceful living.

Under Mr. Browne's direction, the *Monitor*'s London staff covered the Battle of Britain and wrote their daily dispatches after nights of firefighting under the bombs. It was a very capable Bureau, and all of its members are still on the job. Senior among them is Peter Lyne, who has been the paper's parliamentary correspondent since the early 1930's. Though Peter joined the paper's London staff in 1929, he became the golf champion of the Press Gallery of the House of Commons as recently as 1957! He lived in Clandon, Surrey, on a fifteenth-century farm populated by his wife, four children, Daybreak, the cow, Sunrise, her calf, Pigling Bland and Porgy — who identify themselves — and Clara and Petrouchka, the ducks. There were others but these will do, and of course generations and names change. The Lyne household was not nearly as coy as these names suggest. It was lively, and certainly picturesque.

Few correspondents for American newspapers, or for British for that matter, have covered the British government longer or more intimately than Peter Lyne. His dispatches are always crisp, well balanced, objective. Sometimes the *Monitor* runs into the sort of political reader-misunderstandings in Britain which it regularly experiences in the United States. That is to say, some Conservatives think its writing is too favorable to Labor, and some Laborites insist it is unutterably Tory. During the war, Peter kept the *Monitor*'s worldwide readership accurately informed on the steady hand of government in Whitehall.

John Allan May also came to the London Bureau over a quarter of a century ago, and in his cub years drew light illustrations — which often went with Ronnie Stead's sports stories — almost as frequently as he wrote. But as time went on, he developed into a writer of real authority in the field of business and economics, though his sharp and facile pen could handle any story. In addition, he kept on writing humorous articles, which developed into a regular column, "Come What May." This editorial-page feature, along with John himself, was transplanted to the United States for three years of comment on the American scene and service in the Boston office. Thus the humor became, and remains, Anglo-American, which has only deepened its savor.

In 1940, John was called into the Royal Navy, and after a while had his own command, a torpedo boat. He was in the St. Nazaire raid on March 25, 1942, at one of the most costly, and most successful of Britain's spearthrusts into Fortress Europa. He was navigation officer of one of the seven ships out of eighteen that escaped. Two ships were shot from under him. John lost his trusty typewriters on both occasions. When available, the typewriters were never idle. John wrote superb sketches of his naval life, and returned to the London staff just as soon as the Admiralty would permit.

It should be added that many other *Monitor* staff members — all of whom would have liked to be war correspondents — found their places in the armed services. Some became press-relations officers in various theaters of war, often pretty hot, and others were simply on regular duty. Their sacrificial part should not be forgotten alongside the war correspondents who got the by-lines and a considerable share of the glory.

One *Monitor* man, Max K. Gilstrap, was managing editor of *Stars and Stripes* in various points of publication in Europe, and was transferred to the Far East after V-E Day. He made a remarkable pictorial record of the atom-bombed ruins of Hiroshima not very long after peace was declared. He had been natural science writer on the Boston staff. After the war he worked first in the American news department in Boston and then as chief of the Central News Bureau, where he covered a vast area with great distinction.

The *Monitor*'s American news editor in 1958, Robert R. Brunn, was a prisoner of war in Germany from 1942 until the end of the war. He had been shot down in an early American bombing raid over the continent. He first began to write for the paper from the prison camp, sending letters out through the International Red Cross. They were so graphic — despite the inhibitions — that the paper was eager to hire Mr. Brunn as soon as he got back to private life. He served as correspondent in his native San Francisco, and then in Boston.

These are but illustrations of some wartime services of *Monitor* men. There were also several women in service, both in the various forces and in Red Cross work. In short, the staff did their part to keep the great Allied effort going. The lads with those glamorous words "War Correspondent" on their shoulders were not the only heroes!

Two other men who later played large roles in the *Monitor* were also active war correspondents. They were Joseph Harrison, the present overseas news editor, and William H. Stringer, chief of the Washington Bureau. Mr. Harrison covered the first three years of the war in Washington, writing from the

State, War, and Navy Departments. He went to North Africa in late 1942, and took over from Edmund Stevens in 1943. He was on the spot just in time to accompany the New Zealand Division of the British Eighth Army when it broke the Nazi Afrika Korps' Mareth Line in Tunisia by a long and beautifully executed end-run. He sat on a hilltop and described the battle beneath him: massed artillery, attack planes, infantry movements, and a vast supply line stretching 100 miles back in the desert. This battle broke the last serious Nazi resistance in Tunisia.

Mr. Harrison managed to get aboard the first flight connecting the British front in Libya and the American-British front in Algeria. His plane flew between forty and fifty feet above the ground to avoid enemy fighters. When it breasted a sand dune the passengers could hear the tips of desert foliage strike the plane's undercarriage. It was literally at treetop level.

After the North African fighting, Joe went to Greece just as the Greek Communists made their most intense effort to capture control. He was the last correspondent in Athens for a protracted period when the Communist ELAS forces held much of the city. They laid siege to the Grande Bretagne hotel, and Joe knew again the rattle of machine guns and the blast of mortar shells on the hotel. In the co-operative manner of newspapers in an emergency, Joe also covered for the London *News Chronicle* and the London *Observer*. In these manifold capacities, he reported the emergency visit to Athens of Harold Macmillan, then liaison with General Eisenhower, and later Britain's Prime Minister.

From Greece, through the aid of Randolph Churchill, Joe got to Yugoslavia and reported the beginning of Marshal Tito's communizing of the country. In April, 1945, he witnessed the surrender of German forces in Italy, and was taken by Partisans to view Mussolini's body soon after his execution in Milan. He got to Trieste when the Yugoslavs were occupying part of the city and the British the rest. Thereafter, he moved up through Eastern Europe, interviewing Mátyás Rákosi in Hungary and Edouard Beneš in Czechoslovakia. Even then, just as the war was ending, Beneš foresaw the danger to long-term peace which would come from partitioning Germany.

Bill Stringer was sent to North Africa in early 1944. There, from the headquarters which controlled campaigning in the Middle East and the Balkans, he observed and wrote about the conflicts which were to dominate so much of world politics for the next decade and a half. He described the Communist pressures being put on the Balkan countries as the Nazis were slowly driven out. And he saw the beginnings of conflict in the Middle East even as liberation spread along the Muslim crescent.

From North Africa, he went to Supreme Headquarters in Western Europe, and covered campaigns from the Normandy breakthroughs to the crossing of the Rhine. On December 4, 1944, before the Allied setbacks in the Ardennes had reached their most spectacular pitch, he wrote a dispatch pleading for more honesty in the release of information concerning Allied losses. In stark contrast to what was being published elsewhere, he wrote: "Do the folks back home realize the meaning of the fact that some ace divisions of the Americans and British have had replacement of 120 per cent or higher since the Normandy landings?"

In a telling preview of what was soon to come when the Nazis made their great penetrations at the Battle of the Bulge, he wrote: "Newspapers continue to carry headlines and war reports giving the impression that the West-Front campaign is mostly a super-football game. Many soldiers I have encountered do not like such headlines. They want to be sure the American people understand the hardships and toughness of current campaigning. It is not that they want personal sympathy; it is that they don't want the home front to let them down in production, prayers, or postwar programs."

On January 2, 1945, Mr. Stringer carefully analyzed Germany's astounding ability to launch a massive offensive and spelled out the shortcomings in Allied strategy. Many of the points he made have since been developed in technical reviews of strategy. They are part of the history of the time. The

Monitor correspondent's mandate to dig beneath the surface again provided information of permanent value.

Emlyn Williams, too, after a period in governmental service, returned to a correspondent's uniform and followed the drive into Berlin. He was one of the first correspondents to get into Warsaw after its capture. Thereafter he took up his German coverage where he had been forced to leave it off in 1939, and there he has been ever since. His continuing postwar chronicle of the slow regeneration and impressive economic restoration of West Germany is based on profound knowledge and experience.

Much more could be said about the *Monitor*'s war correspondents, both staff and special. But they were only one part of the paper's coverage. Even these correspondents could not cover all the war news that came pouring into the paper's office by the wire services. The *Monitor* did not consider it an adequate reader service just to slap into print the hottest war bulletin to come over the wire on deadline. It processed all the war news each day into a concise, integrated, explanatory summary. This remarkable job of synthesis and careful interpretation was done by Henry Sowerby. It was a massive but highly useful task. It gave readers, every single day, the most important news set in the total context. Often the war summary would lead the paper. It balanced and broadened the individual dispatches. It took a lot of work, and a lot of wisdom and judgment.

Mr. Sowerby's summary, the dispatches of the correspondents at the front, their "war diaries," their "Inside the War" articles, and the many articles from special correspondents all over the world which filled in the chinks were all developed under the supervision and leadership of Charles E. Gratke, the foreign news editor. (This position's title has subsequently been changed to overseas news editor, for a significant reason. Since the *Monitor* is published for readers everywhere, and from a non-nationalistic viewpoint, nowhere is "foreign." "Overseas" is a more accurate way to express the *Monitor*'s attitude to the world outside North America.)

Charles Gratke was a journalist of immense ability and dedication. His loss, when the plane in which he and twelve other American newsmen crashed over Bombay on July 12, 1949, was a sad and severe blow. But he left an unforgettable heritage in terms of skillfully trained staff members, sound precepts of newspapering, inspiring incidents and examples of his careful thinking, and a life of unswerving devotion to Christian Science and to journalism. He began newspaper work for his father's Astoria, Oregon, *Evening Budget.* He was graduated from the University of Oregon, and worked on the Oregon City *Enterprise,* the Portland *Oregonian,* and the Detroit *News* before coming to the *Monitor* in 1927. He worked in the New York Bureau until 1929, as assistant to the executive editor to 1932, as Berlin correspondent in 1932–33, European editorial manager in 1933–34, general news editor in Boston from 1934–37, and as foreign news editor from 1937 to 1949.

The *Monitor*'s files and the memories of its staff are crammed with evidences of Mr. Gratke's great work. Three points among many are these: he was a superb teacher of young journalists, he was a very foresighted planner and administrator of a worldwide force, and he was an extremely vigilant news editor. The stories that he refused to print, at least until they were clearly confirmed, are almost as important as the stories he stimulated and produced. The *Monitor* fell into no booby traps during his period and in his areas. Day in and day out, during the early years of the Second World War, he insisted on accuracy of fact and interpretation, holding both undue pessimism and excessive optimism in check.

For a young man to win his confidence required hard work. He was a rigorous trainer of men. Generations of cubs passed through his department. He would load their desks with work, shrewdly watching for their reactions. He expected others to work as hard as he did. He searched out the limits of men's capacity and explored their teachability. If a man could take criticism and learn from it, he was on the road to confidence. He would cut inadequate copy to ribbons, carefully analyzing every word and sentence so the neophyte might learn. The criticism was pungent, terse, uncompromising. And it applied to old-timers working for his department, as well as the beginners.

Such a training school produced very competent correspondents. Their loyalty to Mr. Gratke was deep and warm. He felt the same way about them, and would strive fiercely for their well-being, especially when they were in tough corners overseas. He used the cable freely to keep in touch with them, to let them know their work was appreciated, to check and correct them when required.

His cables to staff and special correspondents were proverbial in their wit and effectiveness. One day in 1948 the *Monitor*'s special correspondent in Shanghai, Randall Gould, sent a mail piece on a certain subject. Two days later Mr. Gratke ordered that very story by radio. Then, when the mailed copy got to Boston, this cable went to Shanghai: "Mailer seventh received. Isaiah 65:24." Which is to say: "And it shall come to pass, that before they call, I will answer; and while they are yet speaking, I will hear."

Mr. Gratke's system of keeping in touch with his correspondents often involved messages sent by prearrangement to transmit information which otherwise could not be sent in an open cable. Thus he had a verbal agreement with Emlyn Williams that when the end of the war should come in Europe, Emlyn would flash a signal agreed upon in advance. Early in the morning of May 7, 1945, the signal came. With it were other signs. Volney Hurd and Emlyn openly cabled they "would not file until late today." Mallory Browne cabled from London that they "expected important story" coming up later that day. So all the preparations were started for a V–E Day extra.

By 9:35 A.M. when the AP flash came — the dispatch sent by Ed Kennedy in alleged violation of SHAEF agreement — the *Monitor* was well on its way with an extra. Doubtless the extra would not have been published without something more than the tell-tale signal from Emlyn Williams and the hints from the others, but the forethought enabled Mr. Gratke to be sure that the AP was not out on the limb occupied by the

UP in 1918. It was with vivid memories of the UP's unhappy experience in that earlier armistice, that Mr. Gratke made his plans for multiple confirmation of the second war's end.

He plunged into postwar planning with his usual zest. He had been overseas during the war in a notable trip across fighting lines to neutral Sweden. In April and May, 1946, he visited Germany and did a penetrating series of articles. He managed the deployment of *Monitor* correspondents in all the crucial postwar areas. Again in 1947, he went to Germany and Austria. He was decorated by the French government in 1947 and again posthumously. He received a Sigma Delta Chi award for outstanding achievements in journalism in 1947.

In June, 1949, he accepted the invitation of the Netherlands government for a thirty-day tour of Indonesia, then in the throes of the independence struggle. He went, first visiting The Hague. With other skilled journalists, he probed deeply into the bitter situation in Indonesia, and wrote about a dozen articles while still on the spot. His dispatches shed important light on the Dutch accomplishments in Indonesia, on communism's role in the struggle, and on the determination of Indonesians to be totally independent.

William R. Mathews, editor and publisher of the *Arizona Star,* Tucson, who left the ill-fated party at Singapore, wrote: "Charles Gratke . . . was the skilled diplomat of the group. He could always be counted upon to say the right thing at the right time.

"He composed a telegram to Prime Minister Nehru of India asking for permission to land in India. It was his plea that finally melted down President Sukarno of the Indonesian republic in his stern refusal to answer questions. Mr. Gratke was probably the best-liked man of the group. He never got fussed. He never said a mean word; he was always kind and helpful."

But the finest tribute to Charles Gratke, one of the finest ever paid to a newspaperman, and one which in some sense applies to other *Monitor* men in the pursuit of their duties, was written by the hard-boiled editor of the Lubbock, Texas,

Evening Journal: Charles A. Guy. It is a tribute to a single staff member, but many are proud of it. Charlie Guy wrote:

A NEW BEAT FOR CHUCK GRATKE

The wide world was Chuck Gratke's beat and he died the other day while covering it. . . .

There were many good reporters on that Dutch airplane Tuesday morning, but there was none better than Chuck Gratke. In the group there may have been others whose lives were consecrated to good, but there was none more consecrated than Chuck Gratke.

He was a most unusual man, mentally and spiritually. We can say this, because we know it to be true.

. . . Throughout its long and highly respectable career, the Monitor has been home to countless writers and editors of high principle. But none of its people have surpassed Chuck Gratke in that regard and few, we suspect, have equaled the paper's late foreign editor in professional ability.

Chuck Gratke was a very fine newsman, as well as a very fine gentleman.

We can only guess, of course, what happened in those brief, awful moments over Ghatkopar last Tuesday morning . . . But we know there was no fear in the heart of Chuck Gratke, because, long ago, he had banished fear from his life; he had even defeated man's greatest mental enemy: worry. . . .

We had six weeks with Chuck Gratke in the gray, ugly Winter of 1947.

We flew the ocean with him twice. We winged across Europe by day and by night in weather so thick that the sensation was of flying in great rolls of cotton. We were in cold, damp treks by automobile with Chuck Gratke; at midday and past midnight with him we covered the tense Yugoslav frontier and the murky, rubble-strewn streets of a dozen European cities.

We had long talks with Chuck Gratke in the blackness of early mornings; long walks with him under snow-spitting skies.

From him we learned much. From him, more than from anyone else, we discovered that man's disciplining of his own life and thoughts can be a very amazing thing. . . .

One hundred fifty minutes a day, Chuck Gratke gave to study of his religion, its tract, the Bible, and to contemplation of what to him were eternal truths.

His complete mental and physical subservience to duty made him a very strong character. . . .

He made no effort, aside from setting an example, to influence anyone.

But Chuck Gratke's example is one we're sure none of the other members of our group failed to notice. . . .

For the better part of two decades, the wide, wide world was Chuck Gratke's beat.

As always, he was dutifully covering that beat — many miles from his loved ones in Marblehead, Mass. — when the inexorable Blue Pencil of Fate wrote '30' to his earthly assignments.

But if there is a Heavenly Clarion, Chuck Gratke today is on its staff with the whole expanse of the celestial sphere as his new beat.

He's fitted to cover it well.

He trained for the job down here.

✧

PART FOUR

THE MONITOR TODAY

1945–1958

✧

30

Peace and the "Stand-Up" *Monitor*

THE MONITOR moved into the postwar period in much the mood of the Western nations: there were high hopes, but not many illusions.

A strong staff had been sent to cover the United Nations Conference at San Francisco. I could not resist returning to my correspondent's days, and was in charge of the delegation. Roscoe Drummond, as chief of the Washington Bureau, headed the news staff. Neal Stanford, State Department and diplomatic correspondent in Washington, was on the job. Carlyle Morgan, the editorial writer who specialized in international organization, was a hard-working member. And there were two resident members of the Pacific Coast staff: Rodney Brink, chief of the Pacific Coast Bureau, and Kimmis Hendrick, San Francisco correspondent.

It was the same type of staff the paper sends to cover the Presidential nominating conventions. Several of its members were well acquainted with delegates from a number of countries. Their sources of information on the American delegation were first-rate. I had been resident correspondent at the League of Nations in Geneva for several years and so not only knew many people involved but was familiar with the difficulties and successes of the elder peace-seeking organization.

Though the paper covered the birth of the United Nations with this zeal and care, even in those hopeful days it was quite clear that the compromises required in the U.N. Charter would curb the organization's utility. The acceptance of a big-power veto on the Security Council, the paper's dispatches reiterated, meant that if there were not big-power unity there would be deadlock. And big-power unity could not be assumed. On the other hand, it was pointed out that if there were not big-power unity, or at least co-operation, no kind of organization could be successful in keeping the peace.

In those days, it is true, the tremendous difficulties in the way of co-operation with Moscow had not all been revealed. But Mr. Molotov's stubbornness at San Francisco was self-evident. The intransigent attitudes of the Kremlin on many issues were carefully pointed out in *Monitor* dispatches. Few of the idyllic hopes that marked the last months of the First World War and the first weeks of the Versailles Conference, were present at San Francisco. The war against Japan had still to be won. The atomic bomb had not yet fallen. Indeed, V–E Day came only during the midst of the San Francisco conference.

The conference at the Golden Gate was a pleasant and stimulating assignment, and to none more than the *Monitor* staffers who had not been to the Pacific Coast before. Among them were Messrs. Morgan and Stanford. They recall a particularly ebullient moment at a cafeteria along Market Street one midnight. It was the staff custom to write copy late at night or in the early hours of the morning, so that despite the time differential it would reach Boston soon after 7 A.M. About midnight, some of the men would step out of their workroom at the Palace Hotel and get a bite to eat at a nearby cafeteria. On the night in question, the counter was crowded. Neal Stanford leaned over the shoulder of a lady waiting to be served, and gave his order to the counter man in a firm voice.

"Young man," said the lady, "I was here ahead of you."

"Oh, madam," said Neal, "I am ordering these things for you."

"But I don't want them," said the lady.

"In that case," said Neal, "I'll take them."

The *Monitor's* practice of sending an editorial writer to such a meeting as the U.N. Conference has paid big dividends. Similarly, an editorial writer is sent to political conventions, and on regular trips to Washington or other parts of the nation or the world. For several years in the 1930's an editorial writer was maintained as a part of the Washington Bureau, and may be again someday. The paper does not believe in ivory towers. It thinks editorial writers must be in touch with the facts and atmosphere of the news.

The competence and nature of the Pacific Coast Bureau needs explanation. Early in its life the *Monitor* accepted the responsibility of covering with care news of the United States, from coast to coast. Since soon after its establishment, it has had sizable news bureaus in California, Chicago, and New York. From time to time it has also had staff correspondents in such places as Atlanta (1917–19), in Dallas since the 1940's, and in Detroit. In addition, it has always bought much copy from special correspondents in all parts of the country. For many years, it purchased many stories from college campuses. Many a working newspaperman or teacher of journalism got part of his start in writing for the *Monitor,* and remembers it gratefully.

The California Bureau has always been very important. The *Monitor* has many readers on the Pacific slope. Significant news happens there. In 1945, when the U.N. Conference was held, Rodney Brink had been running the Bureau since 1940. He was a Scripps veteran, well known up and down the coast. He had been preceded by Lewis Rex Miller, who had gone to California after being editor of the magazine section in Boston. Preceding Mr. Miller, the Bureau chief for many years was Courtland Holdom, a skilled, *Monitor*-trained journalist who helped establish the paper's reputation on the coast. Nate

White, now the paper's very successful business and finance editor, was San Francisco correspondent early in the 1940's. Kimmis Hendrick has been Bureau chief from 1947 to the present.

The work of the Pacific Coast Bureau calls for examination and insight into the remarkable news and social developments of what is clearly the fastest-growing and freest-thinking area in the nation. New political leaders have grown up apace on the Pacific slope. Industry and technology burgeon. Social experiments are advocated, and many are tried. And it is a window on the Pacific. In many ways it is a newsman's paradise. The Pacific Northwest, as well as California, is teeming with good copy. For all these reasons, the *Monitor* has kept first-rate correspondents there and printed abundant copy from the West country.

The central states, covered mainly from Chicago, are similarly fruitful. They include more great cities, more farmland, and more industrial areas, more natural-resource areas, more transportation, more economic sinews, than any of the other bureaus. From about 1914 the *Monitor*'s Central News Bureau was headed by Frederick W. Carr. He was a conscientious and thoughtful journalist. In the latter years of his *Monitor* service, he covered labor relations from Boston. One of his professional rules was to check the exact language he had used in a story with his sources before it went into the paper. This simple practice won for him, and for the paper, the gratitude of an immense number of people. Long after Mr. Carr had passed on, industrialists and trade union leaders would recall and comment on his scrupulous care in checking facts. This concern was especially appreciated by labor leaders in days when they got short shrift in some newspapers. On at least one occasion, a story by Mr. Carr was accepted by both sides as evidence in the arbitration of a hot labor dispute. He himself served as impartial arbiter in several disputes.

In Chicago, Mr. Carr was ably succeeded by Ralph W. Cessna, another *Monitor*-trained man during the great cubbing period of the 1920's. He was followed briefly by W. Lowrie Kay, a Pennsylvania newspaper veteran, and from 1949 to

1957 the Bureau was headed with great distinction by Max K. Gilstrap. Max has been mentioned as managing editor of *Stars and Stripes* in several of its European editions. This was not his only distinction. He had been a National Park ranger, and in that work became an expert birdsong imitator. His fame justly went far and wide. But his well-informed analysis of events and trends in the great midlands grew more capable year by year. He was very effective at national political conventions, and was well acquainted with the decisive political leaders who lived in his territory. In 1957, Mr. Gilstrap was transferred to Boston for important work, but passed on at the end of the year. He was succeeded by Godfrey Sperling, Jr. One of Mr. Sperling's great journalistic strengths is to get at currents of public opinion in vivid human terms, and his composite interviews always shed much light on thinking and events in the nation's center of gravity.

The *Monitor* is not an Eastern paper, but is nationwide and international in its appeal and responsibility. So it has always been deeply conscious of the great American continent. Its word for that region is not "hinterland." The Boston staff, many of them Westerners, has never considered any other part of the country hinterland. It is perfectly apparent that each section of the nation has an important role to play, and the *Monitor* is committed to its coverage. No section takes priority over the midlands. The *Monitor* has a very large reading public there.

As for New York, the *Monitor* has maintained an active bureau there almost from the beginning, recognizing the significance of the nation's metropolis, its financial, arts, and theatrical center. From 1924 to 1945 the Bureau chief was Alexander H. Williams. Mr. Williams, now retired, was as genial and hard-working as he is slender. He was an old-time New York newspaperman, on close and informal terms with everybody who mattered in the city. He was as intimate with political leaders like James A. Farley as he was with financial moguls like the partners of J. P. Morgan & Company. I know. I have visited both kinds of people with Al Williams, and it was a gratifying experience.

Al Williams also helped train many *Monitor* men who have pulled or are pulling heavy oars in the boat: Charles Gratke; Saville Davis, the present managing editor; Joe Harrison, the overseas news editor; Bill Stringer, chief of the Washington Bureau; Robert M. Hallett, Latin American editor, and so on. He was succeeded in New York by John Beaufort, later by Robert R. Mullen, who left the *Monitor* to write editorials for *Life* Magazine, and by the present New York Bureau chief, Stafford H. Derby. Mr. Derby came to the *Monitor* at the end of its first decade and returned during the Second World War.

Throughout all this time, the *Monitor* sought to keep a firm grip on the sinews of American affairs which are flexed in New York. It has always maintained the strongest possible coverage of the arts centering in New York: music, theatre, ballet, painting, films, and so on. And since the establishment of the United Nations headquarters in New York, it has kept a remarkably strong staff coverage there.

Joe Harrison was the first *Monitor* man assigned regularly to the U.N. in New York. He was soon succeeded by Homer Metz, a copy desk and foreign department veteran in Boston who gave expert coverage until he left to work for the Arabian-American Oil Company in the Middle East. The present U.N. correspondent, William R. Frye, then took over and soon became one of the recognized stars of the U.N. press corps. He is generally regarded as a correspondent who knows the people and practices of the U.N. to a superlative degree. In 1957, he was given a leave of absence in order to make a special study for the Carnegie Endowment for International Peace, which resulted in the book *A United Nations Peace Force.*

At this writing Mr. Frye has held his post for nearly a decade. Thus, like *Monitor* correspondents elsewhere, he has added long and intimate familiarity with the people and issues of his assignment to normal reportorial zeal. He understands the ins and outs of U.N. diplomacy and the background and motivation of many tangled problems. His coverage of the sometimes enigmatic Soviet delegations has been penetrating but fair. This incisiveness once led Andrei Gromyko, now

Foreign Minister of the U.S.S.R. to say that the *Monitor* is "the only serious newspaper in the United States."

Again from its earliest days, the *Monitor* has tried to maintain effective coverage of Latin America, as well as first-rate correspondents in Canada. For two decades now, its chief Canadian writing has been done by Bruce Hutchison, of the Victoria *Daily Times*.

Mr. Hutchison is perhaps Canada's most widely recognized and successful news interpreter to the rest of the world. His books are being justly praised. But week in and week out, for all these years, his *Monitor* dispatches have had comparable quality and insight, and have covered comprehensive areas. Readers of no other newspaper published in the United States have had a wider, deeper flow of information from the great nation to the north. Mr. Hutchison was preceded as the *Monitor*'s chief special correspondent in Canada by Lloyd Roberts, also a well-recognized book-writing authority on Dominion affairs.

The same may certainly be said for Latin America. In the 1930's, the paper's first Latin American editor was Roland Hall Sharp. Dr. Sharp is another of the remarkable people who have enriched the *Monitor*. He took his duties with intense seriousness. An episode which the office remembers with delight is the occasion when he outfitted himself for jungle reportage with a kit comparable to that Henry M. Stanley must have taken when he sought Dr. Livingstone in Darkest Africa. It included a pith helmet, naturally. There was a still — but for making pure water. And Dr. Sharp had procured a surely unique pair of high boots. They were topped with soft leather to which he could affix flypaper or similar adhesive, to entrap any insects that might try to invade the correspondent's person on foot. Of course he wore a mosquito net about his head. Dr. Sharp was quite willing to be photographed with his gear, and the result is an office treasure.

Despite the admittedly comic aspect of this outfit, Roland Sharp was a capable and intelligent correspondent. It was valuable for him to get up the Amazon, to evaluate and introduce realism into its agricultural potentialities. He flew everywhere, interviewed everybody, and wrote with skill and dash. He resembled nothing so much as the British explorers and eccentrics of the nineteenth century. Beneath his individualism was a persistent digging capacity which turned up important copy.

Roland Hall Sharp was followed by Robert K. Shellaby, and later by Robert M. Hallett. Each of these men roamed the Americas by plane, writing regional and composite interpretations of continental affairs. The *Monitor* has always been realistic and soundly democratic in its evaluations of Latin American politics. It has consistently exposed the weaknesses of dictators. It was never beguiled by Peronismo. This freedom and capacity to be strong owes no small debt to the fact that the *Monitor*'s Latin American editor was not actually resident in any single Latin American country. The men rather steadily made the rounds. Between trips they were in Boston ready to edit copy from special correspondents who were resident in various Latin American countries, and to write background articles.

The value of the *Monitor*'s coverage on Latin America is not measured by individual articles or series. Month in and month out the paper makes a conscientious effort to keep track of events in that part of the world before they explode into headlines. Then when the big news breaks, it has a fundamental understanding of the situation which can be passed along to the reader.

There is no doubt that the *Monitor* uses a higher percentage of stories on Latin America than any other general newspaper in the country. Furthermore, unlimited by strict news demands, it is able to develop cultural features and background stories that really give readers a more fundamental understanding of life in the Western Hemisphere.

As the war approached its end, *Monitor* policies and practices were given another careful re-examination. The Board of Trustees set up a Monitor Improvement Committee, which proceeded to dig into all aspects of the paper's news and editorial operation. The chief problem the *Monitor* faced, and still faces, was to make itself valuable to the overwhelming majority of its readers who do not receive the paper, for one, two, or many days after publication. Those who follow the news in any degree will have been exposed to many radio broadcasts and possibly several editions of local newspapers before the *Monitor* reaches them. Therefore the *Monitor*'s basic need is to give them added value beyond the mere reporting of news.

This necessity had always been recognized. Its fulfillment remains technically difficult. The *Monitor* correspondent faces the dual task of writing basic news facts and events which must not be ignored, and then of adding other background or explanatory material so that the copy will be of real utility long after the day of publication. This composite job is challenging to any writer. It runs the risk of falling between two stools: the spot news can be excessively blurred or omitted; the explanation can be tainted and dated by the spot news. Moreover, the explanatory or interpretive copy often seems to be editorial and opinionative in nature — and sometimes it is.

The *Monitor* writer must start with prime news facts, using them as a peg on which to hang his story, but he must make clear to the reader at once that he will learn things from the story which he has not received in other spot news media. To write this sort of copy requires training and experience.

The *Monitor* staff, being highly professionalized, naturally feels a continuing obligation to the news. It has a duty to the event. But mere coverage of the event signals to the distant reader that this story is something he has read or listened to before. Take the problem in a specific case: it is the day of a Presidential election. Not the day after, when the results are known and can be explained and interpreted with exclusive and important background information and judgment. Should the *Monitor* give strong front-page prominence on the day the voting takes place to a story of the election, knowing that the paper will not reach readers on the Pacific Coast until three or four days after the results of the election are known? And yet the election story is the biggest event on the day of publication. The same situation confronts the paper's news editor and writers on any breaking news story.

This hard issue was faced. It was recognized that the only kind of copy worth printing on page one on the day of the election for readers of remote editions would be copy which retained its value when it reached them. This meant rejecting the news editor's normal newspaper judgment to play the election story strongly on the day of the voting. The reasoning applies to every news situation when time does not permit the added-value story.

The mail editions of the *Monitor,* on the other hand, require even more dynamic impact than the editions which reach readers swiftly, for the latter have the advantage of spot news. For the mail editions to become merely daily news magazines would be to forfeit the *Monitor*'s mandate as a newspaper.

Therefore, in the thinking which went on in the mid and late 1940's, it was decided to instruct all correspondents to write every piece of copy they possibly could on a stand-up basis. Only such stand-up copy was to be given prominent display — or, ideally, be run at all — in the mail editions. It was to be made just as strong as possible, through use of relevant background and explanatory material. Typography was to be enlivened through use of more arresting heads, larger and more attractive pictures and brighter drawings.

One step was taken which has proved to be about the most popular technical device the paper ever adopted. All "jumps" from page one to inside pages were stopped. Every story beginning on page one had to be complete on that page. This step had two great advantages. It made reading the paper very much more convenient. Its readers no longer had the nuisance of skipping from a few paragraphs on page one to some inside page, and then back to the front page for another story. And the change also greatly improved the inside pages. They, too, were now composed of complete stories, with strong top heads on all of them. A sense of integration and orderliness was possible.

But there was also a disadvantage: front-page stories had to be either very short or limited in number. A compromise course was followed. Most stories were actually shortened. The effect, on the whole, has been very desirable. It has produced tighter and more economical writing. When stories really needed length, they were permitted it. This cut down on variety and sometimes produced a front page with large masses of unrelieved type. On the whole, the best was made of both worlds. Only a few dissented from the proposition that a front page without jumps, even without so much variety, was better than a front page of bits and pieces.

Every effort was also made to group the news in orderly array. Local news was assigned to certain pages, national news to others, overseas to others. In days of tight newsprint supply and high costs, it is sometimes regrettably necessary to use small areas of space for general news on feature pages, but with this exception, orderly grouping has been achieved.

Make-up based on horizontal rather than vertical display of stories and pictures was applied. Instead of stringing down the length of the page, like long stockings on the clothesline, stories were pulled into compact masses, under broad heads. The talents of staff artists were used for small, light drawings with which to embellish many stories.

Although the *Monitor* did not change its type faces, it did revise and modernize its headline styles, in keeping with, and sometimes in advance of, general newspaper styles. The content of headlines was also important. They could signal the idea of perishable spot news or the value of stand-up quality even more effectively than the story itself. But to give this added value to headlines required almost more technical skill than in the story itself. The task was attempted, and measurably fulfilled.

These changes had the intent of making the *Monitor* look like a stand-up national and international newspaper rather than a local spot-news newspaper. They were introduced gradually, and except when jumps from the front page were dropped, readers scarcely knew what was happening.

Some of the readers, however, have wondered about and occasionally criticized the idea of interpretive writing. The very word is a misnomer. Interpretation suggests editorializing. That is not the fact or purpose of *Monitor* coverage. The word "explanation" is better, or "clarification." The value which the *Monitor* must add to all possible copy is the value of placing the news in its proper perspective and context. It calls for much greater digging, not for less. The task is essentially reportorial. The writer must consult files and sources, in order to show the real meaning of today's news event. He must write objectively, not simply out of his own opinions. He must not obscure the news, but clarify it.

There is a difference, of course, between explanatory news writing and full-fledged columns under a correspondent's byline, identified as a special enterprise. The *Monitor* has had front-page columns almost from its earliest days. From 1908 to 1919 it ran "Monotorials" by Nixon Waterman, a light column of verse and paragraphs. Thus early in its life did it see that bright and lively touches must be added to the serious news. During the next decade, its columns were mainly on inside pages, and were largely reminiscence, although often with valuable political content. In the 1920's, when there were no page-one columns, the editorial page blossomed with many regular columns, including those by H. W. Massingham, Wickham Steed, Lord Lothian, and Willis J. Abbot, the editor himself.

Then there came the 1930's and the inauguration of the Rufus Steele column, "March of the Nations," on the front page, followed by Henry E. Williams' "Tower Views." There were also inside-page and editorial-page columns. In the 1930's two Washington columns were started: "Intimate Message from Washington," in 1933, and "Washington Sideglances," in 1939. The former still continues, on the editorial page. It is an opportunity for analytical and observant copy by the paper's Washington staff. To process their writings in editorial-page column form gives added value and impact to copy which it would be difficult to dignify so effectively in the news columns.

In 1936 the paper began "Economics in the News," followed in 1938 by "This Changing World," by Herbert B. Elliston, its business and financial editor. Mr. Elliston was a talented and experienced journalist. He gave a great deal to the *Monitor*. He was of British birth, had worked many years in

China, and came to the *Monitor* from the staff of the Council on Foreign Relations in New York.

While his primary *Monitor* responsibilities concerned business and finance, his experience and interests covered a far wider field. He wrote about national and international affairs with knowledge and force. His advice and counsel during the re-examinations of the 1930's were most useful, and his departure in 1940 for the great opportunity of running the Washington *Post*'s editorial page left a real gap. His successor, George R. Ericson, wrote interesting financial comment on inside pages and ran the business coverage of the paper with skill.

In 1955 Nate White, who had left the *Monitor* seven years before to take a high-level position with the Committee for Economic Development, returned to the paper's staff as business and financial editor. His many years of contact with leadership in these fields soon brought into the paper's columns a flow of perceptive coverage. Notable in the work he began was an extensive series of articles by officials of the nation's chief economic and financial enterprises, explaining how their companies operate. The articles pulled together the most comprehensive and clarifying profile of American enterprise which has ever been published in a daily newspaper. Mr. White also began a front-page column published weekly, "Trend of the Economy." He developed in depth regular background articles from the *Monitor*'s best overseas correspondents, giving readers a clarifying picture of the world economy.

These and many other undertakings were part of the *Monitor*'s effort to make itself much more than just another newspaper. Both in fact and in appearance, it has to convey to its readers a set of values rarely accepted by the ordinary daily newspaper. To "stand up" is the last thing most newspapers feel called upon to do. But if the *Monitor* were not different it would not exist.

31

The Cold War — and Infiltrators

In the disillusioning decade which began in 1947, the *Monitor* strove its hardest to preserve balance and sane judgment in itself and its readers. It was an early and energetic critic of militant communism. But it could not approve the methods of fighting communism which were called McCarthyism. Furthermore, the *Monitor* refrained from denouncing President Truman when he recalled General Douglas MacArthur from Tokyo, considering the action — however debatable — the executive's prerogative as commander-in-chief. For these positions, it was criticized by some readers who were caught up in the uncertainty and emotionalism of the period, or whose earnest patriotism, nationalism, and conservatism led them to an extreme position.

The fundamentals of the *Monitor*'s editorial commitment bear directly on the issue. The paper is dedicated by its Founder to the blessing of all mankind, which is what its subtitle "An International Daily Newspaper" is intended to convey. It has never supported or endorsed any form of supergovernment. The United Nations, which it has always supported, is of course an organization of sovereign countries. The kind of "one worldism" which the paper supports is the kind Mary Baker Eddy affirmed on its first editorial page.

Since the *Monitor* is published in the United States, the paper has a special interest in the safeguarding and strengthening of American institutions and freedoms. It believes the American Constitution, providing religious and other rights, gave the environment in which the Christian Science movement could be founded and, by consequence, the *Monitor* established. So the paper has always been deeply devoted and vigilant in the preservation of American constitutional and civil liberties.

But it has never been willing to equate progressivism or New Dealism with communism. It has scrutinized each element of the liberal political and economic programs on its own merits, from days of Theodore Roosevelt and Woodrow Wilson to Herbert Hoover — who was also criticized in his time as a dangerous reformer — to Franklin D. Roosevelt, Harry S. Truman, and Dwight D. Eisenhower. Often the *Monitor* has supported separate and concrete elements in these programs, over the half century, but always with careful reservations and conditions.

It has emphasized the need for safeguards against excessively centralized government, against regulations or taxes which hamper and destroy initiative or free competition, against fiscal policies that build up an excessive burden of debt, and against personal political power. It has favored the rule of law. It prefers government as close to the people as possible. It believes government should never do anything that can be done satisfactorily by private initiative.

Its position may best be summarized as old-fashioned liberalism, dedicated to the safeguarding of men's opportunity to fulfill their individual destinies. The paper's position remains rooted in the declarations of its Founder, as the century began, when she denounced under the heading "Insufficient Freedom": ". . . the robbing of people of life and liberty under the warrant of the Scriptures; the claims of politics and human power, industrial slavery, and insufficient freedom of honest competition; and ritual, creed, and trusts in place of the Golden Rule, 'Whatsoever ye would that men should do to you, do ye even so to them.' "

In the bitter political atmosphere generated in the United States by twenty years of one-party control of the executive government, by the disappointments which followed the nation's tremendous efforts in the Second World War, and still more by concern when the Korean War broke out, and by the shocking revelations of treason perhaps even in high places, it is no wonder that the *Monitor* had to stand firm against extremists. The role of moderation and balance, which in political affairs is imposed by the *Monitor*'s nonpartisanship, is sometimes equally exasperating to both extremes.

There have always been critics of the *Monitor*'s political positions. Even when it was striving its hardest merely to report and explain the facts, its objectivity came under attack from both sides. When in 1933 and thereafter I was a Washington correspondent, I was denounced by some few readers as a "Communist" although I was simply trying to report the Roosevelt Administration accurately and without pre-judgment. Other *Monitor* writers have been subjected to similar attack. The fact is ignored that *Monitor* policies are carefully supervised by The Christian Science Board of Directors, and the staff is engaged and closely administered by the Board of Trustees. Neither of these boards would knowingly admit the slightest trace of subversion or infiltration.

The *Monitor* has a remarkable record of freedom from such infiltration. There has been no staff member whose activities could be legitimately called in question before a loyalty investigation. In one of Senator McCarthy's books there is an invidious reference to Richard L. Strout. It is patently false and misleading. It was at once denied in the paper's columns with convincing proof.

However, there are two cases of space writers who have been accused of pro-communism by official investigative bodies.

Neither is an American citizen or ever worked regularly in the United States. Both men, it so happens, had been dismissed as *Monitor* special correspondents before charges were made against them or had even become known. One is Wilfred G. Burchett, the other is Guenther Stein.

Mr. Burchett, an Australian, cabled the *Monitor* from the British Legation in Budapest on May 19, 1949, stating that he was in Hungary for the London *Daily Express* and was free to write for an American paper. He offered his services. He had served as a war correspondent in the Pacific and had written a few dispatches for the paper at that time. Since the *Monitor* had no special correspondent in Hungary, it was glad to try out Mr. Burchett, an experienced and able journalist. He later notified Boston that he had been appointed Balkan correspondent for *The Times* of London. But before long it became apparent to the *Monitor*'s vigilant foreign editor that his work had a pro-Communist twist. By late June, 1950, the *Monitor*'s doubts crystallized, and on July 5, 1950, it notified Mr. Burchett it would no longer accept copy from him.

Mr. Burchett next turned up in Communist China, as correspondent for *Le Soir*, of Paris, a Communist paper. He covered the Korean War from the north side of the 38th parallel and appeared one day at Kaesong, Korea, where the cease-fire negotiations were under way. He was also a participant in one way or another, at the interrogations of some United Nations prisoners. He denied being a Communist. The *Monitor* feels proud that it detected the unreliability in his copy speedily, and broke off relations with him.

Guenther Stein is a more complicated case. He was a rather intimate friend of that sturdy anti-Communist, William Henry Chamberlin, when Mr. Chamberlin was the *Monitor*'s correspondent in Japan. Mr. Stein had been on the staff of the *Berliner Tageblatt* and *Frankfurter Zeitung* in pre-Hitler days. In Japan he was principally employed by the Manchester *Guardian*. On Mr. Chamberlin's recommendation, the *Monitor* accepted copy from him, at first chiefly economic, from Japan and China in the days before the Second World War.

When the Chinese Nationalist government was forced back

to Chungking, Mr. Stein went with them and covered the war against the Japanese. He is favorably mentioned in the book covering this period written by Hollington Tong, the present Chinese Ambassador to the United States. At one point, he journeyed into the areas controlled by the Communists, and wrote about them vividly — as did various other correspondents for Western newspapers. Mr. Stein came to the United States in 1945 and did a few additional articles for the *Monitor*. Then the *Monitor* terminated relationships with him, although it had detected nothing wrong with his copy. There was simply no further use for him. Up to this point, no public charges against Mr. Stein had been made, and none had come privately to the *Monitor*'s attention.

Meantime, as the American occupation forces in Japan dug into the files of the Japanese secret police, they unearthed information allegedly connecting Mr. Stein with the Sorge spy ring which had operated in Japan on behalf of the Soviet Union. Such information was made public at the Defense Department in Washington. Without waiting for any hearing or discussion, Mr. Stein suddenly left the United States for Paris. The *Monitor* has not heard from him since. His case remains somewhat enigmatic. The Defense Department later withdrew some of its adverse statements about the Sorge ring, and then reissued them. There is much about Guenther Stein in the various books and reports on subversion in China.

The semiofficial account of the Sorge spy ring is in *Shanghai Conspiracy*, by Major General Charles A. Willoughby, who was General MacArthur's chief of intelligence. General Willoughby regards Mr. Stein as a "top-level member of the ring." The evidence gathered by the Japanese police, as summarized by General Willoughby and his staff, places him as a courier who carried a message to Hong Kong, and indicates that he permitted his home to be used as a location for the secret radio set by which information was sent to Russians on the Asian mainland.

Mr. Stein's book *Challenge of Red China*, says General Willoughby, "has the outward appearance of the thoughtful reporting of a serious, objective analyst who is neither pro nor anti-

Communist, but who only wants to discover the underlying truth." He adds: "His book had been very effective in perpetuating the legend that Chinese Communists are not Communists and are not in any way connected with the Soviet Union." This may be true, but it does not apply to Stein's writing in the *Monitor*. That falls under General Willoughby's first description of "thoughtful reporting." Indeed, if Mr. Stein were an active Soviet spy, he would have been foolish to write copy that would have given him away. General Willoughby writes that Mr. Stein "is a man about whom too little is known." This is certainly true.

There is no evidence that his writing for the *Monitor* was unprofessional, inaccurate, or slanted. His sudden disappearance was quite contrary to the behavior of other Communist agents, who usually fought their cases long and loudly. Some of his friends still insist that Mr. Stein may have been working for the British secret service all the time, but I have no information on the subject. What matters is that the *Monitor*'s columns were not significantly tainted by Mr. Stein, whoever he was. And the paper broke off with him before the charges erupted.

There is another instance of a corrrespondent with a concealed identity. The paper only learned about it in 1957. David E. Walker, in his book *Lunch with a Stranger,* tells how he was recruited for British intelligence work during the Second World War, was sent to Lisbon, and there got work sending articles to *The Times* of London, the *Daily Mirror*, and *The Christian Science Monitor*. He was a very experienced newspaperman and his stories were excellent. Doubtless his intelligence work made them all the better and enhanced their inside sources. Mr. Walker liked the *Monitor*, too, for he wrote: "To work for the Christian Science Monitor was an undiluted pleasure. . . . With a courage almost unknown in the modern newspaper world, the Monitor never seemed to mind if the news was a day or two late, provided that when it did arrive it was comprehensive, fair and accurate." He wrote for the *Monitor* from mid-1942 to 1944.

Of course a great many suspicious characters have submitted

copy to the *Monitor,* hoping to penetrate its columns. It takes eternal vigilance and prayerful insight to protect the paper from such intrusion. One such effort got into the news in 1950. Early in that year, the foreign news department got a letter from Frank E. Stevens, who had written for the paper on a space basis from Rumania in the early 1930's. He offered to begin his services again, stating that meantime he had been correspondent for Reuters, the New York *Sun,* the United Press, and the Religious News Service.

He was told the paper would very much welcome "a good picture of what is happening in Romania today." When his copy began to arrive, its pro-Communist slant was obvious. None of it was ever printed by the *Monitor.* On July 9, 1950, Mr. Stevens denounced President Truman as a warmonger and announced he had decided to stay in Rumania "to fight for peace, freedom and human dignity." He claimed to be a correspondent of the *Monitor.* The *Monitor* was very glad it had published none of his copy. The State Department announced that for two years Mr. Stevens had been trying to get his wife and two children out of Rumania. Just what tragic human drama lay behind this episode may someday become known.

Every year the *Monitor* buys space copy from some 2000 different individuals. For the last turbulent quarter century in which the Communist conspirators have been trying to infiltrate various innocent enterprises, there could have been some 50,000 opportunities for them to do so via the *Monitor*'s space purchases. Of course, these include many light and trivial items, and many repetitions, so the figures are not quite realistic. But even so, the fact that the *Monitor* seeks and obtains copy from correspondents at the ends of the earth, shows that there has been plenty of opportunity for infiltration. This the paper well understands. So its editors and news staff scrutinize copy with extreme care and a very sharp nose for bias. A phony can usually be spotted. And whenever possible, a responsible staff member gets in personal touch with the space writer and inspects him carefully. But the fact remains that the paper has been wonderfully protected from being misused. On only one or two other isolated occasions has copy briefly been run from writers about whose complete loyalty there later emerged any doubt.

On the positive side, its detection of Communist conspiracies goes back a long way. Mention has been made of William Henry Chamberlin, who covered the Soviet Union with utmost realism after his awakening, not long after his arrival in Moscow. His successor, Demaree Bess, for many later years a special correspondent for the *Saturday Evening Post,* also saw and reported the Soviet situation clearly. Edmund Stevens began by covering the Finnish war realistically from the Finnish side. His Russian coverage during the later war years, when the alliance with the Soviet Union was at its height and Russian patriotic heroism was at its most ardent, was inevitably favorable and generous.

When he returned to Moscow as a resident correspondent in 1947 his copy was as realistic as the rigid censorship would permit. After he left Moscow in 1950, he wrote a scathing and factual series for the *Monitor,* "This is Russia — Uncensored," for which he received the Pulitzer Prize. Thus the *Monitor*'s total record on Soviet coverage adds up well.

The various threats of communism were exposed in the *Monitor*'s columns by nobody more effectively than Reuben Henry Markham. Mr. Markham is one more of the unique and precious persons who helped build and maintain the *Monitor*'s character. His loss in 1949 left a large gap.

Reuben Markham was born in Smith County, Kansas, of Yankee parents. He went to Bulgaria in 1912 as an ordained minister and educational missionary for the American Board of Commissioners for Foreign Missions of the Congregational Church. He saw the Balkan-Turkish War in 1912, the inter-Balkan war in 1913, and the outbreak of the First World War. He returned to the United States at the end of 1917, and was sent by the United States Army on a special mission to Archangel, Russia, in 1918. Thereafter he went to France to work on behalf of Russian prisoners there.

In 1920 he returned to Bulgaria, driving from Paris to Sofia in a Model-T Ford with his wife and three children and the family of a fellow missionary which included two children. There he observed the fierce struggles in the Balkans in the 1920's. His missionary job was a casualty, for a reactionary Bulgarian government forced his organization to accept his resignation. Thereupon he published a new weekly paper called *Svet* (World), which came to be the widest circulated weekly in the country.

In 1927, Mr. Markham began to work for the *Monitor* as a stringer correspondent in Sofia. Soon he was placed on the staff and given responsibility for the entire Balkans. He roamed them as no other American correspondent before or since. He was known and loved by the people, from peasants to politicians, teachers, journalists. He was particularly close to the sturdily anti-Communist leaders of the peasant parties. He saw the tides of fascism and nazism sweep in, driving communism underground. He watched King Carol return to Rumania to establish a royal dictatorship. He was on hand when the Yugoslav royal dictatorship was proclaimed in 1929. No other American correspondent spent so much time as he in Albania.

He was in Vienna when the Socialists and Heimwehr fought through the streets and apartment blocks; he was in town on the day Chancellor Dolfuss was assassinated, and he watched Hitler sweep into Austria. In 1935, the *Monitor* sent Mr. Markham into Ethiopia to cover the tense situation there just prior to the Italian invasion. His writing was spectacular; but his expense account is one of the most extraordinary documents in the *Monitor*'s archives. One of its arresting items is this: "Two mules & saddles Th. 190, sold for Th. 130, leaves Th. 60." Even more provocative is this: "For finding slaves Th. 4." Who the slaves were, and why they had to be found, is not recorded. Another item shows a proper sense of values: "Mule man 9 weeks Th. 23. News scouts 9 weeks Th. 90."

Reuben's mule was a splendid black beast, with scarlet velvet saddle robe, but it had a slow and jolting gait. His retainer's mule, though small and brown, was swift, obedient, and had a delightfully rolling gait. Proper respect for prestige kept the unfortunate correspondent on the big black animal.

After Ethiopia, he went to the Bible Lands and wrote a splendid series of fifty-three articles. Reuben always declared it was the most pleasant assignment he ever had. Then he came back to the United States, did a series on "Rediscovering America" and another on "Mr. Markham Goes to Washington." Other American series followed thick and fast. For his humble, graphic, folksy touch — his love for people everywhere and his fervent patriotism — touched the heartstrings of readers.

In 1942, Mr. Markham was called into the service of the American government, and was a Deputy Director of the Office of War Information in charge of American information and propaganda to the Balkan countries. His chief, Elmer Davis, wrote that Reuben knew the Balkan peoples better than any other American. But he and the government came to a parting of the ways. In Mr. Davis' frank words:

> Eventually, he came to the conclusion that American policy in dealing with the Balkan countries — the support of all elements, including the Communists, that were resisting the Germans — was mistaken. American propaganda policy was of course a reflection of American foreign policy, which was determined on a higher level than Markham's or mine . . . It entailed long-term political consequences of which Mr. Markham, familiar with the Balkans, was perhaps better aware than most American officials.
>
> His predicament was one which was not uncommon in our (or any) wartime government; and his behavior in that situation was impeccable. Having done his best, unsuccessfully, to get American policy changed, and being unable conscientiously to execute the policy which had been determined, he resigned. But he resigned without noise and uproar which might have hampered the execution of the policy on which his superiors had decided. The event proved that the policy which was followed led to precisely the unfortunate results which he foresaw.

Thus Reuben Markham came back to the *Monitor*. After the war, he was sent by the paper again to the Balkans. There he observed the workings of communism in a most intimate manner and described them in much detail. This caused the

Commanding General of the Soviet army in Rumania to order him peremptorily to leave the whole area in the summer of 1946.

It was a poignant leave-taking. As he was hustled out of the country by the Communists, Reuben could not help remembering a day in 1925 when the Fascist-type government of Bulgaria was taking severe reprisals against Communists, and the well-known Alexander Dimitrov had been condemned to death. A day before the date of execution, an Eastern Orthodox priest, wearing his customary long black robe and high black hat, appeared in Mr. Markham's house, accompanied by his wife and daughter, who was the wife of the condemned Communist. They implored him to ask King Boris to save the son-in-law and husband from execution.

It was a moving meeting. In view of the political hatred that divided Bulgaria, causing murders and massacres, the tenderhearted Reuben felt that further executions would only fan the flames. He immediately urged King Boris to suspend Dimitrov's execution, hoping the act of mercy would assuage the danger of civil war. That same evening, King Boris wrote Mr. Markham to tell him the death sentence had been commuted.

But twenty years later the wheel had turned, and the Communists — one of whose lives Mr. Markham had saved — knew that he was one of their most effective and implacable critics. On the afternoon of his expulsion, he went to a reception given for the head of the American military mission. News of his expulsion had just been made known, so the party turned into a spontaneous reception in his honor. A former prime minister, former cabinet members, writers, professors pressed around him to express their regrets and devotion. When he left, the former prime minister, in Balkan fashion, publicly kissed him goodby. That evening another former prime minister, the most beloved leader of modern Rumania, sent the newspaperman a grateful farewell message.

Joseph Harrison entered Rumania in the fall of 1946. As he registered at the Athénée Palace (Bucharest's leading hotel), the desk clerk, when he saw that the visitor was from the

Monitor, looked carefully about the lobby and then leaned over and said, "We all love Mr. Markham."

With his direct knowledge of the working of communism in Eastern Europe, Reuben Markham came back to America. He was crammed with direct information which his old and close friends in Eastern Europe had confided to him. He knew the ways of infiltration and subversion. He had seen the patterns by which societies striving to be free had been brought down. All of this he wrote in the *Monitor* with vivid detail. His accounts of the nature, ends, and strategy of communism did not please those who were still under the wartime spell, or otherwise bemused by the Kremlin's ideology. And so at a time when other liberals or humanitarians — and Reuben was all this in abundance — were refusing to believe in subversion or treason, he pointed out its stark trail from Eastern Europe to America itself.

But he knew the difference between liberalism or progressivism and communism. He would never have condemned a man without evidence. The only guilt he knew was that susceptible of clear and unmistakable proof. He fought communism, or anything else that denied human liberties, with facts and knowledge. His books *Romania Under the Soviet Yoke* and *Tito's Imperial Communism* were timely warnings.

Almost his last work for the *Monitor* took the form of articles uncovering the infiltration of organizations and groups in the United States. These antedated most of the professional red-hunters. His little book *Let Us Protestants Awake* was the fruit of this uncovering.

In 1949, when the American government's policy had again become opposed to appeasement and collaboration with communism, Mr. Markham was summoned back to official service. He had just finished editing another small book, *Communists Crush Churches in Eastern Europe,* and was ready to make a flying trip abroad, when he suddenly passed on, December 29, 1949.

Nobody could have loved people and freedom more than Reuben Markham, or have written about them more honestly and humbly. His work stands almost alone in American journalism for its simplicity, integrity, and direct, personal knowledge. For many years he helped the *Monitor* express this love, which is also the paper's birthright. And then when crisis came, he put the paper in the forefront of those who had seen the dangers, and had given the warning — but a warning based on truth and justice.

32

◇◇◇◇◇◇◇◇◇◇◇◇◇◇◇◇◇◇◇◇◇

The Richer Side of Life

A WOMAN on a remote mountain ranch in western Canada once wrote the *Monitor,* and in simple but touching terms told how its pages had brought to her the rich flow of the world's cultural life and heritage. It had obliterated her isolation and made her one with the company of cultivated persons the world over, and timelessly. Her appreciation was justified. It can be multiplied many thousandfold.

For half a century the *Monitor* has mirrored the world's finest cultural achievements. It has analyzed and criticized performance in the arts, seeking always to improve achievement. It has provided popular entertainment, enjoyment, relaxation. The scope of the *Monitor*'s interest and attention to the fields of fine and popular arts is so large that only summary and sampling are possible here.

Take "The Home Forum," for example. Each issue normally contains five basic features: a major essay or article of sound literary merit, a reproduction of a noteworthy work of art with explanatory comment, one or two well-chosen poems, one or more excerpts from a published literary work, a daily religious article often translated into a foreign language.

If you were to convert the twenty-five to twenty-seven Home Forums published each month into the format of a monthly magazine, you would have a fat product of about 150 pages of highly selective reading matter, plus 25 illustrations of first-rate quality and diversity, expertly explained. The average high-quality monthly magazine may have 70 pages of reading matter, including illustrations. This means that the Home Forum publishes every month the generous equivalent of two monthly magazines.

Translated into annual terms, this is the equivalent of nine profusely illustrated books at least as long as this one. Multiplying the figures by the half century, the Home Forum has given its readers a bookshelf of 450 volumes. Using books like this one, that would mean a shelf some 56 feet long! Such are the staggering proportions of the Home Forum's quantitative contribution to the cultural lives of *Monitor*'s readers. In quality the content is equally impressive.

The page was included in the very first sample copy of the *Monitor* printed on September 15, 1908, and taken to Mrs. Eddy for her approval over two months before the paper appeared in public. It met with her warm endorsement. At the outset it was a composite page, including elements that later became the women's page, children's page, educational page, book review page, and family features page. From the beginning, the page included the religious article, the only explicit statement of Christian Science regularly published in the paper.

Steadily the Home Forum evolved and its cultural qualities deepened. By the 1930's, when it was edited by Miss Margaret Williamson and its art work and commentary were prepared chiefly by Miss Dorothy Adlow, the page reached the form and standard it has maintained and enhanced ever since.

On September 19, 1922, the first translation (French) of the religious article appeared. Thus began one of the most striking and distinctive of the *Monitor*'s features. It is one most commonly noticed and discussed by interested professionals. Today, translations in fifteen different languages appear. No other daily newspaper, as far as can be determined, regularly publishes material in so many languages.

The articles, especially those in the less familiar languages, evoke amazed interest. The translation work is handled by the translations department of The Christian Science Publishing Society, and the religious article itself by the *Sentinal* and *Journal* editorial department. The type is set without fuss in the regular *Monitor* composing room, by operators who often do not know the languages they are using. The Home Forum translations are of course published as a kind of missionary function. Their very novelty and appeal to people whose native tongue is used constitute a very attractive feature.

The cultural enrichment of the Home Forum really began when its editorship was assumed by Miss Margaret Ramsay, in 1922. Prior to that time, the page had suffered from attrition during the litigation, and from the burden of carrying as many as five different feature pages within its confines in earlier years. Its central pictorial feature — the art — had been pleasant but not outstanding. Many of its written contributions were by eager amateurs. They lacked professional quality. In the very earliest years, a substantial part of the copy was reprinted, with credit, from other publications.

But under Miss Ramsay's editorship, the professional quality of the literary material became established at a high level. The prose improved greatly as essayists of real distinction began to write for the page. Many of these contributors still enrich its columns. T. Morris Longstreth, who has published some forty books, has written familiar essays for the page over a third of a century. During the 1920's and 1930's Professor Odell Shepard, the Connecticut teacher and the biographer of the unicorn, wrote light essays in great profusion.

In the days when Miss Ramsay was selecting much of the page's art, the present writer had a poignant lesson in her austere standards. As a very young cub, I had been sent to interview a visiting expert in Persian art and history. The visitor gave me some pictures of Persian rugs which I thought beautiful, and suggested that they might be of value to the Home Forum. I bore them proudly back to Miss Ramsay, of whom I stood greatly in awe, and had seen only at a distance. It was a hot day, and in accordance with newsroom practice, I had taken off my coat. Miss Ramsay made me get it and put it on before I could approach her desk. Only then would she look at the pictures. It took her only a second, and she said, "They won't do at all. I'm not interested." I found enough courage to ask her why.

"Young man," she said, "do you see those marks on the rugs? That is writing. Those words are Arabic. How do I know what they might be saying?"

Miss Ramsay also began to convert the merely pleasant little quotes from books into definite guides to reading. She also commenced the improvement in quality of the poetry.

All these trends were continued and deepened in the editorship of Miss Margaret Williamson, which extended from 1931 to 1952. And Miss Williamson began to avail herself of the valuable judgment of Miss Dorothy Adlow. From that time on, Miss Adlow has supplied most of the pictures and written brief but informative notes about them. Any reader who follows the Home Forum regularly can receive a broad education in the world's art. The page was slow to admit contemporary styles in art, but did so in the 1950's after they had become fully established and recognized as part of the canon by galleries, schools, and critics.

In terms of literature, the page — at least since the 1920's — has offered readers a daily flow of original essays and poems which have been of consistently good quality and occasionally of outstanding merit, supported by book excerpts aimed at encouraging wider reading. Thus readers have been given the means of developing a keener and more literary awareness, a great ability both to judge and appreciate literature. Any regular reader could have enriched and warmed his life experience in the glow of these bright fires.

In terms of literature, the *Monitor* has helped to keep alive the essay form, which is particularly suited to the Home Forum's needs. Many books have been published from the page's essays and sketches. Among the more notable are *Small Moments* by Richard Church, who is perhaps the page's most eminent literary contributor, and *The Harvest of a Quiet Eye* by Odell Shepard. Dorothy L. Pillsbury's New Mexico sketches have been collected in book form. Other collections of essays have been published privately or semiprivately.

In the field of poetry, the Home Forum's most distinguished regular contributor was Robert P. Tristram Coffin, who wrote over sixty poems for the page. Most of them have later appeared in his books. David Morton long contributed fine verse. Others who have regularly written for the page, and have received outside recognition, are Elizabeth Coatsworth, Frances Frost, and Joseph Joel Keith. Later Home Forum poets are: Norma Farber, whose book *The Hatch,* largely composed of poems from the page, appeared in 1955 in Scribner's "Poets of Today" series; Betty Bridgman, whose Home Forum poem "Lullaby for Eggs" was the basis of an illustrated children's book by Macmillan in 1955; and Elizabeth Alsop Shepard, whose "White Fox," 1955, included many poems from the page.

One of the most unusual books to result in large part from Home Forum poems is *Coral Reefs,* by Naoshi Koriyama, a high school teacher in Japan. He is of that small company of bilingual poets, with his languages spanning the gap all the way from Japanese to English. He regards his verse as legitimately hybrid. Beneath the English cloak there beats a Japanese heart. The *Monitor* has published over thirty of his poems. About fifteen books a year have been published by Home Forum writers in recent years.

Often the page fostered good writers in their beginning years. It gave early welcome to V. S. Pritchett, Charles Wharton Stork, Harold Hobson, Doris Peel, and others. That the page has been able to produce so much high-quality material is remarkable because it imposes on writers an unfamiliar and strict discipline. The presence of a religious article means that the page's content must contain nothing of a conflicting nature. This discipline is hard enough for any creative writer to accept, but it is especially difficult for poets. When writers see this discipline as a liberation rather than a limitation, requiring them to turn to deeper currents of spirituality than mere sense experience, they produce finer creative writing than ever before.

While the Home Forum provides background and depth for the cultural experience of its readers, other pages have from the beginning given coverage and analysis of the news in the artistic, literary, and entertainment worlds. In its first few weeks of publication, the *Monitor* carried theatrical criticism and book reviews. By January 26, 1909, it had its own correspondent covering the New York theatre. Soon a music page, a theatre page, and an art page were introduced. A book page was added not long thereafter.

As part of its obligation to local readers, the paper has maintained a critical staff in Boston, covering the great music performed there and keeping a sharp eye on the theatres which continuously handle tryouts for the New York stage. In New York, it maintains a staff member who does theatre and film reviewing. In London it has its own full-time staff reviewer. In Hollywood the *Monitor* has had for many years either a staff correspondent to cover films or the equivalent in special correspondence. And in nearly all the other arts centers of the world, the *Monitor* has special critics who write regular articles.

The *Monitor*'s coverage is especially strong in music, theatre, dance, and painting and sculpture. For many years its art editor as well as its chief music critic was the versatile and uncompromising Leslie A. Sloper.

Following Mr. Sloper as arts editor came Edwin F. Melvin, a drama specialist. He had served for sixteen years on the Boston *Transcript,* partly under H. T. Parker, whom he succeeded. Mr. Melvin's perceptive words on plays coming to Boston before they open in New York have been helpful to generations of authors and producers, as well as to playgoers.

As music critic, Mr. Sloper was succeeded by Harold Rogers, who is not only a journalist-critic but a musician and composer as well.

It isn't often that a lively news story waits nineteen years.

But it happened to Winthrop P. Tryon, who was the *Monitor*'s music critic in New York. In 1916 he detected that a group of concert compositions, played and published by Fritz Kreisler and attributed by him to various music masters of the preceding three centuries, were actually written by Kreisler himself. Mr. Tryon went to the violinist and put it to him directly. Kreisler admitted that he had indeed written and adapted the compositions, but did not place them on programs under his own name because he "found it inexpedient and tactless to repeat my name endlessly on the program."

Mr. Tryon wrote his discovery into an interview, and submitted it to Kreisler. The composer felt it wiser — in 1916 — not to let the secret out of the bag. He asked Mr. Tryon not to publish the interview, and so, in conformity with the *Monitor*'s policy not to print unauthorized interviews, the galley proofs were tucked away with suitable notations. In 1935, Kreisler finally decided he might as well admit the authorship of the compositions. Out of the files came the original Tryon story, and two articles were published under the heads: 1916 and 1935. It made twice as good a newspaper story for being aged in the proof.

In the theatre, the *Monitor*'s critics elsewhere in the United States have been several and distinguished. Ernest C. Sherburne has been referred to earlier. During the 1920's Frank Lea Short covered the New York theatre with one foot on both sides of the street. He was actor, director, teacher as well as critic — a well-known figure on Broadway. Ralph Flint wrote of art and films in New York, and he, too, blended a popular with a fine-arts medium. He visited Hollywood for the *Monitor* as early as 1925, and thereafter spent many summers writing for the paper from the film capital.

After Mr. Sherburne's tour of duty in New York, he was succeeded by John Beaufort, who has been mentioned as a war correspondent. Mr. Beaufort is well established himself as a critic of distinction. His lectures on the theatre are growing in popularity. His expert analysis introduces important moral values into the criticism.

The *Monitor* has always striven to recognize the deeper elements in the arts. If art holds the mirror up to nature, the *Monitor*'s interest has been to persuade artists to hold the mirror up to man's best self — his true selfhood — rather than the tawdry man of human weakness.

In the field of the dance, the *Monitor* has been proud for many years to publish the work of Margaret Lloyd (Mrs. L. A. Sloper). Her book *The Borzoi Book of Modern Dance* is partial evidence of the position she occupies among dance critics. Miss Lloyd's critiques have been followed by leading dancers for many years, as well as by those only interested in the art.

Miss Dorothy Adlow adds art criticism to her work for the Home Forum. Her knowledge and sensitivity are outstanding. She is in great demand as a judge of artistic contests and as a lecturer.

In recent years, the *Monitor* has had regular arts coverage not only from Boston, New York, and London, but from Paris, Dublin, Vienna, Frankfurt, Florence, Sydney, Mexico City, Chicago, St. Louis, San Francisco, Los Angeles, and Philadelphia. Both in scope and penetration, this coverage of the arts is notable, and rare indeed in daily newspapers.

The *Monitor*'s book reviewing has always been a strong feature. The paper turns alike to experienced staff members or to specialists for reviews. For years Leslie Sloper wrote a charming weekly column, "A Bookman's Holiday." Three talented literary critics have most recently edited the page: Doris Peel, Olive Deane Hormel, and Rod Nordell. The *Monitor* finds a great deal to reject in the vulgarity and moral drifting of altogether too much modern fiction. Such books usually it simply ignores. But when a novel is attracting wide public notice, and when it has unquestioned literary merit, the *Monitor* considers it a duty to notify and warn readers of its objectionable content, while striving to identify and explain the author's artistic achievement. Thus its fiction reviewing is on the restrained side. The paper's reviewers try to apply basic moral standards. They make the effort to understand the writer's purposes. The *Monitor* does cover the significant elements of contemporary letters. Sometimes the paper's tolerance for an author's intent far outruns that of its readers.

In one area of fiction, the *Monitor* has no difficulty: it surveys the whole field of juvenile fiction with enthusiasm, recognizing constantly improving standards. Twice a year it publishes large sections devoted to children's literature. For years it published a good deal of juvenile fiction itself, in weekly "Children's" and "Young Folks'" pages. In 1950 these pages were converted into a daily youth section, mostly written by young people themselves, and a weekly three-column story feature for children. The youth section focuses on a teen-age and young adult group. Other pictorial features on the "Family Features" page help meet the needs of younger children.

This page has been the chief home for light and entertaining features in the paper since the 1920's, although *Monitor* humor has not been segregated and the paper has had plenty of it from the outset. The editorial page, for instance, welcomes the lighter touch. It was the *Monitor*'s editorial page that introduced John Gould, Maine's rustic wit, to a national audience. He writes a bright column once a week. Other light essayists abound on the page. Two of the paper's own staff members, Silence Buck Bellows and John Allan May, regularly write witty columns. Down through the years, the editorial page has printed a vast volume of fictional sketches from all parts of the globe: rural America, a Scottish island, the bazaars of Iran, Mexican *casa* — all are long familiar spots.

In the 1920's, the Family Features page began to take its present form. It became the home of the *Monitor*'s comic strips, although juvenile comic strips such as the "Busyville Bees" were published on the Children's page at a much earlier time.

Across the Family Features page for over a quarter of a century there paraded a beloved troupe of characters, animal and human, who endeared themselves to *Monitor* readers. First among them was "The Diary of Snubs, Our Dog," the creation of the *Monitor*'s present political cartoonist, Paul R. Carmack. To create a regular comic strip for the *Monitor* took a bit of doing. The usual blood-and-thunder sequences were not welcome. The *Monitor* also had to have strips exclusive to itself, since it could not publish syndicated material that was available to readers of other newspapers before they could get the *Monitor.* Nearly all other newspapers simply buy comic strips from a syndicate. The total cost is spread over a large number. Elaborate teams of collaborators produce the famous strips. The *Monitor* must pay the entire cost of production of each of its strips.

As if that were not challenge enough, the content of most syndicated strips is either too banal or too bloodthirsty for the *Monitor.* Such strips obviously appeal to many elements in the human mind. Nowadays, carried to an extreme, these horror comics are causing serious trouble for the United States at home and abroad.

The *Monitor's* comics had to be wholesome. Other strips came to join Snubs. One was "The Adventures of Waddles," which not only presented a prepossessing duck family, but was for many years written in excellent jingles. It passed through three generations of drawing and writing by the same family, the Hagers. Then came "Tubby and Buddy & Co." by Guernsey Le Pelley. This comic strip is the only one now regularly run in the *Monitor.* It has a lively story-line of schoolboy adventures.

In 1940 a talented and puckish artist, L. Franklin Van Zelm, joined the *Monitor* staff. He first drew what might be called political illustrations. They were not quite political cartoons, and they were usually run on a news feature page. They were hard-hitting and graphic. But it soon came out that Mr. Van Zelm's heart was in the drawing of little woods creatures and fairies. So a comic strip called the "Vangnomes" came into being, and throve for over a decade. The creatures who passed as Vangnomes delighted many and completely puzzled others. They often included a sly twist.

Other comic strips came and went. But as the 1940's waned, it was concluded that the time for a change had come. And so the paper tackled the herculean task of changing over its comic strips. If anybody questions the word "herculean" let him ask any editor who has ever tried to drop a comic strip, if there is any such editor!

It was the same with the *Monitor.* Some readers were deeply wedded to strips which in the editors' judgment could be vastly improved. For some years the paper had been seeking and obtaining a splendid flow of comic panels. These one-shot drawings, the kind of sketches that embellish the back pages of the most widely circulated national magazines, were available exclusively to the *Monitor* at reasonable rates, and from skilled artists.

Obviously there is an overproduction of comic panels. The *Monitor* — by looking over an artist's rough drawings the very day he sends them in, and making selections — can obtain, at rates it can afford to pay, an excellent selection of drawings comparable to those for which the slick magazines pay a much higher figure. Compared to the paper's former strips, the humor is more adult, more professional, and yet entirely wholesome.

Dropping all the strips except Tubby and Buddy was difficult. Readers who had been brought up on Snubs protested pathetically, despite the fact that Mr. Carmack had been forced to leave him to a contributing artist for some years. It was virtually impossible to retain his original verve and freshness. Waddles had gone correspondingly stale. The Vangnomes were repeating themselves.

The letters the editor received! You would think the paper had suddenly espoused communism, or come out against Home and Mother! Never in any political crisis of war, peace, or Presidential elections, has the paper received more outraged mail. It all amounted to about 600 letters. But the paper stuck to its guns, and readers soon found that the new panels — which always included one for the youngest children — had a more professional appeal and touch. They should have. They are by the same artists who delight millions in the mass-circulation weeklies. Sometimes the distortion which is the stock in trade of cartooning is not understood by some literal readers. However, on the whole the panels have gone very well.

Strips and panels are only part of the Family Features' content. Its oldest and most significant item is the "Sun Dial." Under the motto "I Record Only the Sunny Hours" the *Monitor* has published since January 8, 1925, every single day, the true story of some good and noble deed or event in the contemporary world. No comparable record of encouraging achievement has ever been compiled elsewhere. The supply never runs out. The deeds pour in. Each Sun Dial piece would fill perhaps half a page in this book. The paper has run nearly 10,000 of them. They would fill 5000 pages; or over ten books like this. Truly, the world's supply of the sunshine that reflects human goodness is inexhaustible.

The Family Features page, behind its friendly façade of humor and human interest, is one of the *Monitor*'s closest links with its readers. Its reader participation and interest are not equalled in any other part of the paper. Readers feel the page is theirs and they belong to it. They contribute copiously, not only to the Sun Dial but to the "Small Fry" column and the "Youth Section." Behind the page is the awareness that somewhere in the *Monitor* there must be a place for relaxation, where intellectual demands will not be severe, where readers can put on their slippers and sit before the fire. It calls for no effort. Even the crossword puzzle is a gentle one.

Yet the page rings with authenticity and sincerity. Experiences recorded are simple and true, written by ordinary folk — heart to heart. It is also genuinely inspirational, in naïve and unaffected fashion. Its "Verse for Today," its "Today's Quotation" help supply this need. The family is the essence of the page, as its name indicates.

The development of the Youth Section brought into active participation in the *Monitor* a whole generation of lively and imaginative young people. Early in 1950, younger readers were invited to submit material for publication on a professional basis. Response was tremendous. The section is enthusiastically supported and many writers have gone on to other parts of the paper. The work is very good. A Boston bank recently liked the art work of one contributor and asked for his address, but not his age. The address was London. The age was fourteen!

International friendships are featured through the page's "Mail Bag" and "Youth Round Table." The page is constantly changing, so as to remain fresh, alive, dynamic. Its contents are as interesting and new when they reach Australia, many weeks after publication, as they are in Boston's Back Bay.

In short, the *Monitor*'s entertainment values reach below the surface of mere pleasure. They bind the readership together and to the paper. They are the essence of home and family. And all this, too, is part of the paper's purposes. For it is speaking to a great many people whose major interest is the home.

33

◇◇◇◇◇◇◇◇◇◇◇◇◇◇◇◇◇◇◇◇◇

The *Monitor* Views the Awakening Multitudes

WITH ITS BASIC DEDICATION to the unfoldment of man's birthright as child of God, it was inevitable that the *Monitor* should pay special attention to the great awakening now taking place among the underdeveloped and formerly colonial peoples of the world. India is one focus of this tremendous story. And India has been covered by the *Monitor* with intense interest from 1908 on.

Mention has been made at several points of the clarity with which the *Monitor* discerned, even before the First World War, that independence for India was inevitable. After that war, the paper followed Mahatma Gandhi's crusades intently. Late in the 1920's, it sent an able staff correspondent to India, Alexander Inglis. Mr. Inglis was later hired away from the *Monitor* by *The Times* of London. Thereafter, and during the Second World War, the *Monitor* was served in India by another of the unexpected persons who have given it such unusual quality. This was Miss C. K. Cumming, a quiet little lady who refused to live in the fine Western-style hotels in India, who did not mingle with the foreign correspondent or diplomatic set, but wandered about India using her eyes and ears and getting facts and trends from the people. Her correspondence was most valuable.

It was followed by a flow of perceptive articles from Gordon Graham, from 1945 to 1956. Mr. Graham chronicled the first decade of independent India with insight and diligence. When he was transferred to the United States, he was succeeded by an extremely able Indian journalist, Sharokh Sabavala. These several correspondents have given *Monitor* readers a tremendous awareness of the affairs of the awakening subcontinent. They have never concentrated on the bizarre — no rope tricks or fakirs turned up in their copy — but have probed deeply into social, economic, and political problems.

Direction of the *Monitor*'s coverage of the rise of underdeveloped peoples has for nine years been in the hands of Joseph G. Harrison, its overseas news editor. Mr. Harrison has himself traveled widely in North Africa, the Near East, and Eastern Europe. He knows and understands peasants and senses the revolutionary force of their demand to enter the modern world.

The *Monitor* has found plentiful space for copy from the underdeveloped areas. It believes that in many respects they hold the key to the future. It believes people in the West need to know much more fully and graphically than ever before just what the awakening peoples are thinking and doing and saying. The West, the paper feels, must listen to the voice of these new, but very ancient, societies; must listen and understand.

Believing all this very deeply, the *Monitor* detached one of its ablest men to spend the better part of the year 1955–56 exploring the more remote but revealing corners of Southeast Asia. Saville R. Davis, now managing editor, is a person of great sensitivity and journalistic talent. After a decade as American news editor he felt — and the paper readily agreed — that an assignment in lands with great meaning for the American future would be not only refreshing but productive. So off he and his wife went, to look, listen, and report in Japan,

Taiwan, South Vietnam, Laos, Cambodia, Hong Kong, Thailand, Indonesia, Burma, India, and Afghanistan — with a briefer look at Pakistan and the Middle East.

The purpose of the assignment was well put in his opening article: "Here we are with a world which has come together so fast materially that it is split more deeply than ever spiritually." And he defined the people he was to see in words which were not mawkish in context: "Strangers are just the friends you haven't yet made."

In that mood the Davises crossed the Pacific on a small Japanese freighter. They went to little villages to see the progress of land reform. They found brotherhood in the thick of a Tokyo fire — the worst since the bombings. "Respect for the local inhabitants" they found to be the key for getting things done. Writing from the backwoods of Indo-China, Mr. Davis said: "This is no place for pessimists. So what do you do? You put together a team of self-starting Americans with a gift for pioneer improvisation, a liking for people, and a lively curiosity for how you can get a job done by taking things as they are and working from the inside out — not from the outside in."

In another dispatch, Mr. Davis said: "I had been looking all over Southeast Asia for some way out of the problem of local corruption fattened by American aid . . . How prevent the huge inflow of dollars and American goods from going to the rich man and the racketeer and stopping there, and never reaching the common people, and thereby planting the seeds of violence and revolution later on?"

"Corruption," he wrote later, "is taking the place of imperialism as the number one political issue in Southeast Asia . . . The Americans are being tarred with it, though it is not directly their fault. As the new foreign power in this part of the world, they live in a goldfish bowl and they are seen swimming around with some pretty ugly fish."

Thus were these dispatches compounded of warm and generous idealism, acute observation, and down-to-earth realism. They covered a very wide field. Summarizing the American position in Southeast Asia, Mr. Davis wrote: "The new United States policy toward Asia . . . will consist of helping to enlarge and deepen the integrity, self-reliance, and fundamental democracy of the nations of Asia . . . This will mean less emphasis on military affairs and a shift toward constructive economic and political aid."

Along the way there were a multitude of tender touches, which helped to forge bonds of understanding between the Asians and the peoples of the West. There was the story, written from Bangkok, of the Thai boy who had taken his name from two words in the abridged *Oxford English Dictionary:* "Blooming Highwit." In terms of this boy, Mr. Davis told of shy and eager peoples reaching out for a new life. The dispatch evoked from a Thai girl studying in Boston this letter to the paper: "You are the first to show insight and sympathy for some of the 'nice' characteristics which are hindering the progress of my small, bewildered country very much. Bewildered because we are thrown, unprepared, into contact with so much more sophisticated, worldly people, who many times take our 'great human decency, mutual respect, kindness, tolerance, eager generosity — the gifts native to a simple people' [quoting Mr. Davis] for granted, but rarely return a little of those offerings."

It was to bring about the understanding which would lead to such a return that the Davises took their trip. The *Monitor* ran the articles with strong display for nearly a year. One of the most deeply moving and eloquent dispatches, epitomizing the whole, was from Duck Pond Big, Cambodia. There, where a bluff and kind Belgian named Frans was battling for the forgotten people, Mr. Davis found these words on a tiny blackboard in an open, thatch-covered hut: "I am a man."

To enhance the awareness of that fact, the *Monitor,* in these postwar years, has sought to bring together the universal elements in the human family. Though the Davis trip was a highlight, it was preceded and followed by conscientious and knowledgeable coverage from every corner of the underdeveloped, awakening world.

It has long been a precept of *Monitor* journalism that no correspondent should remain merely in the capital city of the country where he works. The paper has believed that the most important news is not of parliaments but of people. Staff correspondents in Asia and Africa, particularly, are instructed to wander persistently to the real sources of popular movements and conditions.

Under such instructions, the paper's Indian correspondent was the first to discover the land-gift movement of Vinoba Bhave. Gordon Graham unearthed the story in 1951, and the *Monitor* gave it strong display. More recently, Sharokh Sabavala pointed out the significant way in which Bhave was challenging the all too prevalent Indian belief that the individual means nothing and that self needs to be annihilated.

So Sabavala described official India flocking to wherever Bhave happens to be: "In a trice, the humble village square is seething with officials, convoys crawl along dusty, bumpy cart tracks, the President and Prime Minister are jostled by cowherds, and there is only the hard floor of the mud hut on which the reporter can squat as he hammers away at his typewriter."

That is precisely where the *Monitor* wants its reporters to be. That is the front line of today's battle for peace. But the *Monitor* also wants its reporters to be at the laboratories of the great technical institutions and at the seats of government and centers of economic power. It recognizes that in these days power is distributed and balanced in many places. It seeks to report them all.

In another area of crucial importance, the *Monitor* sought in the 1950's to organize balanced coverage. For many years, it had received first-rate copy from special correspondents in Palestine, later the State of Israel. Its Palestinian correspondent was Gershon Agronsky, who later became owner and editor of the Palestine *Post* and mayor of Israeli Jerusalem. Its correspondent when Israel achieved independence was Francis Ofner, a prominent Israeli journalist of Yugoslav birth who has long been close to Premier Ben-Gurion. Mr. Ofner kept up a steady file of thoughtful, independent writing.

At the same time, the paper felt it must make special efforts to report and explain the Arab position, since many interpreters and supporters of the Israeli policy were abundantly available in the American press but few who spoke up for the Arabs. Several staff correspondents visited the Arab lands regularly during the Second World War and thereafter. But in 1951 the paper sent one of its ablest young staff members, Harry B. Ellis, to be resident correspondent for the Middle East with headquarters in Beirut. Mr. Ellis soon made himself authoritative in the area, and ranged widely afield with notebook and camera. He had notable adventures in Saudi Arabia, where — as well as writing excellent copy — he took a splendid personal photograph of the monarch that was later enlarged and presented to King Saud.

Returned to the United States as assistant overseas news editor, Mr. Ellis has produced three valuable books on the Middle East and continues to write background articles about the area. He refreshes his *expertise* with occasional trips back to the Middle East. Succeeding Mr. Ellis, the *Monitor* installed another able staff member, Geoffrey Godsell, with headquarters in Cairo. Though he is of British nationality, Mr. Godsell was very speedily welcomed back to Egypt after the Suez crisis. He found his goods and chattels had been carefully preserved for him by a faithful Egyptian servant, because of widespread recognition of his understanding of the Arab peoples. Like other *Monitor* correspondents, he specializes in vivid, accurate reports of Egyptian politics as seen from the pressure point of the Egyptian peasants, the fellahin.

Farther south on the African continent, another staff correspondent has been set up in a vast area. John Hughes, a British South African who was trained journalistically in the *Monitor*'s Boston office, is headquartered in Johannesburg, but keeps moving from Cape Town to the Sahara. His mission is to get beneath the surface of popular movements in order to show the trends of the future.

The presence on the *Monitor* staff of young Englishmen, South Africans, and others brings to light another point. The *Monitor* seeks the most objective and expert staff that it is possible to recruit. Its men require home-office training or its equivalent. There is no effort to see that they are all Americans, or conversely, to make nationality a point in their selection. They are chosen for their talents and objectivity. In keeping with a paper of universal commitment, it is suitable that there should be men and women of diverse nationalities.

John Delane, of *The Times* of London, sought to employ non-Britishers as his foreign correspondents, since he thought they would write more objectively about British foreign policy. His position was as sound journalistically as it was historically. "Foreigners" are often the most acute observers of a national policy, as the British historians who are expert in American affairs, and vice versa, abundantly prove.

The *Monitor* is proud of the spread of its staff. In the post-war years, two of its ablest acquisitions were young men born of German and Japanese nationality. Each has turned into a splendid journalist. The former German is now a staff correspondent in New York. The Japanese is a specialist on the overseas news desk. Another assistant overseas news editor is the distinguished former editor of a Viennese newspaper. His grasp of Central European political backgrounds and ideologies is of daily value. Another assistant is of British nationality.

It should be emphasized that professional competence is indispensable. Those *Monitor* staff members who had to learn English have done so with complete success. Time was, in the early years, when the paper tried to get copy from eager nationals of various countries whose zeal outran their newspaper and linguistic skills. This stage has long since been left behind.

The *Monitor*'s editorial page has also carried forward the paper's interest in awakening peoples. And perhaps this is as good a place as any to explain the organization and operation of the page. As has been described, basic editorial policy is set by The Christian Science Board of Directors, and is administered through the office of editor. But it has been about thirty years since the person holding the title of editor wrote a preponderant part of the major editorials. During that period, the page has been in charge of a chief editorial writer. Since 1930, the chief editorial writer has been Donovan M. Richardson, who grew up in New Mexico, and once served in that state's legislature and was a Rhodes Scholar at Oxford University. Mr.

Richardson has held the position of chief editorial writer longer than any other person in the paper's history.

Mr. Richardson confers with the editor daily, discussing news and policy. He holds an editorial-page-staff conference each day, in which proposed editorials are discussed at some length. This procedure once more brings to the paper the values of collective judgment. The writers do much of their writing around midday and the page for the next day's publication is made up in midafternoon. Proofs are then sent to the Board of Directors and are studied overnight, both by the Directors and by the editorial page's own staff members and other key persons on the editorial staff. If important overnight news happens, fresh editorials or important changes can be handled right up to the last minute before the various editions go to press.

The editorial-page staff has the difficult task of translating general policy directives and positions into explicit editorials which will be the voice of the paper. Their work is based on long experience. Each has had a wide background. Unlike staff correspondents and columnists, their work perforce but undeservedly must be done anonymously. This is a good time, therefore, to explain their extensive talents. Mr. Richardson not only spent part of his student days in Europe, but has traveled regularly abroad. He has also visited the Orient, in the critical days at the end of the Second World War. He goes frequently to Washington, where he visits valuable sources of news and ideas.

Mr. Richardson's great talent springs from his judicial temperament, capable of fervent indignation at injustice but always fair-minded and careful. More than once he has stuck to a point when those around were influenced by the heat of passing emotion, and he has kept the paper from losing its long-range perspective. The steadiness of his convictions, exemplified in daily writing for over a third of a century, has given the all-important editorial page an anchor as well as a beacon.

The assistant chief editorial writer is Tully Nettleton. After several years as special writer and correspondent, he was placed on the editorial page staff in 1930. He was stationed as an editorial writer in the 1930's in Washington, to give him first-hand familiarity with national affairs. For two years, in the 1940's, he was American news editor. He is a native of Oklahoma, and returns to the Great Plains states from time to time to refresh his contacts with these vital areas. During the Second World War, he was a naval officer stationed much of the time in the Pacific, especially in the Philippines, and he has made writing trips to Europe. In 1937, Mr. Nettleton was national president of the honorary journalism fraternity Sigma Delta Chi.

Carlyle W. Morgan, the only New Englander on the page staff, has been an editorial writer since the 1930's. Previously, since the early 1920's, he had been a member of the financial page staff. He, too, illustrates the efforts which the writers themselves and the paper invest in getting out of the ivory tower. Mr. Morgan has been assigned to cover several international meetings, including the U.N. Charter conference at San Francisco. For several years, he served as European editorial manager, in London. He has made a particular study of the North Atlantic Treaty Organization and recently took leave of absence to make an examination in depth in each of the NATO countries. Mr. Morgan first proposed the idea of a "People's Section" of the United Nations. The project, then taken up by the American Association for the United Nations, was an effort to bring the impact of popular thinking to bear on the U.N., isolated by diplomatic rigidities from enough contact with ordinary people.

Another member of the page staff, Edward B. Orr, is a native Missourian who served as an officer in the Marine Corps in both world wars, and has been a faculty member at colleges and universities in the Middle West. He specializes in domestic topics, and has a wide knowledge of sociological problems. He, too, travels throughout the United States extensively.

Down through the years, the *Monitor*'s editorial page has been staffed by persons of breadth of experience and viewpoint comparable to that of those just mentioned. There are also many editorials, submitted or assigned, from other staff members who have special knowledge of a given subject.

An indispensable associate of the editorial page is of course the paper's political cartoonist, Paul R. Carmack. Mr. Carmack has been mentioned as the originator of a comic strip, "The Diary of Snubs, Our Dog." Not long after this strip began its regular appearance in the *Monitor*'s columns, Mr. Carmack turned his crayon to the field of political ideas. To convert the paper's carefully qualified editorial positions into simple, but eloquent drawing is a task of real magnitude.

Mr. Carmack could not begin to do it without a deep sense of the paper's ultimate mission. The commitment to help and to heal is almost antithetic to the usual political cartooning. But Mr. Carmack has so successfully translated the paper's purposes into pictures that his work is reprinted with great regularity in other newspapers. He ranks with the nation's most eminent cartoonists, although the very essence of his work must be utterly alien to the ruthless scalpels of the Herblocks and Fitzpatricks. That he can cartoon in *Monitor* terms, and find wide acceptance is a triumph.

The important feature of the editorials, as in different degree of the entire paper, is the sense of impersonal, collective responsibility which must be maintained. Even in the case of signed columns and articles, the *Monitor* does not allow the diversity and conflict of expression or of personal opinion that some other papers cultivate. Everything printed in the paper is considered by some readers to express the paper's considered policy, and within reason it does. Hence it must all fall within the range of the *Monitor*'s over-all commitment.

This does not mean a slavish uniformity of expression. *Monitor* policy may be thought of as a lane in a highway, with an agreed and permissible amount of deviation — somewhat in this direction, somewhat in that. One writer's interpretation will be toward one side of the lane, another's interpretation will go in a different direction. Both must stay on the highway. Neither can go into the ditch, or stray into the opposite lane. Every effort is made to define the boundaries clearly.

The Board of Directors, with their basic policy decisions, have long permitted this kind of variation within well-defined limits. They have understood the dangers of overconformity and overgeneralization of instruction. One of the besetting sins of many newspapers is that editors or staff overconform to what they believe owners or publishers desire.

The *Monitor* staff has the immense advantage of being able to submit actual copy to the ultimate policy authority. The Directors rarely say "Never do this," or "Never do that!" Their instructions apply to a particular circumstance or a particular editorial, or to the degree of frequency or prominence given some phase of the news. Their rules, except insofar as they touch basic moral issues, are not arbitrary but based on reasonable, specific judgment.

34

◇◇◇◇◇◇◇◇◇◇◇◇◇◇◇◇◇◇◇

The *Monitor* as a Business Undertaking

JOHN H. HOAGLAND, manager of The Christian Science Publishing Society, was attending the annual meeting of the American Newspaper Publishers' Association. Here he met one of his old friends in the business, for Mr. Hoagland had long been connected with those fine newspapers, the Louisville *Courier-Journal* and *Times*.

"Pretty soft for you!" quipped his friend. "You don't have to worry about budgets and profits and loss. When you need some more *Monitor* revenue, I suppose all you have to do is to turn to the church. Somebody will pass the hat." The misconception could not have been more wrong.

The fact is that the *Monitor* is published and always has been published — under the terms of the Deed of Trust of The Christian Science Publishing Society — in the manner of a straightforward business operation. For the greater part of its fifty years, its circulation and advertising revenues, averaged, have been sufficient to pay its costs of operation. It is not intended that the *Monitor* should produce more than a modest profit. If a great deal more money were earned than is necessary to pay for the *Monitor*, it would undoubtedly be plowed back into a better product. The Publishing Society as a whole does produce substantial earnings which constitute an important part of the church's revenue.

The Publishing House, in which the *Monitor* and the other Christian Science periodicals are produced, like its predecessor was built with funds contributed to The Mother Church by Christian Scientists all over the world. Other capital equipment, as needed, is advanced by the church. This is only proper and sound business, since the net earnings of the publishing operation are turned over to the Board of Directors of The Mother Church at six-monthly intervals. They, and they alone, are legally empowered to maintain the reserve which would be necessary to make capital expenditures.

The position is plainly set forth in the Deed of Trust, of January 25, 1898. In this document, Mary Baker Eddy conveyed to a Board of three Trustees — Edward P. Bates, James A. Neal, and William P. McKenzie — all the properties of The Christian Science Publishing Society. She reserved temporarily the copyright of *The Christian Science Journal,* a monthly periodical, but this too passed to the Trustees later. The conveyance included the real property, publications, equipment, mailing lists, financial assets, and all else belonging to the Publishing Society.

The terms of the trust were that the property and property rights should be managed "exclusively for the purpose of carrying on the business, which has been heretofore conducted by the said Christian Science Publishing Society, in promoting the interests of Christian Science; and the principal place of business shall be in said Boston."

The trustees were required by Mrs. Eddy "energetically and judiciously [to] manage the business of the Publishing Society on a strictly Christian basis, upon their own responsibility, and without consulting me about details, subject only to my supervision, if I shall at any time elect to advise or direct them."

The Trustees were further required to keep accurate books, and "once in every six months . . . shall account for and pay over to the treasurer of 'The First Church of Christ, Scientist, in Boston, Mass.' the entire net profits of said business. The 'net profits' shall be understood to mean the balance remaining at the end of each six months after paying the usual and legitimate expenses incurred in conducting the business. No authority is intended to be conferred upon the trustees to expend the money of the trust for property not necessary for the immediate successful prosecution of the business, or to invest the same for purpose of speculation, or to incur liabilities beyond their ability to liquidate promptly from the current income of the business."

It was further provided that "the business manager shall present to the Trustees, at the end of each month, a full and correct statement of the receipts and expenditures of the month." The Trustees were empowered to "employ all the help necessary to the proper conduct of said business, and . . . discharge the same in their discretion or according to the needs of the business, excepting that the business manager may call in at times of necessity such temporary help as will facilitate the business."

It was significantly required that the Trustees and their successors in trust "shall not be eligible to said trusteeship or to continue in the same, unless they are loyal, faithful, and consistent believers and advocates of the principles of Christian Science as taught by me in my book, 'Science and Health with Key to the Scriptures.'" Vacancies in the Board were to be filled by the remaining Trustees, although it was added that "the First Members together with the directors of said Church shall have the power to declare vacancies in said trusteeship for such reasons as to them may seem expedient."

It is through this last provision, of course, that the ultimate authority is placed in the hands of the Directors. As described in Chapter 16, it was called in question in March, 1919, through litigation. In December, 1921, by decision of the Supreme Judicial Court of Massachusetts, the power to declare vacancies was affirmed to reside in the Board of Directors.

The duties of the Trustees and manager, in conducting the business of the Publishing Society, are thus clearly demarked. There must be a profit and it must be turned over to the Directors at six-monthly intervals. The Trustees can incur no obligation they cannot liquidate promptly from current revenue. They must manage the business energetically and judiciously, on a strictly Christian basis.

The Publishing Society has always been operated in faithful conformity with these rules, except for the brief period of litigation. Its Trustees have been men and women of extensive business or professional experience, with deep dedication to Christian Science. There have been twenty-six of them. Six of their number later became members of the Board of Directors, and one was a Director before he became a Trustee.

Among them have been men of high position in national or worldwide corporations, bankers, publishing executives, lawyers or judges, advertising men. Since 1945, a woman has always been a member of the Board. The Trustees in 1958 were: Leonard T. Carney, elected in 1947; Henry Allen Nichols, elected in 1955; Miss Helen Appleton, elected in 1956.

Previous to devoting her entire time to the practice of Christian Science, Miss Appleton, a Bostonian, was engaged in educational work, being a teacher and dean of a private school. In 1948, Miss Appleton was appointed a member of the Board of Lectureship. She acted in that capacity until June, 1950, when she was appointed Second Reader of The Mother Church, serving in that office until June, 1953. At that time she was reappointed to membership on the Board of Lectureship, where she continued until her appointment as a member of the Board of Trustees in 1956.

Mr. Nichols is a native Californian who attended Bowdoin College in Maine and graduated from the University of California. He was for many years active in education, both as a teacher and as a representative of a publisher of textbooks for colleges and universities. He has been in the public practice of Christian Science healing since 1926. In the First World War he served as an ambulance driver in the United States Army Ambulance Service, attached to the French army. He was awarded the Croix de Guerre with silver stars for devotion to duty under attack. In the Second World War, he was Christian Science Wartime Minister to the United States troops maneuvering in the desert of the Colorado River in California. From 1951 to 1955, he was a member of The Christian Science Board of Lectureship.

Mr. Carney graduated from Grinnell College, in Iowa, and from the Harvard Law School. He is a member of the Iowa and California bars, and practiced law for seven years before entering the public practice of Christian Science. In the First World War, he was a representative of The Mother Church at a large military encampment. He became a teacher of Christian Science and teaches at Beverly Hills, California, where he resided for many years before his present appointment as Trustee of the Publishing Society. From 1943 to 1947 he served as a member of The Christian Science Board of Lectureship.

Such trustees bring to their responsibilities and duties a wide experience in public affairs — educator, publisher's representative, lawyer — and their long-standing dedication to the cause of Christian Science.

The Board of Trustees is no absentee body, meeting once or twice a year or month. They meet several days a week, and are on the job every working day. They take very seriously the requirement to manage the business "energetically and judiciously." The Trustees are thoroughly informed of all vital matters in the publishing operation. Innumerable decisions must be cleared through their Board. All hiring of personnel or dismissal, all salary increases, all special expenditures above a very modest minimum, require Trustees' approval.

In short, the Trustees contribute to the operation of the paper not only a fulfillment of serious fiduciary responsibilities, but a large positive increment of experience and wisdom. They are constantly alert to the well-being of all the operations of the paper, as of the Publishing Society as a whole. They have regular, and many special, meetings with the manager and with individual department heads or executives, to discuss, clarify, and decide numerous problems.

Compared with the operations of typical boards of trustees, this is a most unusual procedure and one that is highly beneficial and fruitful. In effect, the publisher of the *Monitor* is a board which is available for virtually continuous decision. More than being available, it is in fact, a continuous operative collective executive. Thus the *Monitor,* and the other publications, have the rare benefit of steady, experienced, positive, and creative judgment. The importance and value of this kind of responsibility and support can scarcely be overestimated. It is one of the most important factors which have helped make the *Monitor* a success.

The Board of Trustees has under its direction an executive officer, the manager of the Publishing Society. Under a provision of The Church Manual he is appointed by the Board of Directors to serve in this capacity. He works in close collaboration with the Trustees.

There have been eight managers of the Publishing Society. The first of them was Joseph Armstrong, who was called publisher from January 1, 1893, to June 29, 1903, and manager from that time to December, 1907. He also had been a member of the Board of Directors since 1893.

Mr. Armstrong was one of great oaks among Mrs. Eddy's early students and followers. White-bearded, clear-eyed, upright of stature, he was a key figure in the building of The Mother Church and wrote the history of that great endeavor. He had been a successful business man before coming to Boston from Illinois. He dedicated his experience to the important pioneer work as publisher and then manager.

David B. Ogden and John R. Watts were the two managers who were associated with the litigation. Mr. Ogden, who succeeded Mr. Armstrong and served as manager from 1908 to 1917, was one of the litigating Trustees. His successor, Mr. Watts, was an active participant in the litigation. He left in 1922 to co-operate with Mr. Dixon in publishing a magazine in New York.

The managership was filled after the litigation, from 1922 to 1927, by Charles E. Jarvis, who had been corresponding secretary for the Board of Directors. He was succeeded in

1927 by Charles E. Heitman, the New York businessman and Committee on Publication who later became a member of the Board of Directors. Following Mr. Heitman, the manager from 1929 to 1939 was Roland R. Harrison, whose role in the development of the *Monitor* has already been described.

In 1939, A. Warren Norton, an official in O'Meara and Ormsby, a firm of newspaper management consultants, became manager until 1944. He brought to the paper experience in the practical field of newspaper management which was of real value, to which he combined his own activity in Christian Science work.

As a graduate of Massachusetts Institute of Technology and vigorous in its alumni affairs, he helped forge useful links between the *Monitor* and the natural scientists who were then beginning to play an important part in national affairs. Mr. Norton left to assume the presidency of Press Wireless, Inc., a co-operative communications system of which the *Monitor* had been a pioneer member. It still sends much of its overseas copy through the facilities of Press Wireless, though it has ceased to be one of the newspapers maintaining a co-operative ownership of the undertaking.

Mr. Hoagland became manager in 1944, and thus has held the post longer than anybody else save Joseph Armstrong. His experience in many aspects of newspaper work in Louisville, Kentucky, combined with his long background in Christian Science — he is a teacher of Christian Science — enabled him to carry forward to deeper fulfillment than ever the requirements laid down in the Deed of Trust. He is a thoroughgoing newspaper professional, widely respected throughout the newspaper world.

The present writer, who is held accountable for the business operations of the *Monitor's* editorial department by the Trustees and manager, is in a unique position to testify to the effectiveness of the stewardship. I can say, with utmost earnestness, that the editorial operation of the *Monitor* has had full, generous, scrupulous and wise support from the business office. The frictions which prevail in some newspapers between the editorial department and the counting house, the heavy hand which the profit-and-loss ledgers sometimes lay upon the editorial hopes, have been absent. This is not to say that the editorial operation, like all other aspects of the *Monitor,* must not be conducted in a businesslike way under regular budgetary and operational controls.

Such controls are careful and extensive. They have to be, for the manager and Trustees are themselves strictly accountable under the Deed of Trust. And the accountability runs right down the line. But it is carried out with supporting and constructive intent, focusing on orderly productiveness, growth, and deeper and fuller measures of service.

The business operations of the *Monitor* are budgeted on a perfectly normal business basis. They are targeted monthly against income. Rates, both advertising and circulation, are held to just what the advertiser and reader will justify in the light of going commercial newspaper rates.

It would be inconceivable for The Church of Christ, Scientist, actually to subsidize such a big annual operation as the *Monitor* — no less than $6,000,000 overhead per year. The other periodicals, which help to meet the *Monitor*'s need if and when a year comes along when the maintenance of *Monitor* quality standards requires a temporary expenditure beyond earnings, could not provide a subsidy of anything like this magnitude. The Mother Church frankly expects the earnings of the religious periodicals to support its own missionary and extension work.

The *Monitor*'s annual budget in 1957–58 was $6,593,000. Of this amount, $1,259,000 was expended for the Editorial Department; $1,431,000 for the Advertising Department; $623,000 for the Circulation Department; $2,065,000 for the Production Department; and $1,215,000 for other technical operations such as accounting, building maintenance, etc. The operation has risen from $920,112 in 1916, $1,726,313 in 1919, and from $4,350,177 in 1945.

Behind these figures lie many unique facts. The *Monitor* is an exclusively tailored product. Thus it is relatively expensive to produce. Its editorial staff is much larger and costlier than would be required to publish a local newspaper of similar circulation and size. The bureaus and correspondents it must maintain in the United States and overseas are expensive. Revenue cannot be recouped by syndicating their output to other newspapers, though many have wished to buy it. The paper purchases very substantial amounts of space copy from special correspondents throughout the world, both of news and features. Though the paper gets a great deal for its money in its editorial operation, the outlay is substantial.

Since the paper's budgetary figures have never before been made public, I venture that editors and publishers familiar with the budgets of other newspapers and magazines which keep networks of correspondents and carry out careful and extensive editorial operations will be astonished at the modest scale of the editorial expenditure. But the fact remains that it is very costly in terms of over-all circulation and in comparison with local commercial newspapers.

The advertising and circulation costs are similarly high. They must include provision for very special selling of advertising, through the paper's own salesmen, both on salary and commission, all over the world. These salesmen must share closely the *Monitor's* ideals. Because of larger payrolls, branch office maintenance and so on, it costs much more per dollar of income to sell *Monitor* advertising than it costs any other newspaper in the world.

To promote and sell circulation is equally expensive. An overwhelming part of the circulation effort has to be by mail and requires greatly increased paper work. Merely to handle the subscription lists, which cover about 90 per cent of the paper's subscribers, is a mammoth undertaking which does not apply to most other newspapers. The accounting operation is also vastly larger, because both subscribers and advertisers must be dealt with largely by mail and to the far corners of the earth.

The *Monitor* income pattern is very similar to that of American daily newspaper averages these days: about 60 per cent from advertisers and 40 per cent from readers.

As the paper approached its fiftieth anniversary, it had achieved substantially the largest circulation and the greatest income and advertising content in its history. It had grown slowly and surely throughout the half century. It had become a success by virtually all accepted publishing standards. During the period of its growth, nearly 1000 daily newspapers in the United States were sold out, merged, or closed their doors.

The *Monitor* is a business success without several of the customary ingredients for commercial success. It rejects large elements of advertising revenue supposedly essential to daily newspapers: tobacco, liquors, patent medicine, multiple advertising pages from local department stores or food stores. It succeeds in spite of the absence of mass local circulation delivered on the day of publication.

All the managerial efforts would have been unavailing, and the paper would never have attained its drive, vitality, and morale if it had access to a subsidy fund. The *Monitor* has always known that it must not be a failure as a publishing enterprise, any more than it could be a failure as a public service. Its editorial prestige would rest on utterly unsound pillars if subsidy were the presumed support.

A sense of order and of integrity comes to the paper through its requirement to be a success as a business enterprise. It is very easy for an undertaking like a well-endowed foundation, or a rich monopolistic business concern — or a governmental department — to lose its sense of budgetary discipline. There are great positive virtues in having to budget carefully, in having to compete hard and skillfully for business, in having to earn and justify progress at every step of the way.

These invaluable disciplines, controls, and incentives were built firmly into The Christian Science Publishing Society, and the *Monitor,* by the Deed of Trust given by Mrs. Eddy in 1898. They are administered with deep zeal and consecration, as well as practical business acumen, by the Board of Trustees and manager. They are indispensable elements in the *Monitor*'s total success. Without them, the editorial operation would never have been possible. Without them the prestige never would have existed.

35

◇◇◇◇◇◇◇◇◇◇◇◇◇◇◇◇◇◇◇◇

The Role of Advertising

IN THE FIRST ISSUE of the *Monitor* there were fifty-five advertisers. Half a century later, no less than eleven of these firms were still publishing their messages in the *Monitor*. Considering that thirty-eight of the original fifty-five firms have gone out of business, this record says about all that needs to be said of the efficacy and business validity of advertising in the *Monitor*.

Advertising was from the beginning an essential part of Mary Baker Eddy's publishing enterprises. Though her earliest publication was strictly a religious organ, *The Christian Science Journal* began in its first few months of publication to carry paid professional notices. By 1885, commercial advertisements appeared in display space. One was a full-page advertisement of A. Conant and Company, Boston, featuring mirrors. There was another full-page advertisement of W. Kellaway, Boston, book and job printer. There were several other advertisements

— a news company, a piano company, a publishing company, two printing manufacturing establishments.

At the *Journal*'s founding, Mrs. Eddy herself was editor and publisher. She gave the advertisers support in the monthly's columns. It was the custom in those days. The August, 1888, issue of the *Journal* wrote: "Our Advertisers. Take note of them! Go to the old house of Houghton, Mifflin & Co., and see their many books by the best authors, — Whittier, Holmes, Lowell, Aldrich, Norton, Higginson, Larcom, Jewett, Thaxter. Take a thought for their Atlantic Monthly, also!"

When the *Monitor* was founded, Mrs. Eddy took a similar interest in the advertisers and their well-being. When Jordan Marsh Company were celebrating their own centennial, in January, 1947, they reproduced in the *Monitor* their first full-page *Monitor* display.

The paper's first issue carried 5387 lines af advertising. The figures for the year 1956 showed 8,423,800 lines. While the first issue of the *Monitor* carried messages from fifty-five advertisers, the columns in 1956 were used by 31,057 advertisers, exclusive of classified advertisers. A typical day's issue today carries 27,000 lines, from 100 advertisers. The growth of advertising from the beginning has been steady, both in volume and in recognition of the *Monitor* as a valuable medium.

No sooner had announcement been made of the forthcoming daily, in October, 1908, than applications from advertising men and women who were Christian Scientists began to pour in. The first advertising manager was Thomas H. Winans of Pittsburgh. Mr. Winans, a big burly man, was initially in charge of both circulation and advertising. He had been for many years circulation manager of the Pittsburgh *Leader*. Alexander Dodds, the managing editor, was in over-all charge of advertising, circulation, and production for several years after 1908, although undoubtedly much latitude was left the three departmental managers. In his reminiscences, Mr. Dodds recalls the interest with which Mrs. Eddy followed all departments of the paper. He writes: "Her keenness of discernment even to the advertisements is shown by the fact that one Tuesday in February when our advertising was almost nil, she directed her secretary to say to the Managing Editor: 'I see the Monitor does not carry advertising on Tuesdays.' The fact was the Monitor had come under the claim common to all newspapers — that February is a very dull month for advertising."

In 1911, John K. Allen came from Chicago to become advertising manager. He remained in that position until 1917, returning to the paper in 1922 as manager of financial advertising which he held until his retirement in 1935. To Mr. Allen goes much of the credit for building up the *Monitor*'s advertising concepts, practices, and success in its earliest years. He was a nationally noted and respected member of his profession, very active in the Associated Advertising Clubs of America, now the Advertising Federation of America. On many occasions, he was program director of the organization's annual conventions.

He had a great deal to do with the AACA's "Truth in Advertising" campaign. This important movement began to develop at the group's convention in Boston, in 1911. The theme was adopted as a formal slogan in the Toronto convention in 1914, whose program was organized by Mr. Allen. All this began to take place at a time when advertising was just emerging from an irresponsible and reckless era. Spurious claims, especially in the field of patent medicine but unhappily extending to many other areas, had been very widespread.

It was quite apparent that if advertising was to grow and prosper, if it was to play its proper role in the expansion of the American economy through mass consumption of the articles soon to be produced by mass production, advertising needed to clean its own house. This was the doctrine the *Monitor* had been preaching and practicing from its inception. The *Monitor* had no desire to stand out in righteous contrast to its brethren. It hoped for the reform of all advertising. Once more, as in its editorial policies, its commitment was to the achievement of genuine freedom and strength based upon integrity and truth.

When, in 1936, the Advertising Federation of America again came to Boston for its convention, tribute was paid to Mr.

Allen for the pioneer role he played in helping the entire profession get on the right track. The ethical standards he and others set nearly half a century ago remain today as landmarks by which an essential element in the free enterprise system can play its rightful role. The *Monitor* is grateful for the opportunities it saw and seized to help render sane and strong the major economic base for newspaper production.

As was mentioned in Chapter 18, when the paper returned to control of the Directors in 1922, Norman S. Rose, previously of George Batten Company, became advertising manager. Mr. Rose was a thoroughly experienced advertising man. He was imaginative, broad-gauged in his concepts, debonair and forceful. He did much to help restore the paper to its rightful place. The department when he took charge numbered only 36 people. During the next twenty years, it was built up so that in 1942 there were 136 people on the department's staff, in Boston and elsewhere. In 1958 there were 160.

Upon Mr. Rose's retirement in 1942, he was succeeded by M. Alvah Blanchard, who had joined the *Monitor* staff in July, 1928, by way of the New York office. He later managed the Chicago office, and came to Boston in 1934 as manager of national advertising, later as assistant advertising manager. Mr. Blanchard is an advertising man of long experience, wide knowledge, and practical views. He and his seasoned staff have continued the steady growth in *Monitor* advertising down through the years. In the 1950's, month after month and year after year, they were setting new *Monitor* records for linage and revenue.

Such growth takes place despite the fact — and in a fundamental sense because of the fact — that the *Monitor*'s advertising policy is highly selective. Not only the types of advertising accepted, but copy and illustrations must be carefully screened. There is one important difference between the relationship of readers to advertising columns and news and editorial columns. In the latter case, readers are being given information they may find useful, interesting, or essential. Sometimes it is news of distasteful and tragic events, since citizens often need to know such news in order to be adequately informed. Readers, in effect, can "take or leave" such information.

But in the case of advertising, the reader is encouraged to patronize *Monitor* advertisers. The paper seeks to support its advertisers in every proper way. Therefore the obligation the paper accepts for the integrity of its advertising columns is of a different sort from the responsibility it accepts in news columns. A closer scrutiny and somewhat different role must be carried out. In the case of advertisers who are presenting ideas rather than goods or service, the role of advertising is identical with news or editorial columns — the reader is expected to do his own thinking.

On the commercial side, a good illustration of the difference is in the field of book advertising and book reviewing. No book will be advertised which the paper does not feel will be of legitimate interest to some of its readers. But many books are reviewed not only without recommendation but sometimes with active and outspoken disapproval. Readers need to be informed of the flow of current literature, particularly of books which are much in the public eye, even though their contents be distasteful. Merely to ignore them would be no help whatever to the reader. The same criteria apply to the reviewing or the advertising of plays, films, and so on. There is a distinct difference between the function of the review and of the advertising.

In some instances, advertisers just becoming acquainted with the *Monitor* have objected to the careful scrutiny of their copy. When it is explained to them that advertising copy with features distasteful to the vast majority of *Monitor* readers would be in fact a disservice to the advertisers, they understand and co-operate. A good-sized copy department is maintained which has among its duties the task of rewriting copy not suitable for *Monitor* publication. In some instances these changes have later been viewed with such favor that the advertisers have revised according to *Monitor* standards their advertising in other publications.

Only in certain categories are *Monitor* advertising standards rigid. The general policy of permitting only truthful statements, as far as can be determined, without extravagantly worded copy, and excluding all liquor, tobacco, medical, curative, or hygienic advertisements has remained fixed. Any claim of something given away "free" must be genuinely free, not worked for in any way.

Of course, *Monitor* advertising styles have evolved down through the years, just as public taste has varied. And there are regularly many borderline cases, difficult to judge, concerning the suitability of a product or the integrity of its copy. Such cases have to be decided on their own merits. In many classified advertisements, the *Monitor* requires references from reputable and known persons, attesting to the character of the advertiser, as for instance in the case of a person offering rooms to rent or advertising for help wanted.

Monitor advertising possesses extremely high reader confidence and responsiveness. That is one of the secrets of its success. Without the patronage *Monitor* readers give its advertisers, the paper could not obtain the volume of advertising it secures, or at the rates it must charge. These facts are recognized in the profession. Walter E. Thwing, former president of his own New York advertising agency, gave great credit to the *Monitor* as a strong advertising medium, saying: "The *Monitor* is published for its readers, not for its advertisers, and that very fact makes it a superior advertising medium. It demonstrates the principle that a policy of reader service automatically produces advertiser service." From the earliest years, the *Monitor* has received a steady flow of appreciation from satisfied advertisers. The very repetition of their patronage is the best proof.

But it requires a great organization to get the *Monitor*'s advertising and to keep reader support at a sustaining level. To these ends, the paper established branch advertising offices of its own in its first years. In 1913, there were such offices in New York, Chicago, and London. Other offices were opened from time to time in various parts of the United States and Canada, in Europe, Australia, and New Zealand. In 1958 the list of branch advertising offices includes New York, Chicago, Los Angeles, London, Washington, Paris, Detroit, Philadelphia,

St. Louis, Kansas City, Cleveland, San Francisco, Seattle, Portland, Oregon, The Hague, and Geneva.

In addition to these offices, there evolved down through the years the practice of appointing local representatives, to serve in their own communities. In 1957, there were no fewer than 800 such representatives. They are paid on commission, and provide a substantial volume of advertising. Indeed, the advertising produced on this local basis represents about three-quarters of the *Monitor*'s total linage.

It is obvious that this indispensable economic support is possible because the *Monitor*'s readers, in the local communities, support the paper to the point where it is an attractive medium to local advertisers. That essentially local advertising should be valuable in a worldwide newspaper constitutes one of the most remarkable phenomena in the world of advertising, a situation which never fails to call forth astonished comment from professionals.

How remarkable it is, for instance, that the advertising representative in Coeur d'Alene, Idaho, on June 21, 1956, was able to procure almost 4 columns of display advertising, from 29 advertisers, at a cost to the advertisers of $520.19. Or that on October 13, 1956, there were 4 columns from 21 advertisers in Port Arthur, Texas. Or that on December 7, 1957, St. Petersburg, Florida, produced 42 ads in 16 columns, costing the advertisers $1941.76. Or that Salem, Oregon, had 37 ads on April 3, 1957, costing $1213.60. Or that from Salisbury, Southern Rhodesia, on October 12, 1957, came 19 ads costing advertisers $458.80. Or that Melbourne, Australia, had 29 ads in 14 columns on January 28, 1956, at a cost of $904.72. What triumphs of devoted and zealous salesmanship! Church committees and local representatives are responsible. Such results, which are repeated month after month and year after year throughout the world, would not be possible of continuance if the advertisers were not persuaded of their economic value.

The phenomenon of advertising from the far ends of the earth not only impresses readers, but sometimes bewilders them. For a subscriber in Boston to set her heart on a pair of shoes tastefully illustrated and then find that they are purchasable only in Melbourne calls forth expostulation. Many times, of course, the products advertised at a distance can readily be purchased by mail, and so the reader and advertiser alike are being given a marketplace as wide as the world.

Late in 1923 Amos Weston, production manager, and Wendell Wyman, foreman of the *Monitor* composing room, came forward with a plan to modify the editions of the paper which virtually revolutionized its advertising content, improved its editorial content, and saved considerable money for the advertiser and the paper.

Prior to that time, from two to five editions had been published throughout the day. The editions all contained the same advertising, and the news, feature, and editorial matter was varied only to the extent that Boston and New England news was more vigorously included and played up in the local editions. The variations in the editions turned largely on the inclusion of late news. During the litigation, when circulation had dropped precipitously, only a single edition was published, on morning-paper schedules.

In normal times, however, as in 1922 and 1923, the paper ran five editions, beginning in late forenoon and concluding in late afternoon. The changes between the editions were little more than replates in most cases — the substitution of later news for earlier on a few pages.

The plan which Messrs. Weston and Wyman proposed was to divide the paper's circulation into large zones, and to print local advertising only in its zone. News was to be varied somewhat also, with a large nucleus of universal news running through all editions, and a lesser amount of regional news to be distinctive to each. The features were to remain the same throughout. As many advertisers as possible, of course, were to be sold all-edition advertising, but it was recognized that many would prefer only their zone, at a lower rate.

The plan, which was modified and perfected by the thinking of many others, was nothing short of genius. It enabled the paper to save a substantial quantity of newsprint by not running local advertising throughout all the editions. It gave advertisers a lower rate for substantially all the circulation that was of real interest to them. Thus it made the selling of advertising easier and the production of the paper considerably cheaper as far as newsprint consumption was concerned.

As worked out, after several years of settling down, first seven and then six editions were published. As issued today, they are the Pacific, Central, Atlantic One-Star, Atlantic Two-Star, Atlantic Two-Star Dash, and Overseas. Advertising is sold for all editions, or separately for each or for groups of them.

The Pacific edition naturally serves the states west of the Continental Divide, much of South America, and the islands of the Pacific. The Central edition serves the Middle Western states west of the Alleghenies.

The Atlantic One-Star is an early local edition, serving downtown Boston and such New England points as can best be reached by a midday edition. The Two-Star is the late local edition, containing stock market figures and later news. It also serves such Boston and New England points as can get delivery conveniently.

The Atlantic Two-Star Dash reaches the Atlantic seaboard from New York south, some points in Latin America and the Caribbean. The Overseas or Atlantic Three-Star edition goes to all remaining overseas points, as well as most of Canada. The editions are published during the day in the order named, with the first press start at 10:00 A.M. and the final run at 4:35 P.M.

As a result of the change, advertising rates for single editions were dropped by about 50 per cent from what all-edition rates had been before. All-edition rates remained the same. In 1925, the first full year of the zone system, advertising revenue increased 50 per cent over 1923, the last year under the old system. Meantime, the paper saved many pages daily, although readers were getting more reading matter than they had ever received before. In November, 1957, had the old system of all-edition advertising prevailed, the paper would have required 40 pages daily instead of the actual 20. Thus a 100 per cent saving in newsprint was achieved, using the actual proportions of news and advertising which prevailed in 1957. Costs of production, and hence of advertising, would have been substantially higher than they were.

The inclusion of overseas display advertising in the all-Atlantic zone accounts for the Melbourne shoe store advertised in the Boston edition. It gives the remote advertiser a bit of frosting on his cake, and it interests many readers greatly.

Another important result of the over-all advertising work merits more careful explanation. The advertising salespeople and representatives are all Christian Scientists. They are deeply committed to the help and healing of human ills and problems. They are eager to offer a cup of cold water in the Master's name whenever it is proper and welcome for them to do so. The Church of Christ, Scientist does not maintain missionaries as such. Its "practitioners" respond only to requests for their work. They do not proselytize. Christian Science lectures or periodicals are not forced on people. There is no religious sales talk, no door-to-door solicitation.

But a Christian Scientist is always happy and grateful to share what has come into his life with those in need, when they ask for it. Opportunities for this kind of good Samaritan's work arise frequently in the advertising field. The eager face of the religionist is often a very welcome visitor in the stressful business office.

The salesman very definitely and scrupulously does not mix religion with business. But he is a living witness. He will answer questions when asked. Or the advertiser, or potential advertiser, may take home with him a copy of *The Christian Science Monitor*. It may turn his thought, or that of a member of his family, to an investigation of what religion may do for him.

One experience out of hundreds will illustrate the point. An advertising representative in a Southern city called at a grocery store. There this kind-faced, outgiving lady talked with a clerk, who confided in some distress that his children were proving a problem. The lady recommended Sunday School, and the children started attending a Christian Science Sunday School. After a while, seeing how much good was coming to his children as a result of the Sunday School work, which was primarily Bible study, the father started to attend church services. He was followed by the mother, and the mother's young brother. During one of the church services, the father was freed from alcoholism. He later became a church member. His whole life changed. Manifestly he became a better store clerk, ultimately he came to own his own supermarket, but of course the great thing was the new spiritually oriented life which he led. The young brother had many helpful experiences during military service in the Second World War which he attributed to his religious dedication.

Too many such experiences have come to light — I myself have heard too many of them at first hand — to leave them out of this record. Advertising in the *Monitor* is strictly a business proposition. Those who sell it are seeking to offer the advertiser a chance to improve his business. If the advertising does not justify itself in that way, they do not want it. They never intrude with religion. They simply cannot keep it out of their faces since it is so large a part of their lives. They cannot refuse to share the cup of cold water.

36

◇◇◇◇◇◇◇◇◇◇◇◇◇◇◇◇◇◇◇◇

The *Monitor's* Circulation

THERE IS MUCH that is unique about the circulation, and the circulation problems, of the *Monitor.*

No other daily newspaper goes so far afield: to no less than 120 different nations or special geographical areas. The *Monitor* exceeds the circulation of any other national circulated newspaper in two-thirds of the United States. No other daily newspaper reaches so many of its readers by mail — fully 90 per cent of its total circulation. No other daily newspaper reaches so many of them after the day of publication. No other newspaper, one may conclude without available statistical proof, has so many readers per copy. And surely no other newspaper uses gallons of nail polish in its regular circulation operations — no less than thirteen different shades.

The publisher's statement submitted to the Audit Bureau of Circulation shows average net paid circulation for the *Monitor* in the quarter ending March, 1958, was 178,256. During the six months ending March 31, 1958, the total circulation included purchases by churches, corporations, and organizations taking bulk orders of 6441.

The *Monitor* costs $18 a year. This figure of course reflects the inflation of the 1950's. It has risen from $5 ($8 overseas) in 1908, $9 in 1917, $12 in 1938, $14 in 1947, $15 in 1950, and $16 in 1954. Such figures are comparable to those of other important metropolitan newspapers. Its single copy price has risen from two cents in 1908 to three in 1917, five in 1920, and finally in 1957's inflation to ten cents outside Boston.

The *Monitor* circulation has followed a somewhat similar curve. The trend has been consistently upward, with only a few aberrations. In April, 1909, a few months after the paper was first issued, the circulation was 43,000. It rose annually until, on the eve of the First World War, it was 55,000. During the war the rise was sharp. It was stimulated after American entrance by many free copies furnished as a part of Christian Science Camp Welfare activities. Thus, the early 1917 figure of 81,558 rose to 123,080 in October, 1918. This bulge dropped off in early 1919. Then began the cancellations brought about by readers who would not support the paper as long as it was published in contravention to the Church Manual. The official published figure in October, 1921, was 20,939. Undoubtedly the actual circulation in January, 1922, just as the paper was returned to the control of the Board of Directors, was still lower. With the re-establishment of the proper control, a steady increase began again. By early 1924, the pre-First World War figure had been passed. In October, 1924, the total was 103,159. It went progressively up to 135,077 in April, 1930.

The great depression brought about a slip in *Monitor* circulation, although in all probability far less than for most other newspapers. The low point was in 1933 with 122,636. Again a climb began, which resumed a steady march during the Second World War and thereafter. In 1945 it was 153,946; in 1955 it was 172,859.

These figures are as misleading as they are modest. They bear very little comparison to those of any other newspaper, and certainly none to the typical mass-circulation city newspaper. Such a paper is finished on the night of publication.

Its purchaser is through with it. It litters the streets, or wraps up the fish.

On the night after its publication, the *Monitor* has barely begun to circulate. Most of the editions have not even reached their readers. When they do, they have also just begun to circulate. The typical *Monitor* is consulted by several members of a family. It may be shared by some other family. And even then, many thousands of copies are brought to Christian Science churches where they are used as free distribution copies by committees seeking to increase the circulation and use of the paper. Many copies will be marked and mailed to specially interested persons. It is difficult to say by just what number the *Monitor*'s total circulation should be multiplied in order to arrive at a realistic figure, but it is certainly in the order of seven to ten.

The *Monitor*'s circulation bears very little correlation to the total number of Christian Scientists. Nor is it possible to say with any degree of accuracy just how many of the *Monitor*'s subscribers are Christian Scientists. It would be a fair guess that a substantial number of them are; but it is equally evident that many non-Christian Scientists take the paper. It is widely subscribed to by libraries, universities, institutions, public officials, offices, organizations, professional men.

The *Monitor* reaches virtually all its out-of-Boston readers by regular surface mail. Air mail subscriptions are available to remote points, but the rates are still very high. There are a few air mail subscribers in Great Britain, the Pacific Coast, and a scattering at more remote points overseas. For the rest, subscribers get their paper when the steamships, trains, and postmen complete their appointed rounds. The *Monitor* tailored its product to become and remain useful to readers who would perforce get their papers late.

For over a quarter of a century the *Monitor* has investigated carefully all methods that have been proposed for the speedier distribution of newspapers. It intends to overlook no practicable means of improving its delivery time to its readers.

From the outset, the *Monitor* has benefited from consistent efforts to maintain and extend its circulation. Circulation managers and their staffs in Boston have operated with the aid of committees and representatives provided voluntarily by Churches of Christ, Scientist throughout the world. Today, approximately 1600 circulation representatives are actively doing sales work in spots as remote as Ceylon, Guam, Iran, Pakistan, and Tasmania. Approximately 2629 Christian Science Reading Rooms are also *Monitor* sales outlets in many parts of the world, although they serve primarily to acquaint interested persons with the basically religious literature of Christian Science.

The element of voluntary service has always been a principal factor in the *Monitor*'s sales work. Representatives, however, receive commissions for sales they make — a system inaugurated by Mrs. Eddy. Much latitude has always been given to circulation committees in branch churches as to the best promotional methods and systems they should employ.

In the earliest days, the circulation promotion staff in Boston also reflected these elements of the volunteer — one might almost say of the amateur — however zealous, tireless, and often practical they were. As in any other nonprofessional system, there were effective ideas mingled with others less effective. It was not until the 1920's that the central direction of circulation promotion, as well as its implementation in the field, began to take on stronger business-organization methods. Even then, as is also the case today, the paper benefited from the fresh enthusiasm, ingenuity, and dedication of voluntary workers in all parts of the world.

In 1927, Colonel Herbert A. Johnson, an experienced business executive, was appointed circulation manager. He brought his background to bear on the problems of promotion and of servicing the *Monitor*'s circulation. He remained circulation manager until 1942, during which time — including the challenges of the depression — steady progress was made at organizing the circulation effort.

Colonel Johnson was succeeded by H. Phelps Gates, a Californian who had had experience in *Monitor* advertising and editorial work, as well as in sales promotion and advertising agency and public relations work. His technical skill, drive, and perception contributed further to the work. As the years have gone by, the department has become increasingly professional and proficient in its operations. Mr. Gates introduced remarkable innovations and simplifications in the circulation fulfillment process.

Each day approximately 3000 letters, renewals, new subscriptions, and changes of address pour into the circulation department from its far-flung subscribers. Under a highly mechanized system, letters and orders from subscribers receive accurate, same-day handling. Each technical worker is responsible for a particular geographical unit, each one serving the needs of from 5000 to 12,000 subscribers.

A unique system of varicolored lacquers (nail polish!) helps to identify the address plates for various billing purposes. The clerks paint the tops of thousands of address plates with bright-colored lacquer when renewal notices go out. When payments come in, subscription clerks dip these plates in nail-polish remover to credit the subscription. In its simplicity, the system has proved fast and accurate.

Both for time saving and space saving, all subscription correspondence goes on microfilm. A single cabinet, half the size of an average desk, holds upwards of a million pieces of correspondence. In busy times, a file clerk can photograph up to 18,000 pieces of correspondence in a single day.

The simplification and streamlining of the *Monitor*'s circulation fulfillment work resulted in the saving of an entire floor in the Publishing House — 10,000 square feet. When the filing was switched to microfilm, the operation was reduced from 250 to 50 filing cabinets.

The development of geographical area specialists, who could service all the needs of a subscriber in one operation, eliminated sizable correspondence units and adjustment units, and speeded up the work greatly. Job standards and working conditions improved substantially as the result of these changes. In sum, the unique circulation servicing needs of the *Monitor* have been met by carefully thought out methods which utilize the best in mechanization and in personnel skills. It is interesting and significant that these complex processes, though using the best in machines, have greatly enhanced — and require — the skill, dignity and craftsmanlike pride of technical workers.

Since the first issue, the *Monitor* has been on newsstands and home delivery service in Boston. Today the paper is on sale at approximately 1200 newsstands, corners, and stores in Greater Boston. A fleet of cars and trucks deliver the paper to these sales outlets and to rail, bus, and air depots. In one of the great blizzards of 1956, several of the district supervisors spent all night in their cars when snow tied up the traffic.

The circulation department, on the receiving end, constitutes a kind of daily inventory of the *Monitor*'s utility to readers. A steady flow of letters from organizations, scholars, officials, leaders, clergymen of many denominations, from great metropolises and remote jungle villages, all attest to its value the world over.

The *Monitor* did not receive a letter of appreciation from one of its most noted — or notorious — subscribers. Perhaps a better word than subscriber is recipient. In the late 1940's a thoughtful and imaginative reader believed it would be a contribution to peace and understanding if one Joseph Stalin, whose address was then at The Kremlin, Moscow, U.S.S.R., should receive a subscription to the *Monitor*. She thought it might give him a better picture of the United States, and the world, than he was then getting. So she sent along her check for a year's subscription.

The circulation manager pondered the proprieties of the gift, and concluded there was no harm — and just possibly some good — in complying with the reader's wishes. So the subscription was duly serviced, and every day a copy of the *Monitor* was sent off to the aforesaid address. As far as the *Monitor* office was concerned, the subscription went out into a great void. Undoubtedly it got as far as the Soviet Union's postal officials. What happened then is anybody's guess. It's an amusing speculation whether a postal censor, an intelligence officer, a secretary, a clerk in the Kremlin, perused the copy. Since Marshal Stalin's English was never considered very good, it is a melancholy inference that he didn't spend long winter evenings in front of the Kremlin fireplace with his copy of the *Monitor*.

But some people in Moscow do use quite a different kind of subscription. The Soviet Embassy in Washington takes a substantial number of *Monitor* subscriptions. Presumably some of them are flown in the Embassy's diplomatic pouch to the suitable office in Moscow. There a number of research agencies and libraries get regular subscriptions direct. The Soviet press frequently quotes from the *Monitor*, usually to criticize, and sometimes out of context. The *Monitor* is read with avidity in Moscow.

It is also carefully read in all the other capitals of the world. Presidents, prime ministers, foreign secretaries, other cabinet ministers, members of parliament and legislatures, diplomats — indeed, people at all ranks and levels of officialdom — receive the *Monitor*. There is much evidence that they put it to good use. Sometimes they quote from it in official debates. References crop up in public documents, or are reflected in public policy.

During recent years, the United States Information Agency has made extensive use of the *Monitor*, selecting articles and editorials from its columns and cabling them to remote points where it is felt they would do the most good. Often they are circulated to local newspapers by the regional U.S.I.S. posts, and reprinted in substantial volume. Thus, although the paper itself may get to very few readers by air mail, its more important contents are frequently circulated to millions of readers within a few hours of initial publication.

For many years the State Department has excerpted and circulated through its official bulletins a great many quotations from the *Monitor*. Subscriptions also regularly go to official American posts abroad. The paper's views and services are thus available in the implementation of American foreign policy.

Naturally the paper is read carefully on Capitol Hill, in Washington. Its editors have an abundant correspondence with members of Congress who wish to discuss specific matters. The legislators introduce material from the *Monitor* with great frequency in the *Congressional Record,* usually with a pleasant compliment. Similar attention is paid the paper in governors' offices, state legislatures, and lesser centers of authority.

Against all these indices of usefulness, however, must be balanced the *Monitor*'s relatively modest numerical circulation. Although the figures must be multiplied many fold to give a realistic readership total, the fact remains that the paper's circulation could be and should be much larger. Why isn't it?

This is the challenging question which has faced all concerned with the *Monitor* for many years. First, why should not the *Monitor* be taken by a larger percentage of Christian Scientists themselves? While membership figures of the Church of Christ, Scientist, are not given out, under a stipulation of the Church Manual, it is an easy inference that membership and attendance at such churches in the United States alone is many times the total circulation of the *Monitor.* A little simple arithmetic by a resident of any American city can deduce this fact.

No pressure is put on these Christian Scientists to subscribe to the *Monitor,* as is obvious from the figures. There are, of course, some Christian Scientists who take the *Monitor* out of a sense of duty. Such persons do not always read it with particular care. For the most part, those Christian Scientists who take the *Monitor* do so for a combination of reasons. Interest in the paper itself is one of them.

The fact is that the *Monitor,* in addressing Christian Scientists, is speaking to a very diverse audience. Almost the only thing they have in common is their interest in Christian Science. Some of them are highly educated. Others are very simple people. Some are avid readers and students of current affairs. Others read little beside their religious reading. They live in 120 lands. Some of them know little English. Politically speaking, the world over, some of them are conservative, some are liberal, some are in the middle. Some are zealots at the two extremes. They are of many races and historical backgrounds. In the United States, some are Republicans, some are Democrats, and of all varieties of the two parties.

To address all these people simultaneously and acceptably is a major editorial challenge. It is a challenge stylistically and a challenge policy-wise. For some of them, *Monitor* style should be as simple and as popularized as possible. For others, such simplicity would be a drawback, too elementary and uninteresting. They ask for a more scholarly approach. In terms of policy, some of them wish one political slant and some another very different one and some none at all, or think they want none at all.

Quite apart from this complexity of readership, the *Monitor* by its most fundamental commitments is a relatively austere paper, publishing important things for the most part, rather than merely entertaining things. It can, and does, achieve a certain strength and brightness, but only within bounds of sobriety and responsibility. Its concessions to sheer human interest can go just so far and not much farther.

In short, the *Monitor* is a challenge to those human minds which are still wedded to sensationalism and sensuality. Like Christian Science itself, it calls upon its readers to rise to high standards of interest and of citizenship.

While these obligations of the *Monitor* are priceless virtues, they are not always immediately useful in building up circulation among people who have not yet seen and accepted for themselves the serious approach to problems which is the paper's duty.

A pathetic letter reflecting in crude and blunt form the problem afflicting many human minds, though unacknowledged, came to the paper a few weeks after the world's first atomic bomb fell at Alamogordo and a few weeks before the first one fell on human beings. On May 7, 1945, this letter came:

Dear Sir,

Please do not send the Christian Science Monitor paper . . . I'm born ignorant and it pays to stay ignorant. The less I read the better.

Mrs. B —— i.

Some Christian Scientists are displeased when the *Monitor*'s position on a controversial issue does not happen to coincide with their own. They will sometimes criticize it severely. There have been, during the impassioned days of the 1940's and '50's, some attacks on the *Monitor*, mostly from the extreme right wing. Such attacks have had very little effect on circulation, though sometimes they have made quite a lot of noise. The most violent of them was publicized by an individual who had been condemned by the House Un-American Activities Committee as a semi-Fascist fanatic of the extreme right. Another was led by a person who is well known for his participation in other semi-Fascist campaigns. The attacks puzzled some sincere supporters of the paper, who received this hostile literature through the mail, but on the whole they evoked inspiring manifestations of loyalty and support.

Among non-Christian Scientists, the handicaps to more extensive *Monitor* circulation turn largely on the lateness of its arrival at distant points and its religious affiliation. The latter factor as a handicap has diminished steadily. In the local New England area, deterrents to larger *Monitor* circulation are for the most part its inability to include some elements which appeal most vigorously to mass human interest: syndicated comic strips, unlimited publicizing of trivial but sensational crime, extensive death notices, society news, and the fact that absence of a local mass circulation deters local advertising on a massive scale. The *Monitor* has excellent support from Boston advertisers, and serves them well, but its circulation does not yet command advertising to the degree that will tell the housewife about every bargain that is offered.

Fundamentally, however, all these handicaps — for Christian Scientists and non-Christian Scientists alike — reduce to the fact of the *Monitor*'s challenge to the human mind. As mankind responds more intently to the grave problems of our time, as clearer and more responsible thinking deepens in the community, as education and enlightenment elevate thinking, the *Monitor* can confidently expect a growing response. Moreover, the *Monitor* is learning to do its job more effectively and more interestingly. Within the terms of its mandate of significance and responsibility, it can and must make its pages just as lively as the resources of journalism permit. It must fulfill its deepest purposes.

37

◇◇◇◇◇◇◇◇◇◇◇◇◇◇◇◇◇◇◇◇

The *Monitor's* Manufacture

WHEN THE MONITOR's first anniversary edition was being run off, on November 24–25, 1909, a sturdy young schoolboy who had been taking papers off the press and handing them along to the mailers fell asleep on a pile of mail sacks as the unusually long run extended far into the night. He awoke to the smell of a Thanksgiving turkey dinner, prepared by ladies who had come to help the men working overtime for the great edition.

The schoolboy was Herbert T. Stanger, since 1934 production manager of the *Monitor* and production assistant to the manager of the Publishing Society for a still longer period. He has been for many years one of the most widely respected production managers among American newspapers. And the *Monitor* has long enjoyed the technological esteem of its peers. From the beginning, every effort has been made to achieve high-quality standards and first-rate efficiency. The stream of production specialists who come from all parts of the world to visit the Publishing House is a compliment to the paper's attainment of these goals.

In recent years many of these visitors have come to see the *Monitor*'s four-color printing on its Hoe Color-Convertible Presses, which were the first presses of this type to be installed after the Second World War. The paper publishes a substantial volume of color advertising, some of it in delicate process color. From time to time it produces color on its news and feature pages as well. For a period it ran many colored illustrations, and published its own magazine supplement on the Hoe presses. But for some years the publication of editorial color has been rare.

The use of color is one more example of keeping abreast of the technological times. *Monitor* production specialists have always been keenly interested in more efficient and effective ways of manufacturing newspapers, and have pioneered with those which could be applied to its problems. This does not yet include all of the experimental devices now being used in some other newspapers, for many of them do not meet *Monitor* needs. The paper's insistence on quality and efficiency causes it to make certain that new devices are really proven before adopting them.

Typographically, the *Monitor* has always been conservative. It has published banner headlines on page one only when the news was of outstanding importance. Its most typical front-page headline type size is 42 or 48 point, whereas its Boston afternoon paper colleagues regularly use front-page heads running to 120 point and more.

Headlines and type faces have evolved steadily down through the years, being modernized and improved at each change. From the outset, the *Monitor* body type has been the best of available contemporary design. The first type, in 1908, was a lightface 8-point roman letter. This type was easy to read, clear, reserved, and handsome. Headlines of the same period were more austere, in an upright and condensed Gothic — a type that stands erect, with letters close together and many words often crowded into limited space. It is not very easy to read. It does not have the openness, the emphasis, the joy of a more varied type. It was well-named Gothic, for its stiff slimness and close array.

So, in 1913, the *Monitor* changed its headlines to a roman type family, Cheltenham, more in keeping with its body type. This familiar type is smaller in depth and takes fewer letters per line, but it is much more readable, animated, free. It has greater contrast in the width of letters and gives variety and movement to the page.

During the period from 1914 to 1922, these types were printed very gray, and almost no headlines beyond a single column were permitted. The paper had departed from Gothic but it was still perpendicular in make-up. Then came a considerable livening up of make-up and general style. In 1930, the light headlines in previous use were discarded. A blacker, boldface type of the Caslon family was introduced. Headlines were larger, though still conservative. A new body type was required to present a greater contrast with the white paper, which would have delicate curves that would yet stand up under modern printing and not collect ink smudges. After much research, the paper jumped right back over the Victorian interlude and selected a type basically designed in 1828, the Ionic. It was used in 7 point on an 8-point slug — the small metal body on which the type face stands. The present body type is 7½ point Excelsior on an 8-point slug. It is really a trimmed-down 8 point. During the Second World War, for newsprint economy reasons, the same type was set on a 7½ point slug.

In 1933, the headlines were again modernized. The *Monitor* very early joined the now almost universal group of newspapers using lower-case heads: that is to say, heads not set entirely in capital letters. It is agreed that upper- and lower-case heads are easier to read. These technical terms carry us back to old days of handsetting of type, when the small letters, those mostly used, were in the lower part of the case nearest the compositor, and the capitals were farther away in the upper part, since they were not used so much.

In the sections of the paper not devoted to news, much

typographical diversity has always been shown in the *Monitor*, with larger sizes of body type, wider columns, and distinctive heads.

The mechanical production of the *Monitor* shares the same sense of dedication and idealism which marks its editorial work. The first foreman of its composing room, who kept a talented hand on its printing problems for thirty years, was Amos Weston. This gentle person will never be forgotten by those who knew him. His smiling, open face shone with an inner radiance only matched, in his later years, by the silver aureole of his hair. He was also a Sunday School teacher and superintendent, a most devoted religionist who brought his convictions into daily operation.

Mr. Weston had had twenty years of newspaper and magazine experience when he came to the *Monitor* in 1908. He never ceased to explore ways to improve the printing craft. When he went on a vacation trip, it would be to visit important publishing establishments along the way. When he passed on in 1941, the Boston Club of Printing House Craftsmen in dedicating a volume to him summarized the affection his fellow printers felt by saying: "For many years Amos Weston was permitted the joy that lay in his unselfish quest for examples of high artistic merit in the graphic arts. It was a service rich in results for education and craftsmanship. His high conception of the necessity to thus open avenues for the education of the younger members of the craft have made many young men feel profoundly grateful to him for their advancement."

There is indeed much that is intangible, but important, in the approach of *Monitor* technicians to their tasks. The earnest and confident perfectionism that imbued Amos Weston is typical of many others. After Mr. Weston was placed in charge of all printing production, the foreman of the *Monitor* composing room was Wendell W. Wyman. He, too, deeply felt the craftsman's sense of his work. And something of his unusual nature is shown by the fact that he was a justly famous grower of gladioli, running away with a lion's share of the prizes at the Massachusetts Horticultural Society.

Mr. Wyman was assisted in the *Monitor* composing room by Herbert P. Haake, now assistant production manager, an imaginative, versatile, intelligent specialist in production technology. The present composing room foreman is Sidney V. Julin, who handles a complicated and fast-moving operation with great efficiency. These men, who started as apprentices in the *Monitor* composing room, were products of long training in its methods and ideals. Like so many master printers, but with the important addition of a special zeal, they have the artist's attitude toward their jobs, the craftsman proud of his work. As a matter of fact, several of them are artists: Mr. Stanger is a sculptor of real talent. It may not be irrelevant to mention that one of his sons is among the nation's rising conductors of symphony orchestras and choruses.

The *Monitor* is frequently complimented on the quality of its picture reproduction. It has an excellent photoengraving department staffed by a number of genuinely gifted artists. They are also first-rate technicians.

Burt Mader, who has headed the photoengraving department since 1942, is also a talented portrait artist. Again at the risk of irrelevance, it reveals something to say that Mr. Mader is often sought by advertising agencies as a model in their photographs!

Under such men the best photoengraving equipment and techniques were developed. And as often as possible the men were given time to do their jobs well. It is impossible to get real pictorial quality when the photoengraving has to be rushed. The *Monitor*'s photoengravers can do a job when necessary on the swiftest deadlines, and it will be as good as possible. But when editors have difficult copy, they have learned to take the photoengravers into their confidence, asking for their advice and giving them plenty of time. As a result, the artists who turn picture copy into cuts will invariably rise to the occasion, relishing the challenge.

Other vital factors in good photoreproduction are the quality of stereotyping and the presswork itself. Here the *Monitor*'s preference to print a little on the gray side is of great value, for it preserves shadings and separations in the cuts which would be lost in a flood of blacker ink. Since 1941 the stereotyping job — plate casting for the presses — has been supervised by Rupert M. Roaf, a meticulous craftsman who worked up from the bottom rung of the production ladder, beginning in 1924.

The *Monitor*'s editorial art department also deserves its share of credit in turning out a handsome paper. Mention has been made of Dwight C. Sturges, the great etcher who drew so many pictures for the *Monitor* for a quarter of a century. His portraits of public men and women, his familiar and historic scenes, his more mundane handling of cut layouts and retouching, were all the work of a tireless, swift, unerring master.

Frank Saddler, also a portrait artist of distinction, supervised *Monitor* art for a number of years and produced many of its handsome layouts in the magazine section and later. More recently he also handles its big and growing stock of photographs. The pictures are instantly available for any news emergency. They must be skillfully filed, imaginatively selected.

Two artists of very different bent have adorned and enlivened the paper's pages in recent years. Russell Lenz, who has been drawing for the paper since 1928, is a cartographer of national fame. No newspaper map maker has more distinction, accuracy, or cartographic judgment. Mr. Lenz's style is unmistakable. Nowadays, as well as appearing in the *Monitor*, his work embellishes a number of history and geography texts.

Gene Langley is primarily an illustrator. He turns out brilliantly witty sketches for the paper's front-page or editorial-page columns. Toss him a piece of copy, and he will be back in five minutes with half-a-dozen rough sketches. His work is used to brighten the *Monitor*, bringing values which cannot be captured by the camera. Like Emil Weiss, an illustrator who contributes from many great meetings such as those of the United Nations, Mr. Langley brings to the *Monitor* — in an utterly modern vein — some of the perceptive touches newspapers had before they became slaves to the lens.

Uninformed critics have sometimes attributed the *Monitor*'s technical excellence to the absence of normal newspaper pressures. This is not the fact. Indeed, the *Monitor* has some of the most complicated production problems of any American paper. Its six editions, which go to press through the day from 10 A.M. to 4 P.M., require an almost total advertising makeover three times during the day. As explained earlier, the Pacific-edition advertising is largely exclusive to that edition; the Central edition has its own; the Atlantic editions have much the same advertising; but the Overseas has notable changes. The total advertising makeover requires a very substantial editorial makeover.

That is to say, it is necessary for the make-up men in the composing room to take all the Pacific ads out of the forms, replace them by Central ads, and later by Atlantic-edition ads, all in different shapes and sharply variable quantity. One day there may be 45 columns of news room in the Pacific edition and 55 in the Central edition, and vice versa on the following day. No other newspaper has so complicated a makeover problem.

The task was solved by careful organization and co-ordination of advertising, editorial, and production processes. First the advertising department makes dummies — marked quarter sheets — laying out the positions of all the ads. These dummies are prepared in wooden frames with wooden blocks — for all the world like children's blocks — just the proportional size of each ad. The advertising make-up specialist puts the blocks in the frame, draws a line around them, numbers each ad, and presto the dummy is made! This simple system, originated by Mr. Stanger, is believed to be unique.

The dummies showing where each ad will appear on each page are then sent to the editorial department and the composing room. In the newsroom, make-up assistants take lists of news stories from the editors and lay them out on the various pages. The completed dummies go swiftly to the composing room. They are hung, with clothespins, from lines strung over the make-up tables, called imposing stones. Both editorial department and composing room keep careful records of which stories have run in which editions, to avoid repetition of the same story on successive days. This bookkeeping operation is a heavy and unusual responsibility.

Copy having been read, corrected, headlined by copyreaders, passes over a copy control desk, where it is measured for length and recorded to register the copy flow, and goes to the composing room. There it is cut into "takes" and set up by the Linotype operators.

Though copyreading is a function of the editorial department, this is a suitable place to describe it. The *Monitor*'s copyreaders and the head of the copy desk, called a slot man because he sits in the inside curve of a U-shaped desk, are journalists of a very high quality, as they must be on any well-conducted newspaper. They are among the most carefully trained and highly qualified specialists on the paper. They require technical skill, judgment, and ingenuity to write good headlines. On the one hand, this job has some elements of a crossword puzzle or anagram. On the other, it calls especially in the *Monitor* for the capture of stand-up meaning in heads, as well as mere spot news. The copyreaders must know unerringly how to correct spelling, bad grammar, poor style — indeed, inaccuracies, mistakes, anachronisms, and gaffes of all sorts. They save writers from countless blunders committed in the haste of deadline meeting. More, they add the element which any writer, however experienced and skillful, badly needs: the sober judgment of a trained, relentless, and constructive critic.

The *Monitor*'s copy desk includes many of the paper's unsung heroes. Its chief is Harry N. Hazeldine, who has presided in the slot since 1941. He was already a widely experienced copyreader when he joined the staff in 1935. His judgment and skill in training new copyreaders have made a contribution of inestimable value. He was preceded, from 1927 to 1941, by Carroll A. Lake, an ingenious and experienced typographical and make-up specialist who helped vitally in the many technical steps forward that were developed during the 1930's.

These craftsmen work in closest co-operation with the production department in the *Monitor*'s manufacture. In fact, the editorial department has long since learned the great value of taking the mechanical department into its confidence at all stages. And the production specialists have always tried to produce the kind of paper that was being planned. There is no division between those with ink on their hands and those with desks and typewriters. The extraordinarily high standards of the production men have naturally produced deep respect for them in the editorial department. A common morale and deep purpose inspires them both. They speak a common language and feel a common opportunity. Many of them are close social, fraternal, or church friends and colleagues.

The unionization of the mechanical departments, and the absence of unions in the editorial, advertising, circulation, and clerical departments has never constituted a breach. As recorded in Chapter 8, there has never been a strike of cessation of work. The atmosphere and conditions of employment attract journeymen of fine quality. The skills described in the composing and photoengraving rooms are matched by the stereotypers, the pressmen, and the mailing room personnel.

The paper's frequent color printing brings out special skills among the pressmen. Indeed, good press work is one of the *Monitor*'s special distinctions. Since 1917 the press room has been ably headed by Reginald Reed, one more of the paper's trusted craftsmen. The paper has had a steady growth of press capacity down through its half century. The first was a little Goss Straightline two-page-width press. It was thought very grand in those days, but it could only print 20,000 twelve-page papers an hour. Soon, in 1909, a double-width two-unit press was installed and a third unit had speedily to be added. In 1910 growth required a second Goss sextuple press. By 1917 a third high-speed sextuple press was put into operation. In July, 1924, three new octuple Goss presses were installed. By 1947, the two that were used were running at top speed to keep up with circulation. They could print 32,000 an hour. The present Hoe Color-Convertible Presses — a battery of ten press units set up as two presses — are capable of printing 120,000 papers an hour, up to forty pages each, though for quality and efficiency they are not run so fast.

The mailing operation, far exceeding in magnitude that required for the dispatching of any other daily newspaper, is performed by a phalanx of mailing machines which were virtually tailored for the *Monitor*'s needs. The papers are fed to them by conveyor belt. Each machine wraps and addresses single copies at a single operation using a drawer of embossed address plates and dropping the papers at the rate of 12,000 an hour per machine into mail sacks directed to different localities. The sacks go by conveyor belt direct to the loading platform.

These details reveal the efficiency of the present Publishing Society building, which was erected to its particular needs in 1932–34. By that time the work had far outgrown the original Publishing House and spilled over into many adjacent buildings, ill adapted to such use. So, at the depth of the depression, Christian Scientists all over the world were asked to contribute to a building fund. They did so with great enthusiasm, and the massive building was erected on the block from Massachusetts Avenue to Falmouth Street, with Norway and Clearway Streets on its two other sides. With building costs at an all-time modern low, and with great need for providing employment, the undertaking could not have been more timely. For $4,000,000 there was erected a structure which in 1958 would cost at least $16,000,000.

There were many admirable features of the design and construction of the building, for which the architect was Chester Lindsay Churchill. Perhaps the best tribute is to say that if the job were to be done all over again now, twenty-five years later, very few changes would be made. It remains a splendid publishing plant. The design is particularly good for the *Monitor*. The newsroom is spacious, and its work feeds directly into the composing room. At the other end of the composing room is the photoengraving department, and just below are the press and mailing rooms. The operation is performed with no waste motion.

One anecdote connected with the building captures the atmosphere of Anglo-American business folkways. Mr. Churchill, the architect, went to London to buy various materials best available there. The European manager, John Sidney Braithwaite, took him to call on British managing directors of supply firms. None of them, Mr. Churchill thought, really tried to sell him anything, or indeed, took him very seriously! Accustomed to the aggressive ways of American salesmen, he missed being given the high-pressure treatment. The climax came one day when Mr. Braithwaite had taken him to lunch at the Oxford and Cambridge Club, in Pall Mall, with Colonel Pilkington, the managing director of the famous St. Helen's Glass Company. They talked about the weather, the cricket, and the social season. Finally Mr. Churchill rather lost his patience, and said, "Colonel Pilkington, I'll give it to you straight. I'm going to buy our glass from the Pittsburgh Plate Glass Company." To which Colonel Pilkington replied, unmoved, "A capital firm. You couldn't do better." Of course, Mr. Churchill bought much of his glass from the St. Helen's Glass Company.

It must be realized once more that the *Monitor*'s quality down through the half century, as reflected in its clean, restrained, modern typography, make-up, pictures, is due to the dedicated craftsmen who produce it. It is genuinely a quality operation. But it is capable of working at high speed second to none. A news flash can be on page one and rolling from the presses ten minutes after it arrives on the teletype. Day in and day out, the output must be worthy mechanically of the thinking behind it. It is, because it is produced by good men.

PART FIVE

THE FUTURE

38

◇◇◇◇◇◇◇◇◇◇◇◇◇◇◇◇◇◇◇◇

The *Monitor* and Modern Journalism

TO STATE CONFIDENTLY just what the *Monitor* has achieved in modern journalism is more than a little difficult. It has held up a standard. But it has been a standard no other newspaper was ready to follow totally. Many of them could and did follow it in part.

Its influence has undoubtedly been substantial, if elusive. The fact is that for a number of reasons, throughout the half century, the better and more responsible newspapers in most parts of the world have improved in quality and conscientiousness. They have become less biased. They are more conscious of the need for public service.

In many parts of the world, as in the English-speaking nations, newspapers have become journals of information rather than journals of opinion. At the same time, there have been many consolidations and failures of newspapers. But those left are on the whole stronger institutions, tending to serve an entire community instead of only a part of it. The development of one-newspaper cities in the United States has had good as well as bad features, although critics are more conscious of the bad elements.

The so-called monopoly newspaper, as it typically exists in the United States, is far less reckless and biased than its predecessor half a century ago. Such newspapers owe, and many of them accept, an obligation to the total community to do an impartial job of informing, and an honest job of editorializing. Such newspapers are far nearer the standards of the *Monitor* than were any of its contemporaries in 1908. They do not typically have to descend to the depths of sensationalism in order to be successful. The most reckless newspapers in America, and, indeed, elsewhere in the world, are the newspapers in the most competitive situations.

The value in a so-called monopolistic newspaper (none of them are really noncompetitive, since there are many forms of competition — news magazines, radio, television, etc.) is that sooner or later it must acknowledge and fulfill its obligations to the entire community. If it does not do so, ultimately it fails. And in the long run — though happily this day has not and should not come — monopolistic newspapers would fall into the plight of public utilities and suffer public regulation unless they voluntarily meet their obligations.

This acceptance of a high standard of obligation to the community is becoming the price of survival for American newspapers. It comes very close in many respects to the *Monitor*'s standard. Such newspapers can and do find in the *Monitor*'s practices, techniques, and attitudes some ideas which they can apply themselves.

As newspaper consolidations into a community-wide relationship have progressed, another important change has taken place. The newspaper is no longer the exclusive or the most efficient purveyor of spot news. Radio or television can get a news bulletin into the kitchen or the automobile dashboard or the business office quicker than the copy boy can run with the scrap of paper from the teletype machine to the news desk.

Thus all newspapers, and particularly the more alert and responsive among them, have realized their task is becoming increasingly what the *Monitor*'s has always had to be: that of providing background, depth, perspective and meaning for the news. The *Monitor* has developed techniques to this end. From the outset, many of its correspondents have written explanatory and perceptive dispatches.

In the 1930's and 1940's this study and practice of explanatory news-writing was intensively applied by the *Monitor*. The durability of reader-interest was defined as a prime requisite. Every story had to be what newsmen call a "second-day story," which is to say that every story had to have the kind of added value that the news bulletin lacks but which the capable correspondent can gather and impart when he has a little time.

Other newspapers have steadily come to the same awareness. So have the great wire services. Compare the file of the Associated Press, the United Press, the International News Service, or Reuters of today with their file of twenty years ago; the change is very striking. Backgrounded writing is currently very much the rule. News is handled as quickly as possible, but the correspondent seeks as soon as he can to give his copy as much perspective as it is in his capacity to do. This is the *Monitor*'s stock in trade. Its pioneering example has definitely been of assistance to many other newspapers. Meantime, as the other papers and news services approached more and more closely its standard practices, the *Monitor* has to advance further into newer techniques.

The *Monitor* knows the commercial imperatives that govern all newspapers, itself included. It knows that newspapers must retain a high degree of reader confidence and interest if they are to keep going along. Therefore it does not expect many other papers to adopt standards of austerity and moderation which it can and must preserve. In a good many respects, the *Monitor* is ahead of the human mind. It makes demands on its readers, on the whole quite severe demands. Perhaps these demands are too great; certainly at some times in the past they have been too great. It, too, must learn and apply better ways to command the attention of its readers. It does not expect other papers to make themselves over into its pattern.

With immense good will other newspapers and newspapermen have praised and complimented the *Monitor*. At times the compliment has taken the form of a degree of emulation. Some of them have scoffed at the *Monitor* and repudiated its conscientiousness. They have declared it was "out of this world" and have made fun of its news attitudes. Sometimes this criticism had a measure of justification. Those days are going if they are not utterly gone. A realization that problems cannot be solved if they are not faced has become the *Monitor*'s maxim. This fact has become known.

Most of the generous praise that has come to the *Monitor* has been unexpected. It has sprung spontaneously from the desire of other newspapermen to turn toward a nobler model. Why did an utter realist like Charles Guy, of Lubbock, Texas, refer to the *Monitor* as "a great publication respected by newsmen and other discerning readers of current affairs, both in and out of the religious group that sponsors it"? Why did one of newspaperdom's most perceptive cynics, Jenkin Lloyd-Jones, editor of the Tulsa *Tribune,* and recently president of the American Society of Newspaper Editors, write: "The immense popularity of The Christian Science Monitor among non-Christian Scientists, including many godless newspapermen, springs from the fact that the publication is both factual and hopeful. The Monitor knows the score about as well as any American newspaper. It recognizes and describes the weak spots in the dike and the pitfalls in the path. It is capable both of alarm and righteous indignation. But it never gives up the ship. It never discounts its ultimate faith in the triumph of decency."

These generous words do describe what the *Monitor* seeks to be, and what perhaps it has measurably achieved.

One of the most moving tributes to the *Monitor,* one that filled its staff with the deepest humility, gratitude, and sense of challenge, came from the editor of a modest country weekly published at Trout Creek, Delaware County, New York. On its front page, the *West Delaware Tribune* said:

Sometime ago we accepted the offer of the Christian Science Monitor to receive that paper in exchange for advertising. We are increasingly becoming aware that there is not enough space in the Tribune to pay the Monitor for what it brings us.

If it is true that an institution is but the shadow of a man, it can certainly be said that the Monitor is the strong shadow of a faith . . . that man is a spiritual being, created in God's image . . . and the standard of perfection is no less than the likeness of God. This truth is exemplified in the editorials, features, and news columns of the paper.

The Monitor quickens our imagination, crystallizes our principles, restores our faith in journalism as a high profession and makes us proud to be the editor of a country weekly.

The *Monitor*'s influence, not always understood in these terms, on other newspapers and on the public in general, is expressed in many ways. The *Monitor* reaches at least 4500 newspaper offices every publishing day. In many large metropolitan newspapers it may receive short shrift, or be turned over to specialists who want to utilize some special feature. But small newspapers, especially small city dailies and weeklies, find the *Monitor* of tremendous value and interest. They discover plenty in it that is quotable and can be reprinted. There is more that suggests editorial ideas to be developed. As has been mentioned, the *Monitor* reaches substantially more newspaper offices of this sort than any other daily newspaper. Thus its thinking, whenever acceptable and stimulating, is plowed into the soil of local journalism. The secondary influence of the paper, not for any special cause or bias but for the general enlightenment of public thinking, is therefore of very great magnitude.

It extends overseas and is particularly strong in areas of the world where society is going through one kind or another of formative crisis. In different ways, two such areas are Japan and India, although a similar situation prevails elsewhere. To newspaper editors and their readers in such areas, the *Monitor* — though universal in approach — is nevertheless a voice of American idealism. It speaks with understanding and love of the aspirations of peoples in underdeveloped areas.

Its alert coverage of the American occupation in Japan, its sympathy with the better side of Japanese character — perhaps, latterly, the presence of a very able Japanese among its by-lined writers — have helped make the *Monitor* of use and interest in many Japanese newspaper offices. Air mail subscriptions, at substantial expense, are taken by some such newspapers.

In India, the *Monitor's* breadth of sympathy, its humanitarianism, its rejection of materialism, and its extensive coverage of Indian affairs latterly under the by-line of an Indian, have given it an unequaled entree and respect. This means, again, that the better side of American thinking is being brought to Indian editors as contrasted with the tawdry sensationalism which spreads before the world chiefly the rope tricks and the child brides.

In a quite different respect, the *Monitor* has something to offer other newspapers. It is operated by a trusteeship. The mechanics, as well as the fundamentals, of the operation are successful. Perhaps they have something to offer to newspaper owners or their families who wish to provide for the maintenance of the newspaper tradition, character, and success down through the generations.

A number of great newspapers have been placed in various forms of trusteeship, or its equivalent, in recent years. *The Times* of London, the *Observer,* the Manchester *Guardian,* the Kansas City *Star,* the Washington *Post and Times-Herald,* the Milwaukee *Journal,* the Chicago *Tribune* — these and other papers have been set up in one way or another so that there is a check on the perpetuation of their character.

The Christian Science Publishing Society formula works. It works, as has been made clear, for rather special reasons. Nevertheless, there is something in its experience which may be of value to others. And nowadays more than a few newspaper owners are seeking ways to provide for perpetuation more significant than the ties of blood.

The *Monitor* experience impels several criteria. For one thing, there must not be divided ultimate authority. The last word must lie clearly in a single place. Otherwise there will be conflict and confusion. Drafters of wills should keep this in mind.

For another thing, it is important that those who must make decisions daily about editorial commitments or business operations should have ready and frequent access to the source of ultimate authority. Perhaps there is something to be said for the delegation of extensive authority. Perhaps there are cases where a board of directors or board of trustees can delegate business and editorial control of a newspaper to a business manager and an editor and wash their hands of the operation for months on end. Such a system may go on happily for years. It is, after all, the pattern in much American business, education, foundations, and other institutions.

As one who works daily in a system with continuous access to the source of authority and serves on half a dozen boards of the other kind, I prefer the former. If I were setting up a system for preserving the character and well-being of a newspaper, I would try my hardest to insure that the decision-making power was primary and continuous, rather than delegated and spasmodic.

As a third safeguard, I would make certain that the news and editorial side of the operation had direct access to the ultimate authority, rather than passing through a business office. This is, of course, self-evident. But altogether too frequently in newspaper organization it is contravened. For his policy direction the editor should have the right to go straight to the fiduciary body that stands for the owner. On business affairs, such as budget and personnel, he should be under the business office. But if the power of the purse as administered by the business office ever is exercised to alter editorial or news policy — as it may very readily do — the editor should have direct access to the ultimate ownership body. The business manager will have direct access as well, and the case can be judged between them.

These conditions were all provided for in The Church Manual and the Deed of Trust by which the operations of the

Christian Science Publishing Society are governed. Efforts to alter them have failed. They continue as a guarantee of strength and freedom in the deepest sense.

The *Monitor* arrangement has immense advantages which perhaps it would be difficult if not impossible to duplicate elsewhere. It is most unlikely that two boards — of directors and of trustees — could be set up in other operations on a daily working basis. And without the special religious dedication which prevails in this case, the arrangement would be doubly difficult. Without that factor, the collective executive might break down in jealousy and spite.

Nevertheless, anybody interested in a novel and workable form of newspaper fiduciary control is recommended to study the *Monitor* example. It has a great deal to contribute.

39

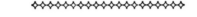

How to Publish a *Christian Science Monitor*

SUPPOSE THE Ancient and Honorable Order of Freemen, or the University of Metropolis, or some eminent church body, decides it will publish a daily newspaper. What must it have as indispensable ingredients? What are the essential elements in the success of *The Christian Science Monitor?*

First, you must have some measure of the kind of vision that came to Mary Baker Eddy: the transcendent sense of idealism, of service to mankind, of practical judgment, which put and kept the *Monitor* on the straight path.

Second, you must get a substantial body of dedicated, interested people who will support the circulation of such a paper.

Third, you must organize a method of getting and keeping a considerable volume of advertising, which must return continuing value to the advertiser.

Fourth, you must get staff, executives, officials with first-rate journalistic skills, business and mechanical experience, and basic wisdom and judgment, plus heart-felt loyalty to the deepest goals of the paper.

Fifth, you must produce a good newspaper — interesting, readable, significant, challenging, entertaining, important.

With these ingredients, you will be on your way.

Here is how it is done at the *Monitor* itself.

The Christian Science Board of Directors sets basic policies, keeps a sharp and continuous eye on their application, settles any problems. It corresponds to the owner in other newspapers, but an owner who is always active, interested and decisive in the daily operation.

The Board of Trustees and the manager of the Christian Science Publishing Society correspond to publisher. They settle all matters relating to the business operation, though fundamental issues go to the Directors for final decision. The constant daily role of the Trustees and manager is to support, safeguard, and implement the well-being of the publishing enterprise. The circulation, advertising, and production managers and other department heads are directly responsible to the Trustees and manager. The editor of the *Monitor* is also responsible to the Trustees and manager for business operations of the editorial department, and to the Directors for news and editorial policy.

This arrangement is singularly effectual. It is of great importance that the Directors and Trustees are active boards, functioning daily and continuously. There is no sense of absentee ownership. Authority is closely integrated rather than merely delegated. At the same time, department heads and lesser executives are encouraged to show the utmost autonomy and enterprise in the fulfillment of their responsibilities.

While the operation is one that might be called "closely held" it is at the same time one that brings out the fullest zeal and initiative in individuals right down the line. This is because everybody is working together, with a commitment to common goals rather than simply to earning money for an absentee owner, family, or even stockholders. Incentives are inherent.

In the editorial department itself, the same kind of participation up and down the line prevails. There have been no ivory tower editors. The present writer, who has been chief editorial department executive since January, 1941, has functioned most of that time as a managing editor as well as an editor. I have maintained over-all direction and responsibility for the entire department. Editorial writing has been largely delegated to the editorial-page staff. The chief editorial writer has been given great initiative in the implementation of editorial policy, though the exact text of editorials is carefully cleared with the Board of Directors.

A typical day in the *Monitor* editorial department may show how the operation works. Since the paper is published on afternoon-paper deadlines, most of the staff is on duty at an early hour. The editor, managing editor, and news department staffs are at their desks by seven-thirty, some of them earlier. Their job is to survey the news of the day and get the flow started for the editions.

The American news editor will receive schedules of stories to come over the leased wire from the Washington and New York Bureaus. Stories or schedules will be filed from the Chicago and California Bureaus, from staff or special correspondents elsewhere in the country. Some material will come in by air mail.

The overseas news editor will similarly receive copy or schedules from Bureaus and correspondents throughout the world. The New England news editor will assign his staff to the important local stories, many of them research jobs exclusive to the *Monitor*. The sports and financial editors will also be surveying the news in their areas and organizing their copy.

At eight-forty the news editors and the head of the copy desk meet in the editor's office to submit their lists of important stories and to make up page one for the first local editions. There is brief discussion of the main items and co-ordination of effort between the news areas.

As the stories start pouring into the office — and the news services of the Associated Press and Reuters are virtually continuous — the news editors and their staffs are busy editing copy for basic policy, content, and style. A great deal of cutting and selection must take place. The work of columnists, especially news-deadline columnists such as the authors of the page-one column "State of the Nations." must be very carefully scrutinized.

The closely integrated operation means that no important copy goes into the paper without the thoughtful study of several specialists. Much as the news desk members respect the work of the paper's brilliant writers out in the field, both editors and writers are convinced that any and all copy can be improved by skillful editing. Each of the news editors is expert in a particular field. Most of them have served long periods as correspondents.

The copy desk is just as important and expert. Its members, rigorously trained in copy-editing for style, mistakes, brevity, and head-writing, perform an invaluable function. The *Monitor* is fortunate in having had for many years a copy desk of high professional talent. Its members often catch policy points that have slipped through the news desks.

General news copy and financial copy is read on the universal desk. Sports copy, editorial-page copy, art news copy, and the copy for all the feature pages are read by members of these specialized staffs, and they write the heads. Broadly speaking, feature-page copy is handled prior to the day of publication.

In earlier years, like most other newspapers, the *Monitor*'s pages were made up in the composing room by a make-up man who worked in shirtsleeves right at the imposing stone, with guidance from news editors, particularly on page one. But after the *Monitor* had begun to regionalize its advertising in different editions, calling for many makeover changes between the editions, the old system proved cumbersome and inefficient.

The system was then changed, so that all pages in all editions are fully and carefully dummied in the newsroom. That is to say, editors or make-up assistants prepare full designs of each page, showing where every story is to be placed. The advertising department first lays out the advertising for each inside page, and provides blank dummy sheets with only the location of the advertising marked on them. The editorial department then takes these sheets and makes its news layout on them. The sheets next go to the composing room and are used by the make-up man to put the paper to bed!

An extensive bookkeeping system is required in order to keep track of articles that have run in one edition and not in another, so that duplication does not occur.

All day long, the news continues to pour into the office, through news service wires and leased wires. Much of the overseas news comes by radio through Press Wireless, Inc. Very little comes by telephone.

The technical secret of this operation is quality of personnel. Newspapermen know this. Their most frequent inquiries of the *Monitor* are: How do you recruit? How do you train?

Recruitment is not difficult. The *Monitor* attracts potentially able people. Since its reputation is worldwide, eager persons from all parts of the world seek opportunity to join the staff. The problem is one of selection. This task is more difficult. It is necessary to recognize real newspaper talent. Droves of people apply for jobs to the *Monitor* who are filled with good will and the best intentions but no newspaper flair. Their motives are appreciated, but the *Monitor*'s staff must be of the best technical competence.

Fortunately, the editorial department normally has to employ a dozen or more copy boys or girls each year. This is an excellent tryout spot. Young people who are willing to come and start at the bottom rung of the ladder will soon show whether they can develop newspaper skills or not. In recent years, the most valuable staff acquisitions started at this level.

The paper has about 150 people in the editorial department. This includes copy boys, clerks, and secretaries. It includes the entire staff, at home and abroad. It does not include special correspondents, who are not employed full time. Of these people, 15 are in the New England news division, 21 in American News, 20 in Overseas News, 30 are on the staffs of various feature pages, 26 in technical and clerical operations, 12 in copyreading, and 3 in executive offices.

It will be seen that this is a staff of very moderate size, as newspapers go. The *New York Times* in 1951 had an editorial staff of no less than 1350 men and women, but of course the *Times* prints a much larger daily edition and a mammoth Sunday paper.

It is no mean achievement that the *Monitor* is able to publish a newspaper of quality, originating all its own news copy, with the exception of the moderate amount of wire service copy it prints, with a staff of 150 persons. Again, quality of personnel is the secret.

Another frequently asked question is whether *Monitor* editorial staff members have to be Christian Scientists. The answer is No. Down through the years, many persons who were not Christian Scientists have been hired when they were the best available applicants for a given job. During the last quarter century, however, more and more Christian Scientists who were also promising and well-qualified journalists have been available.

It would be possible to staff several *Christian Science Monitors* from the promising Christian Scientists who would like to work on the daily newspaper. Because Christian Scientists of equivalent newspaper talent may be presumed to understand the paper's goals and objectives somewhat more fully than non-Christian Scientists, and may be expected to give the paper an extra measure of dedication, they are nowadays hired when available. But nobody has given the paper more able, loyal, and effective service than the non-Christian Scientists who have worked for it down through the years.

If recruitment is not difficult, training is something else again. There is no formal course of training. It is all on-the-job. From time to time writing workshops are held, with voluntary attendance; but, mainly, staff members are trained by senior editors, rigorously and painstakingly. The methods used down through the years by Paul Deland and Charles Gratke have been described. Others carry on the same kind of work today. They are seeking to develop in young people a sense of good writing, of news judgment, of policy implementation, of responsibility about words and their meaning. There are no secrets about this training, except that skilled and earnest journalists are trying to instill into young people, intimately and with abundant daily personal contact, in a small-group atmosphere, the lessons they have learned themselves.

The educational background of *Monitor* staff members is very diverse. Virtually all, especially the younger people, have had the equivalent of liberal arts college work. A small minority have had journalism school experience. A few have taken law school or business school post-graduate degrees. In the main their education has been in terms of breadth and stimulation rather than in technical newspaper training before they came to the *Monitor.* Some have worked on other newspapers, and in most cases this has been clearly beneficial. Even so, the great part of their technical training had to come after they joined the *Monitor* staff.

Monitor experience establishes that a solid general educational background is of utmost value. Journalism school work on top of this may be useful, but perhaps less so in the case of the *Monitor,* where ability to think and evaluate is of paramount necessity, and the technical training comes in large part on the job.

Recruitment and training are only the beginning of *Monitor* staff development. Opportunity and incentive play a vital role. While the size of the staff is small, and opportunity for promotion not too great, there is nevertheless some considerable staff movement. A young man or woman of ability, coming to the *Monitor,* can see others much like himself who have been able to advance quite rapidly into work of genuine challenge and interest.

Often it takes six or seven years from the time a young college graduate goes on the copy boy staff to the moment when he is well advanced in the reportorial category, or is making progress on the copy desk, or has been sent out as a staff correspondent. Sometimes the period is substantially less. It is not an overly protracted period of seasoning and training, provided the young person can see some distance along the road as he progresses.

At times young people feel they are not going forward and see greener pastures in other jobs somewhat related to journalism. The *Monitor* editorial structure is inevitably pyramidal. It cannot promote into topnotch jobs as many good men and women as it can and must hire at beginning levels. Some of them will leave, and it can't be helped. Many leave at later times, when they have progressed to what they believe are their limits on the *Monitor,* and still have not attained the responsibility or salary level they are capable of reaching. Like other newspapers, the *Monitor* has contributed many experienced and talented men and women to various similar lines of work.

Monitor salary scales are modest in the higher brackets, where some persons may feel tempted to other jobs. At lower levels, in the job classifications customarily covered by union contract (the *Monitor* has no Newspaper Guild union organization, although its mechanical employees are organized) it has long been the paper's policy to pay salaries at least as good as those reached by union negotiation on the average of other Boston newspapers. The *Monitor* is somewhat in the category of an educational institution or a profession, where salary scales are not the only form of genuine compensation.

Salaries therefore are no particular incentive in the obtaining and keeping of a strong staff. The real incentives are in terms of the job to be done and the circumstances. Every effort is made to give able staff members an opportunity to develop their careers to the limit of their vision and ability. They are encouraged to take initiative, to develop their own ideas, to be creative and imaginative, to lift their craftsmanship just as high as they can reach. Thus there is opportunity for many staff members to become specialists in one field or another.

And the job is consistent with the staff member's sense of idealism and spiritual fulfillment. He is not called upon to debase his sense of right and wrong. He is required to lift his concepts, rather than to lower them. He does this in the comradeship of a group of like-minded, stimulating, and congenial fellow workers. The atmosphere is both wholesome and exciting. It is no wonder, then, that the *Monitor* attracts and holds its share of first-rate journalists. Its ideals make their jobs possible, and their ideals joined to its, make its accomplishment successful.

40

◆◆◆◆◆◆◆◆◆◆◆◆◆◆◆◆◆◆◆◆

The *Monitor* and the Future

THE YEAR is 1958.

The *Monitor* ends its half century. The ferment of forces and ideas, some new and some very old, stirs the world. Under the silent whirl of the satellites, in the shadow of the mushroom cloud, mankind needs more than ever to awaken from the false dream of security in materialism. The time for spiritual solutions is at hand.

Thus the mission of *The Christian Science Monitor* is more urgent than ever before. That mission is — with honesty, moderation, foresight and candor — to help give humankind the tools with which to work out its salvation.

What are these tools?

The first of them is information. People must be told the facts, as clearly and closely as they can be determined. The precise nature of the ghastly breach of contact and understanding between the rulers and people of the Communist nations and the government and peoples of the free world must be defined. We must learn what to do about it.

In the face of every problem of life, a first necessity is information. The improvement of civic affairs, the preservation of the home, the education and training of the tempestuously increasing population, the restoration of values, the release from mass-ism — all these challenges need first to be identified.

The second tool comes with explanation of the information. The newspaper's task of digging deeper into the news, giving perspective to events, relating today to yesterday and tomorrow, is a role pioneered by the *Monitor*. It, too, is more urgent today than ever before, as the modern world grows more complex and filled with voices. The meaning of the news is sometimes the most important news of all. To understand it gives the citizen the means of action.

The third tool follows from the first two — it is the arousing of dormant thinking. Too many people in the so-called free world have been drifting on the drowsy seas of materialistic self-satisfaction. Glutted with goods, some of them have forgotten the sacrifice, the denial of self, the moderation and restraint, of truly spiritual living. Each citizen, each person, must accept an individual responsibility for good and effective government, for a healthy and progressive total society. There are other tools which the newspaper provides. But all of them have one end: to protect, preserve, and advance the values and opportunities which make up what we call the free way of life.

The first, and perhaps the last, place where these tools must be used is within the individual. Each of us needs to master in himself the aggressions of materialism and of totalitarian thinking. Once the people who make up the free world have awakened to the dangers which must be met in themselves and in their own societies they will be ready to meet whatever dangers are presented by external threat.

No factor in society can be more effective in bringing about this awakening than the newspaper. It is one of the primary means by which the voice and thinking of leadership reach the people. It is one of the primary means by which people learn how to choose their leadership. It is a dynamic, never dormant, network of true integration. It is part of the cement of society.

A central and indispensable factor in the awakening of human thought is the definition and affirmation of spiritual values. This is the heart of *The Christian Science Monitor.* Despite the paper's proudly borne name, it is a nondenominational and nonsectarian affirmation. The paper does not ask readers to turn to a particular religious approach, but to God. It defines God, as does Christian Science itself, in the broadest and deepest terms.

This fundamental concern with spiritual values gives the paper its confidence in man's best self and in the triumph of decency. It does not impair, but enhances, its ultimate realism.

It has been given to the *Monitor,* to its staff, to all humankind in this half century, to live through some of the great days of history. These are surpassing times. Perhaps they are apocalyptical. At any rate, they are not over.

We move, as the paper's second half century opens, into an age which calls for the best-informed people, the most fully awakened people who have ever trod the globe. We are the generation who lift not only our eyes and our hearts but our bodies toward the stars.

For that task, we need first to find our way on the earth.

Dedicated and equipped as it is, *The Christian Science Monitor* is ready to be a pathfinder. The path will not be easy. These are days of struggle and of danger. But they are also days of transcendent opportunity.

The opportunity is to carry to all mankind the great news of our time: the fact that men do not need to destroy the society they have been so long and arduously building. The fact that men have the truth on which the edifice of peace and of individual rebirth can rest.

Long years ago William Wordsworth saw something of what the printed word, spiritually illuminated, could do for society. He wrote:

Discourse was deemed man's noblest attribute,
And written words the glory of his hand;
Then followed Printing with enlarged command
For thought — dominion vast and absolute
For spreading truth, and making love expand.

For the service of such ideals, *The Christian Science Monitor* was founded. To their fulfillment, as its second half century opens, it stands committed.

Index

Index